God and the Little Grey Cells

God and the Little Grey Cells

Religion in Agatha Christie's
Poirot Stories

Dan W. Clanton, Jr.

t&tclark

LONDON · NEW YORK · OXFORD · NEW DELHI · SYDNEY

T&T CLARK
Bloomsbury Publishing Plc
50 Bedford Square, London, WC1B 3DP, UK
1385 Broadway, New York, NY 10018, USA
29 Earlsfort Terrace, Dublin 2, Ireland

BLOOMSBURY, T&T CLARK and the T&T Clark logo are trademarks
of Bloomsbury Publishing Plc

First published in Great Britain 2024

A catalogue record for this book is available from the British Library.

Library of Congress Cataloging-in-Publication Data

Names: Clanton, Dan W., Jr., author.
Title: God and the little grey cells : religion in Agatha Christie's Poirot stories /
Dan W. Clanton.
Description: London ; New York : T&T Clark, 2024. |
Includes bibliographical references and index.
Identifiers: LCCN 2023051069 (print) | LCCN 2023051070 (ebook) |
ISBN 9780567696076 (hardback) | ISBN 9780567715760 (paperback) |
ISBN 9780567696083 (pdf) | ISBN 9780567696106 (ebook)
Subjects: LCSH: Christie, Agatha, 1890–1976–Criticism and interpretation. |
Christie, Agatha, 1890-1976–Religion. | Poirot, Hercule (Fictitious character) |
Detective and mystery stories, English–History and criticism. | Religion in literature.
Classification: LCC PR6005.H66 Z585 2024 (print) | LCC PR6005.H66 (ebook)|
DDC 823.912—dc23/eng/20240223
LC record available at https://lccn.loc.gov/2023051069
LC ebook record available at https://lccn.loc.gov/2023051070

ISBN: HB: 978-0-5676-9607-6
         ePDF: 978-0-5676-9608-3
         eBook: 978-0-5676-9610-6

Typeset by RefineCatch Limited, Bungay, Suffolk

To find out more about our authors and books visit www.bloomsbury.com
and sign up for our newsletters.

Contents

Acknowledgments

This was my pandemic project, one of the things that sustained me during that difficult period. M. Poirot, Miss Jane Marple, and Agatha Christie's other memorable characters—not to mention the presence of David Suchet, Hugh Fraser, and other cast members of *Agatha Christie's Poirot*—kept me company amidst impromptu Zoom classes, spraying Lysol on groceries and pretty much everything, and worrying almost all the time about my family, friends, and future. I owe them, and I hope this book repays that debt in some small way.

Some of the content in this book has been presented elsewhere:

- A version of Chapter 3 was presented in the "Bible and Popular Culture Workshop" that Amy Balogh, Elizabeth Rae Coody, and I facilitated at the Rocky Mountain/Great Plains Regional AAR/SBL Meeting in March 2019. I later delivered a longer and more formal version of the paper at the National AAR/SBL Meeting in November 2022.
- Much of Chapter 4 was presented in the Religion & Culture Area at the Annual Conference of the Popular Culture Association/American Culture Association in Washington, DC in April 2019 under the title, "God and the Little Grey Cells: Bible in Agatha Christie's Poirot." An expanded version was then delivered asynchronously in September 2022 for the International Agatha Christie Festival.
- A good deal of Chapter 13 was presented as "'Frightfully Decent': Jews in Golden Age Crime Fiction," at the Thirty-Fourth Annual Symposium on Jewish Civilization in Omaha in October 2022.

I'd like to thank my co-facilitators, fellow presenters, and our audiences for their helpful feedback on my work. Thanks also to Leonard Greenspoon and Tony Medawar for their graciousness in inviting me to deliver two of these presentations.

Much of the research for this book was supported by Doane University via the generosity of the Walt Olsen family, and I'm grateful not only to the Olsen family, but also to Drs. Pedro Maligo and Lorie Cook-Benjamin. A special thanks goes to Tammy Roach, whose assistance in locating sources and good humor made my work so much easier. Support your librarians, y'all.

As always, my wife Missy and our daughter Hannah supported and sometimes even tolerated me during the writing of this book. I love them for that, and for so much more.

This book is dedicated to our son Danny, who watched Poirot with me and of whom I'm so proud. Love you, Boo.

Preface

It must've been a Sunday afternoon, because that's when they had movie matinees on the TV. I was spending time with my mother's parents in their small town in south Arkansas, a little less than fifty miles north of the Louisiana border. My Mamaw Lu (short for Lucille) had made me a pallet in the middle of the living room floor to put my toys on and lounge. The TV was on, and I watched half-heartedly for a few minutes, then seemed to have forgotten all about my toys. There'd been a murder on a fancy train somewhere in Europe (which might've been Mars, for all I knew). And there was a strange-looking man whose name I couldn't exactly pronounce who was asking all the passengers about it. I knew what a detective was. I was familiar with the Lone Ranger and Batman (I had *Superfriends* bedsheets, after all). But this odd fellow was different. He didn't throw any punches or have any special gadgets (although he did a trick with a hat-box I thought was pretty cool). He just asked questions and used his imagination, and he solved it. Everyone seemed to underestimate him, to think that because he was different that he couldn't get at the truth, but he did. After the movie ended, I went back to playing with my toys, but something about that guy stuck with me.

A few years later I ran into that guy again at the local movie duplex in our own small town. My friend's mom took us to see *Evil Under the Sun* after it was released in early 1982. I would turn eleven later that year, and was a pudgy, not-particularly-athletically-inclined kid who preferred a good book. Even though the version of Poirot (I could say his name by now) I saw on the big screen wasn't the same one I remembered from my grandparents' TV, I had the feeling again that here's someone whose mind was going to get the better of all these flashy, snobby people, one of whom was a murderer. Even though it's difficult to remember now exactly how I felt after seeing that movie (partly because I've rewatched it so many times) somehow the whole idea of brains over brawn appealed to me particularly.

Although he faded into the background for a bit, Poirot was still with me in high school. Evidence of this is found in a present I received from my high school sweetheart Sally. For my sixteenth birthday, she thoughtfully bought me a paperback copy of *Murder on the Orient Express*. I read and re-read this, then sought out other Poirot novels at our local used bookstore. I enjoyed these, but once again, Poirot seemed to dwindle in my mind. Until David Suchet came along and returned him to my life.

Suchet is, of course, the actor who portrayed (embodied, really) Poirot in the British TV series *Agatha Christie's Poirot*, a set of adaptations of Christie's Poirot stories that ran intermittently from 1989-2013 and eventually rendered every single Poirot story she wrote (save one) for the screen.[1] After I started graduate school, got married, and

---

[1] The lone, un-adapted, story is "The Lemesurier Inheritance," which first appeared in the 1951 short story collection *The Under Dog and Other Stories*.

we had our son Danny, I remember being awake one night when it was my turn to feed him. There wasn't much on the TV, but we managed to catch part of an episode from the Poirot series on our local PBS station. Here was a Poirot utterly different than the ones I'd seen onscreen before, one that seemed much closer to my recollections of the Christie novels I'd read years earlier. I watched a few more episodes, and to my delight, Suchet became *my* Poirot. That is, his mannerisms and affectations, the supporting cast, the sets, the wardrobe, everything seemed to cohere with Christie's vision of the characters. And slowly, Poirot began working his way back into my life.

Even though I was trained as a biblical scholar, I did quite a bit of research, teaching, and writing in the area of religion and popular culture in and after grad school. After working on a textbook on the subject in 2012, I started thinking about Poirot again. There were a lot of press and stories around that time about *Agatha Christie's Poirot*, since it was coming to an end, and would air its last episodes in 2013. I hadn't done much work on religion and popular literature, and I remembered how much I'd enjoyed Christie's Poirot stories and the adaptations in that series. I wasn't sure I wanted to take on such a large topic right then, so I contented myself with reading the odd novel for pleasure and watching an episode now and then. After I finished a large research project in 2020, I decided to look more closely at religion in the Poirot stories and their various adaptations, and was surprised both at what I found, and what I didn't find.

What I found was a character who clearly and strongly identified as a Catholic, one whose world was recognizably Christian, and one who was written by an author who herself identified as a Christian. I was also surprised to see how central religious language and imagery was to the stories, and how key religious literacy is to understanding them, especially so in some cases. At the same time, I was fascinated at how religion was presented, augmented, or erased in the adaptations of the Poirot stories in radio, TV, and film. Finally, what I didn't find was much research on religion in the Poirot stories. This was somewhat shocking to me, considering what a wildly popular author Christie is and how prominent Poirot continues to be in popular culture. I'll say more about this lack of scholarly engagement later, but suffice it to say that this lack left an opening for someone interested in religion and popular culture to fill. And that's what I hope to do in this book.

Introduction

It's generally acknowledged that Agatha Christie (1890–1976) is the most popular novelist of all time, and according to the official Agatha Christie website, only "the Bible and Shakespeare" have "outsold" her.[1] In terms of sheer numbers, Jeremy Black claims that by 2016 "her sales . . . exceeded two billion books in over 100 languages."[2] The vast majority of her works fall into the genre of crime and/or detective fiction, and are a primary example of what scholars refer to as the Golden Age of that genre. In those works, Christie has created two of the most enduring detectives in the genre: Miss Jane Marple, and M. Hercule Poirot.

Despite that Golden Age being mainly confined to the period between the two World Wars, Christie's works remain widely available and popular today, with new and authorized novels with Poirot, as well as three recent big-budget Poirot films from director and actor Kenneth Branagh. Because of Christie's ongoing popularity, many scholarly works have analyzed and engaged various facets of her output and the later interpretations of them. Very few of these works have engaged religion in Christie's output, though. In some ways, this is understandable, given the sheer size of her work. Because of that, I'll be more modest in what I hope to accomplish in this book. That is, what I want to do generally is examine the presence and role of religion in Christie's Poirot canon. And there are two good reasons for doing so.

The Poirot Canon

The Poirot canon consists of all the works Christie published between 1920 and 1972 in which Hercule Poirot appears as a central character. These amount to thirty-three novels, fifty-one short stories, and five plays (several of which were adaptations of novels). Interestingly, three of these plays actually omit Poirot as a character. In this book, I also examine later radio, TV, and film adaptations of Christie's Poirot canon, most notably the series *Agatha Christie's Poirot* (1989–2013).

---

[1] See http://www.agathachristie.com.
[2] Black, *The Importance of Being Poirot* (South Bend, IN: St. Augustine's Press, 2021), 184.

One reason this book is necessary is that Christie's works have been extraordinarily popular, and as such are not only ripe for, but need to be analyzed if we wish to understand better the cultural traditions (including religion) and historical events that lie behind them. Popular works like Christie's are a much more helpful representation of a culture's mores, values, and practices than elite or more narrowly targeted aesthetic products.[3] And the former are certainly more significant in that they function more obviously as avenues of meaning-making for their wide audiences. In a discussion of how Christie differs from some of the other "modernist" literature of the time, e.g., Virginia Woolf, Black clarifies this point, noting, "Modernism in literature was frequently elitist, had only a limited commercial appeal, compared with many of the 'middle' and 'low' brow writers of the period, and had little airing on the radio." This means, claims Black, that "'Middle' and 'low' brow writers offered a much more authentic reflection of popular culture than anything Modernism could provide."[4] Even though the distinction between "high" and "low" culture is more often subjective and arbitrary than not, Black's comments do help us understand why Christie's works offer a better mirror of her particular socio-historical and religious milieu than works with a far more limited audience and a much higher barrier to accessibility. After all, if one was interested in understanding American culture in 1951, for example, would it be more useful to study the TV series *I Love Lucy* (then in its first season on CBS) or Elliott Carter's nebulous and difficult forty-minute String Quartet No. 1? Which cultural product would provide a more rounded understanding of a wider swath of American culture? I trust you get my point.

Another, more specific justification for this book is what I have previously mentioned: almost no one has paid thoroughgoing attention to the role of religion in Christie's Poirot works. For example, consider Gillian Gill's comment on this issue in her book on Christie and her work:

> Religion is a subject rarely discussed in Christie's mystery novels, but it provides the framework for all her writing. Unlike her great mystery-writer contemporary Dorothy L. Sayers, Agatha Christie wrote no Christian mystery plays or Anglican polemics. Christie had had no formal education in philosophy or political thought, was no linguist, had none of the scholarly talents needed to write about religion and theology. All the same, Christie was as serious about her religious faith as Sayers, and, unlike Sayers, as she grew old, she saw her work as a humble but acceptable way of expressing certain values she held dear.[5]

[3] Alison Light, "Agatha Christie and Conservative Modernity," in *Forever England: Femininity, Literature and Conservatism between the Wars* (London & New York: Routledge, 1991), 63–64, notes that the very popularity of Christie's output have led scholars to view it pejoratively.
[4] Black, *Importance*, 61. This contrast is undercut by the work of Light, who persuasively argues that Christie's work should be seen as modernist in her "Agatha Christie," *passim*. Black doesn't engage Light's work, so her claims go unchallenged in his book.
[5] Gill, *Agatha Christie: The Woman and Her Mysteries* (New York: Free Press, 1990), Kindle edition, ch. 6, "Mary Westmacott: Death Comes as the Beginning."

While it is true that Gill's purpose isn't to examine religion in Christie's works, she neither elaborates on the "framework" she alludes to, nor does she return to the issue of religion in her book. Similarly, Black admits that "even though clerics are not thick on the ground, that does not mean religion is absent, either in terms of the lay religiosity of the characters or with reference to the role of the author. Far from it."[6] Yet while Black is clearly interested in what he calls the "moral framework" or "ethical force" of Christie's work, he doesn't elaborate on the bases of that framework or force.[7] Finally, in much the same way, Earl F. Bargainnier includes a section in his book on Christie in which he explores the "Allusions, Nursery Rimes, and Titles" she includes in her works. It's telling, then, when he doesn't so much as mention *any* biblical references or allusions.[8] In addition, researchers have also by and large neglected to examine the narrower issue of Poirot and his religious identity. These gaps are all the more striking when we consider just how broad and regular the presence of religion is in Christie's works, especially her Poirot canon. Hopefully, this book will remedy these gaps, at least in part.

*   *   *

Now, let me lay my cards on the table. In this book, I'll treat Christie's works as belonging to the genre of Golden Age crime/detective fiction and as situated in socio-cultural and historical contexts characterized by Christian normativity and hegemony. But I also see her as a modernist author engaged in creative confrontation with those contexts, a process of pushback that I call resistant reception. I'll explain all of this in more detail in Part One, in which we'll examine how Christie's Poirot stories both exemplify and contest Christian hegemony and normativity. We'll see that in her works, Christianity is depicted as a cultural discursive given. That is, her works presuppose that readers understand biblical language and Christian imagery, as these form the basis for the worldview shared by Christie and her audience. Chapter 1 situates Christie in her chronological and literary context by providing a brief introduction to Golden Age detective fiction. In Chapter 2, I'll examine the Christianity of Christie's time, argue that it's both hegemonic and normative, and detail how Christie both reflects and resists it in her works. Establishing this ideological baseline will be important before we explore how Christie interrogates it.

In Part Two, I'll then deepen our engagement with Christianity in Christie through case studies (or "Deep Dives") by exploring how often language with religious (and specifically Christian) content occurs in the Poirot canon and how central that language is to certain stories. Put differently, Christie assumes a certain level of religious literacy

---

6 Black, *Importance*, 12–13.
7 See ibid., 122.
8 See Bargainnier, *The Gentle Art of Murder: The Detective Fiction of Agatha Christie* (Bowling Green, OH: Bowling Green University Popular Press, 1980), 168–170. Similarly, in her 1990 "biography" of Poirot, Anne Hart points out his fondness for Shakespeare, but says nothing of Bible. See *Agatha Christie's Poirot: The Life and Times of Hercule Poirot* (London: HarperCollins, 1997), 196. I've collected all of the biblical references I've noticed in the Appendix, and hope the reader will forgive me if I overlooked any.

in her readers as reflected by the regular inclusion of this language. Yet she also pushes her readers to think differently about the biblical texts she engages, and in this way, Christie offers a subtle resistant reception to the normative Christianity of her day.

If Parts One and Two focus on the language and imagery in Christie's works that underpins yet problematizes the dominant Christian worldview of her day, Part Three will take a broader approach, and ask what we can reconstruct of Poirot's own worldview. We'll begin in Chapter 6 by exploring the religious language characters use to describe/refer to him and his views on key issues, such as murder and truth. Chapter 7 will examine Poirot's religious identity via two case studies before we focus more closely on TV and cinematic adaptations of Christie's Poirot stories in Chapters 8–10.

Part Four will examine the presence of discordant or minority religions and religious practices in her Poirot stories. By looking more closely at how Christie treats groups like a heterodox Christian "cult" (Chapter 11), Spiritualism (Chapter 12), Judaism (Chapter 13), and Islam (Chapter 14), we'll be in a better position to indicate how she tactfully shows that practitioners of these movements and traditions—as well as some of their characteristics and practices—lie outside what was normally considered acceptable forms of religious behavior and belief. Even so, I'll note how Christie allows for the partial inclusion of these groups (with the telling exception of the Christian "cult") in the societies she constructs in her Poirot stories, i.e., they're not assimilated, to be sure, but neither are they rejected out of hand from participating in and even marrying into English culture(s). Finally, in my Conclusion, I'll answer the "So what?" question, briefly summarize what we discover along the way, and mention a few possibilities for future research that might help us understand Christie and religion and popular culture more deeply.

Before we get started in earnest, let me say something briefly about my approach in this book and the research process behind it. The approach is predicated on Corinne Carvalho's Three Worlds model of biblical interpretation.[9] I've used her model for several years now in the classroom, and have found that it's a tidy way to think about how we engage with texts. Rather than adopt an approach in which we only survey Christie's words on the written page (*the world of the text*), Carvalho's model asks us to pay attention to *the world behind the text*, namely, the history and culture and other background data current at the time of writing that might've influenced the way in which the text was written. That is, while my book is not a biography, I'll mention socio-historical and biographical data where pertinent, and by so doing hopefully illuminate Christie's stories in a more holistic fashion. However, many (or most?) people do not encounter Poirot in his original literary contexts. That is, far more people have been exposed to Poirot via "mediated" renderings and interpretations of the stories and novels in various other genres, including plays, films, television series, BBC Radio productions, and even new, authorized Poirot novels not written by Christie. As such, the book engages the reception of the stories in these various genres in what Carvalho terms *the world the text creates*, since the process of adapting the original narrative plots involves, at times, large-scale changes and additions.

---

[9]   See Carvalho, *Primer on Biblical Methods* (Winona, MN: Anselm Academic, 2009), *passim*.

As for my research process, I mention in my Preface that I was trained as a biblical scholar. This means that I was taught how important it is to read primary texts thoroughly and critically before making any claims about them or moving on to secondary sources that comment on them. So, even though I'm not an English professor or a scholar of British literature, I brought that same method to bear on this project. More specifically, I read every story and novel in the Poirot canon in chronological order, making handwritten notes as I went.[10] After I completed that step, I went back and transcribed my notes, re-reading all the primary texts in the process. I then watched all the adaptations in *Agatha Christie's Poirot*, as well as the assorted feature films and made-for-TV movies I could access before moving on to the BBC Radio 4 productions and the various dramatic adaptations of Poirot stories (most of which remove Poirot as a character, so they don't feature in this book). Then came the biographies; other Christie novels and stories; monographs; and additional secondary sources, the majority of which you can find in the Bibliography. After this admittedly lengthy process, I was more convinced than ever that there was something worth pursuing here, that a book discussing religion and Poirot would be both helpful and illuminating. I hope that what follows hits those marks.

---

[10] Unbeknownst to me, this is very similar to the way in which David Suchet prepared for his work as Poirot. See Suchet and Geoffrey Wansell, *Poirot and Me* (London: Headline, 2013), 25.

Part One

Literary and Historical Background

Introduction to Part One

In the Introduction, I introduced the work of Agatha Christie and outlined my plan for what follows. In Part One, we'll dig more deeply into the three worlds of Christie's works. We'll learn more about Christie's writing in Chapter 1 by situating it as an example of a particular genre of fiction and noting how she creates her own closed, "fictional world" in her works. We'll also examine the changing socio-historical and material contexts in which she began writing, as well as how those changing contexts affected her gendered audience. Finally, we'll situate Christie as a modernist author who challenged and questioned her religious, cultural, and literary inheritances. In Chapter 2, we'll continue this focus by examining English Christianity in Christie's time as well as her own religious identity. There, though, we'll extend our discussion to the world of the text and the world the text creates by modeling our approach to Christie's work with an examination of her first and final Poirot novel.

1

Golden Age Crime Fiction and Agatha Christie

Literary historians normally classify the period between the two World Wars as the "Golden Age" of crime fiction.[1] Although there's no critical agreement as to why this period is "Golden," there does seem to be a consensus as to the primacy of the "clue-puzzle" or "plot puzzle" component in the works included under that moniker.[2] In his work, Stephen Knight has identified a list of twelve characteristics found in the major stories and novels of this period that will help us understand the genre of detective fiction.[3] First, "Murder is now essential as the central crime," and that the crime is "enclosed" in its physical setting, as is obvious from the popularity of murders in locked rooms or large houses on rural estates.[4] Third, the bounded nature of the crime is also felt in how "socially enclosed" the classes of the character are—on the higher end, he means—and the way in which the "wider politics of the context are ignored."[5] Fifth, the murder victims come in for special consideration in Knight's analysis, as he notes, "The victim will be a man or (quite often) a woman of some importance and wealth, though that position is rarely of long-standing or antique respectability: instability is constant. The victim is also a person of little emotive value; he or she is not mourned, nor is the real pain and degradation of violent death represented."[6] The minimal emotion displayed at the demise of the victim is in keeping with the logical methods employed by the semi-

---

[1] In her work, Lucy Sussex presents what she calls a "polygenetic" view of the origins of crime fiction that lays a heavy emphasis on newspaper reporting, the intersection between real crimes and the literature that sprang up around it, and literary genres like the Gothic novel. See chapter one of *Women Writers and Detectives in Nineteenth-Century Crime Fiction: The Mothers of the Mystery Genre*, Crime Files (Hampshire & New York: Palgrave Macmillan, 2010), 6–25. Also, Black's first chapter in *The Importance of Being Poirot* (South Bend, IN: St. Augustine's Press, 2021), 1–23, provides an overview of detective fiction/writing prior to Christie's work in which he pays special attention to the links between newspaper crime reporting and crime fiction.

[2] As noted by Richard Bradford, *Crime Fiction: A Very Short Introduction* (Oxford: Oxford University Press, 2015), Kindle edition, ch. 2, "The Two Ages: Golden and Hard-Boiled." See also Marion Shaw and Sabine Vanacker, "Women Writers and the Golden Age of Detective Fiction," in *Reflecting on Miss Marple*, Heroines? (London & New York: Routledge, 1991), 13–14.

[3] For these components, see Knight, "The Golden Age," in *The Cambridge Companion to Crime Fiction*, ed. Martin Priestman (Cambridge & New York: Cambridge University Press, 2003), 77–79. For a more extensive discussion, see Knight's book *Crime Fiction since 1800: Detection, Death, Diversity*, 2nd edn (New York: Palgrave, 2010), especially 85–89.

[4] Knight, "The Golden Age," 77.

[5] Ibid., 77–78.

[6] Ibid., 78.

professional or amateur detective in these works. As Knight notes: "Detection is rational rather than active or intuitional, a method which fits with the unemotional presentation of the crime."[7] Seventh, he also points out that the central detective "will focus strongly on circumstantial evidence and will eventually ratify it, properly interpreted, as a means of identifying the criminal."[8] In the course of the investigation, the reader will encounter "a range of suspects, all of whom appear capable of the crime and are equipped with motives," yet unlike earlier "Sensation Novels," in Golden Age fiction, "Romance is rare – though it can occur, both between two suspects and between the detective and a possible suspect."[9] And endings—both of the plot and the criminal—are key for this genre, as "The identification of the criminal is usually the end of the story. It is very rare for execution to be included, though suicide or an appropriate accident can intervene; if the police arrest the murderer this is represented without melodrama: as with the victim's death, the tone is cerebral and contained."[10] Knight also notes the stylistic implications that accompany such plot choices, noting, "The writing style will usually match the rational circumstantial detection in being decidedly plain ... with neither authorial voice nor characters given any elaboration."[11] Twelfth and finally, Knight notes what he terms "the most widely known and most unusual element of the clue-puzzle form," namely, "the fact that the reader is challenged to match the detective's process of identifying the murderer."[12] To facilitate this challenge, the author must play fairly, that is, "the reader must be informed of each clue that the detective sees."[13] Anyone reading this who's familiar with Christie's works might be nodding in assent as they think about how Knight's characteristics are reflected in her books, and rightly so.

In keeping with Knight's list, many scholars note that Christie constructs a kind of hermetically sealed world in which to set her plots. For example, literary critics have pointed out that in typical Christie works like *The Murder of Roger Ackroyd* (1926) and *The Murder at the Vicarage* (1930), she creates a literary charade, a false vision of England. Colin Watson famously termed this world "Mayhem Parva"—"Parva" being often found as the second name of English villages, coming from the Latin, meaning "little" (as opposed to *magna*, meaning "big"). Watson calls this world a "dream, but not of marble halls. The picture was of familiar homeliness and it was populated with stock characters observing approved rules of behaviour according to station, and isolated utterly from all such anxieties and unpleasantness as were not responsive to religion, medicine and the law."[14] It was, he continues, "self-contained and largely self-sufficient," with—especially significant for our purposes—"a well-attended church."[15] Even so,

---

[7] Ibid.
[8] Ibid.
[9] Ibid., 79.
[10] Ibid.
[11] Ibid., 78.
[12] Ibid., 79.
[13] Ibid.
[14] Watson, "The Little World of Mayhem Parva," in *Snobbery with Violence: Crime Stories and Their Audience* (London: Eyre & Spottiswoode, 1971), 169. See also the revision of his chapter titled "The Message of Mayhem Parva," in *Agatha Christie: First Lady of Crime*, ed. H.R.F. Keating (New York: Holt, Rinehart and Winston, 1977), 96–110.
[15] Watson, "Little World," 169.

Watson writes, it was "a mythical kingdom, a fly-in-amber land. It was derived in part from the ways and values of a society that had begun to fade away from the very moment of the shots at Sarajevo; in part from [a] remarkably durable sentimentality."[16]

In sum, Mayhem Parva "offered not outward escape, as did books of travel, adventure, international intrigue, but inward – into a sort of museum of nostalgia."[17] Building on Watson's work, Robert Barnard describes Mayhem Parva as "a world shut off from the political and social preoccupations of the day. It cares little about what happens in London, and Europe might not exist, for all it cares. It is a world on which the nineteenth century has made little impact, and which accepts the twentieth century only slowly and grumblingly."[18]

Even though this is much truer of some of Christie's earlier works and isn't universally applicable, Watson and Barnard are certainly onto something. That is, Christie was never especially interested in providing too many details of setting or characterization.[19] Barnard is helpful here, as notes that Christie's stories are set in "places which are, to a lesser or greater degree, remote, enclosed, uncomplicated by the disruptions and distractions of the greater world. Here the attention could concentrate itself where, in Christie's view, it truly belonged, on the beautiful, naked simplicity of the problem to be solved."[20]

Christie herself wrote that this problem is essentially a moral one. Musing on her early writing career, she wrote,

> When I began writing detective stories I was not in any mood to criticise them or to think seriously about crime. The detective story was the story of the chase; it was also very much a story with a moral; in fact it was the old Everyman Morality Tale, the hunting down of Evil and the triumph of Good. At that time, the time of the 1914 war, the doer of evil was not a hero: the enemy was wicked, the hero was good: it was as crude and as simple as that.[21]

Similarly, in his analysis of crime fiction as a literary genre, Bargainnier writes that "A continuously changing society, often confusing and frightening, is not one in which good and evil can be markedly differentiated as they are in detective fiction. There it is

---

[16] Ibid., 171.

[17] Ibid.

[18] Barnard, *A Talent to Deceive: An Appreciation of Agatha Christie* (New York: Mysterious Press, 1980), 26. See also David Suchet and Geoffrey Wansell, *Poirot and Me* (London: Headline, 2013), 77.

[19] Lucy Worsley notes as much when she writes, "The criticisms of her books are longstanding and valid. Her characters are wooden and she cannot conjure up atmosphere, even while her plots and dialogue are excellent" (*The Art of the English Murder: From Jack the Ripper and Sherlock Holmes to Agatha Christie and Alfred Hitchcock* [New York & London: Pegasus Crime, 2014], Kindle edition, ch. 20, "The Duchess of Death").

[20] Barnard, *Talent*, 35.

[21] Christie, *An Autobiography* (1977; reis. New York: HarperCollins, 2011), 437. As I mentioned, Black reinforces this emphasis on the "moral dimension" of Christie's work. In *Agatha Christie: Investigating Femininity*, Crime Files (New York: Palgrave, 2006), Merja Makinen points out that while this is generally true, "this passage is ambiguous" and as such should be applied with caution (136).

accepted that moral good *is* good and evil *is* evil."[22] He then ties this moral outlook to a corresponding function of crime fiction, noting,

> Classic detective fiction is a type of escape fiction, and no one wishes to escape into uncertainty, terror or poverty. The escape it provides is to a world of political and social order, moral certitude, and usually of wealth and culture. Though the peace of this world is broken, the reader can be assured that it will be restored or have a new birth by the end.[23]

John Ritchie concurs with this assessment, commenting, "At the conclusion of each novel there is the happy ending. With the criminal apprehended, the wicked punished, the good rewarded, and the unbalanced world restored to harmony, Christie reverts to cosy sentimentality giving a feeling that all is well with society and that the old standards have been vindicated."[24] R. A. York concurs, emphasizing the didactic function of endings, i.e., this "sense that the endings of the novels represent a possible establishment of a morally significant state of affairs ... is also a kind of rhetoric, assuring the reader that reading the novel is not just a self-indulgence, but that it also offers a kind of learning experience."[25]

Gillian Gill agrees, writing that Christie's "fictional world" is characterized by "the sparseness, the directness, the narrative pace, and the universal appeal of the fairy story, and it is perhaps as modern fairy stories for grown-up children that Christie's novels succeed."[26] Noting the stylistic choices that Christie makes as well as the characteristics of Golden Age detective fiction which her work contributed to/reflects provides a helpful starting point in understanding her literary works. But what about the socio-historical and material contexts behind those works? How did Christie respond to these contexts? Did she simply reflect them, or did she attempt to resist and/or reshape them?

*   *   *

As I noted, Christie is one of the chief examples of Golden Age authors, and more specifically is considered one of the four so-called Queens of Crime from this period, alongside Margery Allingham, Ngaio Marsh, and Dorothy L. Sayers. In her survey of British attitudes towards and engagement with murder in the nineteenth to twentieth centuries, Lucy Worsley asks why these authors came to the fore during this period and remain popular today when so many other authors—especially male ones—have succumbed to history.[27] As a partial answer, she addresses the socio-historical changes

---

[22] Bargainnier, *Gentle Art*, 10.

[23] Ibid., 10–11. See also Watson, "Message," 108–109.

[24] Ritchie, "Agatha Christie's England, 1918–39: Sickness in the Heart and Sickness in Society as Seen in the Detective Thriller," *Australian National University Historical Journal* 9 (1972): 6.

[25] York, *Agatha Christie*, 48; see also pp. 125–127.

[26] Gill, *Agatha Christie: The Woman and Her Mysteries* (New York: Free Press, 1990), Kindle edition, Afterword: "The Secret of Success." Knight, "'... done from within' – Agatha Christie's World," in *Form and Ideology in Crime Fiction* (London & Basingstoke: The Macmillan Press, 1980), 117–118, links this "fictional world" to the economic and class interests of Christie's audience. See also Shaw and Vanacker, "Women Writers," 22–23.

[27] Worsley, *Art*, ch. 19, "The Women Between the Wars."

as well as developments in publishing and the availability of books as these impacted the popularity of Golden Age fiction. She claims that "the pleasures of Golden Age detection were just the thing to steady the nerves after the First World War."[28] Put differently, the melodrama and sexual innuendo of the Penny Dreadfuls and Sensation Novels gave way in the reading habits of the middle-class to works like Christie's early novels, books that were "deliberately unsensational, a better fit for a nation in mourning, where nearly every house had lost a son."[29] As such, Worsley notes, authors like the Queens of Crime "were writing not to challenge society or to stir things up. They were using their pens to heal."[30]

Worsley might be overstating her case here slightly, since characterizing Christie's early novels as "unsensational" seems to me to discount works like *The Secret Adversary* (1922), *The Man in the Brown Suit* (1924), *The Secret of Chimneys* (1925), and *The Big Four* (1927). All of these contain sensational elements like international conspiracies, diamond heists, secret societies, and even action scenes. I'm certainly not claiming these examples are among Christie's best works, but they do qualify somewhat Worsley's claim that Christie is writing sedate, calm works in her first authorial decade. Even so, Worsley is spot-on in her implication that Christie was actively, if subtly, engaging and challenging inherited forms, beliefs, and practices. Let's explore that claim briefly by looking a little more closely at how the Great War impacted not just fiction, but women as well.

Alison Light examines Christie's work in an interwar context, and points out that gender and sex roles were changing then in myriad ways:

The decimation of the British male population coincided with (and no doubt contributed to), increased female emancipation, politically, socially, sexually. The flapper and the neurasthenic can be read as shocking reversals of earlier norms and expectations of what women (or rather ladies) and men might be, but these were only the most visible examples of a continual alarm over the meaning of gender differences after the war.[31]

In the same vein, Marion Shaw and Sabine Vanacker point out the Great War "had opened up work opportunities and the knowledge that accompanied them" for women, including "greater access to higher education."[32] It is in this context that we see more women writers, but Shaw and Vanacker remind us that, "In spite of increased opportunities and widening horizons, the majority of these writing women remained . . . very much like their Victorian counterparts in being ladies, who wrote about the lives of

---

[28] Ibid., 225. Watson concurs in his work that Christie's early works offered "subtle comfort" after the "Great War." See "Message," 102.

[29] Worsley, *Art*, ch. 19.

[30] Ibid. In his work, Watson ties the "detective-story game" to the popularity and escapist function of games in the wake of World War I. See "Message," 108.

[31] Light, "Agatha Christie and Conservative Modernity," in *Forever England: Femininity, Literature and Conservatism between the Wars* (London & New York: Routledge, 1991), 8.

[32] Shaw and Vanacker, "Women Writers," 27.

ladies like themselves, often within a context of romance and domesticity."[33] In the post-War context, they continue, as writing and reading detective fiction "assumed a new respectability," women authoring works in that genre "could escape from or subordinate romance in the exercise of ratiocinative and game-playing faculties."[34] Put another way, "What the interbellum form of the genre offered to women writers, and their women readers, was the opportunity to remain within the respectable and domestic, to keep within the women's sphere, yet at the same time to use that sphere in a different way to satisfy different needs."[35] In essence, female crime fiction authors like Christie are subtly pushing back against not only their inherited literary traditions, but also the societal and religious expectations and mores that were beginning to change as well.[36]

Light agrees, and her central point is worth quoting in full, as it helps us understand how Christie's work fits into a broader socio-historical context:

> It is my own view that in these years between 1920 and 1940, a revolt against, embarrassment about, and distaste for the romantic languages of national pride produced a realignment of sexual identities which was part of a redefinition of Englishness. What had formerly been held as the virtues of the private sphere of middle-class life take on a new public and national significance. I maintain that the 1920s and '30s saw a move away from formerly heroic and officially masculine public rhetorics of national destiny and from a dynamic and missionary view of the Victorian and Edwardian middle classes in "Great Britain" to an Englishness at once less imperial and more inward-looking, more domestic and more private – and, in terms of pre-war standards, more "feminine."[37]

Importantly for us, Christie's focus on what Light calls "the virtues of the private sphere of middle-class life" in her works represented a modernist challenge to the literary forms she inherited.[38] In Light's words, Christie had a "modernist spirit" that aimed "to upset the Victorian image of home, sweet home."[39] Among other female detective fiction authors, she was both reflecting and revising the traditions and attitudes with which she grew up. Light makes this clear in a comment about "the whodunit as a form of popular modernism." She writes, "What has come to seem to us the epitome of the

---

[33] Ibid., 27–28.
[34] Ibid., 28.
[35] Ibid.
[36] As an example of how Christie received and resisted gender norms, see Makinen, *Agatha Christie*, 67, 135, and *passim*. See also Mary Anne Ackershoek, "'The Daughters of His Manhood:' Christie and the Golden Age of Detective Fiction," in *Theory and Practice of Classic Detective Fiction*, eds. Jerome H. Delamater and Ruth Prigozy, Contributions to the Study of Popular Culture, 62 (Westport, CT & London: Greenwood Press, 1997), 120.
[37] Light, "Agatha Christie," 8.
[38] In addition to Light, see also the claims of Nicolas Birns and Margaret Boe Birns on pp. 123–124 in "Agatha Christie: Modern and Modernist," in *The Cunning Craft: Original Essays on Detective Fiction and Contemporary Literary Theory*, eds. Ronald G. Walker and June M. Frazer (Macomb, IL: Yeast Printing/Western Illinois University, 1990).
[39] Light, "Agatha Christie," 61.

old-fashioned and the genteel, arguably began life as a modernising, de-sacramentalising form, emancipating itself from the literary lumber of the past. In popular fiction as much as in high culture, older models were to be broken up, self-consciously redeployed, parodied, pastiched, pilloried."[40] It's in this light that Light examines Christie's output as a form of popular modernism. In order to understand her claims about Christie as a modernist, let me selfishly employ an analogy from jazz.

In the second of his biographies of jazz icon Louis Armstrong, Thomas Brothers writes, "The 1920s was a decade when the reach of the modern was extending in all directions. . . . Modernism meant progress, the articulation of fresh forms, sophistication, something of consequence. It meant inventions of daring and speed, the Chrysler Building in New York City, talking movies, flappers, jazz, consumerism, and distance from Victorian conventions."[41] Brothers goes on to claim that Armstrong "invented not one but two modern art forms," in much the same way Christie codified the modern whodunit.[42] And just as Christie achieved this in dialogue with her own socio-historical and literary context, Armstrong "did this with vigorous commitment to means of expression derived from the black vernacular he had grown up with."[43]

The first of Armstrong's forms was his development of "a new melodic idiom" that "was pitched primarily to the black community," encapsulated in what we now regard as his classic jazz recordings. And Brothers notes, "His second modern formulation was the result of efforts to succeed in the mainstream market of white audiences. The key here was radical paraphrase of familiar tunes," i.e., Armstrong "invented a fresh approach to this old tradition, creating a song style that was part blues, part crooning, part fixed and variable model, plastic and mellow, the most modern thing around."[44] In sum, "Armstrong used what he learned from Eurocentric music to infuse the African-American vernacular with new intensity and possibilities."[45] In a similar move, Christie absorbed her Victorian and Edwardian backgrounds and its literature, but reshaped them into something new for a new time and audience.

Light expounds on this view of Christie as a creative retooler of preexisting forms and claims that Christie's "light reading" that embraces "the young idea" should be seen as a "modernist alternative to the virtuous qualities of nineteenth-century realism."[46] More broadly,

> It is as a literature of convalescence that we might understand something of the sea-change which came over detective fiction after the war. For what is most noticeable about the appearance of the whodunit, and most paradoxical, is the removal of the threat of violence. The crime story was the one place where the

[40] Ibid., 66. In his work, Black emphasizes the parodic aspect of Christie's work, especially how "Modern literature is mocked" in characters like Salome Otterbourne in Christie's *Death on the Nile* (*Importance*, 61).
[41] Brothers, *Louis Armstrong: Master of Modernism* (New York & London: W. W. Norton & Company, 2014), 8–9.
[42] Ibid., 9.
[43] Ibid.
[44] Ibid. For the "fixed and variable model," see Brothers, pp. 5–7.
[45] Ibid., 11.
[46] Light, "Agatha Christie," 69.

reader might reasonably expect violence, but what had formerly been enjoyed as one of the most aggressive of literatures, became distinctly pacific in its retreat from old-fashioned notions of the heroic.[47]

Foreshadowing Worsley's claims regarding the "unsensational" nature of Golden Age crime fiction, Light elaborates, "The whodunit between the wars came rapidly to be as insensible to violence as it could be. As a literature of convalescence it developed a strongly meditative framework, relying upon a kind of inturned and internal ratiocination rather than on what would stir or shake the reader."[48] Light further claims that the "effect" of interwar detective fiction "is preoccupying, the mental equivalent of pottering, which works more to relieve generalised anxiety than to generate strong emotion."[49] The need for new ways of dealing with violence based on the horrors of the War is seen in the foregrounding of the plot puzzle approach, and is echoed in the unheroic type of detective one finds in popular crime fiction in this period (for example, Poirot).

Along with the traumatic emotional and physical changes wrought by the War—not to mention the new opportunities and literary forms open to and employed by women writers—we must also recognize that the material culture of publishing and distributing of books evolved as well.[50] Worsley points out that around the time when Christie's first novel, *The Mysterious Affair at Styles*, was published in 1920, one finds

> changes to reading habits and to the publishing industry that saw the short story published in magazines like the *Strand* being replaced by the longer novel, and very often the novel involving crime. In Britain, the 1920s also saw the development of commercial libraries, such as those run by W. H. Smith or Boots, and publishing imprints such as Victor Gollancz's "Gollancz Crime" or William Collins' "Crime Club" met their voracious appetite for new books for circulation.[51]

Watson also highlights the importance of libraries during this period, both for authors and readers.[52] He writes,

> The novelist's main hope was to receive the custom of libraries, and of these the most useful to the writer of entertainment such as detective stories was the private lending or "chain" library that flourished in every suburban and provincial high street.... During the inter-war years it was virtually the only source of reading matter for those who could neither afford to buy books outright nor find the kind of undemanding entertainment they wanted in the public libraries, with their emphasis on non-fiction and "serious" novels.[53]

---

[47] Ibid., 69–70; see also 86 and 106.
[48] Ibid., 70.
[49] Ibid., 71.
[50] Black, *Importance*, examines some of these emotional and physical changes in his second chapter.
[51] Worsley, *Art*, ch. 19.
[52] See also Black, *Importance*, 61–62.
[53] Watson, "Message," 100.

Additionally, Light informs us that "By 1939 one-quarter of all fiction published was detective fiction and it was established as the majority reading of the 'coffee break and commuter classes.'"[54]

So, along with developments in material culture connected with publishing, we also must recognize the impact of these developments on gender and audience. That is, more books were more readily available, many of these books were classified as crime fiction, and many of those reading them were women, who were reading crime stories written by other women. In fact, Knight claims that "lending libraries which ... were the basic medium for dissemination of the new clue-puzzle novels had a 75 percent female audience."[55] In another work, Knight elaborates on Christie's relationship with this female audience, noting,

> Her stories realised the attitudes and resolved the anxieties of many people, especially women, whom earlier crime stories did not interest or satisfy.... As a woman she had no interest in the active male narcissism common to much crime fiction; being of upper-middle-class background she firmly believed and recreated the values of the English property owning bourgeoisie.[56]

John Scaggs uses Knight's work to argue similarly that, "Christie's consumers ... consisted of respectable, suburban readers (often women) who shared Christie's upper middle-class, property-owning, bourgeois ideology, and were keen to have it confirmed."[57] This emphasis on a shared worldview and socio-economic status between author and audience is important for our purposes. As we have seen, early Golden Age detective fiction represented a modernist challenge to previous literary forms and foci, and in so doing it both reflected and challenged the sensibilities and/or ideology of its audience. In the same way, readerly appreciation of Christie's works was dependent on her audiences' ability not only to recognize and understand the references, allusions, and images (many of which are religious) in the language she used, but also to mark the subtle shifts in the way she employed and explored them if they were to grasp their use in her plots.

This audience, as well as other readers of Golden Age detective fiction, devoured Christie's stories and novels and have made her not just one of the most popular mystery authors of the twentieth century, but one of the most popular authors of all time. Again, though, it behooves us to recall that Christie's literary context and tendencies are situated within this loose category of Golden Age of detective fiction. Doing so allows us to understand how she constructs her fictional worlds and, subsequently, how we can discuss the presence/role of religion therein.

Even though Christie sets what Gill calls her "fairy stories" in nearly closed narrative systems, obviously we can still address religion in those systems. I'll examine Christie's

---

[54] Light, "Agatha Christie," 65.
[55] Knight, "The Golden Age," 81. Watson also highlights the determinative role women played in choosing what their families would be reading. See "Message," 100.
[56] Knight, "'... done from within'," 107.
[57] Scaggs, *Crime Fiction*, The New Critical Idiom (London & New York: Routledge, 2005), 38. For more, see Black, *Importance*, 22–23 and 42ff.

religious beliefs briefly later on, but we need to recognize that those beliefs are of limited value in understanding her works. That is, it's painfully clear that she viewed her writing as a professional obligation, not a confessional one.[58] Building on the work of Barnard, Mary Anne Ackershoek examines what she terms "Christiean misdirection" in her fiction, and posits on this basis that "we do not have a reliable way of knowing what Christie's intentions as an author were."[59] Even so, scholars are in agreement that we can observe some influence of her personal experiences on her work in terms of content. Many also point to a series of six novels written under the name of Mary Westmacott, which they view as thinly disguised autobiographical fiction.[60] We may still glean some important data regarding Christie's own religious background and views, nonetheless. One helpful indicator of her engagement with religion is the fact that she wrote some explicitly religious work, like the 1965 collection *Star Over Bethlehem and Other Stories*, published under the name Agatha Christie Mallowan. Additionally, she was often obvious about her scriptural allusions, as in the titles *Evil Under the Sun* (an allusion to Ecclesiastes) and—what is most likely her first published short story—"The Wife of the Kenite" (a reference to the character of Jael in Judges 4–5). Further, her 1958 novel *Ordeal by Innocence* begins with an epigraph from Job 9:20 and 28 (King James Version) and its final chapter includes a citation from the English Standard Version of Job 9:23.[61] Finally, *The Crooked House* mentions Jezebel, the mark of Cain, and the Scarlet Woman of Babylon.[62] Clearly, here is a woman who knew her Bible and mined it for plot schemes and character paradigms. However, these allusions also obviously reflect the normative Christianity present in England during this period.

Even granting these examples, we should be mindful of trying to gauge the tenor of her work based on her own religious beliefs and practices, as it assumes too porous a boundary between author and work.[63] For her part, Gill connects this to Christie's chosen genre, noting, "As a creative yet opaque literary medium, detective fiction was perhaps uniquely fitted to the character of Agatha Christie, a woman obsessively concerned to avoid self-revelation."[64] Gill continues, echoing Knight's observation regarding Golden Age "writing style," pointing out for us that,

---

[58] See, e.g., Christie, *An Autobiography*, 358 and 413.
[59] Ackershoek, "'Daughters'," 123. Barnard sees this withdrawal of authorial presence as an outgrowth of Christie's famous disappearance in 1926. See *Talent*, 48–59, especially 52. York, *Agatha Christie*, 129, also comments on the extent to which Christie's novels reflect the external world of their author.
[60] This is a basic and thoroughgoing assumption in biographies like that of Laura Thompson, *Agatha Christie: An English Mystery* (London: Headline, 2007); repr. *Agatha Christie: A Mysterious Life* (New York: Pegasus Books, 2018), Kindle edition, e.g., *passim*. Several secondary sources also focus on Christie's Westmacott novels and make the same assumption. See chapter nine in Mary S. Wagoner, *Agatha Christie*, Twayne's English Authors Series (Boston: G. K. Hall & Co., 1986), 110–118.
[61] See *Ordeal by Innocence* (1958/1959; reis. New York: HarperCollins, 2011), Kindle edition, Epigraph and ch. 24.
[62] See, e.g., *Crooked House* (1949; reis. New York: HarperCollins, 2011), Kindle edition, chs. 10, 12, 13, and 14.
[63] A point made by Janet Morgan, *Agatha Christie: A Biography* (London: William Collins Sons & Company, 1984; repr. New York: Alfred A. Knopf, 1985), 108.
[64] Gill, *Agatha Christie*, Introduction, "The Hidden Author." See also Makinen, *Agatha Christie*, 7; and Worsley, *Art*, ch. 19.

Consciously, her novels are an attempt not to reveal but to mask the self, yet even as she succeeds in eliminating personal opinions and autobiographical information, Christie thereby gives free rein to her unconscious. Hers is a fictional world in which the author is hidden, and which fixes readers' minds upon the analysis of emotionally neutral elements, such as cigarette butts and railway timetables, while sweeping their fantasies along on an effortless, unthinking race to the denouement.[65]

In sum, aside from autobiographical works and perhaps her Westmacott novels, Christie's own life and views aren't center stage in her fiction, and this is especially true of her Poirot canon.[66]

Christie's audience hasn't seemed to mind this authorial reticence, as evidenced by her aforementioned astounding sales and the popularity of the characters she created. In fact, a good deal of Christie's success is directly related to the point Knight and Scaggs made earlier: to a great extent, she and her reader share the worldview underlying her fiction. Again, Gill writes,

In the postwar world . . . as the fame of many of Christie's contemporaries waned, she remained popular. In fact, the world she had first created in her novels reached new audiences through the stage, film, and, at last, television. This success, which continues unabated today, points to a deep and remarkable consonance between Christie's world view and that of an enormous public, yet the definition of that world view proves to be enormously difficult.[67]

I'm much more optimistic than Gill that the worldview shared by Christie and her readers can be defined. One issue related to that worldview that I think is especially important for us to mention is a longing to return to the time period(s) that occasioned it. That is, as I mention earlier in reference to Watson's research, amidst all the radical cultural and religious shifts Christie herself experienced in the mid-twentieth century, her Poirot stories contain undoubtable nostalgia for the Victorian and Edwardian eras.[68] As Patricia D. Maida and Nicholas B. Spornick write, Christie "found sustenance in the well-worn values of the past. . . . Her perspective shaped a nostalgic Eden out of England's Victorian and Edwardian past."[69] This means that "Nostalgia provides

---

[65] Gill, *Agatha Christie*, Afterword.

[66] Barnard, *Talent*, 57, sees this as an advantage in her writing.

[67] Gill, *Agatha Christie*, ch. 6, "Mary Westmacott."

[68] See, for example, Mark Aldridge, *Agatha Christie's Poirot: The Greatest Detective in the World* (London: HarperCollins, 2020), 256. Also review Watson, "Little World," 171. Not all critics agree that this nostalgia is present, benign, and/or univocal. In her *Agatha Christie: An Elusive Woman* (New York: Pegasus Crime, 2022), Worsley claims that "Christie to her first readers wasn't 'nostalgic'" (Kindle edition, Preface). Further, see Ackershoek, "'The Daughters of His Manhood'," 120ff.; and Gill Plain, "'Tale Engineering': Agatha Christie and the Aftermath of the Second World War," *Literature & History* 29, no. 2 (2020): 179–199, who is careful to note "the contradictory amalgamation of nostalgia and modernity that underpinned the hopes, aspirations and fears of postwar reconstruction" (180).

[69] Maida and Spornick, *Murder She Wrote: A Study of Agatha Christie's Detective Fiction* (Bowling Green, OH: Bowling Green State University Popular Press, 1982), 193.

nurturance as Christie feeds the public's appetite for security and stability."[70] Christie's audience, too, has seen societal and technological upheavals of an unimaginable magnitude in the late twentieth to early twenty-first century. It's only natural to expect that her readers find a respite from our confusing times in the comfortable nostalgia of the illusion of a simpler time.

In Chapter 2, we'll delve more deeply into that "simpler time," to understand better the nature and reach of Christianity in Christie's time, as well as her own religious identity. These data will help us in comprehending how she represents Christianity and uses biblical literature in her works as well as challenges their hegemonic and normative status.

---

[70] Ibid., 193.

2

Christianity in England and Agatha Christie

This chapter will begin by discussing the theoretical concepts of Christian hegemony and normativity before examining the pervasive presence of Christianity and biblical literacy in nineteenth- and twentieth-century England. Building on that, we'll then examine the issue of Christie's own religious identity before discussing her first and final Poirot novel to demonstrate our approach. All of this will aid us in understanding how Christie relies on shared religious and biblical language that she expects her audience to comprehend, presents Christianity as a normative presence, yet subtly resists that normative Christianity in a modernist sense.

*   *   *

Let's begin with a brief discussion of the socio-cultural and historical position of Christianity in the Victorian (1837–1901) and Edwardian (1901–1910) eras, a position we'll describe as hegemonic and normative. As a way of understanding these terms, we're going to employ the work of Khyati Y. Joshi on the dominance of Christianity in the US. She helps us understand Christian hegemony, writing, "*Hegemony* refers to a society's unacknowledged and/or unconscious adherence to a dominant worldview. Hegemonic ideologies are perpetuated through the cultural norms, policies, and practices which set those ideologies up as 'business as usual.' *Christian hegemony* thus refers to the predominance and endorsement at the national level of Christian observances, beliefs, scriptures, and manners of worship."[1]

Similarly, the term "Christian normativity" implies that the symbols, language, and values from Christianity are taken to be "ordinary and expected," and generally applicable in socio-political discourse as well as aesthetic productions of a given time.[2] The normative position of Christianity has pejorative implications for non-Christian individuals and groups, though. As Joshi claims, we must acknowledge "the presence of a Christian norm within the US, and the existence of a religious consensus around monotheism (and theism itself) that ignores or trivializes, denigrates and alienates citizens from marginalized faith communities and nonbelief convictions."[3] Shifting to

---

[1] Joshi, *White Christian Privilege: The Illusion of Religious Equality in America* (New York: New York University Press, 2020), 4.
[2] Ibid., 3.
[3] Joshi, "Diversity, Pluralism, Secularism," in *Proceedings of the Fifth Biennial Conference on Religion and American Culture* (Indiana University & Purdue University, Indianapolis: The Center for the Study of Religion and American Culture, 2017), 42.

focus on civic organizations and ideology, she notes that "Christianity dominates by setting the tone, and establishing the rules and assumptions about what belongs or does not belong and what is acceptable and not acceptable in public discourse. It is embedded in our institutions in ways that provide advantages to Christians and disadvantages for members of minority religious groups."[4]

Admittedly, there are obvious differences between the socio-cultural and religious context(s) Joshi is addressing and those we find in the nineteenth to twentieth centuries in England. However, in both one finds Christianity at the nexus of ideology, politics, and identity; that is, the hegemonic position of Christianity determines the very discourses that define individual and group identity, whether in civic, political, religious, and/or personal life. This is even more obvious in England, due to the established position of the Church, as opposed to the US, in which disestablishment is supposed to be the norm. It's this determinative quality that we'll find assumed and reflected in Christie's works, along with our subsequent assessment of non-Christian religious practices and identities (discussed in Part 4). At the same time, I'll argue that Christie is pushing back against the ideologies and practices assumed to be normative in these times.

Joshi also includes a useful distinction in her work between what she calls external (structural) and internal (attitudinal) dimensions of Christian privilege. She defines the former as

> the construction of what is normal and not normal, what is acceptable and unacceptable, as decided by society. Privileged groups define the mainstream culture—behavior patterns, symbols, institutions, values, and other socially constructed components of society. They are what is "normal;" groups that do not fit this mainstream norm are marginalized. Sometimes they are described as "subcultures"—literally "under" the (mainstream) culture.[5]

Examples of this structural dimension include phenomena like Christian language, imagery, and even the social recognition of Christian holidays in calendars, not to mention the proliferation of Christianity through material culture and architecture. Moving on to the second dimension, Joshi writes, "The *internal/attitudinal* dimensions of privilege are the beliefs and thought patterns that reify the idea that members of the dominant group have some specific right to their position and its advantages."[6] As we'll see in Part 4, there is an unspoken (though sometimes verbalized) assumption that Christianity is a superior religion and that other kinds of religious identity are odd, socially unacceptable, and even dangerous.

Both of these dimensions help us see better why it's important to reckon with religion in Christie's Poirot stories. If we understand better the kinds of assumptions

---

⁴ Ibid. See also Paul Hedges, *Religious Hatred: Prejudice, Islamophobia, and Antisemitism in Global Context* (London & New York: Bloomsbury, 2021), 21–22.

⁵ Joshi, *White*, 129.

⁶ Ibid., 130.

Christie is working with, engage the presuppositions held by the society in which she was socialized (the world behind the text), and examine how religion is treated in her work (the world of the text) and its renderings (the world the text creates), we can develop a deeper sense of the impact of her work. That is, because of how popular Christie remains, how Christianity and other religious practices are portrayed in her work matters, as her corpus of stories functions as not only entertainment, but also a resource for meaning-making for her ever-growing audience. And as Joshi reminds us, this is not some ivory tower discussion, as "Very real everyday consequences result from a situation in which the Christian way of doing something comes to be understood as the normal way of living."[7]

Joshi's emphasis on Christian normativity leads us to consider another important point. As Matthew Grimley writes, "church membership figures do not tell the whole story of Christian influence."[8] That is, "the churches employed both 'hard power'—their membership base—and 'soft power,' their broader cultural, political, and ethical influence."[9] Grimley's point is that the numbers belie the ideological and ceremonial roles played by Christianity in English culture more broadly. These roles lie at the heart of Joshi's Christian normativity, so it'll be helpful to spend a little time with this idea of soft power.

Grimley's use of the term is indebted to Joseph S. Nye, Jr., who wrote about soft power in the context of post-Cold War international politics. Nye argued that the US's position in global politics was actually much better than analysts thought; this was due to a reckoning with America's outsized cultural influence as opposed to focusing on military or economic power. Nye claimed, "The ability to affect what other countries want tends to be associated with intangible power resources such as culture, ideology, and institutions."[10] More broadly, he pointed out,

> Soft co-optive power is just as important as hard command power. If a state can make its power seem legitimate in the eyes of others, it will encounter less resistance to its wishes. If its culture and ideology are attractive, others will more willingly follow. If it can establish international norms consistent with its society, it is less likely to have to change.[11]

Stated differently, Nye felt that hard power resources—such as economic influence or military might or even a sheer advantage of numbers—weren't the sole or even the most important loci of power in the late twentieth century. Instead, "such resources as cultural and ideological attraction" were the key to "co-optive" or "soft power."[12] As we'll see, despite its numerical decline, Christianity—and especially the established Church—retains this soft power in various ways, perhaps most importantly "the way in which Christianity infused public culture and was adopted by individuals, whether

7 Ibid., 3.
8 Grimley, "The Religion of Englishness: Puritanism, Providentialism, and "National Character," 1918–1945," *Journal of British Studies* 46, no. 4 (2007): 887.
9 Ibid.
10 Nye, "Soft Power," *Foreign Policy* 80 (1990): 166–167.
11 Ibid., 167.
12 Ibid., 168.

churchgoers or not, in forming their own identities."[13] This deep reach of Christianity into identity-formation, both on an individual and communal level, obviously reinforces Joshi's claim of the normative and hegemonic status of Christianity. For now, though, let's briefly examine Christianity in England in the nineteenth and early twentieth centuries. Spoiler alert: we'll see that Christianity was both hegemonic and spawned that normativity that Joshi mentions.

*   *   *

It may seem obvious, but it is nevertheless vital to keep in mind that Christie was most definitely a creature of her contexts and the beliefs and values of her times—the world behind the text—are reflected in her work, even as she interrogates them. For example, in their analysis of Christie's *oeuvre*, Patricia D. Maida and Nicholas B. Spornick write, "The happy combination of imagination, practicality and respect for those late Victorian values became the mainstay of her fiction. Christie's world – the servants, money, class, traditions, concepts of good and evil – became the vital forces in her detective fiction."[14] Likewise, Mary S. Wagoner points out that in her *Autobiography*, Christie "explains attitudes that inform her detective fiction, such as her essentially Victorian social and moral conservatism, her views on the importance of discovering the guilty in order to protect the innocent, her notions on the built-in imbalance that keeps criminals from applying brakes as ordinary citizens do, and her skepticism about new ideologies for perfecting the human condition."[15] However, Gillian Gill (among others) agrees with my seeing Christie as resisting and reframing those Victorian beliefs and mores. She notes,

> Just like everyone else, Christie was the product of a specific time and place, and she was certainly no revolutionary thinker. Nonetheless, Christie was significantly less enslaved by the ideology and structural prejudices of her culture, time, and class than [her] contemporaries. . . . The racism, the classism, the sexism that make the huge majority of popular novels written in the thirties and forties unreadable today are relatively unimportant in Christie's work.[16]

Gill's claim clearly echoes the views of Nicholas Birns and Margaret Boe Birns, as well as Alison Light, in seeing Christie as a modernist author, one who challenges and reorients previous aesthetic forms and moral beliefs.[17]

---

[13] Callum Brown, *The Death of Christian Britain: Understanding Secularization, 1800–2000*, 2nd edn (London & New York: Routledge, 2009), 8.

[14] Maida and Spornick, *Murder She Wrote: A Study of Agatha Christie's Detective Fiction* (Bowling Green, OH: Bowling Green State University Popular Press, 1982), 62.

[15] Wagoner, *Agatha Christie*, Twayne's English Authors Series (Boston: G. K. Hall & Co., 1986), 133.

[16] Gill, *Agatha Christie: The Woman and Her Mysteries* (New York: Free Press, 1990), Kindle edition, Introduction, "The Hidden Author."

[17] See Birns and Birns, "Agatha Christie: Modern and Modernist," in *The Cunning Craft: Original Essays on Detective Fiction and Contemporary Literary Theory*, eds. Ronald G. Walker and June M. Frazer (Macomb, IL: Yeast Printing/Western Illinois University, 1990), 120–134; and Light, "Agatha Christie and Conservative Modernity," in *Forever England: Femininity, Literature and Conservatism between the Wars* (London & New York: Routledge, 1991), 61–112.

Regardless, the importance of focusing on these eras is that they encompass her childhood and as such exerted an obvious influence on Christie's upbringing, including her early religious rearing and literary socialization. Put differently, since Christie was born on 15 September 1890, it's key for us to understand religion and Christianity during this period in order to shed light on her formative experiences attending religious services and her introduction to reading, especially the Bible. This world behind the text is clearly important to our understanding of Christie's use of and challenge to her natal religion in her Poirot stories, even as we keep in mind that this world isn't completely determinative in its influence.

In his book *Religion and Society in England, 1850–1914*, Hugh McLeod claims that "organised religion was highly visible and accessible, and available in a variety of forms suited to a wide range of tastes."[18] Callum G. Brown agrees with him, echoing Joshi's attitudinal dimension I mention earlier: "In 1900, there was almost universal certainty in British government and the major institutions (including the churches) that Christianity was the only legitimate religion, that it was obviously superior to every other religion, and that without it social morality and civil order would collapse."[19] Both authors note Joshi's structural dimension as well, what McLeod calls the "massive presence of Christianity in so many areas of daily life."[20] An example of this presence is religious buildings, i.e., "almost ever [sic.] street had a church, chapel, mission hall, Sunday School, parish hall, or institute."[21] Brown also notes the material presence of Christianity in this period, claiming, "Religious structures – like churches with spires – stood proud of the landscape, whilst religious ritual punctuated the lives of virtually all of our forebears every week and every year. Christian culture interspersed the seasons and the week, in the form of rituals, clothes and ways of marking time."[22]

Picking up on Christianity's impact on the lived experience of believers, McLeod explores Joshi's dimensions further by describing the exposure to and impact of Christianity on the life-cycle of the "great majority of the population," beginning with "infant baptism," then "the learning of prayers" and the content thereof, before discussing the pervasiveness and centrality of Sunday School in terms of education, socialization, and potential "material benefits."[23] As John H. R. Moorman reminds us, in 1882 compulsory elementary education had been mandated, and in 1891 the government made this education free of cost. More to the point, by 1891 "the voluntary, or non-provided, schools numbered over 14,000 of which by far the majority belonged to the Church of England."[24] As such, Christian influence and discourse could be found

---

[18] McLeod, *Religion and Society in England, 1850–1914*, Social History in Perspective (New York: St. Martin's Press, 1996), 72–73. See also John R. H. Moorman, *A History of the Church in England*, 3rd edn (Harrisburg, PA: Morehouse Publishing, 1980), 393.

[19] Brown, *Religion and Society in Twentieth-Century Britain* (Harlow: Pearson Education Limited, 2006), 2.

[20] McLeod, *Religion and Society*, 71.

[21] Ibid., 72.

[22] Brown, *Religion and Society*, 5-6. Likewise, Sarah C. Williams, "Is There a Bible in the House? Gender, Religion and Family Culture," in *Women, Gender and Religious Cultures in Britain, 1800–1940*, eds. Sue Morgan and Jacqueline deVries (London & New York: Routledge, 2010), 23, notes the "sheer material presence of Christianity in every dimension of nineteenth-century culture."

[23] McLeod, *Religion and Society*, 80. See also Moorman, *History*, 414.

[24] Moorman, *History*, 411.

in day, grammar, and public schools, all of which—even if "independent of any church control"—would have led to a "sense of sectarian identity" once the student exited the school system.[25] Once they did, their "sectarian identity" or religious adherence also factored into "where they found work," since "religious screening ... religious connections ... [and] sectarian preferentialism" were all significant factors in seeking gainful employment.[26] McLeod even claims that, "Religion might also determine where people spent their free hours, as so many leisure facilities were provided by churches or chapels. The role was particularly important in small towns and rural areas, where the range of alternatives was likely to be relatively narrow."[27] Sarah C. Williams seconds McLeod's judgment here. Writing of the Nonconformists (non-Anglican groups like Presbyterians, Congregationalists, and Wesleyans/Methodists), she notes, these "groups likewise fostered a higher degree of association between family and chapel culture in this period [1850–1914] such that members' lives were in every detail constrained by the norms of their particular denominational association."[28]

Finally, McLeod points out that "Religious issues played a major part in politics throughout this period, and religious affiliation was a major influence on voting."[29] Brown sums up the influence of religion on how people understood themselves, noting, "It governed ... how they felt about each other and about themselves. Personal identities were heavily constructed on religious frameworks.... Everyday British culture was a moral maze, defined by a Christian core, which constantly berated the irreligious and praised the 'true Christian.'"[30] Determining who exactly counted as a "true Christian" is difficult in any time period, but we do have some help in terms of measuring church attendance and membership. In general, we can observe a decline in church membership from the end of the Great War until the end of World War II, at which point we see a brief uptick in membership and attendance before a precipitous drop-off during the 1960s.[31]

Clearly, we've already seen evidence for Christian hegemony and normativity, but let's deepen the baseline we've thus far established by moving solidly into the twentieth century and discussing the impact of World War One. We'll begin with the work of Mary Anne Ackershoek, who notes "two cultural attitudes" that are important for us to understand: "First, the perception that the world was crippled, that the Great War had irrevocably damaged, at least, that world of order and security that England felt to be peculiarly its own."[32] And second, "the deaths of so many men in World War I had left

[25] McLeod, *Religion and Society*, 83.
[26] Ibid, 86.
[27] Ibid., 88.
[28] Williams, "Is There a Bible in the House?" 19.
[29] McLeod, *Religion and Society*, 91. Nevertheless, as McLeod notes, there were "important limits to this influence" (121, see also 122).
[30] Brown, *Religion and Society*, 6.
[31] See, e.g., Brown, *Death*, 5; and Grimley, "Religion," 886–887.
[32] Ackershoek, "'The Daughters of His Manhood': Christie and the Golden Age of Detective Fiction," in *Theory and Practice of Classic Detective Fiction*, eds. Jerome H. Delamater and Ruth Prigozy; Contributions to the Study of Popular Culture, 62 (Westport, CT & London: Greenwood Press, 1997), 119–128, 119.

a gap in the structure of a society that could, and must, be filled by women, including women acting in what had previously been male roles."[33] The importance of this second point is to reinforce the bald fact that "signs of societal change were everywhere," and especially for women, the "war years were to some extent emancipatory."[34] That is, as Marion Shaw and Sabine Vanacker and Alison Light also note, inherited gender expectations and codes were in flux as a result of the conceptual and pragmatic results of the War.[35]

In a broader sense, Philip Jenkins argues convincingly that "The First World War was a thoroughly religious event, in the sense that overwhelmingly Christian nations fought each other in what many viewed as a holy war, a spiritual conflict."[36] More important for our purposes, Jenkins also claims, "In 1914, something like Christendom was clearly the accepted political-religious order in much of Europe."[37] And he continues, writing that, "In the immediate aftermath of the war, moreover, parts of Europe still notionally remained within the scope of Christendom, in that many states defined themselves as Christian and gave preferential or even exclusive status to a particular church. Such establishment continued to be the situation in Great Britain."[38] Jenkins's claim here resonates nicely with Joshi's description of Christian hegemony, but we're able to demonstrate the hegemonic status of Christianity in more detail.

Given the crises in population and identity noted by Ackershoek as well as the claims of Christian hegemony from Jenkins, it's not surprising that we find attempts to solidify the nation's character that employ religion. As an example of this, let's recall Light's comment about Englishness undergoing a redefinition after the War and explore Matthew Grimley's work on Englishness as a kind of religious identity. Utilizing research on the literary and material presence of Christianity in the Interwar period, Grimley pains a clear picture of what he calls "the connection between Englishness and Protestant Religion" in the period after World War I.[39] That is, Grimley reviews primary texts such as "books exploring national character and poetry, sermons, political speeches, and film," and finds what he calls "an imaginative identification between Englishness and a tolerant, undemonstrative form of Protestantism [which] remained strong in the first half of the twentieth century."[40] However, this was "a common English Protestantism" that's exemplified by the way in which these various primary sources treat the Bible as a symbol of a "common religious heritage … that straddled the Anglican and nonconformist traditions."[41] According to Grimley, the aesthetic authors

---

[33] Ackershoek, "'Daughters'," 119.
[34] Ibid.
[35] See Shaw and Vanacker, "Women Writers and the Golden Age of Detective Fiction," in *Reflecting on Miss Marple*, Heroines? (London & New York: Routledge, 1991), 9–34; and Light, "Agatha Christie," *passim*.
[36] Jenkins, *The Great and Holy War: How World War I Became a Religious Crusade* (New York: HarperOne, 2014), 5.
[37] Ibid., 192.
[38] Ibid., 193.
[39] Grimley, "Religion," 885. Grimley is reliant on and cites McLeod, "Protestantism and British National Identity, 1815-1945," in *Nation and Religion: Perspectives on Europe and Asia*, eds. Peter van der Veer and Hartmut Lehmann (Princeton: Princeton University Press, 1999), 44–70.
[40] Grimley, "Religion," 885.
[41] Ibid., 891 and 895. See also McLeod, "Protestantism," 44.

and cultural creators he examines "invoked shared religious traditions as a way of inspiring a sense of community against a number of secular challenges in the 1920s and 1930s."[42] At this point we should remember that the majority of the texts Grimley discusses aren't religiously authoritative, even if they are prescriptive in their construction of Englishness. That is, most of these texts aren't drawn from the Church hierarchy, yet they're engaging and employing religion and religious language/imagery in order to redefine "Englishness." In his conclusion, Grimley makes this clear:

> Religion remained central to the articulation of the idea of national character in the first half of the twentieth century. When commentators referred to the English as a Christian people, they were referring not to their propensity (or otherwise) for churchgoing but to a belief that Christianity (and specifically Protestantism) had shaped the distinctive political, legal, and associational culture of the nation. The frequency with which they did this suggests that the idea still resonated with a public that still saw itself as Christian.[43]

If you flip back a few pages and review Joshi's definition of Christian normativity, you'll see clearly that this is exactly what Grimley is describing: the belief that Christianity is the "norm" in a given society, despite what actual numbers might indicate (remember our discussion of "soft power"?). And if we combine this with Jenkins's claim regarding Christian hegemony during and immediately after the Great War, then it seems obvious that Christie's early work should be seen as a response to and a wrestling with these issues.[44]

These issues are also found in Aimee E. Barbeau's research on "official publications by the church during the war."[45] Therein, she claims that "Anglican clergy responded to the war using the language of national crusade" which "evokes an image of England as a Christian nation with the vocation of redeeming worldwide Christendom."[46] More specifically, Barbeau points out that numerically, the Church in 1914 was flourishing with an impressive reach, but that it was also "losing ground in British society" and "stood in need of reform."[47] She notes several reasons for this loss of ground, including "the alienation of the working class," overseas missionary expansion, and internal conflicts in the form of three new inner-groups: evangelicals, Anglo-Catholics, and modernists.[48] In essence, "Though Britain in 1914 was still largely Christian by many

---

[42] Grimley, "Religion," 897.
[43] Ibid., 906.
[44] As Ackershoek, "'Daughters'," 120, exhorts us to do. Along with Christie's work, pageants are another example of a popular cultural phenomena functioning didactically and ideologically to represent shifting socio-cultural and religious practices and identities. For more on this subject, see Arthur Burns, "A National Church Tells its Story: The English Church Pageant of 1909," and Amy Binns, "Nobility, Duty and Courage: Propaganda and Inspiration in Interwar Women's and Girls' Pageants', both in *Restaging the Past: Historical Pageants, Culture and Society in Modern Britain*, eds. Angela Bartie, et al. (London: UCL Press, 2020), 56–79 and 132–157, respectively.
[45] Barbeau, "Christian Empire and National Crusade: The Rhetoric of Anglican Clergy in the First World War," *Anglican and Episcopal History* 85, no. 1 (2016): 27.
[46] Barbeau, "Christian Empire," 27.
[47] Ibid., 28. On a broader scale, Jenkins agrees. See *The Great and Holy War*, 192.
[48] See Barbeau, "Christian Empire," 29, 31, and 60–61.

measures, the Anglican Church was losing ground in a secularizing and materialistic society. Among the lower ranks of society, industrialization, urbanization, and socialism were eating away at the church's influence; at the top, it was Darwinism, modernism, and agnosticism. Everywhere, the church was gradually losing touch with society."[49] According to Barbeau, the first World War "appeared a godsend opportunity to shift the spiritual tide of the country in the Church's favor."[50] However, this didn't happen: "The war did not permanently restore the fortunes of the Church of England, but neither did it eliminate it as a force in British life."[51] Even with this equivocal impact, the programs and experiences of the Church led to a number of reforms and modernizing efforts.[52] As such, even though the Church of England still exercised a great deal of soft or co-optive power, the numerical and political (i.e., "hard") power of the Church began to wane significantly after World War Two.[53]

Even from this brief survey, it should be obvious by now that both of the dimensions of Christian privilege Joshi discusses in her work were amply present during the Victorian and Edwardian periods, the Great War, and the Interwar years, and this provides sufficient evidence of Christian hegemony and normativity. But what about Christie herself?

* * *

Christie describes her early experiences with religion in her *Autobiography*, and her own religious views were evidently a mixture of her father's and those of "Nursie," her childhood Nanny. In Chapter 11, I'll say more about her mother Clarissa's religious eclecticism, but Christie characterizes her father Frederick as "a simple-hearted, orthodox Christian. He said his prayers every night and went to Church every Sunday. His religion was matter-of-fact and without heart-searchings."[54] Christie writes of "Nursie" that she was "a Bible Christian. She did not go to Church but read her Bible at home. Keeping the Sabbath was very important, and being worldly was a sore offence in the eyes of the Almighty."[55] Bible Christians were "an overwhelmingly rural Methodist sect," and because of the centrality of the Bible and its "literal" interpretation thereof, held a more progressive view which resulted in "a more active religious role for women" than other sects.[56] In fact,

---

[49] Ibid., 61.

[50] Ibid., 33.

[51] Ibid., 61.

[52] Ibid., 60–61.

[53] Miss Marple herself attests to this decline in the hard power of the Church. In the 1971 novel *Nemesis*, she remarks that in her youth, village life revolved "around the church," but that "Nowadays of course it's rather different." See *Nemesis* (1971; reis. New York: HarperCollins, 2011), Kindle edition, ch. 10, "'Oh! Fond, Oh! Fair, the Days That Were'."

[54] Christie, *An Autobiography* (1977; reis. New York: HarperCollins, 2011), 25.

[55] Christie, *An Autobiography*, 25. See also Janet Morgan, *Agatha Christie: A Biography* (London: William Collins Sons & Company, 1984; repr. New York: Alfred A. Knopf, 1985), 11; and Maida and Spornick, *Murder*, 19.

[56] McLeod, *Religion and Society*, 34, 162. In fact, the influence of Nursie on a kind of pure, unadorned, primitive Christian practice finds a voice in Christie's 1934 novel *Three Act Tragedy*. Therein, a young woman called Miss Hermione Lytton Gore (nicknamed "Egg") launches into a full-blown critique of Christianity after a Vicar named Babbington is killed. Egg's preference for a hypothetically pure Christianity, devoid of its later accoutrements, parallels the austerity and conservatism of Nursie's conception of Christianity.

as Jennifer M. Lloyd notes, Bible Christians actively recruited female itinerant preachers early after their formation in 1815, and after several slack years, began seeking women to travel and preach again right around the time of Christie's birth in 1890.[57] As such, Nursie's influence on Christie may have broadened her receptiveness to a more progressive view regarding women's role(s) in religious contexts.

In terms of her own religious views, she recalls, "I was myself insufferably smug in my conviction of being one of the 'saved';" that is, the young Agatha refrained from playing games or music on Sunday, and had "terrible fears for the ultimate salvation of my father, who played croquet blithely on Sunday afternoons," and joked about religious figures.[58] Additionally, she recounts how Sunday Church attendance was "one of the highlights of the week."[59] Christie also claims that her father had contributed money in her name to assist the building of a larger church for the parish when she was born, and because of this, she was keen to attend church. "'When can I go to church?' had been my constant demand—and at last the great day came. I sat next to my father in a pew near the front and followed the service in his big prayer-book. . . . I enjoyed church services on Sunday very much."[60] All of this tells us that at a young age, Christie would have been familiar with the dominant form of Christianity in England, and regular Church attendance was not only expected of her, but eagerly anticipated on her part. We can assume that little Agatha would've attended Sunday School and been exposed to biblical stories both there and during the services she looked forward to attending. In fact, in her *Autobiography*, Christie mentions the Bible in a section discussing what she liked to read as a child. She writes,

> And there were, of course, Old Testament stories, in which I had revelled from an early age. . . . At home previously there had been special story-books only allowed to be read on Sundays (which made a treat of them) and books of Bible stories with which I was familiar. There is no doubt that the stories of the Old Testament are, from a child's point of view, rattling good yarns.[61]

To illustrate how Christie's recollections situate her into the normative discourse of Christianity during her childhood, let's return to McLeod's work. After examining the components of Christian influence and its presence in society, he also points out that "Nineteenth-century English Christianity found typical expressions in three cultural features which, to a considerable extent, crossed the boundaries of class, politics and denomination: knowledge of and reference to the Bible as a final authority; the love of hymns; and the observance of Sunday as a day set apart."[62] We've already seen the

---

[57] See Lloyd, "Women Preachers in the Bible Christian Connexion," *Albion: A Quarterly Journal Concerned with British Studies* 36, no. 3 (2004): 451–452.

[58] Christie, *An Autobiography*, 25.

[59] Ibid., 49. As Christie notes, this would have been "the parish church of Tor Mohun . . . the oldest church in Torquay" (49–50).

[60] Ibid., 50.

[61] Ibid., 49–50. See also York, *Agatha Christie*, 143, for an assessment of "Christie's culture."

[62] McLeod, *Religion and Society*, 100.

importance of Sunday and its observance in Christie's household.[63] It's also worth mentioning that since Christie was an accomplished singer and talented pianist, we may assume that hymns were also important to her, even if she doesn't mention performing them in her *Autobiography*.[64] Obviously, though, the first of McLeod's "typical expressions" is most central to our examination of shared religious language in Christie's work. He claims that "The chief foundation of Victorian Christianity was the Bible, and a detailed knowledge of the Bible was general among those who made any claim to be religious."[65] Timothy Larsen agrees with McLeod, noting "the remarkable extent to which the Bible was a dominant presence in Victorian thought and culture."[66] Commenting on the Bible as the "focal point" of "English popular religion," McLeod writes,

> There were no doubt many households where the function of the Bible was more symbolic than practical. But even those who never read the Bible inevitably had considerable experience of hearing it read. Education in Sunday Schools, church day schools or Board Schools ensured that almost everyone had at least some knowledge of the Bible. Church services almost always included readings from the Bible, and, even more important, the focal point of the Protestant service was a sermon based on a biblical text.[67]

Even among those who lampooned the the Bible and/or those who relied on it, a familiarity with biblical literature is assumed. So, how did this knowledge of the Bible function?

In an answer that resounds with Christie's recollection of the Bible from her childhood, McLeod notes, "The Bible provided an inexhaustible supply of dramatic stories, colourful characters, and memorable sayings, to which keen readers repeatedly returned as their own experience provided parallels with what they had read."[68] As we'll see, Christie mines her childhood fascination with biblical stories to develop and employ narratives, characters, and sayings in her works. Observant readers will not only catch these references, but will see how important they are for understanding her stories. As Larsen reminds us, we must recognize that "the centrality of the Bible in the Victorian age is amply revealed in its literature. The Scriptures were the common cultural currency of the Victorians."[69] Even though Christie is a modernist engaging

---

[63] See Ibid., 100–104, for more on the practice and importance of "the quiet Sunday," especially the "eight characteristic ingredients" listed on p. 103.

[64] It seems Christie wanted very much to be an opera singer, and she trained very hard to achieve that goal. Even though it wasn't to be, she never lost her love for opera, especially Wagner.

[65] McLeod, *Religion and Society*, 116.

[66] Larsen, *A People of One Book: The Bible and the Victorians* (Oxford & New York: Oxford University Press, 2011), 1.

[67] McLeod, *Religion and Society*, 106–107.

[68] Ibid., 108.

[69] Larsen, *A People*, 2. J. C. Bernthal seems to argue against a central role for the Bible in Christie's works, but he nonetheless acknowledges "the reliance on biblical themes and narratives in constructing plots." See his "'A Dangerous World': The Hermeneutics of Agatha Christie's Later Novels," in *The Bible in Crime Fiction and Drama: Murderous Texts*, eds. Alison Jack and Caroline Blyth; Scriptural Traces: Critical Perspectives on the Reception and Influence of the Bible, 16; LHB/OTS, 678 (London & New York: Bloomsbury, 2019), 173.

yet interrogating Victorian (and Edwardian) views and forms, it's clear that she, too, assumes a great level of biblical literacy in her work. This assumption, again, is an example of the soft power or assumed normativity of Christianity I mentioned a few pages previously.

*   *   *

One of the central arguments of Parts One and Two is that this knowledge and function of the Bible and other religious language is found obviously and recurrently in Christie's Poirot stories. That is, Christie employs language that references, alludes to, and/or specifically cites terms, images, themes, symbols, and scripture drawn from religious traditions of her time, in virtually every case from Christianity. One may simply see these as mimetic reflections of the kind of language current in Christie's social and religious circles and the literature to which she was exposed. R. A. York explains what I mean when he writes,

> Christie's characters are overwhelmingly middle class.... In Christie's time this meant that they were likely to share a fairly wide familiarity with literature and other arts, and some respect for them. A certain number of the cultural references in the works may seem to do little more than establish that characters (and readers) are members of the same club, so to speak.[70]

However, the cumulative effect of such language—not to mention the dominant role it plays in understanding and/or unlocking the thematic key(s) of her works—is to create a shared worldview between author and reader, one that is evidence of Christianity's broader presence and cultural reach and predicated on what we're calling Christian normativity.

This is not to say that religious language is the *only* kind of shared language we find in her Poirot stories. Fluency in Shakespeare's works is assumed in several stories—especially *Othello*, which Christie references numerous times—and other kinds of shared literacy is helpful in unraveling the crime, as with *Cards on the Table* and its reliance on an understanding of the game of bridge.[71] Again, York helps us to understand the function of these "cultural references," i.e., they "do not simply demonstrate the level of education of author and reader. They serve also to imply the *values* by which the events of the novels ... are to be assessed. So they often form part of a conception of enjoyment and refinement. They afford a sense of beauty, elegance and sophistication."[72] What's different with Christie's religious and scriptural language is how pervasive and presumptive it is, i.e., it recurs with remarkable regularity and the

---

[70] York, *Agatha Christie: Power and Illusion*, Crime Files (Hampshire & New York: Palgrave Macmillan, 2007), 141–142.

[71] Poirot references Iago in "The Mystery of the Spanish Chest," in *The Harlequin Tea Set and Other Stories* (1997; reis. New York: HarperCollins, 2012), Kindle edition; chapter 9 of *Peril at End House*; and several times in *Curtain* (as we'll see in Chapter 8). In his *The Importance of Being Poirot* (pp. 182–183) Black points out the prevalence of Shakespeare in Christie's work, as does York, *Agatha Christie*, 158. With regard to bridge, see York, p. 108.

stories presume that their readers have enough religious literacy to grasp the sense of it.[73] At the same time, though, Christie's work represents not just a reflection of that soft power of Christianity, but also can be seen as a modernist revision of the symbols, texts, and outlooks of her inherited Christian faith, what I'm calling resistant reception.

Even so, this language serves as evidence for Joshi's structural dimension of Christian privilege which, as we've seen, is a key indicator of the hegemonic and normative presence of Christianity. As Larsen writes in his study of the Victorian views of the Bible, "The Bible provided an essential set of metaphors and symbols. Scriptural knowledge is a required pre-requisite for entering into a Victorian author's imaginative world. . . . [Further] the Bible provided an irreplaceable linguistic register not only for novelists and poets, but for the Victorians in general."[74] There was simply no getting around the Bible in the "Scripture saturated culture" into which Christie was born and in which she was reared.[75]

∗ ∗ ∗

As a way of understanding Christie's employment of shared Christian language and imagery, let's examine two brief examples of the world of the text before we move to the three biblically focused "Deep Dives" in Part Two. In order to demonstrate the steady recurrence of shared religious language, we'll examine not only Christie's first Poirot novel (*The Mysterious Affair at Styles*) but her last one as well (*Elephants Can Remember*). Separated by over fifty years, these novels nevertheless both employ shared religious language, the recognition and comprehension of which is important for understanding the progression of the plot and the thought processes of their characters, especially Poirot.

The Mysterious Affair at Styles

Published in the US in 1920, then in England the following year, the first Poirot novel, *The Mysterious Affair at Styles*, confronts the reader with religious language even before Poirot appears in the narrative.[76] Before we examine that element of the book, let me provide a brief summary. Our narrator, Captain Arthur Hastings, is injured and invalided from the War, and receives an invitation to stay with an old friend called John

---

[72] York, *Agatha Christie*, 145 (emphasis mine).

[73] York helpfully points out this readerly assumption when he notes that "Some of Christie's cultural references . . . are not clearly related to characters' consciousness, but signal the author's expectation as to the reader's culture" (*Agatha Christie*, 142). Even so, he only mentions the Bible in passing on pp. 147–148.

[74] Larsen, *A People*, 4.

[75] Ibid., 6.

[76] For a more detailed summary or background information on *The Mysterious Affair at Styles*, I would refer the reader to Charles Osborne, *The Life and Crimes of Agatha Christie: A Biographical Companion to the Works of Agatha Christie*, rev. and updated ed. (London: HarperCollins, 1999), 5–18; and more recently, Mark Aldridge, *Agatha Christie's Poirot: The Greatest Detective in the World* (London: HarperCollins, 2020), 2–10. Three critical examinations are also helpful: Maida and Spornick, *Murder She Wrote*, 63–67 and 90–92; the second chapter Gill's *Agatha Christie*; and Black, *Importance*, 27ff.

Cavendish at Cavendish's mother Emily's estate (the titular Styles). Emily has recently married a much younger man named Alfred Inglethorpe, of whom neither John nor his brother Lawrence are fond. Emily's longtime friend and secretary Evelyn Howard finds Inglethorpe especially loathsome, so when Emily dies from an apparent overdose of strychnine, she's convinced he's to blame. In the meantime, Hastings has run into an old acquaintance of his in the midst of a group of Belgian refugees Emily was sponsoring. This old friend is none other than Hercule Poirot, and with John's permission, Hastings asks Poirot to help investigate Emily's death. Of course, Poirot discovers a surprising solution to the murder, namely, that Evelyn and Inglethorpe are actually romantically involved and plotted together to kill Emily. At the end of the novel, it's hinted that Poirot and Hastings may "hunt together again," and of course they do just that, partnering and even living together for several years.[77]

Let's begin with the first of two examples of religious language in the novel. At the beginning of the story, John Cavendish and Hastings arrive at Styles and meet Evelyn Howard, who's working in the flower garden. After John asks if tea will be taken inside or outside, he says to her, "Come on then, you've done enough gardening for one day. 'The labourer is worthy of his hire,' you know. Come and be refreshed."[78] The quote here comes from the King James Version (aka, the Authorized Version) of Luke 10:7, which is an instruction of Jesus's to the seventy ministers/apostles he sends to towns "before his face" (10:1). He tells them to carry nothing with them and to go to houses to see if they're welcome. If they are, they should stay there, "eating and drinking such things as they give: for the labourer is worthy of his hire" (10:7). This exhortation is odd, though, as these ministers haven't technically done any work. In Matthew's version of this saying, it occurs in the context of Jesus sending out the twelve apostles specifically to the Jews and he mentions not manual labor, but curing the sick, raising the dead, cleansing lepers, and casting out demons (10:8). And here it's "laborers deserve their food" (NRSV) or "the workman is worthy of his meat" (KJV).

Once we recognize the biblical reference(s), we can now ask how these texts regarding workers and ethical action might apply to Evelyn's crimes against Emily Cavendish, and if Christie employs them to call into question the values of her inherited culture. Perhaps paying attention to the biblical echo helps to explain or elaborate on the motives of Evelyn, since she's the "labourer" in John Cavendish's analogy. However, Evelyn clearly isn't doing any proselytizing or performing any miraculous healings like the apostles Jesus is sending out. Rather, Evelyn is complicit in a murder and in so doing, is clearly a discordant example vis-à-vis the prescriptions one finds in the antecedents of the Lukan reference John Cavendish makes. Specifically, Luke 10:7 is reliant on Leviticus 19:13, a text that prescribes, in the course of exhortations about holiness, that one shouldn't "defraud your neighbor" or "steal" or "keep for yourself the wares of a laborer until morning." The fact that Cavendish equates Evelyn with Jesus's disciples when she is actively defrauding her neighbor creates a situation of irony, that

---

[77] Christie, *The Mysterious Affair at Styles* (1920; reis. New York: HarperCollins, 2010), Kindle edition, ch. 13, "Poirot Explains."
[78] Ibid., ch. 1, "I Go To Styles."

is, a discrepancy in knowledge between characters and readers. Put differently, because we as readers will ultimately know that Evelyn is already conspiring to kill Emily when John refers to her as the "labourer" and John obviously does not know that, the irony of the situation demonstrates that Cavendish's scriptural reference is askew.

Even at the end of the novel, the narrator (Hastings) doesn't provide us with any interior monologue or confession or response to Poirot's summation of his solution from either of the guilty parties (Alfred and Evelyn), so we're forced to take Hastings's word (as narrator) as to Poirot's description of their plan and pecuniary motive. Again, though, if we return to Cavendish's scriptural allusion, we might be helped. That is, what if Evelyn's plan was occasioned by Emily's thrift? Did Emily "keep the wages of a laborer until morning," and this is what caused Evelyn to put her plan into motion? We know the house was being run with great economy—it *is* the War, after all. Could this have supplied the motive? We don't know, but again, an informed engagement with the biblical text here opens avenues of insight that would be closed to those unable to recognize the quotation.[79]

The second scriptural reference occurs in chapter five, after Poirot has been recruited to investigate the murder. In the course of interviewing the family and the staff, he speaks to Evelyn, who is certain that Emily was murdered by Alfred. So sure is she that she tells Poirot that "Hanging's too good for him. Ought to be drawn and quartered, like in good old times." The mention of hanging occasions a reference to the book of Esther from Poirot, as can be seen when Poirot tells Evelyn, "Believe me, Miss Howard ... if Mr. Inglethorp is the man, he shall not escape me. On my honour, I will hang him as high as Haman!" And Evelyn is "enthusiastically" satisfied with his pledge.

Esther is an especially appropriate source for this allusion, and for *The Mysterious Affair at Styles*.[80] Its story concerns hidden identities and a surprising "Big Reveal" which exposes the villain while protecting and preserving the good-hearted heroine. Briefly, the titular character of Esther is chosen to be queen after the bumbling king Ahaseurus gets drunk and sends his wife Vashti away for not obeying a royal order that would've endangered her dignity, if not her bodily safety. Esther is a Jew and is kin to another Jew called Mordechai, who's made an enemy of the king's right-hand man, Haman. Haman decides that not just Mordechai, but all Jews in the kingdom deserve to die because of Mordechai's disrespect. Ignoring the danger, Esther hosts a dinner for the king and Haman at which she identifies Haman as the one who's endangered her and her people, and the king orders Haman to be hung (impaled, really) on the gallows Haman himself had built to execute Mordechai.

Returning to the scriptural echo from Poirot, we see just how Christie playfully recasts the story of Esther. Since Inglethorpe is equated with Haman (both being culpable), and Poirot ultimately exposes Inglethorpe's guilt, then Poirot emerges as the

---

[79] That missing motive is supplied in the world the text creates, via the 1990 feature-length adaptation of the novel in Series 3 of *Agatha Christie's Poirot*. In this film, it's made clear that Evelyn and Alfred committed the crime for money.

[80] For my own reading of Esther and how it's been variously adapted in cinema, see my "'If I Perish, I Perish': Esthers in Film," in *Daring, Disreputable, and Devout: Interpreting the Hebrew Bible's Women in the Arts and Music* (New York & London: T&T Clark, 2009), 111–141.

equivalent of Esther. And while we don't want to push an allegorical reading of the allusion too far—since Evelyn doesn't fit neatly therein as Alfred's lover and co-conspirator—we can nevertheless see clearly that Poirot occupies the role of heroine. By feminizing him via a scriptural analogy, that is, Christie is at odds with both the tradition of detective fiction—with its manly and physical protagonists—and the gendered expectations of normative Christianity in her day.[81]

Speaking of challenging cultural norms, we should remind ourselves that *The Mysterious Affair at Styles* is Christie's first novel, and as such we shouldn't expect her modernist challenge to inherited Victorian and Edwardian mores and assumptions to be in full view. To wit, Light notes that while the novel contains "All the paraphernalia of an already well-worked genre," we also see that "Christie's conservatism is less noticeable than the lack of emotional charge attached to any of the moral and social values which underpin the plot."[82] That is, inherited assumptions regarding faithful familial conduct, the sanctity of marriage, and even the otherness of the foreign interloper are challenged. As Light puts it, "For the reader of Conan Doyle these transgressions, though thrilling, would ultimately be deemed contemptible. In Christie's world nothing is sacred. Crime makes not for tragedy, nor even for the shudders of melodrama, but oddly and startlingly, for a laugh."[83] Even so, we must admit that the brevity and colloquial nature of Poirot's allusion to Haman should forestall us against making too much of it.[84]

Elephants Can Remember

Similarly, the last Poirot novel Christie wrote, *Elephants Can Remember* (published in late 1972), contains several examples of religious language, including one especially important Old Testament reference.[85] The novel is quite similar to another Poirot story, *Five Little Pigs* (1943), the 1971 Marple novel *Nemesis*, and several of Christie's Mr. Quin stories in that it hinges on an imaginative reconstruction of a past crime from the vantage point of the present, what Matthew Bunson helpfully terms "retrospective analysis."[86] Poirot's

---

[81] For the unheroic and feminine characterization of Poirot, see Knight, "'. . . done from within' – Agatha Christie's World," in *Form and Ideology in Crime Fiction* (London & Basingstoke: The Macmillan Press, 1980), 108–111; and Ackershoek, "'Daughters'," 120.

[82] Light, "Agatha Christie," 67.

[83] Ibid., 67–68.

[84] Again, in the world the text creates, the quotation from Esther is absent from the 1990 adaptation in *Agatha Christie's Poirot*. Both scriptural quotations are found in the 2005 BBC radio rendering (produced by Enyd Williams with a dramatization by Michael Bakewell). Further, this radio adaptation also includes another example of additional shared language when Emily quotes "England to Her Sons," a poem by William Noel Hodgson composed in August 1914 against the backdrop of World War I. By incorporating this poem—which contains imagery obviously connected to the nationalistic and religious rhetoric we saw in the work of Barbeau and Grimley earlier in this chapter—and the quotation from Luke, the radio production assumes its listeners possess the requisite religious literacy to understand the worldview they reflect.

[85] I would refer the reader looking for a more comprehensive summary to Osborne, *Life and Crimes*, 347–350; and Aldridge, *Agatha Christie's Poirot*, 285–289. Black, *Importance*, 178ff. also discusses this novel.

[86] Bunson, "Elephants Can Remember," in *The Complete Christie: An Agatha Christie Encyclopedia* (New York: Pocket Books/Simon & Schuster, 2000), 56.

friend, the mystery writer Ariadne Oliver, is approached by a woman called Mrs. Burton-Cox, who's concerned about the young women her son Desmond has chosen to marry. This young woman, Celia Ravenscroft, is actually Miss Oliver's goddaughter, and Mrs. Burton-Cox worries that Celia might be tainted in some way because her parents died in what was apparently a murder-suicide, though no one ever discovered who killed whom first. Miss Oliver appeals to Poirot for help, and he eventually reconstructs the events as they happened, bringing some much-needed closure to Miss Ravenscroft.

In one of their first meetings, Celia Ravenscroft tells Poirot that she wants the truth about the suspicious deaths of her parents. She then says, "When it's a double suicide, one thinks of it as one death. Is it in Shakespeare or where does the quotation come from—'And in death they were not divided.'"[87] Readers with a modicum of biblical literacy will note that it's not, in fact, Shakespeare; it's 2 Samuel 1:23, referring to Saul and Jonathan.[88] The quotation is from a poem, a lament uttered by David in 1:19-27 on hearing of Jonathan's death and Saul's subsequent suicide. The lament keens for the loss of both men, repeating the refrain, "How the mighty have fallen," three times (1:19, 25, 27). It's telling, though, that Celia omits part of 1:23; the complete phrase is, "Saul and Jonathan were lovely and pleasant in their lives, and in their death they were not divided." The King James (or Authorized) Version obscures the form of the lament at this point, and other translations do it more justice. For example, Robert Alter renders it, "Saul and Jonathan, beloved and dear, / in their life and their death they were not parted."[89] Alter's translation makes it plain that David is claiming that father and son were united, of one mind in both life and death. However, this is clearly not the case, as Alter points out in his commentary. He writes that David's description of Saul and Jonathan is "an extravagant idealization . . . since father and son were almost estranged and twice Saul was on the point of killing Jonathan."[90] Recognizing this flawed characterization of the relationship between Saul and Jonathan should make the reader question the appropriateness of Celia's application of this verse to describe her parents' relationship. And as the reader will discover, they're absolutely right to do so, as just as in David's lament, memory, and nostalgia become entangled, leading to deception. Nevertheless, this is clearly an important thematic text for the novel, as it's referred to twice more.

In the very brief eighteenth chapter, Poirot goes to a churchyard cemetery to view the names of the Ravenscrofts.[91] On those tombstones, he encounters not only quotations from Matthew 6:12 and the Book of Common Prayer, but also our text, 2

---

[87] Christie, *Elephants Can Remember* (1972; reis. New York: HarperCollins, 2011), Kindle edition, ch. 12, "Celia Meets Hercule Poirot."

[88] Jennifer Stevens, "The Victorians and the Bible," in *The Historical Jesus and the Literary Imagination 1860–1920*, English Association Studies, 3 (Liverpool: Liverpool University Press, 2010), 22, addresses the relationship between the Bible and Shakespeare.

[89] See Alter, *The David Story: A Translation with Commentary of 1 and 2 Samuel* (New York & London: W. W. Norton, 1999), 200.

[90] Ibid., 200.

[91] Poirot also visits a cemetery in *Dumb Witness* (1937), where he finds scriptural epitaphs. In chapter fourteen of the 1969 novel *Hallowe'en Party* he does the same, and the conversation he has with the gardener therein also contains scriptural language.

Samuel 1:23, again.[92] Finally, after Poirot's "court of enquiry" in which he explains everything, Celia tells him

> "I like to think—oh, it seems a silly thing for me to say"—she looked doubtfully at Hercule Poirot. "Perhaps you won't think so. I expect you're a Catholic, but it's what's written on their tombstone. 'In death they were not divided.' It doesn't mean that they died together, but I think they are together. I think they came together afterwards."[93]

We get no specific comment on this from Poirot, but clearly Celia has added another layer of wistful romanticism onto David's mischaracterization in 2 Samuel 1:23 that extends the false sense of indivisibility into the afterlife.[94]

* * *

What this examination into Christie's first and last Poirot stories shows is a consistent use of religious language to add specifics to her plots and provide the reader with additional layers of information about characters. At the same time, Christie inverts and/or problematizes readerly expectations that arise out of the use of this language. Put in more academic parlance, this language serves to reflect but also to question a socio-cultural ideology of Christian hegemony and normativity—a context in which references to Scripture and the Book of Common Prayer create a shared worldview between author and audience predicated on a common educational and religious experience. In Part Two, we'll see how this worldview is replicated yet interrogated in a series of more detailed discussions of some of Christie's most celebrated works.

---

[92] Remember: shared religious language isn't the only kind of shared language one finds in Christie's work. For example, here, after reflecting on what he's learned, Poirot quotes from the last line of "East Coker," the second poem of T. S. Eliot's *Four Quartets* (1943; reis. San Diego & New York: Harcourt Brace & Company, 1971), 32. For the use of this quotation in Christie, see York, *Agatha Christie*, 150–151.

[93] Christie, *Elephants Can Remember*, ch. 20, "Court of Enquiry."

[94] The centrality of the references to 2 Samuel in the novel is ignored in the 2013 film version from *Agatha Christie's Poirot*. Interestingly, the 2 Samuel reference is retained, both from Celia and the headstones, in the BBC 4 radio performance of the novel, which aired in January 2006 (directed by Enyd Williams with a dramatization by Michael Bakewell).

Part Two

The Bible in Christie's Poirot Stories

Introduction to Part Two

As I noted in Part One, Agatha Christie's work often employs terms and phrases with biblical/religious content, assuming that both characters and readers understand them. These offhand phrases establish a shared worldview between author and reader in which religious and biblical literacy is taken for granted. Part Two will discuss three "Deep Dives" to illustrate this shared religious language and how it creates a set of cultural values the reader must understand if a given story is to be comprehended fully. My purpose is to illuminate the centrality of this shared religious language and imagery in the Poirot stories and the ways in which Christie subtly—and at times more explicitly—resists the values and mores indicated in/by that language and imagery, what I call her resistant reception.

In the three "Deep Dives" in Chapters 3–5, we'll examine more closely Christie's use of religious, and specifically biblical, language in works which most obviously reflect and challenge the Christian normativity I examine in Part One.[1] Each of the chapters in Part Two will discuss not only a novel and/or story (the world of the text) but also later radio, TV, and/or film adaptations (the world the text creates) to track how the presence of shared religious language evolves, or in some cases disappears. We'll begin by focusing on two novels, *Death on the Nile* and *Evil Under the Sun*, that both contain a central, defining scriptural reference that lies at the heart of its plot or focus. Finally, our third example will differ slightly, in that instead of centering on a specific story, we'll examine Christie's use of one particular biblical text (the parable of the Prodigal Son in Luke 15:11-32) in both a short story ("The Mystery of the Hunter's Lodge") and a novel (*Hercule Poirot's Christmas*). In the Appendix I've gathered these and other biblical references, allusions, and echoes I've found in Christie's Poirot canon, and they bear witness to her lifelong engagement with the Bible as a resource for her work.

---

[1] Obviously, there are many other examples I could've chosen to examine in this context. For example, in *One, Two, Buckle My Shoe* (1940), Poirot attends an Anglican church, and the biblical literature he encounters here in the liturgy (excerpts from Psalm 140 and 1 Samuel 15) becomes the key for him to synthesize his evidence and develop his solution. Additionally, the image of a "new heaven and new earth" from Revelation 21 plays an important role in several chapters.

3

Death on the Nile

In her 1937 novel, *Death on the Nile*, Christie tells the story of a love triangle.[1] This was a theme with which Christie was unfortunately familiar. In 1926, the same year in which her beloved mother Clarissa died, Christie's first husband Archie had told her he was in love with another woman, a Miss Nancy Neele.[2] These twin punches bewildered Christie, and most of her biographers believe they led to her famous ten-day "disappearance" in early December 1926.[3] Perhaps it's no coincidence that Christie returned again and again to the theme of the "eternal triangle," and not only in her Poirot works.[4]

To return to the novel at hand and its specific love triangle, wealthy socialite Linnet Ridgeway has stolen the fiancé of her longtime friend Jacqueline de Bellefort, a simple, unassuming man named Simon Doyle. After Linnet and Simon marry, they embark on a lavish honeymoon, travelling across the continent to Egypt. Inexplicably, Jackie has managed to follow them wherever they go, much to the chagrin of Linnet and her new husband. The situation has become intolerable, and so when Linnet spies the famous Belgian detective Hercule Poirot at the Cataract Hotel on the banks of the Nile in Assuan, she approaches him after dinner and asks—assuming he'll agree—to act on her behalf to dissuade Jackie from continuing her harassment. He refuses her request, but speaks to Jackie on his own, telling her to "Bury your dead." He also exhorts her, "Do not open your heart to evil," and elaborates, saying, "Because—if you do—evil will

---

[1] To be clear, except in setting this novel is totally different from the short story of the same name featuring Christie's character J. Parker Pyne, which was first published in the US in April 1933. Again, for a more comprehensive summary, see Charles Osborne, *The Life and Crimes of Agatha Christie: A Biographical Companion to the Works of Agatha Christie*, rev. and updated ed. (London: HarperCollins, 1999), 146–151; and Mark Aldridge, *Agatha Christie's Poirot: The Greatest Detective in the World* (London: HarperCollins, 2020), 127–132.

[2] See, e.g., Janet Morgan, *Agatha Christie: A Biography* (London: William Collins Sons & Company, 1984; repr. New York: Alfred A. Knopf, 1985), 123–134.

[3] These events—especially Christie's infamous "disappearance" after her first husband Archie told her he wanted to leave her—have been the subject of much speculation, documentation, and interpretations. Readers can consult Morgan, *Agatha Christie*, 123–161; and Gwen Robyns, *The Mystery of Agatha Christie: An Intimate Biography of the First Lady of Crime* (Harmondsworth & New York: Penguin Books, 1978), 90–143.

[4] In addition to the novels discussed in this chapter, this theme of the "eternal triangle" can also be found in the 1936 short story "Triangle at Rhodes," the Miss Marple short story from 1930 titled "The Herb of Death," and the chapter titled "Snow White and Red Rose" in Christie's novel *Towards Zero* (1944).

come . . . Yes, very surely evil will come . . . It will enter in and make its home within you, and after a little while it will no longer be possible to drive it out."[5] In the end, he fails to convince her to relent. When Jackie somehow follows Linnet and Simon on the Karnak to travel the Nile, Poirot is worried. As it turns out, his concern is validated when Linnet is found murdered. In one of Christie's more celebrated plots, Poirot reveals that Jackie and Simon had been and still were lovers and collaborated to kill Linnet. The novel ends with Jackie killing Simon then herself with a pistol that Poirot knew she had in her possession, thus granting his implicit permission for her actions.

Especially important for our examination are the conversation between Poirot and Linnet and the request for his aid she makes of him. Poirot points out first, that he is on holiday and as such cannot take on any cases, but also that Jackie technically has broken no laws, so there is no "legal redress against such a thing," to use Linnet's words.[6] In order to provide some context for the situation, Poirot tells Linnet about a scene recounted earlier in the novel, in which he overheard Jackie and Simon in a restaurant in London planning their honeymoon, and how obvious it was to him that Jackie was "in love—heart, soul, and body—and she is not of those who love lightly and often. With her it is clearly the life and the death."[7] He then relates how he recently heard Simon's voice again, but this time he was on his honeymoon with another woman. Linnet clearly feels guilty about the situation, but not too guilty. She admits to Poirot, "Of course the whole thing was very unfortunate. But these things happen, Monsieur Poirot."[8]

At this point, Poirot asks Linnet if she is "of the Church of England," and when she, somewhat confused, replies that she is, he remarks: "Then you have heard portions of the Bible read aloud in church.[9] You have heard of King David and of the rich man who had many flocks and herds and the poor man who had one ewe lamb and of how the rich man took the poor man's one ewe lamb."[10] Linnet strenuously objects to Poirot's implication that she "stole my friend's young man," arguing that while Jackie did love Simon very much, that "he may not have been equally devoted to her."[11] Poirot, while not disagreeing, points out that,

> You are beautiful, Madame, you are rich, you are clever, intelligent—and you have charm. You could have exercised that charm or you could have restrained it. You had everything, Madame, that life can offer. Your friend's life was bound up in one person. You knew that—but though you hesitated, you did not hold your hand. You stretched it out and like King David you took the poor man's one ewe lamb.[12]

---

[5] Christie, *Death on the Nile* (1937/1938; reis. New York: HarperCollins, 2011), Kindle edition, ch. 5.
[6] Ibid.
[7] Ibid., ch. 4.
[8] Ibid.
[9] 2 Samuel 12 is part of the Lectionary of the Church of England, meaning that it would've been used as part of a worship service on a regular basis.
[10] Christie, *Death on the Nile*, ch. 4. Hannah M. Strømmen also focuses on this scene and its use of biblical archetypes in her "Poirot, the Bourgeois Prophet: Agatha Christie's Biblical Adaptations," in *The Bible in Crime Fiction and Drama: Murderous Texts*, eds. Alison Jack and Caroline Blyth; Scriptural Traces, 16; LHB/OTS, 678 (London & New York: Bloomsbury, 2019), 160–161.
[11] Christie, *Death on the Nile*, ch. 4.
[12] Ibid.

Linnet has no substantive response to Poirot's accusation, as it's obvious that Poirot is correct in his assessment. Nevertheless, he agrees to speak to Jackie "in the interests of humanity."[13]

In order to understand the importance of Bible in the novel, I'd like to focus more specifically on the analogy Poirot makes between Linnet and the rich man. The story is from 2 Samuel 12:1-4, and is told by the court prophet Nathan to King David. The point of the story is to dramatically illustrate the injustice perpetrated on the poor man by the rich man's theft of his one lamb, who was "like a daughter to him" (12:3).[14] David is full of righteous indignation at the rich man's actions; in vv. 5-6, he pronounces that the rich man "deserves to die ... because he did this thing, and because he had no pity." Seeing his opening, Nathan then announces, "You are the man!" Nathan then recounts for the reader the events of 2 Samuel 11, in which David decides that he must have a woman named Bathsheba, and so puts in motion events to get her husband, Uriah, out of the way.

David, Bathsheba, and Uriah in Christie

Christie was obviously fond of the love triangle between David, Bathsheba, and Uriah, as she had already used it twice in minor ways. *The Secret of Chimneys* (1925) contains a brief mention of the biblical triangle in chapter 15. A woman called Virginia is recounting a time when a foreign prince wanted to marry her. When another character asks what the prince planned to do about her existing husband, she replies, "Oh, he had a sort of David and Uriah scheme all made out." Similarly, in her 1940 novel *And Then There Were None* (originally published as *Ten Little Niggers* in 1939), we learn in chapter 5 that one of the guests on Soldier Island is a former military general who learned of an affair between his wife and one of the officers under his command. He subsequently sends that officer on a mission he knew would lead to his death, and the parallel with David and Uriah is stated outright. Since we know that Christie had a lifelong interest in love triangles— perhaps because of her own experiences—the use of David, Bathsheba, and Uriah shouldn't surprise us, but it does demonstrate Christie's familiarity with and adaptations of biblical literature.

David succeeds, Uriah is killed in battle (11:17), and Bathsheba becomes one of David's wives and bears him a son (11:27). Now, though, Nathan announces God's judgment on David for both what he did and did not do. That is, at a basic horizontal level, David acted to "take" Bathsheba and in the process affected the death of Uriah. But on a vertical level David presumed to act beyond his kingly prerogative, to act like God or to take what he wanted without petitioning for or trusting God to provide what he

---

[13] Ibid.
[14] All biblical quotations taken from the NRSV unless otherwise noted.

wanted. The judgment announced by Nathan is inclusive of both violations: not only will God "raise up trouble against you from your [David's] own house," but also, "the child that is born to you shall die" (12:11, 14). Indeed, as subsequent chapters in 2 Samuel show, Nathan's pronouncements come to pass, as David's reign devolves into personal and national chaos.[15]

It's important to understand just how Poirot's analogous use of 2 Samuel 12 works in the context of the novel, as is demonstrated in Table 3.1.

As one can see, in applying the analogy of 2 Samuel 12, Poirot gender-flips the story of David and Bathsheba. That is, Poirot functions as Nathan, as he's the one telling the story. This self-identification as a prophetic figure will be important to my understanding of Poirot's religious identity, as we'll see in Part Three. However, Nathan tells the story to David, whereas Poirot speaks to Linnet. So, Linnet is David in this analogy, which makes sense, given that that the killings subsequent to Linnet's murder are analogous to the spiraling crises that befall David's family after the incident with Bathsheba. Barbara Green notes the central point Nathan makes on behalf of God in criticizing "David's presuming to act on his own, brazenly and grossly. The parable exposes David's culminated arrogance, contempt, and presumption."[16] If this description of David sounds like Linnet Doyle, then you've been paying attention. And as if that identification wasn't enough, the novel takes pains to establish that Linnet has everything she could possibly want; in addition to being David, she is obviously "the rich man" in the analogy.[17] Since Linnet "stole" Simon from Jackie, the implication is that Simon is Bathsheba and Jackie is Uriah.[18] However, the obvious difference here is that it's not Uriah/Jackie who's killed, but rather Linnet/David. This, in a way, is a more satisfying resolution to the story of the rich and poor man, as it's the rich man/David who violates not only God's law but also the reader's sense of fair play. As we discover, though, Linnet's "stealing of the lamb" is a ploy to get her money on the part of Jackie and

Table 3.1 Poirot's Gender-Flipping of 2 Samuel 12

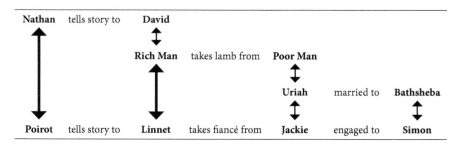

[15] See, e.g., the comments by Robert Alter, *The David Story: A Translation with Commentary of 1 and 2 Samuel* (New York & London: W. W. Norton, 1999), 258–259.

[16] Green, *David's Capacity for Compassion: A Literary-Hermeneutical Study of 1-2 Samuel*, LHB/OTS 641 (London: Bloomsbury T&T Clark, 2017), 202.

[17] See, e.g., Christie, *Death on the Nile*, chs. 1 and 2.

[18] This emphasis on "stealing" or "taking" parallels the reading of Nathan's parable by David Janzen, "The Condemnation of David's 'Taking' in 2 Samuel 12:1-14," *JBL* 131, no. 2 (2012): 209–220.

Simon. As such, it's a kind of revenge fantasy by the "wronged" parties in 2 Samuel 12, that is, if Uriah and Bathsheba somehow exacted revenge on David for his actions. As it stands in the novel, though, everyone assumes that Linnet's killed for what she has—all her money, power, influence, enemies, etc.—which, of course, she is, but the genius of Jackie's plan is to make it seem that the best motive for Linnet's murder is revenge for what she's taken away, viz., Simon. In this way, the brief story from 2 Samuel 12 becomes the key to understanding the entire plot of the novel, containing as it does both the motive behind Linnet's murder, but also the respective and unexpected roles the characters play.

It is in the context of these unexpected roles that we find Christie's modernist challenge to her inherited socio-religious cultures. The most obvious example here is her gender-flipping the characters between the biblical context evoked by Poirot's reference and the plot of the novel. That is, Christie upends not only the expectations of her genre by creating an unheroic, feminine detective while at the same time creating a murderous female protagonist who dominates and controls her male partner. And by framing these relationships with an analogy drawn from Scripture, Christie also exhibits a playfulness and willingness to realign plots and characters from her biblical source text as needed.

Many scholars have noted the innovative nature of Poirot as a character construct, pointing out that Christie creates an unheroic, decidedly un-Sherlockian figure that is old, slow-moving, a cosmopolitan, urban-dwelling foreigner, a Catholic, and most certainly not a "man of action."[19] Marion Shaw and Sabine Vanacker connect this characterization with the generic development of "feminized detective fiction" that's especially foregrounded in the work of the Queens of Crime (mentioned in Chapter 1). They note as well that "their male detectives have a feminine appeal" in the "mixture of the effete, the exotic, and the comic that these outsiders present."[20] Similarly, Alison Light calls Poirot an anti-hero, notes his "parodic" and "theatrical" function, but also writes,

> Poirot could afford his readers some necessary relief from those lantern-jawed fellows who bludgeon their way out of innumerable tight spots in the more backward-looking fiction of the period.... [He was] the best of both worlds, a dispossessed modern, belonging nowhere in particular, and a comic upholder of the values of the past. Like so much else in Christie's fiction he could offer her readers the pleasures of modernity without its pains.[21]

---

[19] See, e.g., Stephen Knight, "'... done from within' – Agatha Christie's World," in *Form and Ideology in Crime Fiction* (London & Basingstoke: The Macmillan Press, 1980), 108–111; Mary Anne Ackershoek, "'The Daughters of His Manhood': Christie and the Golden Age of Detective Fiction," in *Theory and Practice of Classic Detective Fiction*, eds. Jerome H. Delamater and Ruth Prigozy; Contributions to the Study of Popular Culture, 62 (Westport, CT & London: Greenwood Press, 1997), 120; and Nicolas Birns and Margaret Boe Birns, "Agatha Christie: Modern and Modernist," in *The Cunning Craft: Original Essays on Detective Fiction and Contemporary Literary Theory*, eds. Ronald G. Walker and June M. Frazer (Macomb, IL: Yeast Printing/Western Illinois University, 1990), 128–129.

[20] Shaw and Vanacker, "Women Writers and the Golden Age of Detective Fiction," in *Reflecting on Miss Marple*, Heroines? (London & New York: Routledge, 1991), 30–31.

[21] Light, "Agatha Christie and Conservative Modernity," in *Forever England: Femininity, Literature and Conservatism between the Wars* (London & New York: Routledge, 1991), 74. See also p. 78.

Additionally, it seems that the character of Jackie, as a murderess, also pushes back against traditions of genre and culture. This is ably argued by Merja Makinen, who examines texts contemporaneous with Christie such as "newspaper coverage of female murderers, popular books on female murderers and the [then] current criminological explanation of female offenders."[22] After analyzing those available data from the 1920s–50s, Makinen claims that Christie's "representations of female murderers do not accord with the contemporary textual stereotypes of female misbehaviour, since they grant them a reasoned efficiency in their murderous plans in the novels which challenge dominant gender discourses, asserting the potential and powerful possibilities of transgressive femininity."[23] What this demonstrates is that in her early and middle periods, Christie's characterization of female murderers is part of a broader challenge to gender stereotypes and other inherited viewpoints and practices.

Applying her lens to our novel, Makinen focuses on the character of Jackie and writes,

> A central part of the novel therefore dwells on her character, her motives and her retribution. The denouement reveals that her actions are more calculating and intelligent but, in a very real sense, the conundrum of *Death on the Nile* held always before the reader is the figure of a jilted young woman, unforgiving, vindictive and passionate and the question of just how far her unleashed malevolence will take her. . . . Feminine jilted vengeance and the lengths to which it will go, once it is unleashed from the civilised and decorous behaviour decreed by patriarchy, becomes the main focus and enquiry of the body of the novel.[24]

Even though Jackie's vengeance will be shown at the end to be part of a plan to obtain both Simon and Linnet's fortune, Makinen is correct in noting the almost frenzied passion Jackie holds for Simon and the fatal lengths she'll go to in order to protect her plan to have all she wants. Clearly, then, in her choice of detective and murderer, Christie is mounting a challenge to the genre of crime fiction, but how does her use of the Bible push back against the assumptions and Scripture of the Christianity of her day?

I've already mentioned the most obvious aspect of Christie's use of the Bible, namely, her gender-flipping of the story of David, Bathsheba, Uriah, and Nathan in 2 Samuel 11–12. To review, Poirot situates himself in the prophetic role of Nathan and casts Linnet as David (the rich man), who steals Bathsheba/Simon (the one lamb) from Jackie/Uriah (the poor man). As I just noted, Christie's creative inversion of gendered stereotypes is evident in her depiction of Jackie, but it's also present in portraying Simon as little more than a passive stooge following out Jackie's orders. Both of these characters seem to be reflecting and also contesting prescriptive gender patterns within Christianity in the Interwar years.

[22] Makinen, *Agatha Christie: Investigating Femininity*, Crime Files (New York: Palgrave, 2006), 140.
[23] Ibid., 149.
[24] Ibid., 174.

Callum G. Brown points out that even while "the representation of ideal femininity" was changing in terms of fashion and body shape during these years, a resurgent puritan streak led to "sustained sexual restraint" as well, leaving women in something of a "moral maze."[25] Brown also claims that "moral disciplining" for men focused somewhat on sex, but more targeted were "games, gambling, and drink," exactly what one would find on a foreign, exotic honeymoon.[26] Even so, the broader focus on "declining sexual morality" was a major concern amidst arguments over the increased availability of contraception and regularity of sex before/outside of marriage.[27] I don't think it's surprising that both the scriptural text from 2 Samuel and Christie's "eternal triangle" plot revolve around these issues of sexual morality. By flipping the gender-script, then, Christie challenges the assumptions regarding active male sexuality and female passivity. In the biblical text, Bathsheba is entirely passive, acted upon, whereas David holds the power and authority, even over Uriah, who is both a subordinate and a foreigner, even if he is surprisingly depicted as more morally upright than his commander. This changes in the novel, in which we find Linnet seduced by Simon and duped by Jackie into marrying Simon so that Linnet can be murdered. Jackie—representing Uriah/the poor man in Nathan's story—is the one here who has power, even though as a jilted, unmarried, poor girl, she should have none, especially in comparison with Linnet. Jackie emerges as the more active, even masculine of the two, and her murderous plan parallels David's in terms of organization and concealment.[28] Even so, Poirot (in his analogical identity as Nathan the prophet) sees through the veil and correctly identifies Jackie and Simon as the culprits. And so, as I note earlier, we have a far more appealing conclusion to Nathan's story than the death of Uriah and Bathsheba's first child by David.

On a broader note, we need to realize that it's not simply the gender-flipping of the biblical story, it's also the fact that Christie felt free to engage and playfully modify the scriptural text in such a way. In their history of the interpretation of the Bible in England, Stephen Neill and Tom Wright note that prior to the rise of higher biblical criticism in the mid-nineteenth century, "The doctrine of the verbal inspiration and inerrancy of every part of Scripture, treated as one single whole without any recognition of the differing value of different parts, made an intelligent and imaginative approach to the Bible almost impossible."[29] Certainly, Christie's use of the Bible in *Death on the Nile* is both "intelligent and imaginative," but I venture to say that the usage we've been discussing was only possible because of a decline in a traditional view of biblical inerrancy and infallibility. Prior to what we now recognize as the dawn of critical biblical scholarship,

[25] Brown, *Religion and Society in Twentieth-Century Britain* (Harlow: Pearson Education Limited, 2006), 122.
[26] Ibid., 123.
[27] Ibid., 127.
[28] Along this line, it's important to note that there are several comments on how Linnet is more "manly" than Simon in her handling of business affairs. See, e.g., Christie, *Death on the Nile*, ch. 9.
[29] Neill and Wright, *The Interpretation of the New Testament, 1861-1986*, new ed. (Oxford & New York: Oxford University Press, 1988), 4.

Traditional Christian reverence held a view of Biblical inspiration which separated it off from every other book; these were the authentic words of God himself; and though up to a point grammatical, textual, and linguistic criticism might have their place, all awkward questions were supposed to be stilled by the protection of inspiration. It must be remembered that at that time almost all good Christians in England were what would now be called 'fundamentalists'.[30]

As Neill and Wright note, with the explosion of German higher criticism in the mid-nineteenth century, "the question that orthodox Christians had to face was this: 'Is the Bible to be treated like any other book or not?'"[31] Certainly Christie treated it "like any other book" in the sense that she mined it for imagery, quotations, and plots for her work alongside other texts and literary corpora. As we saw in Chapter 2, though, the Bible played a key role in Christie's upbringing, religious socialization and home life, and I'd hazard to say that in the final analysis, it was more than just any other book for her. In the absence of more direct evidence of that point from Christie herself, let's move on to ask how her novel has been interpreted in the world the text creates.

To date, there have been three film adaptations of *Death on the Nile*: a major studio motion picture with an all-star cast released to great fanfare in 1978; a feature-length episode in *Agatha Christie's Poirot*; and another big-budget, star-studded film released in February 2022. The first of these renderings treats the key scene in which Poirot compares Linnet to the rich man/David very simply: it omits it in its entirety.[32] All we hear is Linnet (Lois Chiles) ask if she may speak with Poirot (Peter Ustinov), then the scene shifts to his conversation with Jackie (Mia Farrow), including his admonition to "not open your heart to evil." The effect of not rendering this thematically important scene is to diminish Poirot's analysis of Linnet's culpability in the love triangle. To make up for this, the film includes several scenes between Linnet and other characters in which we're shown past and ongoing conflicts that serve as possible motives for her eventual murder. For example, Linnet's filed a libel suit against Mrs. Otterbourne (Angela Lansbury); she has openly critiqued the clinic run by Dr. Bessner (Jack Warden) among her social circles; and her father financially ruined the family of Miss Bowers (Maggie Smith). Of these encounters, none appear in the novel, and we never hear anything in the film referencing 2 Samuel 12 at all.

Similarly, the 2022 version—one of two recent Poirot films directed by and starring Kenneth Branagh—deals with the scene between Linnet (Gal Gadot) and Poirot in a different fashion than we find in the novel.[33] In keeping with what appears to be Branagh's plan to "retcon" Poirot, his film heavily revises this scene so that both Linnet and Simon (Armie Hammer) ask Poirot for help, and Linnet is adamant that Jackie (Emma Mackey) will commit a crime if not stopped.[34] After Poirot prevents Linnet

[30] Ibid., 33.
[31] Ibid., 32–33.
[32] For more information on this film, see Mark Aldridge, *Agatha Christie On Screen*, Crime Files (London: Palgrave Macmillan, 2016), 141–144.
[33] For more on this film, see Aldridge, *Agatha Christie's Poirot*, 443–447.
[34] By "retcon," I mean "retroactive continuity." I'll say more about this term in Chapter 9.

being bitten by a cobra, he simply listens and makes no reply. He then meets with and advises Jackie to give up what she's doing, but she breaks down, telling him that she loves Simon too much. Again, Poirot just listens and makes no reply. Finally, he advises Linnet and Simon to go back home and start their life together where Jackie can't reach them. As a result of these directorial choices, the scriptural basis for the love triangle plot is removed, and Poirot is depicted as much more of a man of action than of moral consideration, as we find in the novel.

On the other hand, the 2004 TV interpretation hews closer to Christie's novel in that it includes the scene in which Linnet (Emily Blunt) asks Poirot (David Suchet) for help in dealing with Jackie (Emma Malin). As in the novel, after Linnet pleads her case, Poirot notes that Jackie's within her rights to follow them around, as she hasn't threatened or harmed them. At this point, the episode skips right over the important biblical analogy from the novel, but instead has Poirot say simply that Jackie is "aggrieved." Interestingly, Linnet's next line consists of her response to Poirot's allusion to 2 Samuel 12 in the novel, which fails to move Poirot to act. He firmly refuses her offer of money and turns his full attention to enjoying one of his little cigarettes. Poirot then notices Jackie crying by herself. With little to no prompting, Poirot tells her to "bury your dead," and that she "must look to the future." Like the novel and the 1978 film, he adjures her, "Do not open your heart to evil. . . . If you do there will be no turning back." Jackie replies that Linnet "has taken everything from me . . . and I want to hurt her."

The latter film contains a recurring theme that is absent from the 1978 rendering related to the unstated biblical analogy, viz., Poirot's goal of preventing Jackie from "following her star" to ruin. The relation of this goal to 2 Samuel 12 is implicit rather than explicit. That is, Nathan's critique of David's actions regarding Uriah rests on an implicit concern for Uriah as a victim of the king's royal power, as well as the hope that David will admit his guilt, which he does (12:13).[35] Since, in Poirot's analogy, Jackie is Uriah, Poirot (as Nathan) shares a corresponding concern for her. Additionally, since Linnet (as the David in this story) is murdered and thus is not allowed the possibility to admit her guilt and repent, Jackie becomes Poirot's focus for potential redemption. Several scenes between Poirot and Jackie show us this concern, but perhaps the most telling occurs after Poirot reveals Jackie and Simon's (JJ Feild) plan to the passengers. In this scene, as in the novel, Jackie admits, "It's so dreadfully easy—killing people." Her admission, as well as the fact that both she and Simon confessed to their crimes, completes the terrible transformation Poirot had been trying to prevent all along. That is, unlike 2 Samuel 12, there's no redemption or forgiveness here for any of those involved in the love triangle; there's only death.

---

[35] Alter, *David*, spells this out: "As king, his [David's] first obligation is to protect his subjects and dispense justice, especially to the disadvantaged. In the affair of Bathsheba and Uriah, he has done precisely the opposite" (257). In this regard, it's also important to mention Psalm 51, which contains the following superscription: "A Psalm of David, when the prophet Nathan came to him, after he had gone in to Bathsheba." In other words, this psalm supposedly consists of what David said to the Lord when he "pleaded with God" in 2 Samuel 12:16. (It's no coincidence that the Church of England Lectionary pairs 2 Samuel 12 with Psalm 51). See Alter's moving translation in his *The Book of Psalms: A Translation with Commentary* (New York & London: W. W. Norton & Co., 2007), 180–183.

It's in this tragic light that the film ends. Unlike the marginally happier ending of the 1978 film, here Jackie kills Simon and then herself on the loading dock once the ship arrives at port. Poirot's friend and investigative aid Colonel Race (James Fox) asks Poirot if he knew Jackie had another pistol in addition to the one that was used to kill Linnet, which had been confiscated after Simon threw it overboard. With considerable trepidation and sadness—as the camera lingers on his face—Poirot responds in a near-whisper, "It is not always that simple." In other words, Poirot did indeed know that she had the means to avoid a trial and kill herself, and he allowed her to do so, perhaps out of his own feelings of failure and guilt at how Jackie turned out. The tragic, melancholy ending of this adaptation, in which no one is saved or redeemed, echoes the eventual downfall of the house of David in the books of Samuel and Kings. Unlike Nathan, though, Poirot will continue to try to protect and rescue the innocent, and Christie will continue to draw upon biblical literature and images to describe his endeavors, adventures, and worldview.

4

Evil Under the Sun

Our second example of Christie's use of shared religious language is one of her more popular Poirot novels, *Evil Under the Sun* (1941).[1] The story takes place on a secluded island in a resort hotel called the Jolly Roger Hotel, and involves the murder of a well-known and beautiful woman called Arlena Marshall. Arlena has clearly taken to another guest named Patrick Redfern, who's vacationing with his seemingly demur and decidedly retiring wife Christine—thus, another love triangle. When Patrick discovers Arlena's corpse, Poirot sets out to find the murderer, and in a similar plot to that of *Death on the Nile*, reveals that the Redferns are both responsible for her murder, and are not all they seem.[2] As with *Death on the Nile*, let's focus our examination more closely on just one component of the plot, namely, the theme of evil and the scriptural language and paradigms the novel uses to elaborate on it.

At the outset of the novel, Poirot is talking to a woman named Emily Brewster, who opines that their surroundings are too idyllic for anything like the murders Poirot has encountered. Poirot disagrees, remarking that "there is evil everywhere under the sun."[3] Another character named Father Stephen Lane comments soon thereafter,

> "I was interested, M. Poirot, in something you said just now. You said that there was evil done everywhere under the sun. It was almost a quotation from Ecclesiastes." He paused and then quoted himself. *"Yea, also the heart of the sons of men is full of evil, and madness is in their heart while they live."* His face lit up with an almost fanatical light. "I was glad to hear you say that. Nowadays, no one believes in evil. It is considered, at most, a mere negation of good. Evil, people say, is done by those who know no better—who are to be pitied rather than blamed. But, M. Poirot, evil is *real*! It is a *fact*! I believe in Evil as I believe in Good. It exists! It is powerful! It walks the earth!" He stopped. His breath was coming fast. He wiped his forehead

---

[1] To supplement my brief summary, readers may consult Charles Osborne, *The Life and Crimes of Agatha Christie: A Biographical Companion to the Works of Agatha Christie*, rev. and updated ed. (London: HarperCollins, 1999), 186–188; and Mark Aldridge, *Agatha Christie's Poirot: The Greatest Detective in the World* (London: HarperCollins, 2020), 160–164.

[2] Others have pointed out the close similarities between these two novels. See Robert Merrill, "Christie's Narrative Games," in *Theory and Practice of Classic Detective Fiction*, eds. Jerome H. Delamater and Ruth Prigozy; Contributions to the Study of Popular Culture, 62 (Westport, CT & London: Greenwood Press, 1997), 88–90.

[3] Christie, *Evil Under the Sun* (1941; reis. New York: HarperCollins, 2011), Kindle edition, ch. 1.

with his handkerchief and looked suddenly apologetic. "I'm sorry. I got carried away."[4]

Poirot agrees with Lane, noting, "I understand your meaning. Up to a point I agree with you. Evil does walk the earth and can be recognized as such."[5] Minutes later, as if on cue, the rich, beautiful, and married actress Arlena Marshall makes her entrance, and everyone stops to notice her. Miss Brewster even comments, "You talked about evil just now, M. Poirot. Now to my mind that woman's a personification of evil! She's a bad lot through and through."[6] Not long after this, Poirot observes Lane watching Arlena Marshall flirting with the handsome, young, and married Patrick Redfern when Lane

> turned suddenly to Poirot. There was a stern, fanatical light in his eyes. He said: "That woman is evil through and through. Do you doubt it?" Poirot said slowly: "It is difficult to be sure." Stephen Lane said: "But, man alive, don't you feel it in the air? All around you? The presence of Evil." Slowly, Hercule Poirot nodded his head.[7]

Poirot's claim regarding "evil everywhere under the sun," is not only, obviously, the basis for the title of the novel, but is also an allusion to Ecclesiastes 6:1 and 10:5. Lane's scriptural quotation is also from Ecclesiastes, this time from 9:3b. As such, it behooves us to examine what Ecclesiastes means by these claims, and how that might help us understand the novel.[8]

First, what does "under the sun" mean in Ecclesiastes? The Hebrew phrase usually translated as "under the sun" appears twenty-nine times, and most likely "means simply 'in the world', and is equivalent to 'under the heavens.'"[9] As R. N. Whybray notes, the phrase's "function is to stress the universality of the human condition and of human experience."[10] This realm of human existence is sometimes seen by scholars as the opposite or converse of the heavenly realm, where things are not so transitory or fleeting.

As for how Ecclesiastes understands the word normally translated as "evil," this is a much more complicated and difficult subject.[11] By my count, it appears thirty times, and can refer to an unexpected situation or the opposite of what might be expected to

---

[4] Ibid. A similar statement regarding in evil is made by Ruth van Rydock in chapter one Christie's *They Do It with Mirrors*, and much is made in the novel of the inability of Carrie Louise Serrocold to discern the reality of evil in the world.
[5] Christie, *Evil Under the Sun*, ch. 1.
[6] Ibid.
[7] Ibid.
[8] This isn't the only instance in which Christie engages the book of Ecclesiastes. In chapter six of her Miss Marple mystery *The Moving Finger*, Ecclesiastes 1:9 is quoted.
[9] R. N. Whybray, *Ecclesiastes*, NCBC (Grand Rapids, MI: Eerdmans, 1989), 3.
[10] Whybray, *Ecclesiastes*, 4.
[11] Scholars have long noted the composite nature of Ecclesiastes, and if this is indeed the case, we shouldn't expect a coherent understanding of evil or any other topic within the book. For a discussion of the issue of the integrity of Ecclesiastes, see Whybray, *Ecclesiastes*, 17–22. Another reason it's difficult to assess what "evil" means in Ecclesiastes is that the Hebrew word rendered as "evil" is used in various contexts. This leads to an interpretive problem which some scholars seek to solve by using alternative translations depending on those contexts.

be fair or equitable. For example, when someone who's worked hard leaves all their wealth to one who never worked for it (2:20-23), or when one has all the money and possessions they could ask for, but they're not able to enjoy them (6:1-6). Both of these situations are referred to as "evil" in Ecclesiastes (cf. 5:13-17; 10:5-7). "Evil" can also refer to a moral category describing humans and/or their actions (as in 5:1-7 [4:17–5:6 in Hebrew]; 7:15-18; 8:10-13; 9:2-3; and 12:14), but unlike other examples of Old Testament Wisdom Literature, this evil doesn't mark one human as being qualitatively different from another human.[12] In fact, one of the central assertions of Ecclesiastes is that the "same fate happens to everyone," rich and poor, good and evil.[13] As W. Sibley Towner writes in reference to 9:1-12, "the ultimate destiny of the good person is no better than that of the evil person," and that is, "all the achievements of life do not guarantee escape from death or obliteration. In no way does good behavior guarantee good results."[14] As such, "evil under the sun" in Ecclesiastes most likely refers to a challenge to commonly held moral assumptions or a regularly accepted pejorative value judgment on someone's behavior. Either way, these assumptions or value judgments are undercut by Ecclesiastes' repeated claims that everything is transitory and that everyone suffers the same fate in the end.

This kind of ambiguity is certainly not found among the vast majority of the characters in Christie's novel. As I noted earlier, Arlena is viewed negatively by nearly every character.[15] She's variously referred to as a "gold-digger," "a man eater," "a woman of that kind" who's "bad" with an "unsavoury past," who was "rather notorious in her conduct" and "never made much of a pose of respectability."[16] In short, she is "evil."[17] The most acerbic assessment of Arlena comes from Rev. Lane. After Arlena's strangled, the police and Poirot question him, and he says,

I knew instinctively as soon as I saw her that Arlena Marshall was a focus of evil. She was Evil! Evil personified! Woman can be man's help and inspiration in life— she can also be man's downfall. She can drag a man down to the level of the beast.

---

[12] In other canonical Jewish Wisdom Literature, one finds echoes of what some refer to as Two-Ways theology, found most often in texts like Leviticus 26 and Deuteronomy 11:26-32, 30:15-20. That is, there are two ways one can act: in accordance with God's statutes and ordinances (in which case one will receive blessings) or against these statutes and ordinances (in which case one will receive curses). Evidence of this mode of thought in Israelite Wisdom Literature can be found in Proverbs 4:4 and 7:2; and in the speeches given by Job's friends in his eponymous book, e.g., 4:7, 8:3-10, 11:13-20, and 22:12-30. It seems clear that in adapting the Two-Ways theology, the biblical wisdom texts are implying a value judgment on human behavior, but this judgment seems absent in Ecclesiastes.
[13] W. Sibley Towner, "The Book of Ecclesiastes," in *The New Interpreter's Bible*, gen. ed. Leander E. Keck (Nashville: Abingdon Press, 1998), 5:339.
[14] Ibid., 339. This equivocal view most likely offends Poirot's Catholicism (and in that regard he probably prefers Ecclesiastes 12:14), but also probably accords with his professional experiences.
[15] R. A. York, *Agatha Christie: Power and Illusion*, Crime Files (Hampshire & New York: Palgrave Macmillan, 2007), 29, mentions this characterization as an example of how in some of Christie's works "conception of character is subject to variety and bias and this may affect the whole understanding of a crime."
[16] Christie, *Evil Under the Sun*, chs. 2 and 7.
[17] Ibid., ch. 7.

The dead woman was just such a woman. She appealed to everything base in a man's nature. She was a woman such as Jezebel and Aholibah. Now—she has been struck down in the middle of her wickedness![18]

Lane's references to Jezebel and Aholibah are telling, as these women have traditionally been viewed negatively because of their sexuality and sexual actions. It's important for us to understand why he views Jezebel and Aholibah as he does before we move any further, as these pejorative views regarding female sexuality seem to be shared by other characters in the novel, as we've seen, even if they don't go as far in their negative opinions of Arlena as Lane does.

Let's take each of these women in turn. First, Jezebel is probably the most notorious female character in the Bible, aside from possibly Delilah. Jezebel was the princess of Sidon, one of the main cities in Phoenicia (1 Kings 16:31), and was married to Ahab, the king of Israel from 869–850 BCE. Some of the most important stories about Jezebel have to do with her conflicts with Elijah, who's introduced in 1 Kings 17. We're told in 1 Kings 18:4 and 13 that Jezebel was killing off the prophets of the Lord, and this action has sometimes been taken to mean that since Jezebel opposed the religion of the Lord, she eliminated its representatives.[19] In the account of the prophetic contest on Mt. Carmel, Jezebel is clearly aligned with the prophetic opponents of Elijah and the Lord, since they're eating at her table (1 Kings 18:19). After Elijah wins the contest, he orders that all the prophets of Baal be seized, and the people murder them, an act which directly parallels Jezebel's murders of the Lord's prophets in deed, but not in motive.[20]

After this contest, Ahab tells Jezebel what has happened, and Jezebel sends a message to Elijah (1 Kings 19:2). There are three points to note here: first, these are the first words spoken by Jezebel, and they're quite powerful and intimidating. Second, it seems that roles are reversed: Ahab as the king should be the active one, and not Jezebel. And third, Elijah is scared of Jezebel and her message: he is "afraid" and "flees for his life" from her (1 Kings 19:3). After Elijah flees, he goes to Mt. Horeb, where he'll experience his famous theophany, or encounter with the Lord in a "still small voice" (as the King James Version translates 1 Kings 19:12). His absence allows the narrator to mention the incident of Naboth's vineyard in 1 Kings 21. Ahab wants the vineyard of a man named Naboth, and the latter refuses the king's request. Ahab goes home and pouts until Jezebel insults him a tad and vows to get the vineyard for him. She then sends out her second message, this time ordering all the elders and noblemen in Jezreel to bring a false charge against Naboth, so that he'll be stoned and Ahab can then take possession of the vineyard. The plan works, but Elijah is made aware of the incident, and curses Ahab and Jezebel (1 Kings 21:20-24). Ahab repents, and thus is spared for a while, but we get no response from Jezebel.

---

[18]   Ibid., ch. 8.
[19]   Contra this view, see Claudia V. Camp, "1 and 2 Kings," in *Women's Bible Commentary*, eds C. A. Newsom and S. H. Ringe, expanded edn, with Apocrypha (Louisville, KY: Westminster/John Knox Press, 1998), 109–110.
[20]   See Janet Howe Gaines, "How Bad Was Jezebel?" *Bible Review* 16, no. 5 (2000): 17.

She then disappears from the narrative until 2 Kings 9, where she dies. By this time, 20–30 years after Ahab began ruling, Jehoram is now king of Israel and Ahaziah is king of Judah. Jehu, Jehoram's military commander, is attempting a coup and both Jehoram and Ahaziah meet him at, of all places, Naboth's vineyard. Jehu kills Jehoram, who is married to Jezebel's daughter Athaliah. Jehu then proceeds to Jezreel, where Jezebel is waiting for him. In preparation for him, she "painted her eyes, and adorned her head, and looked out of the window" (2 Kings 9:30). While many scholars have taken these actions to imply that she's trying to seduce Jehu, a more sympathetic reading demonstrates other motives. Jezebel by this time is already a grandmother, so seducing Jehu is probably not her motive. Rather, her self-adornment could be seen as an attempt to excite her followers. She even taunts Jehu by calling him "Zimri," a famous assassin who committed suicide to escape the attack of Omri. In the end, though, Jezebel is thrown out of her window by her own eunuchs. Her body is trampled by horses, and then is presumably eaten by dogs, because when Jehu orders her to be buried, all that is left is her skull, feet, and hands. Upon hearing this, Jehu utters an oracle loosely based on Elijah's curse of Jezebel in 1 Kings 21:23.

In the end, what are we to make of Jezebel? Many interpreters have certainly viewed her as Lane seems to do, i.e., as a wanton, evil woman who deserved the punishment she received in 2 Kings 9. However, feminist scholars paint a different picture of her, one which asks us to consider her point of view. One such scholar is Janet Howe Gaines, who concludes her treatment of Jezebel with this summary:

> Jezebel emerges as a fiery and determined person, with an intensity matched only by Elijah's. She is true to her native religion and customs. She is even more loyal to her husband. Throughout her reign, she boldly exercises what power she has. And, in the end, having lived her life on her own terms, Jezebel faces certain death with dignity.[21]

In a similar way, Poirot himself will ask not only Lane but also the novel's readers to see Arlena in a different light, one in which Lane's comparison of her to Jezebel no longer holds.

The other woman that Lane mentions in connection with Arlena is Aholibah. Also known as Oholibah, we find her story in Ezekiel 23, in which the prophet relays a divine message regarding a symbolic analogy between two sexually promiscuous sisters (v. 3) who represent Samaria (Oholah) and Jerusalem (Oholibah) (v. 4). Ezekiel first briefly describes the lustful dalliances of Oholah in vv. 5-10, relating how she "played the whore" (v. 5) with the Assyrians prior to the Lord delivering "her into the hands of her lovers . . . the Assyrians," (v. 9) who rape her, "seized her sons and daughters," and then "killed her with the sword" (v. 10). As a result, "she became a byword among women" (v. 10). The prophet then turns a more elaborative eye to Oholibah in vv. 11-35.

As I mentioned, in this symbolic analogy, Oholibah represents Jerusalem, so it makes sense that more invective would be heaped upon her, given the covenantal relationship

---

[21] Ibid., 23.

between God and Israel that, according to this text, she has violated through her "whorings." Indeed, Oholibah is described initially as "more corrupt than [her sister Oholah] in her lusting and in her whorings, which were worse than those of her sister" (v. 11). As evidence of this claim, the prophet notes that not only did Oholibah lust after all different kinds of Assyrians, she also lusted after and actively sought out the Babylonians (vv. 14-17). As a result of Oholibah carrying "on her whorings so openly" and flaunting "her nakedness," Ezekiel notes that God "turned in disgust from her" (v. 18). But this only caused Oholibah to increase "her whorings" (v. 19).

In response to Oholibah's wanton ways, God announces that he "will rouse against you your lovers from whom you turned in disgust," and that he "will bring them against you from every side" (v. 22). All of Oholibah's former lovers will then surround her, "in order that they may deal with you in fury" (v. 25). These lovers will then attack Oholibah, and the biblical text here is specific in its graphicness: "They shall cut off your nose and your ears, and your survivors shall fall by the sword. They shall seize your sons and your daughters, and your survivors shall be devoured by fire" (v. 25). And in case there's any doubt as to who's to blame for this terrible punishment, God notes in vv. 29-30, "Your lewdness and your whorings have brought this upon you, because you played the whore with the nations, and polluted yourself with their idols." But Ezekiel isn't done with these sisters quite yet.

The remainder of chapter 23 (vv. 36-49) consists of an additional judgment on the sisters with even more punishments and even more specifics regarding their culpability. The latter is seen in vv. 35-45, and includes more descriptions of the sexual excesses of the sisters. One particularly interesting charge—given our discussion of Jezebel earlier—is found in v. 40, in which God notes, "For them you bathed yourself, painted your eyes, and decked yourself with ornaments." In the end, God again condemns the sisters in terms reminiscent of v. 25, but no less chilling: "Bring up an assembly against them, and make them an object of terror and of plunder. The assembly shall stone them and with their swords they shall cut them down; they shall kill their sons and their daughters, and burn up their houses" (vv. 46-47). Unlike the first judgment of Oholibah, this joint judgment has a goal, a specific objective, which the prophet states in v. 48: "Thus will I put an end to lewdness in the land, so that all women may take warning and not commit lewdness as you have done." In the end, then, the emotional and physical violence the sisters endure serve as a warning to other women as well as a reminder that God's the alpha male here. Or, as God puts it in the final verse in the chapter: "I am the Lord God."

Like the stories about Jezebel, it's a safe bet that the material in Ezekiel 23 was written by men primarily for other men. As such, we don't get the viewpoint of Oholibah here, any more than we get the viewpoint of Jezebel in 1–2 Kings. The importance of noting the androcentric viewpoint of the text lies in the negative view of female sexuality and the violence against women in Ezekiel 23. In her work on Ezekiel, Katheryn Pfisterer Darr writes that "his use of female imagery is problematic, for he depicts female sexuality as the object of male possession and control, presents physical abuse as a way to reclaim such control, and then suggests that violence can be a means toward *healing* a broken relationship."[22] Many scholars have pointed out the impact of

---

[22] Darr, "Ezekiel," in *Women's Bible Commentary*, 198.

such views on the lives of real, flesh and blood women (and men).[23] For our purposes, perhaps it's most important to note how Lane's simile—in which he mentions "Aholibah"—as well as his other references to Arlena build upon this pejorative understanding of female sexuality and the appropriateness, even the necessity, of severe punishment for such women.

Now that we've unpacked the symbolism Lane employs to describe Arlena, let's return to the novel and point out that it undercuts his view by three means. First, Poirot refers to Lane as a "fanatic" and a "religious maniac," and we're told that Lane resigned his post and spent over a year in "a nursing home for mental patients."[24] In fact, one of the investigators, Inspector Colgate, reveals that Lane's "trouble was an obsession about the devil—especially the devil in the guise of a woman—scarlet woman—whore of Babylon."[25]

The Whore of Babylon

The so-called "whore of Babylon" is an image taken from Revelation 17–18, in which the author continues the practice found in the Hebrew Bible of portraying cities or countries as sexually shameless women and depicting their deserved punishment for their promiscuity. In Revelation, "Babylon" is a cipher for Rome, who's described as a "great whore" (17:1) and "drunk with the blood of the saints and the blood of the witnesses to Jesus" (17:6). This woman will be attacked by "peoples and multitudes and nations," which will "make her desolate and naked [and] devour her flesh and burn her up with fire" (17:16). This imagery echoes that of Ezekiel 23, but here it's even more obvious the deleterious effect this "whore" has on the faithful. As a result, her punishment is not simply connected to her sexual activities; it's also necessitated on account of her persecution of the followers of Jesus. In Evil Under the Sun, the implied connection(s) between this "whore" and Arlena seem obvious, even though Lane himself never states them outright.

The effect of this data is to render any views or evidence given by Lane suspect because of his mental condition.[26] Secondly, despite the fact that, as Colgate remarks, "The late Mrs Marshall was a pretty good example of what a clergyman would call a Scarlet

[23] Among others, see Joseph Blenkinsopp, Ezekiel, IBC (Atlanta: John Knox Press, 1997), 99; and Jacqueline E. Lapsley, "Ezekiel," in Women's Bible Commentary: Twentieth-Anniversary Edition, eds. Carol A. Newsom, Sharon H. Ringe, and Jacqueline E. Lapsley (Louisville, KY: Westminster John Knox Press, 2012), 289.
[24] Christie, Evil Under the Sun, chs. 6, 11 and 12, respectively. Similarly, in the 1924 short story "The House of Lurking Death," Christie also includes an elderly maid called Hannah who's marked by "religious mania," characterized by severely eschatological Bible reading.
[25] Christie, Evil Under the Sun, ch. 11.
[26] This characterization of Lane, with his excessive religious mono-mania, as mentally unbalanced and emotionally unstable seems to parallel other Christie characters like Emily Brent in And Then There Were None.

Woman—hair and goings on and all," and that in his view "it's not impossible he may have felt it his appointed task to dispose of her," Lane is soon excluded as a suspect, since he's not involved in either the blackmail or drug ring the investigation has uncovered.[27] That is, despite Lane's religious predisposition against Arlena, his alibi precludes his involvement in what the police assume to be the criminal activities related to her murder.

The third and final way in which the novel challenges Lane's biblically informed views about Arlena is through Poirot's own understanding of the "evil" he and Lane discussed at the outset of the story. After Poirot dramatically reveals the solution to the murder, he reflects,

> It was that day that we spoke of evil—*evil under the sun* as Mr. Lane put it. Mr. Lane is a very sensitive person—evil affects him—he perceives its presence—but though he is a good recording instrument, he did not really know exactly where the evil was. To him, evil was focused in the person of Arlena Marshall, and practically everyone present agreed with him. But to my mind, though evil was present, it was not centralized in Arlena Marshall at all. It was connected with her, yes—but in a totally different way. I saw her, first, last and all the time, as an eternal and predestined *victim*. Because she was beautiful, because she had glamour, because men turned their heads to look at her, it was assumed that she was the type of woman who wrecked lives and destroyed souls. But I saw her very differently. It was not she who fatally attracted men—it was men who fatally attracted her.[28]

Poirot's view of Arlena as the victim of men, rather than a predator definitively refutes Lane's impression of her as a "Jezebel" or a "whore of Babylon."

One could pursue this further and note that Poirot's view of Arlena as victim actually serves as a corrective to Lane's interpretation of Ezekiel 23. As we have seen, Oholibah is clearly a victim of divine sexual abuse due to anxiety over her exercise of her own sexuality. Given that Lane's simile also expresses concern about female sexuality and endorses punishment of women who act outside generally accepted societal mores, his view represents a typical, androcentric interpretation of Ezekiel 23, one which doesn't take into account the victimization and subjectivity of women. Poirot's view of Arlena, though, looks beyond the superficial, androcentric understanding of her as a strumpet/"man-eater"—advocated even by some female characters—and affords her a more rounded appraisal, far more in line with the feminist comments I mentioned earlier.

This view of Arlena by Poirot also is in keeping with the theme of reversal of expectation found in Ecclesiastes, the source of the book's title. That is, in Ecclesiastes, as we saw earlier, the author delights in providing examples of what people normally assume to be the case and then refuting them, for example, "under the sun the race is not to the swift, nor the battle to the strong, nor bread to the wise, nor riches to the intelligent, nor favor to the skillful; but time and chance happen to them all" (9:11). This is precisely what Poirot accomplishes at the end of the novel: he paints a

---

27 Christie, *Evil Under the Sun*, ch. 11.
28 Ibid., ch. 13.

sympathetic picture of Arlena as a victim in the face of widespread assumptions to the contrary.[29] And in so doing, he shows that this, too, is an "evil under the sun."

It should be clear that again in this novel, Christie is pushing the needle, so to speak, in terms of gender assumptions, not to mention critically engaging with the category of "evil" in dialogue with Ecclesiastes.[30] The former is seen in Poirot's refusal to accept the standard cultural assumptions regarding Arlena's sexuality and promiscuity. As I mentioned earlier, Lane's biblically informed view represents the conservative, inherited view of female sexuality, even if it's an extreme caricature thereof. Poirot's more nuanced approach is shown ultimately to be more accurate, and it's no coincidence that his willingness to embrace the viewpoint of Arlena instead of summarily condemning her is more in line with the approach of feminist biblical critics. In adopting this approach, the novel shows Poirot—the feminized male, foreign outsider—undercutting Lane's more recognized authority and stance, thus calling them into question.

At the bottom of this questioning is Christie's engagement with the notion of "evil" in Ecclesiastes. As we saw, by taking up this notion, making it prominent in Lane's view, then pulling the rug out from under that view via Poirot's more sympathetic assessment of Arlena, Christie shows a remarkable sophistication in her use of the Bible. As Hannah M. Strømmen puts it, she "sets up a stark contrast between [Poirot's] brand of religious rhetoric and the fanatic clergyman [Lane] also present on the scene."[31] That is, by replicating key themes in Ecclesiastes—the most important of which is the reversal of expectation or the challenge to common assumptions—Christie uses the Bible to interrogate inherited scripturally based assumptions regarding female sexuality and behavior by putting them in the mouth of an Anglican priest and showing them to be inapplicable via a foreign, diminutive Catholic. But, do we find this sophisticated challenge present in the world the text creates?

* * *

There are two cinematic interpretations of *Evil Under the Sun*, and one of these is a big-budget film with the same actor playing Poirot (Peter Ustinov) and the same screenwriter (Anthony Shaffer) as *Death on the Nile* (1978). This film was released in 1982 and is, for lack of better term, campy, in the sense that many of its characters are wildly flamboyant and snarky, and they spend a good deal of their screen time vamping and chewing scenery.[32] However, like the 1978 *Death on the Nile*, this film also totally

[29] In my article, "The Divine Unsub: Television Procedurals and Biblical Sexual Violence," in *The Bible in Crime Fiction and Drama: Murderous Texts*, eds. Alison Jack and Caroline Blyth; Scriptural Traces, 16; LHB/OTS, 678 (London & New York: Bloomsbury, 2019), 125–148, I address the issue of female victims of sexual violence in the Bible not being allowed an opportunity to voice their experiences. In announcing his alternative view of Arlena, Poirot is likewise challenging the narratorial flatness of Arlena's character as well as the assumptions made about her by other characters.
[30] Of course, "evil" is an important theme in Christie's output in general. See, e.g., Earl F. Bargainnier, *The Gentle Art of Murder: The Detective Fiction of Agatha Christie* (Bowling Green, OH: Bowling Green University Popular Press, 1980), 191 and 197.
[31] Strømmen also focuses on this scene and its use of biblical archetypes in her "Poirot, the Bourgeois Prophet," in *The Bible in Crime Fiction and Drama*, 156.
[32] See Aldridge, *Agatha Christie On Screen*, Crime Files (London: Palgrave Macmillan, 2016), 149–151.

ignores the biblical elements I have mentioned previously through a very simple maneuver: the character of Stephen Lane is omitted entirely. As such, all of the biblical echoes and allusions are absent from this frolicking film, save for Poirot's semi-quotation from Ecclesiastes, "The sky is blue, the sun is shining, and yet you forget that everywhere there is evil under the sun." Given that Lane isn't present in this adaptation, Poirot's pronouncement serves only to ground and reference the film's title in the pared-down plot.

In contrast, the 2002 feature-length episode of *Agatha Christie's Poirot* that adapts the novel includes numerous scenes with Lane (Tim Meats), and it's through these scenes that we see a deeper engagement with the biblical issues I noted earlier. The film opens with Lane giving a sermon in which he retells the story of Jezebel in 1 Kings 21:11-15 (reading from the King James Version). Following this, Lane remarks that,

> [Jezebel's] name has come to stand for the wickedness of women. The painted Jezebel of 2 Kings, chapter 9, a woman who was shallow and profane, it was she who persuaded her husband Ahab to kill Naboth, and for this she was punished. 'And of Jezebel also sp[o]ke the Lord, saying, The dogs shall eat Jezebel by the wall of Jezreel' [1 Kgs 21.23; KJV]. She had sold herself to work evil in the sight of the Lord, and the punishment was death. This is the God of the Old Testament: wrathful, unforgiving. We may find this at odds with our understanding of Christianity. But for the Jezebels of this world, death is the price that must be paid.

Here we see a fleshing out of Lane's position in the novel. That is, the material here on Jezebel expands on his identification of Arlena with Jezebel in the novel, and this sermon also makes an obvious connection between the biblical Jezebel and the punishment Lane sees as fitting for her modern-day analogs. The stress on a suitable punishment for the transgressive woman here also echoes Lane's reference in the novel to Oholibah and her divinely sanctioned and enacted punishment. Visually, his sermon is also interspersed with scenes from the murder of a woman named Alice Corrigan, which not only takes place in Lane's parish, but also forms an important precedent to Arlena's murder. In these scenes, Lane is present at the Coroner's Court, and is visibly shaken by their finding of "murder by person or persons unknown."

We next encounter Lane at a seaside health resort, the Sandy Cove Hotel, where Poirot and his close friend Captain Hastings (Hugh Fraser) are spending some medically prescribed time after Poirot collapses at the opening of Hastings's new Argentinian restaurant. Hastings notes, "Surely no one could think of murder in such a beautiful place," and Poirot—as he does in the 1982 film—ominously retorts, "No, Hastings. It is romantic, yes. It is peaceful. The sun shines, the sea, it is blue. But you forget, *mon ami*, there is evil everywhere under the sun." As he says this, the camera follows his eye from Patrick (Michael Higgs) and Arlena (here surnamed Stuart; played by Louise Delamere) playing in the water up to a cliff, where Christine (Tamzin Malleson) is watching them. At this point, Lane appears and agrees with Poirot, repeating nearly verbatim his response in the novel.

Here, though, the episode departs from the novel in the first of several scenes which, I suggest, attempt to redeem Lane from the characterization of the deranged religious fanatic one finds in the novel. Poirot inquires if Lane is "of the Church," and Lane responds cryptically, "I was, but then I was ill. My wife, you see . . . Well, it's a long story. But that's why I'm here. It's for my health." His face hardening, Lane continues, "Anyway, you don't have to be of the Church to recognize evil, Mr. Poirot." Looking now at Arlena, he says, "I see it there. I recognize it. It's real."

After Arlena's murder, Lane is interviewed by Poirot and Scotland Yard Chief Inspector Japp (Philip Jackson). Therein, he reveals that he's no longer a Vicar because "There was a scandal. My wife. . . . You see, she left me. She ran away with a member of my congregation. She was a wicked woman. She should be punished." We also learn that Lane has a prescription for an opioid (Morphine) that he takes for his nerves. As opposed to the novel, then—which, as we saw, dismisses Lane as a religious fanatic/maniac—this film depicts him more sympathetically, as someone who's had a nervous breakdown because of his wife's behavior and is seeking the help he recognizes he needs.

In contrast, the 2002 adaptation retains the novel's emphasis on Arlena's victimhood in Poirot's eyes. This is most notable during the "Big Reveal" segment, and here Poirot draws on Lane's comments to posit his understanding of Arlena. He notes, "*La pauvre* Arlena. To Monsieur Lane, as he watched her swimming at the beach, she was the focus of evil, eh? Of evil under the sun." For extra emphasis, the film here flashes back to the scene in which Lane makes his comments, so we as viewers are reminded of his statement. Poirot then continues, "But, to my mind, the evil was connected with Arlena Stuart in a different way. I saw her first, last, and all of the time as a victim, eternal and predestined." Poirot then, sadly, refers to Arlena as a "target, and a very easy one." There was, he opines, a "weakness in her that was fatal, that she was attracted always to men who took of her only the advantage." Of course, his prime example of the "men [who] preyed on her for her money" is Patrick Redfern who, once he bilked her for all he could get, had to kill her.

After Poirot identifies Redfern as the killer, he turns to address Lane. "I know you have not been well. You have suffered from the nerves most bad." Again, we flash back to the Coroner's Court scene where Lane looks at the distraught fiancé of Alice Corrigan, whom we now recognize as "Patrick." Poirot continues, "But perhaps, the evil you saw that day on the beach, it was the same evil you glimpsed in the courtroom two years before." Lane—looking now again at "Patrick"—agrees, saying, "Yes, he looks different now, but it was him." Following this, Patrick attacks Poirot, grabbing his throat. After he's subdued, Poirot exclaims, "The face of evil, it remains always the same."

This adaptation, then, not only portrays Lane in a much more positive light than the novel, even going so far as to portray him as the crucial eyewitness, but it also employs the imagery of evil from Ecclesiastes found in the novel in a more thoroughgoing manner than the 1982 film. In so doing, it replicates the achievement of the novel in restating the ambiguity and equivocality of Ecclesiastes. That is, Suchet's Poirot refuses to see Arlena as Lane and others see her—as a wicked trollop like Jezebel or Oholibah, who deserved the punishment she received—and he likewise feels sympathy for Lane. He recognizes and understands the evil that exists in Redfern's "mind that was brilliant," but like the speaker in Ecclesiastes, is not content to embrace nihilism in the face of either evil or the realities of human suffering. No, Poirot instead follows the advice of passages like Ecclesiastes 3:17, 8:12-13, 11:9, and 12:13-14, passages which speak of fearing God, keeping the commandments, and the inevitability of God's judgement of the righteous and the wicked. It's no coincidence, in my opinion, that this film ends with all four of the main characters of the series—Poirot, Hastings, Japp, and Miss Lemon (Pauline Moran)—together, laughing, about to go share a meal. This, after all, is what Ecclesiastes posits is "good" under the sun (see 2:24, 3:12-13, 5:18-20, 8:16, and 9:7-10).

In conclusion, the example of *Evil Under the Sun* helps us see the ways in which Christie skillfully employs biblical texts and images in order to complicate and problematize the ideologies of Christian hegemony and normativity which she inherited. By showing Lane's androcentric scriptural analogies and religiously informed worldview to be lacking in sophistication through Poirot's more empathetic understanding, Christie offers a subtle critique of the Church and the way its officials interpret the Bible. In so doing, she shows herself to be a fully modernist author, and far more critical of social and religious institutions than her "cozy" reputation might lead us to believe.

5

The Prodigal Son

In both the romantic plot of *Death on the Nile* and the extended meditation on human evil in *Evil under the Sun*, we find Poirot stories which Christie bases on and constructs around a central scriptural image or paradigm, while at the same time demonstrating both a playful and questioning attitude towards Scripture. For our third and final example of how Christie critically engages biblical literature, we'll examine two works where Christie employs a single New Testament text, the story of the Prodigal Son in Luke 15:11-32, to characterize and illuminate familial relationships that drive the plots of the stories.[1] As I argue at the outset of Part Two, focusing on Christie's engagement with and variations on this parable, as well as other biblical texts, helps us understand better the Christian normativity she reinforces yet challenges for her audience.

Before we examine how Christie uses the story of the Prodigal Son, let's recall what happens in that particular parable in Luke. Put briefly, a man's younger son asks his father for all his inheritance, moves away, and squanders it all (15:12-13). The younger son hires himself out as a servant who feeds pigs, but then realizes his father's servants probably have it better than he does, as he can't even share the pigs' food.[2] So, he decides to return home and admit his mistake in the hopes that his father would welcome him back. On seeing him, his father runs to him, embraces him, and (after his son admits his mistake) orders his slaves to bring out his best robe, a ring and sandals, and to slaughter a calf that has been fattened so they could celebrate.[3] The father even cries out, "This son of mine was dead and is alive again; he was lost and is found!" (15:24). Upon learning what's transpired, the older son becomes angry and refuses to attend the celebration, telling the father he's worked "like a slave" for him for years and has received nothing.

---

[1] Imagery associated with the prodigal son is also present and important in the Miss Marple novel *A Pocket Full of Rye* (1953; reis. New York: HarperCollins, 2011), Kindle edition, chs. 5, 6, 11 and 19. At five points throughout the novel, Lancelot Fortescue is referred to as the "prodigal son" either by himself or other characters. And, his position relative to his brother Percival, who, like the Lukan text, stayed at home to mind the farm, so to speak, is quite similar to the brothers in *Hercule Poirot's Christmas*. The key difference is that Lancelot (the prodigal son) turns out to be the murderer of, among others, his father. We also find a mention of the prodigal son in "The Case of the Caretaker," a Marple story first published in 1950.

[2] As Sarah Ruden points out in "The Good News according to Loukas," in *The Gospels: A New Translation* (New York: Modern Library, 2021), 223.

[3] Ruden writes that this would've been a "weaned calf kept in a stall and fed on grain—human food—so that its meant would be particularly rich and tender, and butchered while it was still relatively small," and "a great luxury" (ibid., 224).

Yet, the fatted calf has been slaughtered for his younger brother "who has devoured your property with prostitutes" (15:30). The father responds, "Son, you are always with me, and all that is mine is yours," before reiterating his previously stated rationale for the celebration (15:21; cf. 15:24). Various commentators note the themes of "restoration and communal celebration" in the parable.[4] They also point out that the father's actions not only subvert or contradict the expectations of Jesus's audience, as most parables do, but also that those actions model and echo an "unforgettable picture of divine grace."[5] So, how does Christie use this parable? Let's focus on two key examples.

*   *   *

"The Mystery of the Hunter's Lodge."

Christie first uses this parable in a short story published in May of 1923 called "The Mystery of the Hunter's Lodge." Therein, a fellow named Mr. Havering comes to secure Poirot's services after his uncle has been murdered.[6] Since Poirot is bed-ridden with the flu, he gives the enthusiastic Hastings permission to go investigate in his stead. Once they are underway on the train, Havering describes himself to Hastings as "somewhat of a prodigal son myself," and that this "rather increased than diminished his [his Uncle's] affection towards me. Of course I am a poor man, and my uncle was a rich one—in other words, he paid the piper!"[7]

Here, Mr. Havering identifies with the younger son who asks for, receives, then squanders the inheritance from his father. Obviously, this isn't an exact analogy, since Havering has no brother who stayed behind, but Havering does claim his uncle (presumably the father in this scenario) had more affection for him because of his absence, despite the fact that he was paying the bills. However, as we discover, the biggest discrepancy between the two stories is that Luke's "prodigal son" doesn't collude to murder his father, as Havering colludes with his wife to murder his uncle.[8]

At the end of the story, the Haverings escape prior to Inspector Japp laying hands on them. After Poirot recovers and explains the solution of the murder to Hastings, the little detective comments, "To bring that precious pair to justice, that is another matter. Well, Japp must do what he can—I have written him fully—but I very much fear, Hastings, that we shall be obliged to leave them to Fate, or *le bon Dieu*, whichever you prefer."[9] Hastings responds, "The wicked flourish like a green bay tree," to which Poirot

---

4   John T. Carroll, *Luke: A Commentary*, NTL (Louisville: Westminster John Knox, 2012), 313, Kindle edition, "15:11-32 A Parable about a Father's (and a Brother's) Response to the Loss and Restoration of a Son."

5   Ibid.

6   The story was originally published in *The Sketch* on 16 May 1923, then collected the following year in Christie's first short story collection, *Poirot Investigates*. All citations and references from the story are taken from Christie, *Hercule Poirot: The Complete Short Stories* (New York: HarperCollins, 2013), Kindle edition.

7   Christie, "The Mystery of the Hunter's Lodge."

8   As I have previously noted, Christie replicates this arrangement thirty years later in her novel, *A Pocket Full of Rye*. Therein, Lancelot Fortescue seduces then tricks the gullible maid Gladys Martin into poisoning his father, Rex, after which he murders her, too.

9   Christie, "The Mystery of the Hunter's Lodge."

replies, "But at a price, Hastings, always at a price, *croyez-moi!*"[10] We do learn the fate of the murderers, though. Hastings relays that "Nemesis did overtake them, and when I read in the paper that the Hon. Roger and Mrs. Havering were amongst those killed in the crashing of the Air Mail to Paris I knew that Justice was satisfied."[11]

Hastings's comment about the "green bay tree" provides us another scriptural reference, as it's an allusion to Psalm 37:35. In the King James Version, this text reads, "I have seen the wicked in great power / And spreading himself like a green bay tree." This is another of Christie's favorite scriptural images. It appears three times in her Poirot works: once here, once in the 1923 short story "The Chocolate Box," and once in the 1955 novel *Hickory Dickory Dock*.[12] In all three cases, the phrase is used to describe the seeming success of a wicked person in evading the consequences of their evil actions. That's certainly the case here, as Hastings quotes the Psalm in a sense of resignation, as if to say that there's nothing more they can do, since the wicked here have escaped justice—or, as Poirot says, *le bon Dieu*. This use of the Psalm certainly tracks with its overall tone and message. Robert Alter helpfully summarizes that message for us, writing that Psalm 37 expresses "the idea that the wicked, however they may seem to prosper, will get their just deserts and the righteous will be duly rewarded. The distinctive note in all this is a plea for equanimity: The good person is enjoined not to get stirred up by the seeming success of the wicked."[13] Just so, the ending of the story undercuts Hastings's cynicism, as we learn that a kind of "Justice" has indeed prevailed. Yes, the Haverings did inherit Mr. Pace's fortune through his murder, but they were killed shortly thereafter in a plane crash. This, evidently, is the "price" they paid for their "flourishing," as Poirot puts it. In his narration, Hastings anthropomorphizes "justice," saying their deaths "satisfied" Justice (even though there were presumably other casualties and fatalities in that plane crash), thus aligning the moral of the short story with the theology of the Psalm. By the juxtaposition of the Lukan parable of the Prodigal Son and the imagery from Psalm 37, Christie demonstrates a deft usage of biblical materials in presenting a story in which greed and deception seem to belie familial kindness, until the wicked are rightly and justly punished.

Given its early situation in Christie's output and its brevity, it's difficult to determine if or how Christie is using this biblical allusion to resist Christian hegemony, even if we already see the willingness to alter and even distort the Bible that will become more prominent in her later work. Unfortunately, the 1991 adaptation of the story in *Agatha Christie's Poirot* isn't much help, as it fails to include any of the biblical references we've examined in this brief story. As such, the world the text creates adds little to our

---

[10] Ibid.

[11] Ibid. I should note that Miss Marple is referred to as "Nemesis" at least twice. First, in an attempt to wake an old man called Mr. Rafiel, she uses the term to refer to herself in chapter 24 of *A Caribbean Mystery*. And second, we obviously find the term used in reference to Marple several times in the last Miss Marple novel Christie wrote—but not the last one she published—called *Nemesis* (1971).

[12] It also appears at the conclusion of the Marple novel, *At Bertram's Hotel* (1965; reis. New York: HarperCollins, 2011), Kindle edition, ch. 27.

[13] Alter, *The Book of Psalms: A Translation with Commentary* (New York & London: W. W. Norton & Co., 2007), 129.

discussion of prodigal son imagery thus far. But perhaps a novel fifteen years later might shed some light.

Hercule Poirot's Christmas

The 1938 novel *Hercule Poirot's Christmas* tells the story of a Christmas gathering of the Lee family.[14] The near-invalid patriarch of the family is a malicious old man called Simeon, who enjoys tormenting his children for his own amusement. Of these children, his dull son Alfred and his wife Lydia live on an estate with Simeon, and the old man also invites two other sons (David and George) along with their wives (Hilda and Magdalene, respectively) to the estate for Christmas. Simeon is a scoundrel, though, and has also invited two extra guests for Christmas. One is Pilar Estravados (a woman he believes is the Spanish daughter of his deceased daughter Jennifer) and his estranged son Harry, who's spent years abroad, and is something of a scandal to the family. Once all these various and not particularly affectionate characters are assembled, Simeon is promptly murdered in what can only be described as a spectacular fashion.[15] The local Constable, Superintendent Sugden, is close by and after an initial investigation, calls Colonel Johnson, the Chief Constable, to inform him . . . and Johnson just happens to be hosting Poirot for Christmas. Once Poirot begins his investigation, the family's secrets will be exposed, and an unlikely killer will be revealed.

The parable of the Prodigal Son is mentioned three times in this novel, so understanding how it functions therein is key in grasping the novel's emphases on family, sons, and legacy/inheritance. In Part 1 ("December 22nd"), Simeon tells Alfred that Harry is returning. Alfred, stunned, asks Simeon, "You—you are having him back here? After everything?" Simeon replies, "The prodigal son, eh? You're right. The fatted calf! We must kill the fatted calf, Alfred. We must give him a grand welcome."[16] When Alfred again objects, Simeon says, "No need to recite his crimes! It's a long list. But Christmas, you'll remember, is the season of forgiveness! We'll welcome the prodigal home."[17]

If this were the only mention of the "prodigal son" imagery, then it'd be curious, but certainly not determinative. However, once Harry comes back to the house, he asks their aged butler Tressilian if Alfred's "looking forward to seeing" him, to which the

---

[14] For a brief discussion of this novel, see Barnard, *A Talent to Deceive: An Appreciation of Agatha Christie* (New York: Mysterious Press, 1980), 71–77; Charles Osborne, *The Life and Crimes of Agatha Christie: A Biographical Companion to the Works of Agatha Christie*, rev. and updated ed. (London: HarperCollins, 1999), 163–166; and Mark Aldridge, *Agatha Christie's Poirot: The Greatest Detective in the World* (London: HarperCollins, 2020), 139–143.

[15] As noted by R. A. York, *Agatha Christie: Power and Illusion*, Crime Files (Hampshire & New York: Palgrave Macmillan, 2007), 17–18.

[16] In her Miss Marple novel *A Murder is Announced*, Christie also uses the image of the "fatted calf" in chapter six. However, it's not connected to any other imagery from the "prodigal son" story, and is simply mentioned on its own.

[17] Christie, *Hercule Poirot's Christmas* (1939; reis. New York: HarperCollins, 2011), Kindle edition, "December 22nd."

servant replies, "I expect so, sir." Harry, though, counters this polite response, and his reply is worth quoting in full:

> I don't! Quite the contrary. I bet it's given him a nasty jolt, my turning up! Alfred and I never did get on. Ever read your Bible, Tressilian? . . . Remember the tale of the prodigal's return? The good brother didn't like it, remember? Didn't like it at all! Good old stay-at-home Alfred doesn't like it either, I bet.[18]

Finally, Harry asks Tresslilian to lead him into the house, quipping, "Lead on, old son . . . The fatted calf awaits me! Lead me right to it."[19]

Later still we find a third and final reference to the Lukan parable. After Simeon's murder, Poirot and Sugden are conducting interviews. When it's Harry's turn, Poirot asks if he's been away a long time. Harry laughs and replies, "You might as well hear straight away—someone will soon tell you! I'm the prodigal son, gentlemen! It's nearly twenty years since I last set foot in this house."[20] When Poirot asks him why he returned, Harry again invokes "prodigal" imagery, telling them, "It's the good old parable still. I got tired of the husks that the swine do eat—or don't eat, I forget which. I thought to myself that the fatted calf would be a welcome exchange."[21]

As it turns out, Simeon is actually killed by Sugden, an illegitimate son of his, i.e., one not "born the right side of the blanket."[22] As Poirot puts it, "It is Simeon Lee's own blood that rises up against him."[23] This phrase of Poirot's could be an allusion to Micah 7:5-7, which in the King James Version reads in part, "For the son dishonoureth the father, the daughter riseth up against her mother, the daughter in law against her mother-in-law; a man's enemies are the men of his own house." In this section in Micah, a speaker is bemoaning the pitiful and desperate state in which they find themselves. Their lament in 7:5-7 serves "to acknowledge the justice of the judgment [of God] upon a population lacking in justice (7:2b-4) and in the faithful devotion (7:2a, 5f.)."[24] The focus on the population and their actions narrows in 7:5-6 to encompass what Hans Walter Wolff terms the "primary unit of all community life, the family."[25] As Wolff notes, the picture painted in these verses is one in which "the family is disintegrated by disrespect and strife. When the nucleus of all community—certainly the first and last place where security is experienced—is undermined, then every refuge is turned into chaos. This is the end of all community."[26] This allusion to Micah, with its terrible portrait of mistrust and degenerating relations among kin, helps us see that the plot of the novel represents *a reversal* of the seemingly more positive familial imagery of the story in Luke 15:11-32, similar to "The Mystery of the Hunter's Lodge." As we saw in

---

18. Ibid., "December 23rd."
19. Ibid. Harry also refers to Alfred as "the good dutiful stay-at-home stick-in-the-mud son" in "December 24th."
20. Ibid., "December 24th."
21. Ibid.
22. Ibid.
23. Ibid., "December 27th."
24. James Luther Mays, *Micah*, OTL (Philadelphia: Westminster, 1976), 151.
25. Wolff, *Micah: A Commentary*, CC, trans. Gary Stansell (Minneapolis: Augsburg, 1990), 208.
26. Ibid.

our examinations of *The Mysterious Affair at Styles* and *Death on the Nile*, Christie's willingness to contort and even reverse the plot(s) of her biblical target text signals a resistant reception of scripture that is modernist in its execution. But how is this execution present in *Hercule Poirot's Christmas*?

Once we look closer at the relationship between the parable and the novel, we see that the plot of the novel both echoes and inverts the parable in nine ways. First, numerous commentaries point out that the parable is, in fact, focused on the father, not the sons (despite its colloquial title, "The Prodigal Son").[27] In the same way, Poirot asserts numerous times that the murder hinges on "the character of the dead man," or "victim" or "Simeon Lee himself."[28] We hear from several characters about the vengeful and spiteful character of Simeon. It's obvious that his actions and attitudes towards his sons are a far cry from the father in the Lukan parable, and we search in vain for any trace of the divine grace the father embodies in that story. Second, like the younger son, Harry stole "several hundred pounds," forged his "father's name to a cheque" before leaving home, and habitually sent home "for money to get out of a scrape."[29] It's also clear how the family views Harry, as when George tells his wife Magdalene, "We don't mention him. His behaviour was disgraceful. We haven't heard anything of him for some years now. He's probably dead."[30] Third, even though Harry connects his return with "the good old parable," it wasn't his decision to return home. That is, there's no moment of self-realization as in Luke 15:17, when the younger son decides it'll be better for him at home, since he's starving in the "real world."[31] Simeon summoned him home, not because he missed him, but because he wanted to rile up Alfred (the good, older brother who stayed at home). Fourth, there's no great, compassionate reunion between Harry and Simeon, unlike in the parable. In fact, Harry's first dialogue with Simeon begins with the question, "Do you really want me to stay here, Father?" further noting that Alfred "resents my presence here."[32] Simeon replies, "The devil he does! . . . I'm master in this house." This is obviously a far cry from the welcome that the younger son in Luke's story receives from his rejoicing father in 15:22-24. We've seen that Harry has no great love for Simeon, even though Simeon has a begrudging appreciation for Harry's vitality.

Fifth, unlike the parable, here the two brothers have a reunion of sorts in the chapter titled "December 23rd." They say hello, then Harry remarks, "'Well, well. Feels funny to be here again!" Alfred responds, "I expect so—yes. A good many years since you—got out." Harry then notes, "'Yes, I'm glad I have come'—he paused to bring out the word with greater significance—'home . . .'"[33] Clearly, all the emotions both brothers are feeling are bottled up, as Pilar astutely observes. Sixth, obviously, there's no celebration with "music and dancing" or a "fatted calf" in the novel, as Simeon's killed before the

---

[27] See, e.g., Fred B. Craddock, *Luke*, IBC (Atlanta: John Knox Press, 1990), 187; and Joseph A. Fitzmyer, *The Gospel According to Luke*, AB 28 & 28A (New York: Doubleday, 1970, 1985) 2:1084-1085.

[28] Christie, *Hercule Poirot's Christmas*, "December 24th," "December 25th" and "December 27th."

[29] Ibid., "December 22nd" and "December 26th."

[30] Ibid., "December 22nd."

[31] See Fitzmyer, *Luke*, 2:1088.

[32] Christie, *Hercule Poirot's Christmas*, "December 24th."

[33] Ibid., "December 23rd."

Christmas celebration. In Part 3 (the chapter titled, "December 24th"), the two brothers and father are all together, and a scene plays out very similar to that in Luke 15:30, in which the older son criticizes the actions of the younger to the father. Alfred does so in an oblique way, but unlike 15:29, doesn't laud his own faithfulness. And obviously, Simeon would never say the kind things to Alfred the father in Luke's parable does to his older son in 15:31, despite the fact that, as Lydia points out, Alfred "worships" his father.[34] As Poirot tells Sugden, this is "a family affair. It is a poison that works in the blood—it is intimate—it is deep-seated. There is here, I think, hate and knowledge."[35]

Seventh, speaking of the "fatted calf," in the parable, the slaughter of that calf serves as a kind of sign or ritual connected to the prodigal son's reincorporation to the kin group. In the novel, though, the murder of Simeon Lee is itself a kind of sign/ritual, as Poirot explains to Sugden: "So much blood—that is what Mrs Alfred said.[36] It takes one back to ancient rituals—to blood sacrifice, to the anointing with the blood of the sacrifice. . . . There are all sorts of deep instincts in man of which he himself is unaware. The craving for blood—the demand for sacrifice!"[37]

Sacrifice in Christie

Sacrifice seems to have been on Christie's mind in the 1930s. *Hercule Poirot's Christmas* falls after two other stories that deal with sacrifice and more specifically the city of Petra. First, in the 1933 Parker Pyne short story "The Pearl" (retitled "The Pearl of Price" in the 1934 collection *Parker Pyne Investigates*) the titular character solves the mystery of a pearl earring that went missing on the High Place of sacrifice. Second, the other Poirot novel published in 1938, *Appointment with Death*, takes place in Jerusalem and Jordan and chapter 12 contains a scene in Petra in which several characters gather at the High Place and ruminate on religion and sacrifice. Interestingly, it seems that Christie and her second husband visited Petra, so she might've been familiar with this site.

In the same exchange, Poirot talks of David Lee's feelings about how Simeon treated his mother, and David's reaction at seeing Simeon dead: "Retribution! Payment! The wrong wiped out by expiation!"[38] Eighth, Poirot identifies one key component of the motive for Simeon's murder in conversation with Sugden. The latter had commented that Simeon was "as proud as Lucifer," and Poirot seizes on that observation. Sugden questions him, "You don't mean that he was murdered because he was proud?" but

---

[34] Ibid., "December 22nd." See also Craddock, *Luke*, 188.

[35] Christie, *Hercule Poirot's Christmas*, "December 25th."

[36] The quotation here in the chapter called "December 24th" is spoken by Lady Macbeth in *Macbeth*, Act 5, Scene 1, Lines 26–40.

[37] Christie, *Hercule Poirot's Christmas*, "December 25th." York, *Agatha Christie*, 17, echoes Poirot's view of the murder as functioning as a kind of sacrifice.

[38] Christie, *Hercule Poirot's Christmas*, "December 25th."

Poirot replies, "I mean that there is such a thing as inheritance. Simeon Lee transmitted that pride to his sons."[39] Of course, inheritance—or the lack thereof—seems to be a central motive for Sugden, but inheritance is also an important issue in the parable. The son who leaves wastes all his inheritance and is forced to work a lowly job, while the loyal son who remains behind could still expect his inheritance after his father dies. Sugden, though, as a son "born on the wrong side of the blanket" wouldn't have access to either inheritance or familial recognition.[40] Alfred, on the other hand, receives half of Simeon's fortune in his father's will, so here at least, the "loyal and devoted son" gets his reward for such filial piety.[41] Finally, the biggest difference is that in the novel the father is murdered by an illegitimate and "prodigal" son. The overriding imagery in the parable of joy for that which has been lost is turned inside-out in the novel, as a "lost" son seeks out and returns to his father, only to confront and murder him, not in the spur of the moment, but in a carefully thought-out and executed plan. And when Poirot reveals him to be the killer, this son (Sugden) doesn't declare his worthlessness to his father, as in 15:18-19, 21, but instead exclaims, "God rot his soul in hell! I'm glad I did it!"[42]

These nine examples should serve to exemplify how Christie playfully twists her Lukan text, but this isn't the only example of interpretive intransigence to a dominant ideology of Christianity. In addition to this, we should also note that the inversion of the Lukan parable strikes a mightily discordant tone within the Christmas setting of the novel. As Christie's audience might've expected, this setting is supposed to be filled with nostalgia, kindness, and harmony.[43] Even Simeon himself connects welcoming Harry back with Christmas being the "season of forgiveness," and even says that Christmas "promotes solidarity of family feeling."[44] Earlier, Colonel Johnson utters to Poirot, "Christmas time. Peace, goodwill—and all that kind of thing. Goodwill all round."[45] Poirot takes his time in refuting that sentiment and the Colonel's claim that crime is less likely during Christmastime, and it should be clear from our discussion that the events in the novel are certainly not filled with good cheer.

Even so, we do get a hint of the kind of English idyll a reader in 1938 might have expected at the end of the story, when Lydia is making a new garden arrangement. Using additional scriptural imagery, she describes it as, "an attempt at the Garden of Eden. A new version—without any serpent—and Adam and Eve are definitely middle-aged." Alfred then tells her, "Dear Lydia, how patient you have been all these years. You have been very good to me," to which Lydia responds, "But, you see, Alfred, I love you. . ."[46] This ending is also interesting for how it extends the focus of the parable: here

[39] Ibid.
[40] However, York, *Agatha Christie*, 74–75, reminds us that while Sugden may not inherit any material goods or monies, he has certainly inherited physical and behavioral traits of Simeon.
[41] Christie, *Hercule Poirot's Christmas*, "December 27th."
[42] Ibid.
[43] Both Barnard, *Talent*, 71, and Osborne, *Life and Crimes*, note the paucity of "Christmas atmosphere" in the novel (164). Christie's audience would be especially interested in yuletide atmosphere, as her books were usually published yearly and were marketed as a "Christie for Christmas."
[44] Christie, *Hercule Poirot's Christmas*, "December 22nd" and "December 24th."
[45] Ibid., "December 24th."
[46] Ibid., "December 28th."

we see the "good son" finally achieve a measure of happiness and community denied to him in Luke's story.

*   *   *

This happy ending is replicated in the worlds the text creates. Both the 1986 BBC radio adaptation—which aired appropriately enough on 24 December—and the 1995 television version, which was broadcast on New Year's Day, end with joy and restoration. The former retains some of the Lukan imagery, e.g., the initial exchange between Simeon and Alfred ("Ah, the prodigal son, eh? You're right. We must kill the fatted calf, Alfred. We must give him a great welcome.").[47] Unlike the novel, though, this production omits the prodigal son imagery when Harry returns and converses with Tressilian, as well as Harry's self-referential comments when Poirot and Superintendent Sugden are conducting interviews. Even so, this is a greater inclusion of the Lukan material in the novel than we find in the version from Series 6 of *Agatha Christie's Poirot*.

In that adaptation, the absence of the expected goodwill and cheer associated with Christmas in the novel is tempered, as the viewer is flooded with Christmas imagery. The structure of the episode follows the chronological pattern of the novel, with scenes divided up by day, beginning with 21 December and ending on 25 December (the novel covers 22–28 December). The first three days in the episode begin with choirs or groups singing Christmas carols: "It Came Upon a Midnight Clear," "I Saw Three Ships," and "Ding-dong! Merrily on High." This Christmas mood is broken on the penultimate day, as 24 December opens in a mortuary, but by 25 December it's clear that Christmas is at hand. At the outset of that segment, we see Alfred (Simon Roberts) and Lydia (Catherine Rabett) going to a morning service and Poirot opening his present from Inspector Japp (a pair of large gloves that Poirot will clearly never wear). It's also on this final day that Poirot reveals the murderer and restores a sense of Christmas to the Lee household. Indeed, the episode's closing scenes are introduced by a choir inside the Lee house singing the Christmas hymn "Angels from the Realms of Glory."

As is the case in some other *Agatha Christie's Poirot* adaptations, the biblical material in *Hercule Poirot's Christmas* is diluted significantly. In fact, the only mention of anything related to Luke 15:11-32 comes when Japp asks Harry (Brian Gwaspari) why he decided to return to England after so many years. Harry tells him, "I thought the fatted calf would make a welcome change." When Poirot asks what Alfred thought about his returning, Harry replies, "Alfred's always been jealous of me. You see, he was the good, stay-at-home, stick-in-the-mud son." Aside from the reference to the "fatted calf," the film completely ignores the biblical parable around which the novel is organized, but it supplies something the novel doesn't: a concrete motive for Sugden's crime.

The movie opens in 1896 in South Africa with a young Simeon Lee (Scott Handy) killing his partner to steal his diamonds. Simeon is wounded in the struggle and is nursed back to health by a woman named Stella (Liese Benjamin), whom he sleeps with before stealing her horses and abandoning her. Obviously, this Stella will become

---

[47] This program was dramatized by Michael Bakewell and directed by Enyd Williams.

the mother of Sugden (Mark Tandy), and we see several scenes with her later in the film. The film then executes a forty-year time skip to London, where we're told it's 21 December 1936. We next see an older Stella (Olga Lowe) on 24 December, examining Simeon's body in the mortuary, and on the following day, Christmas, Poirot leads the main characters to her house for the "Big Reveal" scene. This scene is key, as it fills the aporia of Sugden's motive left open in the novel. There, the reader is left to assume that Sugden murders Simeon because he wasn't given his due as a son. Here, there's no such ambiguity. Stella freely admits that she was the driving force behind the murder: "I saved Simeon Lee's life. And he used me, and he stole from me, and he deserted me and my child. . . . Simeon Lee earned his death as he earned nothing else in his whole life." While the episode does away with the Prodigal Son imagery so prevalent in the novel, it does allow us a deeper understanding of Sugden's motivation for killing Simeon. Perhaps this motivation—in the form of his mother Stella—also fills in a gap in the Lukan story, similar to how the ending of the novel enlarges our understanding of Alfred as the "stay-at-home" son, as I note earlier. After all, we're not privy to any reactions or feelings of any female characters to the absence or return of the son or the father's treatment of any of the sons. By providing us access to Stella's thoughts and her admission of her role in the murder, we hear some of the possible resentment and hurt the Prodigal Son's mother might've experienced, and by framing Stella in such a way, her bitterness and Sugden's resentment and rage become more comprehensible.

Conclusion(s) to Part Two

In Part One, we introduced ideas like Christian hegemony and normativity, then briefly examined Christianity in England in the nineteenth to the mid-twentieth century to discuss how these ideas were present. We then turned in Part Two to specific examples of Christie's work and saw again and again the use of specifically Christian language and imagery in her Poirot stories. And I've argued that this use is evidence for what Khyati Y. Joshi terms Christian hegemony and normativity. In her work, she points out how language and imagery—Joseph F. Nye Jr.'s idea of "soft power"—work to reinforce cultural and religious hegemony in the US, writing that these become "so ingrained in everyday life, they might seem inconsequential. But understanding them deeply, and knowing when and how to wield them, distinguishes Christians, and Protestants in particular, from all others. They hold the additional cultural capital of being 'natives' of these cultural mores, while the rest of us operate from a place of relative cultural disadvantage as a result."[48] By extension, Christie's recurrent use of scriptural citation and allusion presupposes a level of religious literacy on the part of her middle-class, mostly female audience; they are the "natives" in Joshi's quotation. This repeated use of shared language reinforces the sense—buttressed by other components of Joshi's structural dimension of Christian privilege—that Christianity and its attendant language, symbols, and practices are simply the "natural" order of things in England.

---

[48] Joshi, *White Christian Privilege: The Illusion of Religious Equality in America* (New York: New York University Press, 2020), 148.

However, we've also seen that Christie not only receives this Christian normativity, but also interrogates it via her treatment of the biblical texts she uses. Put differently, as a modernist, Christie felt free to contort and invert biblical plots and characters in her work, and this freedom holds an implicit challenge to the hegemonic position of Christianity during this time. Understanding this aspect of Christie's work helps us to see that the impression of normative Christianity is always an ideological construct, one that requires a selective gaze and a willful ignorance of other ways of being in the world in order to support the internal dimension (one's belief in the superiority of one's Christian views/status) that Joshi adumbrates.

In Part Three, we'll continue our examination of normative and hegemonic Christianity in Christie's Poirot works by focusing on how she constructs his religious identity as a foreign Catholic, as well as how renderings of Poirot's religiosity in the world the text creates deepens, augments, and even retcons Christie's works.

Part Three

Poirot, Religion, and Christianity

Introduction to Part Three

In Part One, we examined how Christie's Poirot stories and their later renderings reflect and resist the Christian normativity of her times through the use of shared religious language and images. Part Three will focus on the little Belgian himself, i.e., the ways in which Poirot's actions, attitudes, and identity are described using religious language, as well as how later interpretations deepen this religious identity in the world the text creates.

In Chapter 6, we'll explore nine themes in the portrayal and perspective of Poirot, including describing him as a prophet, his view of murder and truth, his suspicious nature, how he values the innocents impacted by murder, and his own self-understanding. We'll then get our hands dirty in Chapter 7 with a search for data regarding Poirot's own religious identity or other significant information that might help us understand him as a religious figure by examining two primary examples from the Poirot canon. Finally, in Chapters 8–10, we'll expand on the discussion of Poirot's religious identity in the world of the text by focusing more closely on the world the text creates in a series of "Deep Dives," asking how later TV and film adaptations deepen or omit religious language, imagery, and/or issues.

6

Poirot's Religious Identity, Part 1

Background and Nine Themes

Let's begin by examining the world behind the text to contextualize Poirot in order to understand the character better. We'll start with Christie's oft-quoted explanation for the origin of Poirot. In her *Autobiography*, she describes how she formulated the idea of her first novel (1920–21's *The Mysterious Affair at Styles*). One of the most pressing questions was, "Who could I have as a detective?"[1] In reminiscing on that query, Christie provides a detailed explanation of how Poirot came to be:

> Then I remembered our Belgian refugees. We had quite a colony of Belgian refugees living in the parish of Tor. Everyone had been bursting with loving kindness and sympathy when they arrived. People had stocked houses with furniture for them to live in, had done everything they could to make them comfortable. There had been the usual reaction later, when the refugees had not seemed to be sufficiently grateful for what had been done for them, and complained of this and that. . . . Why not make my detective a Belgian? I thought. There were all types of refugees. How about a refugee police officer? A retired police officer.[2]

Christie's choice of a Belgian refugee leaving a career as a police officer, and a Catholic one at that, is not only indicative of her positioning Poirot as an acceptable outsider, but also taps into a larger concern for Belgium and its people current in England in the early twentieth century.

Christophe Declercq analyzes the way in which the English press and popular culture depicted and understood these Belgian refugees and claims that "these Belgians on the run" represented something larger than themselves.

> They contributed – or through press coverage were manipulated into contributing – to the greater good as the victimised civilians of Gallant Little Belgium, a nation that prepared to stand up against the German war machine, as well as the ultimate

---

[1] Christie, *An Autobiography* (1977; reis. New York: HarperCollins, 2011), 256.
[2] Ibid.

destitute from Poor Little Belgium, the nation that needed help: Britain's grand gesture of empathy emerged.[3]

Thanks to entities like the War Refugees Committee (established in August 1914) along with "the publication of various charity books," such as the 1914 *King Albert's Book*, and the 1915 Bryce Report on "alleged atrocities committed by the German troops" in Belgium (sometimes called "The Rape of Belgium")—which consisted of mostly unsubstantiated and uninvestigated testimony—there was a tremendous initial outpouring of support for Belgian refugees.[4] Christie's own testimony in her *Autobiography* reflects this support, but as Declercq argues, once the propagandistic utility and symbolic value of these refugees waned, so did their presence in popular culture and the press.[5]

Fortunately, we know quite a bit about Belgian refugees coming to England, thanks to a Register of Belgian Refugees which was created in late October 1914. According to T. T. S. de Jastrzebski, whose paper about the Register was published in March of 1916, registration of Belgian refugees was required by law beginning in December 1915.[6] Based on the data available then, Jastrzebski claimed,

> The numbers therefore of the refugees coming to this country up to the end of November last were nearly a quarter of a million. Of these 95 per cent. are Belgians and 5 per cent. of some other alien nationality, mostly Russian Jews. Some 15,000 of Belgian nationality are known to have left the country, independently of those thousands who have joined the Belgian army. . . . This leaves about 200,000 refugees in round figures as in the country at the end of November, 1915.[7]

Jastrzebski also includes data on the professions of Belgian refugees, and correlates that data with the 1900 Belgian census to provide an idea of the professional makeup of the immigrant population. Under the heading "police," we're told that 6,961 Belgian men were employed as police officers in 1900, whereas only 203 refugees listed "police" as their former occupation in Belgium on the Register.[8] If this data is accurate, then the historical potential for someone like Poirot as an urban policeman refugee fits nicely with how Christie envisions him as a fictional character.

I should mention that there have been several attempts to identify the "historical Poirot," and some make a strong case that our Hercule was inspired by a Belgian refugee called variously Jacques Hornais or Jacques Joseph Hamoir, who'd been a policeman

---

[3] Declercq, "The Odd Case of the Welcome Refugee in Wartime Britain: Uneasy Numbers, Disappearing Acts and Forgetfulness Regarding Belgian Refugees in the First World War," *Close Encounters in War Journal* 2 (2019): 9.

[4] See Ibid., 10, 11, and 12–13.

[5] Ibid., 14.

[6] de Jastrzebski, "The Register of Belgian Refugees," *Journal of the Royal Statistical Society* 79, no. 2 (1916): 134.

[7] Ibid., 136. In his work, Declercq questions the veracity of the quarter of a million estimation. See "Odd Case," 15.

[8] See de Jastrzebski, "Register," 149.

prior to the War.[9] Since Christie herself never addresses any historical model for Poirot, suppositions like this are of limited value to us. More pertinent is the view of Declercq when he focuses on Poirot and writes, "His character became almost entirely assimilated, with connotations of its Belgian origins perhaps remaining in place to some extent but still lacking any connection with the refugee(s) that stood as a model for the inspector."[10] Declercq continues, and provides a helpful bridge from the world behind the text to the world of the text:

> Poirot as a representative of the entire chapter of Belgian refugees in Britain is perhaps missing the point of the entire history. In the end, the Belgian refugee-detective moves in upper class circles, mirroring – at best – the opportunities seized on by the Belgian happy few, but also moving as a one-dimensional character, stripped of his refugee status and allocated mannerisms only, a non-descript caricature nearly.[11]

Here Declercq views Poirot the character as historically removed from the majority of Belgian immigrants due to his successful assimilation into English society. While this may be so, it is still illuminating and helpful to understand his socio-historical roots, as these inevitably impact his religious identity as well as how Christie's characterization of him undercuts inherited tropes. Now that we've placed Poirot historically, let's remind ourselves what he is in terms of Christie's chosen genre of crime fiction.

Poirot exists first and foremost as a character in Christie's fictional contributions to this genre. That is to say, as a fictional detective, we may assume several things about Poirot from the get-go. In his work on Christie, Earl F. Bargainnier describes the role of the "great detective" in the development of crime fiction as follows:

> He is able to judge because he is given the power of distinguishing absolutely between good and evil. Having this power, he can perform his task of lifting suspicion, distrust and guilt in whatever community he may find himself. In the classic detective story, he achieves this social cleansing by recreating the crime in his mind from the evidence he obtains, a process of imaginative, intellectual reconstruction; once he has completed this reconstruction, he can then establish truth, free the innocent and condemn the guilty.[12]

Mary S. Wagoner similarly focuses on the function of the detective in the restoration of order and the reaffirmation of a society's values, writing that they must "show a mind coping with events and must effect [sic.] a restoration of the social order."[13] That is, the

---

[9]　See, e.g., Alison Flood, "Hercule Poirot's real-life model may have been detected in Torquay," *The Guardian*, 13 May 2014; available online at https://www.theguardian.com/books/2014/may/13/hercule-poirot-real-life-model-belgian-gendarme.

[10]　Declercq, "Odd Case," 21.

[11]　Ibid., 22.

[12]　Bargainnier, *The Gentle Art of Murder: The Detective Fiction of Agatha Christie* (Bowling Green, OH: Bowling Green University Popular Press, 1980), 42.

[13]　Wagoner, *Agatha Christie*, Twayne's English Authors Series (Boston: G. K. Hall & Co., 1986), 35.

detective's "performance must justify classic detective fiction's basic premise that reason can triumph, that events make sense."[14] Further, "When the detective provides an explanation of the past event, he also isolates the agent of violence, the murderer, from society, thus demonstrating that human intelligence can promote justice."[15]

Despite this emphasis on justice and values and the restoring of order, many authors include no treatment of Poirot and religion in their examinations.[16] I hope to remedy this lacuna in Part Three. We'll start in this chapter by exploring key, recurring themes— nine in all—found in how Christie characterizes and depicts the worldview of Poirot, including describing him as a prophet, his view of murder and truth, his suspicious nature, how he values the innocents impacted by murder, and his own self-understanding.

*   *   *

Our first theme is readily apparent: at various times, myriad characters use language with a hue of religion to describe Poirot. One way they do so, as Hannah M. Strømmen notes, is to refer to Poirot's detecting skills as some sort of prophetic gift.[17] This is already evident in Christie's first Poirot novel, *The Mysterious Affair at Styles*, where Hastings expresses that Poirot had correctly predicted how John Cavendish's trial would proceed by calling him "a true prophet."[18] Similarly, in *The Murder on the Links*, Hastings refers to Poirot as "omniscient," and calls him a "fairly true prophet."[19] Even so, Poirot is not entirely comfortable with being equated with a prophet. A woman called Katherine asks Poirot if something he said was a "prophecy" in *The Mystery of the Blue Train*. He replies, "I never prophesy ... It is true that I have the habit of being always right—but I do not boast of it."[20] Nevertheless, in that same novel, Poirot seems to view

[14] Ibid. See also John Ritchie, "Agatha Christie's England, 1918-39: Sickness in the Heart and Sickness in Society as Seen in the Detective Thriller," *Australian National University Historical Journal* 9 (1972): 6; and R. A. York, *Agatha Christie: Power and Illusion*, Crime Files (Hampshire & New York: Palgrave Macmillan, 2007), 98.

[15] Wagoner, *Agatha Christie*, 35.

[16] Bargainnier, *Gentle Art*, allocates twenty-two pages to Poirot and doesn't mention religion once. Similarly, Patricia D. Maida and Nicholas B. Spornick mention Poirot's religion only in passing and only once (*Murder She Wrote: A Study of Agatha Christie's Detective Fiction* [Bowling Green, OH: Bowling Green State University Popular Press, 1982], 87-88). Even in larger works focused solely on Poirot, religion plays a minor role. For example, apart from a paragraph on his Catholic upbringing, Anne Hart only spends two pages (including excerpts from three novels) on the issue of religion. See *Agatha Christie's Poirot: The Life and Times of Hercule Poirot* (1990; reis. London: HarperCollins, 1997), 8 and 127–129. More recently, Mark Aldridge's generously illustrated and informative survey of the history of Poirot (*Agatha Christie's Poirot: The Greatest Detective in the World* [London: HarperCollins, 2020]) doesn't include much data at all on religion. And while I understand the limitations of space, genre and market focus, the omission of virtually anything to do with religion is still surprising.

[17] This is the central claim made by Strømmen in her very helpful piece titled "Poirot, the Bourgeois Prophet: Agatha Christie's Biblical Adaptations," in *The Bible in Crime Fiction and Drama: Murderous Texts*, eds. Alison Jack and Caroline Blyth; Scriptural Traces: Critical Perspectives on the Reception and Influence of the Bible, 16; LHB/OTS, 678 (London & New York: Bloomsbury, 2019), 149–166.

[18] Christie, *The Mysterious Affair at Styles* (1920; reis. New York: HarperCollins, 2010), Kindle edition, ch. 11, "The Case for the Prosecution."

[19] Christie, *The Murder on the Links* (1923; reis. New York: HarperCollins, 2011), Kindle edition, ch. 17, "We Make Further Investigations" and ch. 28, "Journey's End."

[20] Christie, *The Mystery of the Blue Train* (1928; reis. New York: HarperCollins, 2011), Kindle edition, ch. 10, "On the Blue Train."

his involvement in the case at hand as divinely commissioned, almost as if he was "called" for this task. Another character, Rufus van Aldin, asks Poirot why he's assisting the police if he's retired, and Poirot responds that "the good God thrust it upon me."[21] Even at the end of that novel, Poirot seems quite content to claim some sort of special knowledge related to the divine in an exchange that is revealing for our understanding of his outlook on life. He tells a woman named Lenox, "Life is like a train, Mademoiselle. It goes on. And it is a good thing that that is so. . . . Because the train gets to its journey's end at last." He and Lenox joke about whether she'll find love on that journey, and Poirot both reassures and exhorts her: "Trust the train, Mademoiselle, for it is *le bon Dieu* who drives it. . . . And trust Hercule Poirot – *He knows.*"[22] This knowledge requires discernment, though, as we hear Poirot ask Hastings to be quiet so that he can arrange his "ideas with order and method," in *Lord Edgware Dies.* Hastings comments that he then "maintained a discreet silence until such time as the oracle should speak."[23] In *Murder on the Orient Express*, Poirot announces that he "will make a prophecy" as to the location of two important clues, a red kimono and a Wagon Lit uniform.[24] Finally, Hastings mentions in *Curtain* that he was grateful for a bit of a respite from "the deep anxieties that Poirot's revelations had given me."[25]

Commenting on similar data that identify Poirot as prophetic, Strømmen writes,

> Christie constructs this prophetic role through Poirot's abilities as supreme puzzle-solver – always knowing more than other characters and more than the reader, as if in exclusive consultation with a divine voice that keeps him two or three steps ahead of the hoi polloi. In this sense, Poirot is certainly a prophet who succeeds, building up an authoritative as well as comforting status in his ability to solve all – however impossibly complicated – puzzles.[26]

This view of Poirot as prophet is perhaps most obvious in the 1937 story, "Triangle at Rhodes," in which we find a second specific example of this prophetic theme.[27] At one point in the story, Poirot ascends to the Mount of the Prophet, where we're told he "at last was at peace—removed from cares—above the world."[28] This site is known locally as Mount Profitis Ilias, i.e., the Mountain of the Prophet Elijah, and is home to a Byzantine monastery built in 1712 called the Prophetes Elias. After Poirot sits on the Mountain, he engages in some overt theological speculation, musing to himself, "Doubtless *le bon Dieu* knows what he does. But it is odd that he should have permitted

---

[21] Ibid., ch. 16, "Poirot Discusses the Case."

[22] Ibid., ch. 36, "By the Sea."

[23] Christie, *Lord Edgware Dies* (1933; reis. New York: HarperCollins, 2011), Kindle edition, ch. 4, "An Interview."

[24] Christie, *Murder on the Orient Express* (1934; reis. New York: HarperCollins, 2011), Kindle edition, Part 2, ch. 13, "Summary of the Passengers' Evidence."

[25] Christie, *Curtain: Poirot's Last Case* (1975; reis. New York: HarperCollins, 2011), Kindle edition, ch. 7.

[26] Strømmen, "Poirot, the Bourgeois Prophet," 153.

[27] This story was originally published on 2 February 1936 in the US in *This Week* before being published in May of the same year in *The Strand* under the title, "Poirot and the Triangle at Rhodes." All citations and references here are to Christie, *Murder in the Mews: Four Cases of Hercule Poirot* (1937; reis. New York: HarperCollins, 2011) Kindle edition.

[28] Christie, "Triangle at Rhodes."

himself to fashion certain human beings. *Eh bien*, here for a while at least I am away from these vexing problems."[29] Poirot's visit to the mountain parallels that of its namesake in some ways. In 1 Kings 19, God tells Elijah, who has come to Mount Horeb to escape the wrath of Jezebel (19:3), to go "stand on the mountain before the Lord" (19:11). It's at this point that Elijah has his great theophany (an encounter with the sacred), discovering the Lord in a "a still small voice" (KJV), or a "sound of sheer silence" (NRSV), after which he goes about his prophetic business. Similarly, Poirot—who is seeking peace from crime—goes to the mountain to find such peace and muses about the creational proclivities of "*le bon Dieu*." However, Poirot gets no peace, as a character called Marjorie Gold disturbs him to ask for his help. Poirot's response to her is to tell her to leave Rhodes "before it is too late."[30] He reiterates his advice, but Mrs. Gold demurs, and she eventually is revealed to be one of the murderers in the story.

Second, this characterization of Poirot as a prophetic figure is buttressed by language describing characters having faith in him. In *The Big Four*, for example, Hastings says simply that he "had faith in Poirot."[31] Later, when Poirot tries to explain his idea about the Big Four to a group of government officials, they, of course, don't believe him. He predictively tells them that, "each fresh event that comes along will confirm your wavering faith."[32] In much the same way, at one point in *The Murder on the Links*, Poirot even tells Hastings that he "was hurt at your want of faith in me."[33] It's not just Hastings who has faith in Poirot, though. As he is trying to persuade Poirot to take on the case of the murder of Ratchett in *Murder on the Orient Express*, the railway employee Bouc tells his little friend, "I have faith in you!" Poirot responds "emotionally," and says, "Your faith touches me, my friend."[34] In *Curtain*, Hastings reveals that he always had "faith" in Poirot; later he acknowledges his "own inherent belief in Poirot's acumen."[35]

Our third theme is that Poirot himself instructs characters to have faith in him. We see this in "The Veiled Lady," when he exhorts Hastings to "have faith in Papa Poirot," and in "The Adventure of Johnny Waverly," when Mrs. Waverly is told the same thing.[36] This appellation of "Papa Poirot" is a fairly common arrow in Poirot's third-person quiver, and he refers to himself in this way quite often.[37] The familiarity assumed in such a title is related to its function, that is, Poirot and others see him as a "father confessor," one to whom they can tell their secrets and will keep their confidences, at least until they're relevant for his case. That function is easily observed in works like *The Mysterious Affair at Styles*, when Poirot offers his services to Mary Cavendish, telling her, "If you ever need a father confessor, madame . . . remember, Papa Poirot is

---

[29] Ibid.

[30] Ibid.

[31] Christie, *The Big Four* (1927; reis. New York: HarperCollins, 2011), Kindle edition, ch. 4, "The Importance of a Leg of Mutton."

[32] Ibid., ch. 15, "The Terrible Catastrophe."

[33] Christie, *The Murder on the Links*, ch. 26, "I Receive a Letter."

[34] Christie, *Murder on the Orient Express*, Part 1, ch. 5, "The Crime."

[35] Christie, *Curtain*, chs. 3 and 4.

[36] Both of these are found in Christie, *Hercule Poirot: The Complete Short Stories*.

[37] See, e.g., *The Murder on the Links*, ch. 7, "The Mysterious Madame Daubreuil;" "The Disappearance of Mr. Davenheim," in *Hercule Poirot: The Complete Short Stories*; and *Mystery of the Blue Train*, ch. 21, "At the Tennis."

always at your service."[38] He tells a woman called Lily something similar in "The Under Dog:" "Impossible to deceive Hercule Poirot; once realize that and all your troubles will be at an end. And now you will tell me the whole story, will you not? You will tell old Papa Poirot?"[39] And in *Hercule Poirot's Christmas*, Poirot remarks to himself after Hilda Lee comes to speak with him that "As I have always said, me, I am the father confessor!"[40]

This understanding of his function as father confessor is obviously related to the necessity of gathering evidence, but the image of a father confessor also relates to the significant fourth and fifth themes in our examination: Poirot's views of murder and truth. The former is encapsulated in what might be described as Poirot's "catchphrase," namely, "I do not approve of murder."[41] We first hear it in the 1936 short story "Problem at Sea," and in 1966's *Third Girl*, the narrator provides a helpful (if a tad pompous) précis of his outlook.[42] In the latter, the narrator states, "He was Hercule Poirot – the avenger of the innocent. Did he not say (and people laughed when he said it) 'I do not approve of murder'. They had thought it an understatement. But it was not an understatement. It was a simple statement of *fact* without melodrama. He did not approve of murder."[43] Even with this grandiose claim, Poirot's opinion of murder isn't hard to discern in earlier works. In *Lord Edgware Dies*, he calls murder "the most repugnant of human crimes," and in *Death on the Nile*, Poirot tells Jackie that "it is the unforgivable offence—to kill."[44] In the conclusion of the "Murder in the Mews," Poirot passionately decries murder while speaking to Jane Plenderleith, saying murder is the "wilful destruction of one human being by another human being," and that it's "horrible."[45] He even accuses Jane of the "attempted murder of [a man called] Major Eustace."[46] Ultimately, Poirot concludes that the victim in the story, Barbara Allen, killed herself, and Jane has made it to look as if Major Eustace killed Barbara. In trying to convince Jane to tell the truth and save Eustace from execution, Poirot again says that she's committing murder: "Murder can sometimes seem justified, *but it is murder all the same*."[47] He tells Jane that Barbara's suicide was her decision, her act: "Your friend died, in the last resort, because she had not the courage to live. We may sympathize with her. We may pity her. But the fact remains—the act was hers—not another." He asks Jane, "Do you really wish, of your own volition, to destroy the life—the *life*, mind—of *any* human being?"[48] Jane says she doesn't, and thus Major Eustace is saved.

---

[38] Christie, *The Mysterious Affair at Styles*, ch. 10, "The Arrest."

[39] Christie, "The Under Dog," in *Hercule Poirot: The Complete Short Stories.*

[40] Christie, *Hercule Poirot's Christmas* (1939; reis. New York: HarperCollins, 2011), Kindle edition, "December 25th."

[41] This blanket claim appears in *Sad Cypress* (1940; reis. New York: HarperCollins, 2011), Kindle edition, Part 2, ch. 1; *Hallowe'en Party* (1969; reis. New York: HarperCollins, 2011), Kindle edition, ch. 10; and *Curtain*, ch. 15. Laura Thompson makes this point clear in her biography of Christie, writing that both Poirot and Miss Marple "are unambiguous in their condemnation of murder" (*Agatha Christie: An English Mystery* [London: Headline, 2007]; repr. *Agatha Christie: A Mysterious Life* [New York: Pegasus Books, 2018], Kindle edition, "English Murder").

[42] "Problem at Sea" is found in *Hercule Poirot: The Complete Short Stories.*

[43] Christie, *Third Girl* (1966; reis. New York: HarperCollins, 2011), Kindle edition, ch. 21.

[44] Christie, *Lord Edgware Dies*, ch. 6, "The Widow;" and *Death on the Nile* (1938; reis. New York: HarperCollins, 2011), Kindle edition, ch. 5.

[45] "Murder in the Mews," in *Murder in the Mews.*

[46] Ibid.

[47] Ibid.

[48] Ibid.

Again, in *Appointment with Death*, Poirot reiterates his view of murder in the face of a claim from a character called Sarah that one mustn't take into account the character of the victim. Poirot says that she does take it into account, but that he doesn't: "The victim may be one of the good God's saints—or, on the contrary, a monster of infamy. It moves me not. The fact is the same. A life taken! I say it always, I do not approve of murder."[49] That the identity of the victim is irrelevant speaks to a larger issue behind Poirot's view here: his disapproval of murder is also linked with his theology. For example, in *Cards on the Table*, Poirot makes it clear that in his opinion, life and death are the purview of God. If, then, someone "is imbued with the idea that he knows who ought to be allowed to live and who ought not.... [Then] He has usurped the functions of *le bon Dieu*."[50] We might add that such a person has willfully placed themselves on what Poirot would perceive to be the wrong side of God's ethical system—especially if they find it easier and easier to kill—as does anyone who finds murder less than abominable. This sentiment is also found in *One, Two, Buckle My Shoe*, when Poirot is visiting an awfully rude young man called Raikes after Poirot's dentist is found dead. The young man "scornfully" asks, "What does the death of one miserable dentist matter?" Poirot's reply not only sets the tone for his investigation, it's also repeated at several points in the novel: "It does not matter to you. It matters to me. That is the difference between us."[51]

This difference is based on Poirot's need to uncover the truth in his investigations, and his view of truth is an important component of his worldview. Closely related to his almost obsessive need for order, his desire to discover the truth lies at the core of his approach to crime and his life. As an example, in *Three Act Tragedy*, Mr. Satterthwaite asks Poirot what he gets out of his work. After admitting that part of the "excitement" is the "chase," Poirot says, "there is more . . . It is – how shall I put it? – a passion for getting at the *truth*. In all the world there is nothing so curious and so interesting and so beautiful as truth."[52] Again, when he brings all the suspects together in *The Murder of Roger Ackroyd*, he warns them, "Understand this, I mean to arrive at the truth. The truth, however ugly in itself, is always curious and beautiful to the seeker after it."[53] He implores those present to "tell me the truth—the whole truth," but none do.[54] It's clear that not everyone shares Poirot's view of the truth, as we see in *Appointment with Death*. Poirot

49   Christie, *Appointment with Death* (1938; reis. New York: HarperCollins, 2005), Kindle edition, Part 2, ch. 4.
50   Christie, *Cards on the Table* (1936; reis. New York: HarperCollins, 2011), Kindle edition, ch. 19, "Consultation." In her examination of *Cards on the Table*, Gillian Gill echoes this sentiment, as she notes the presence in that novel of "what in Christie's world view is the ultimate sin against God and man—the taking of human life" (*Agatha Christie: The Woman and Her Mysteries* [New York: Free Press, 1990], Kindle edition, ch. 5, "Mrs. Mallowan: Last Trump for Shaitana"). This view seems to be shared by Miss Marple. In *At Bertram's Hotel* (1965; reis. New York: HarperCollins, 2011), Kindle edition, she tells Chief-Inspector Davy that "Murder—the wish to do murder—is something quite different. It—how shall I say?—it defies God" (ch. 20).
51   Christie, *One, Two, Buckle My Shoe* (1940; reis. New York: HarperCollins, 2011), Kindle edition, "Five, six, picking up sticks."
52   Christie, *Three Act Tragedy* (1934; reis. New York: HarperCollins, 2011), Kindle edition, ch. 5, "Division of Labour."
53   Christie, *The Murder of Roger Ackroyd* (1926; reis. New York: HarperCollins, 2011), Kindle edition, ch. 12, "Round the Table."
54   Ibid.

tells Colonel Carbury that he's always felt "The truth . . . is curious and beautiful." Carbury snorts and replies that at times it's "damned unpleasant," but Poirot is unperturbed. "You take there the personal view. Take instead the abstract, the detached point of vision. Then the absolute logic of events is fascinating and orderly."[55] At the same time, though, Poirot warns those who seek his help that when he finds the truth, they may not like it. Whether it's Dr. Lord in *Sad Cypress* or Gladys Nevill in *One, Two, Buckle My Shoe*, Poirot reiterates that he doesn't take sides or play favorites when it comes to the truth.[56] For him, it's simple, as he claims in *The Mystery of the Blue Train*: "I have only one duty—to discover the truth."[57] The discovery of truth, however, is made possible by a central feature of Poirot's personality and our sixth theme: his deep suspicion of others.

A central and recurring component of Poirot's worldview is this omnipresent suspicion, and it behooves us to examine it. We find it early on in Christie's works, as in 1923's *The Murder on the Links*. Therein, Poirot and Hastings debate whether a man called Jack could've killed his own father, and Poirot tells him, "You continue to be of a sentimentality unbelievable! I have seen mothers who murdered their little children for the sake of the insurance money! After that, one can believe anything."[58] This ubiquitous distrust, this experience-based orientation to believe the worst about people and their motives will become more obvious as we move forward through the stories. For example, in *The Murder of Roger Ackroyd*, one of the recurring themes in the book is that everyone has something to hide.[59] This axiomatic belief of Poirot's is clearly connected with his default orientation to the world: suspect everyone.[60] For example, Poirot tells James that a "suspicious attitude" is "necessary."[61] Similarly, Dr. Sheppard asks Poirot, "You don't think—?" to which Poirot responds, "I dare to think anything," i.e., he must be able to ignore common assumptions and suspect everyone in order to account for the evidence and arrange his "little ideas."[62] Another example of this outlook is found in *After the Funeral*, where the narrator comments on Poirot's suspicious nature, noting that "by nature and long habit he trusted nobody until he

---

[55] Christie, *Appointment with Death*, ch. 15.

[56] For the former, see *Sad Cypress*, Part 2, ch. 1. The latter reference is in *One, Two, Buckle My Shoe*, "Thirteen, fourteen, maids are courting."

[57] Christie, *The Mystery of the Blue Train*, ch. 32, "Katherine and Poirot Compare Notes."

[58] Christie, *The Murder on the Links*, ch. 18, "Giraud Acts."

[59] Poirot states this outright to James in ch. 7, "I Learn My Neighbour's Profession," and James repeats that adage in ch. 9, "The Goldfish Pond."

[60] See also "Dead Man's Mirror," in which Poirot's suspicious nature is again evident: "Me, I can suspect everybody!" (in *Hercule Poirot: The Complete Short Stories*). His view is reiterated in *Dumb Witness* (1937; reis. New York: HarperCollins, 2011), Kindle edition, ch. 22, "The Woman on the Stairs:" "Suspect everyone." Other examples can be found in *Five Little Pigs* (1943; reis. New York: HarperCollins, 2011), Kindle edition, Book 3, ch. 1, "Conclusions;" *Hickory Dickory Dock* (1955; reis. New York: HarperCollins, 2011), Kindle edition, ch. 8; and *Dead Man's Folly* (1956; reis. New York: HarperCollins, 2011), Kindle edition, chs. 12 and 16. This attitude is also expressed by Sir Henry Clithering in the Miss Marple short story "The Case of the Perfect Maid," in *Miss Marple: The Complete Short Stories* (1985; reis. New York: HarperCollins, 2011), Kindle edition. And Marple herself admits that she shares this outlook as well in *Nemesis* (1971; reis. New York: HarperCollins, 2011), Kindle edition, ch. 11, "Accident;" and in *Sleeping Murder* (1976; reis. New York: HarperCollins, 2011), Kindle edition, ch. 23, "Which of Them?" and ch. 25, "Postscript at Torquay."

[61] Christie, *The Murder of Roger Ackroyd*, ch. 13, "The Goose Quill."

[62] Ibid., ch. 10, "The Parlourmaid."

himself had tried and proved them."[63] Relatedly, Poirot comments that, "one has to examine *everything*. Oh! it is true enough – it is an old maxim – *everyone has something to hide*. It is true of all of us."[64]

Similarly, the novel *Peril at End House* raises the question of what it must be like to be Poirot, to be always suspicious, mistrustful of everyone, and guard. An example of this is found when, after Hastings calls him "a suspicious old devil,"[65] Poirot tells him, "You are right, mon ami. I am suspicious of everyone — of everything."[65] In fact, as the end of the novel makes plain, his greatest mistake in this case is a lack of suspicion, to trust what Nick told him. By the time of *Murder on the Orient Express*, Poirot seems to have learned his lesson. As in previous stories, Poirot is clearly suspicious of everyone, but at the outset of his investigation, he makes a point of telling Bouc, "Me, I suspect everybody till the last minute."[66]

We hear more of Poirot's suspicious and mistrustful nature in *Death in the Clouds*. Poirot explains his method, telling a woman called Elise, "It is part of my business to believe nothing I am told – nothing, that is, that is not proved. I do not suspect first this person and then that person; I suspect everybody. Anybody connected with a crime is regarded by me as a criminal until that person is proved innocent."[67] Put differently, "That is how one must proceed. Suspect everyone in turn and then wipe him or her off the list."[68] In fact, Poirot takes this method to its logical conclusion when he advises Japp not to leave him off the list of suspects, telling him he has "too trustful a nature."[69]

Speaking of a trustful nature, in *Peril at End House*, we also find our seventh theme: that Hastings's good heart, trust in others, and optimism regarding human nature is the necessary supplement to Poirot's normal position of suspecting the worst from everyone based on his own experiences.[70] This is also evident in *Lord Edgware Dies*, where Hastings blames himself for Ross's murder, but Poirot tells him he shouldn't because "the good God has not given you a suspicious nature to begin with," unlike Poirot himself.[71] In *Dumb Witness*, this distinction is again highlighted. In contrast with his own suspicious, doubtful nature, Poirot tells Hastings that, "Doubt is not your strong suit. Simple faith is more characteristic of you."[72]

---

[63] Christie, *After the Funeral* (1953; reis. New York: HarperCollins, 2011), Kindle edition, ch. 14. In "The Incredible Theft," we hear much the same thing in Poirot's comment to Mayfield: "*Trust no one*" (in *Hercule Poirot: The Complete Short Stories*).

[64] Christie, *After the Funeral*, ch. 14.

[65] Christie, *Peril at End House* (1932; reis. New York: HarperCollins, 2011), Kindle edition, ch. 5, "Mr. and Mrs. Croft."

[66] Christie, *Murder on the Orient Express*, ch. 6, "A Woman?."

[67] Christie, *Death in the Clouds* (1935; reis. New York: HarperCollins, 2008), Kindle edition, ch. 10, "The Little Black Book."

[68] Ibid., ch. 16, "Plan of Campaign." We hear a similar sentiment in *Dumb Witness*, when Poirot also reaffirms his suspicious nature to Hastings, noting "I believe nothing that anyone says unless it can be confirmed or corroborated" (ch. 12, "Poirot Discusses the Case").

[69] Christie, *Death in the Clouds*, ch. 7, "Probabilities."

[70] See, e.g., *Peril at End House*, ch. 4, "There Must Be Something!" and ch. 11, "The Motive." This low view of human nature and the opinion that the world is a wicked place seems to be shared by Miss Marple. We hear it expressed in the short stories "The Bloodstained Pavement," "The Blue Geranium," "Strange Jest," and "Tape-Measure Murder," in *Miss Marple: The Complete Short Stories*. It's also found in *At Bertram's Hotel*, ch. 12.

[71] Christie, *Lord Edgware Dies*, ch. 26, "Paris?."

[72] Christie, *Dumb Witness*, ch. 25, "I Lie Back and Reflect."

The abhorrence of murder and the near-monomaniacal focus on truth becomes even clearer when we discuss our eighth theme: Poirot's focus on the "innocents" impacted by crime.[73] In his work, R. A. York isn't totally convinced by my claim regarding Poirot's view of murder as repugnant, writing, "Poirot's frequent assertions that he disapproves of murder are a strangely faint attempt to revert to morality," but at the same time, he avers, "Poirot's more frequent and explicit assertions of the need to protect the innocent are a stronger moral factor."[74] That is, it's to be expected that Poirot would seek justice for the victims of murder, but there are instances in which he seeks to protect and/or vindicate innocent parties who've been caught up in the web of murder.[75] Take the particularly revealing exchange between Poirot and Jane and Norman Gale (who eventually is identified as the murderer) in *Death in the Clouds*. Poirot asks them what is "the most important thing was to bear in mind when you are trying to solve a murder?" Jane responds, "Finding the murderer," while Norman says, "Justice." Poirot "shook his head" and replies, "There are more important things than finding the murderer. And justice is a fine word, but it is sometimes difficult to say exactly what one means by it. In my opinion, the important thing is to clear the innocent."[76] We see a similar emphasis on protecting innocent lives taken to logical, if shocking, conclusions in *Dumb Witness* and *Curtain*.

In sum, the examples here show first a concern on Poirot's part for uncovering the truth, no matter what the cost or impact to those involved. He has an almost platonic reverence for the truth as a salve to the existential crises of crime and murder, and this seems clearly related to his function as a detective in the genre of crime fiction. As we saw at the outset of this chapter, the role of detectives in this literature is to identify and expel the source of societal disruption to reestablish a state of equilibrium. We can also attribute this emphasis on truth to Poirot's extensive background as a policeman. That is, discernment of the true events of a crime is part and parcel of his identity in the context of law enforcement, as is his distrust of suspects. This context might also contribute to his view of murder, but I'd argue that a more significant contributing factor to that view is his Catholic background.

Before we engage our "Deep Dives" into Poirot's own religious identity, it'll be helpful to investigate our ninth and final theme: his self-understanding. That is, how does Poirot see himself and his vocation vis-à-vis that religious identity? The data we have just examined regarding Poirot's view of murder and protecting innocents is

---

[73] Obviously, this isn't a theme confined to Christie's Poirot stories. In the 1930 Marple short story, "The Four Suspects," Sir Henry Clithering emphasizes this aspect of justice, as does Miss Marple herself in "The Case of the Perfect Maid" (1942).

[74] York, *Agatha Christie*, 89.

[75] In addition to the examples from the Poirot canon, this is also a key theme in *Ordeal by Innocence* (1958/1959), voiced especially in chapters two and twenty-four.

[76] Christie, *Death in the Clouds*, ch. 15, "In Bloomsbury." I should also mention *The A.B.C. Murders*, where Poirot focuses on the effect of crime/suspicion on the "innocent," that is, the ways in which the murders touch the lives of those closest to the victims or the crime(s). At Mr. Clarke's prompting, Poirot gathers these "innocents," the family members of the victims, together to create a kind of think-tank to help solve the crimes. Twenty years later, in *Dead Man's Folly*, we hear several comments from Poirot regarding "murder unavenged," "the spilling of innocent blood," and the "shadow" that casts, but at the same time, he warns "It is *never* finished with a murderer" (ch. 16).

obviously useful, but we get a more detailed glimpse into this issue in chapter 12 of the 1928 novel, *Peril at End House*. In an exchange about Nick's repeated brushes with death, Hastings suggests that her escapes are due to "providence." This leads to a very significant response from Poirot.

First, Poirot responds to Hastings by noting, "Ah! *mon ami*, I would not put on the shoulders of the good God the burden of men's wrongdoing. You say that in your Sunday morning voice of thankfulness — without reflecting that what you are really saying is that *le bon Dieu* has killed Miss Maggie Buckley."[77] Hastings interjects, "Really, Poirot!" and Poirot retorts, "Really, my friend! But I will not sit back and say '*le bon Dieu* has arranged everything, I will not interfere.' Because I am convinced that *le bon Dieu* created Hercule Poirot for the express purpose of interfering. It is my *métier*."[78] Right after this, Poirot tells Hastings that, "I am on the side of the innocent. I am on the side of Mademoiselle Nick because she was attacked. I am on the side of Mademoiselle Maggie because she has been killed."[79]

Poirot here resists a kind of resigned determinism or fatalism, i.e., the idea that since God is ultimately in control of everything that humans should simply accept their fate. In Catholic Christianity especially, humans have free will and can participate in the process of their own salvation. Poirot's Catholic identity, then, conditions him to live in the tension between divine omnipotence and human free will. To wit, Poirot points out that if Hastings ascribes Nick's survival to God's providence, he must also admit that God is responsible for Maggie's murder.

Poirot also rejects the stance of complacency and passivity in the face of God's power and providence by vowing to "interfere." Further, he feels God created him for this very purpose. In adopting this attitude, Poirot's stance echoes certain biblical characters, most obviously Abraham and Job. In Genesis 18, Abraham challenges God's plan to destroy Sodom and Gomorrah without considering the possibility of there being righteous people living in the cities. Abraham eventually convinces God to change God's mind, but the cities are ultimately destroyed. This action accords perfectly with Poirot's insistence that he is on the "side of the innocent." Job, of course, argues against the seemingly arbitrary punishments he received in passages like 23:1-24:17. In the end, though, Job acquiesces to God's providence and authority. As we'll see in the remainder of Part Three, the situation is more complex for Poirot. That is, in Chapters 7–10, I'll examine several examples of Poirot's Catholic identity that problematize a simplistic view of his faith, as we'll see him struggle, question, and perhaps even violate his faith.

---

[77] *Peril at End House*, ch. 12, "Ellen."
[78] Ibid. In a very significant parallel, Miss Marple also sees her vocation in religiously specific terms. We hear in *A Caribbean Mystery* (1964/1965; reis. New York: HarperCollins, 2011), Kindle edition, ch. 16, "Miss Marple Seeks Assistance," that "Miss Marple, feeling rather like a humble deputy of the Almighty, almost cried aloud her need in Biblical phrasing. *Who will go for me? Whom shall I send?*" This language is very close to and modeled on the prophetic commission found in texts like Isaiah 6. Despite some ambivalence in other novels, in *Nemesis* (1971; reis. New York: HarperCollins, 2011), it's clear that Marple understands herself as on a divine mission of sorts in which she's an "emissary of justice," the embodiment of "Nemesis" (Kindle edition, ch. 21, "The Clock Strikes Three"). One character even refers to her in this novel as an "avenger" (ch. 22, "Miss Marple Tells Her Story").
[79] Christie, *Peril at End House*, ch. 12.

7

Poirot's Religious Identity, Part 2

"The Chocolate Box" and *Taken at the Flood*

In this chapter, we'll delve into more specific detail regarding Poirot's religious identity by examining two key examples, starting with the 1923 short story, "The Chocolate Box."[1] This story details the detective's early interaction with religious extremism as well as forms a significant moment in the scant background Christie provides for him. That is, here Poirot details to Hastings one—and perhaps the biggest—of his failures.

The story—all of which all told as a flashback by Poirot, except for the beginning and ending—is set in Belgium against the background of what Poirot calls "the terrible struggle in France between church and state."[2] What he's referring to is the historical context of anti-clericalism in France in the Third Republic (1870–1940). Tensions between Catholics and those distrustful of the papacy had long existed in France, but these were exacerbated by the 1789 Revolution. As William Fortescue writes, because of persecutions and the loss of "most of its wealth, privileges and independence" in the Revolution, Catholics developed a deep distrust of republicans, and vice-versa.[3]

This period is also marked by anti-Protestantism and antisemitism, culminating in the infamous Dreyfus Affair (1894–1906).[4] The end point of the Dreyfus Affair is significant for the world behind the text, as 1906 is also the year in which Christie's mother Clarissa took a young Agatha to Paris to search for "a *pensionnat* at which Agatha might pursue her desultory education."[5] After time at a school run by "Mademoiselle T"

[1] As we've seen, Christie's short stories often have confusing publication histories. For example, the American version of the short story collection *Poirot Investigates* (1925) includes three stories absent from the UK version. These stories are also reprinted in the collection *Poirot's Early Cases*, published in 1974 in the UK. One of these is "The Chocolate Box," which was originally published in *The Sketch* on 23 May 1923 as "The Clue of the Chocolate Box."

[2] Christie, "The Chocolate Box," in Christie, *Hercule Poirot: The Complete Short Stories* (New York: HarperCollins, 2013), Kindle edition.

[3] Fortescue, *The Third Republic in France, 1870–1940: Conflicts and Continuities*, Routledge Sources in History (London & New York: Routledge, 2000), 43.

[4] For the former, see Steven C. Hause, "Anti-Protestant Rhetoric in the Early Third Republic," *French Historical Studies* 16, no. 1 (1989): 183-201. An accessible brief overview analyzing the Dreyfus Affair within the history of antisemitism can be found in Phyllis Goldstein, *A Convenient Hatred: The History of Antisemitism* (Brookline, MA: Facing History and Ourselves, 2012), 207–215.

[5] Laura Thompson, *Agatha Christie: An English Mystery* (London: Headline, 2007); repr. *Agatha Christie: A Mysterious Life* (New York: Pegasus Books, 2018), Kindle edition, "The Young Miss Miller."

where her older sister Madge had been a student, they eventually settled on "Miss Dryden's, a small finishing school in Paris kept by the sister-in-law of Auntie-Grannie's doctor."[6] Laura Thompson tells us that "Agatha stayed in Paris for almost two years and was eventually very happy there," as Christie herself confirms in her *Autobiography*.[7] As such, Christie was herself in Paris studying music and other pursuits during a time of religious hostility, one that she captures in "The Chocolate Box."

If the religious situation in France is pertinent to the world behind the text, then so is the context of the narrative flashback in Belgium. When Belgium revolted against the Dutch and was recognized as an independent state in 1830, it was already almost a completely Catholic one.[8] However, this Catholic hegemony had to exist with other political entities, most notably the Liberal party, with whom it collaborated in a relationship called "unionism."[9] It was this unionism that permitted the development of a constitution (modeled on that of the British) that was fashioned in 1831. This constitution had to balance long-standing "Catholic resentment" on the one hand and the political power and social capital of Catholics on the other.[10]

Bernard A. Cook describes the content of the constitution vis-à-vis the two main parties, and what the Catholics gained:

> Liberals conceded to the Church an extraordinary degree of freedom. Church appointments were to be independent of state interference, and Catholic schools were to be independent of state control. The state would provide financial support to the Church.... The Catholics, for their part, agreed to compensation for all religious ministers and accepted the requirement of civil marriage, even for those who wished the blessing of the Church for their weddings.[11]

However, Cook also reminds us that all was not peaches and cream in the new state: "The Liberals, though many were nominally Catholic and some even practicing Catholics, were anti-clerical, that is opposed to the domination of education by the Church and to a political role in Belgian society for the Church or its clerics."[12] Even granting this anti-clerical tension, the unionism that enabled the constitutional compromise "continued for fifteen years and insured that the Constitution would be interpreted in a manner favorable to the Catholic Church. A whole series of legislative and administrative acts enhanced the position of the Church in Belgian society."[13]

[6] Janet Morgan, *Agatha Christie: A Biography* (London: William Collins Sons & Company, 1984; repr. New York: Alfred A. Knopf, 1985), 23.
[7] Thompson, *Agatha Christie*, "The Young Miss Miller." See also Christie, *An Autobiography* (1977; reis. New York: HarperCollins, 2011), 155.
[8] For more specifics, see Karel Dobbelaere and Liliane Voyé, "From Pillar to Postmodernity: The Changing Situation of Religion in Belgium," *Sociological Analysis* 51 (1990): S2.
[9] See Thomas J. Shelley, "Mutual Independence: Church and State in Belgium: 1825-1846," *Journal of Church and State* 32, no. 1 (1990): 49.
[10] Ibid., 50.
[11] Cook, *Belgium: A History*, Studies in Modern European History, 50 (New York: Peter Lang, 2002), 61. See also Ellen L. Evans, *The Cross and the Ballot: Catholic Political Parties in Germany, Switzerland, Austria, Belgium and the Netherlands, 1785-1985*, Studies in Central European Histories (Boston: Humanities Press, Inc., 1999), 25.
[12] Cook, *Belgium*, 63.
[13] Shelley, "Mutual Independence," 59.

Cook concurs, writing that the constitutional freedoms enjoyed by the Church combined with their near-hegemony in Belgian society allowed Catholics to expand their influence, most notably in "the free development of religious orders and Church organizations," and the development of a "comprehensive system of Catholic educational institutions."[14] Curiously, it was in the area of education that battles between Catholics and Liberals came to a head.

In 1842, Catholics managed to pass a law that granted them control over education at the elementary school level and required religious education in both private and public schools be performed by clergy, with "a provision for exemption for Protestants and Jews, a tiny minority in Belgium."[15] This law—and other political and electoral gains by Catholics—led to a hardening of political partisanship, and pushed Liberals to mobilize and gain political power via the dissolution of unionism. Thomas J. Shelley elaborates: "The year 1846 was a turning point in the history of 'mutual independence,' for in that year unionism perished. The Catholic-liberal alliance broke up, when the liberals moved farther to the left and demanded a greater secularization of society. For the next thirty years, there were bitter political battles between liberals and Catholics, especially over the question of education."[16] One notable example in these battles was the 1879 law, passed by Liberals, that effectively secularized education.[17] As Cook points out, this law had a polarizing impact on the educational system—or systems—in the country.[18] The backlash from Catholics was swift and decisive: after regaining political power in 1884, the Liberal law of 1879 was repealed, and by 1895 state funds were again being allocated for religious schools and "instruction in Catholic religion for Catholic students again became compulsory in all public schools."[19]

The reason this focus on education is helpful for our interest in the world behind the text should be obvious. If, as Anne Hart proposes, Poirot was "born between 1849–1854," then he would've been a beneficiary of the primacy of Catholicism and Catholic educational entities in Belgium.[20] Put differently, because of the near total dominance of Catholicism in Belgium in the nineteenth century, Poirot would've been reared in a hegemonic context of Christian normativity—just like Christie was in England. And since it wasn't until 1879 that Belgium "established its own laicized [secularized] school system," we can say with some confidence that Poirot would've attended a Catholic school for some or most of his education and would've received instruction from a Catholic clergy member in the tenets of Catholicism.[21] Again, though, while Christie does provide some biographical tidbits about her little Belgian, her purpose is not to furnish us with a full dossier of Poirot's childhood and how it shaped him. We can,

---

[14] Cook, *Belgium*, 64.
[15] Evans, *The Cross*, 28. See also Cook, *Belgium*, 65.
[16] Shelley, "Mutual Independence," 62.
[17] See Evans, *The Cross*, 138–141.
[18] Cook, *Belgium*, 79.
[19] Ibid.
[20] Hart, *Agatha Christie's Poirot: The Life and Times of Hercule Poirot* (1990; reis. London: HarperCollins, 1997), 3.
[21] Dobbelaere and Voyé, "Pillar," S2.

though, pick up some clues regarding his background in her stories, and it's to the first of two examples of these that we now turn.

*   *   *

In "The Chocolate Box," Poirot tells Hastings of the murder of a member "among the bitterest of the anti-Catholic party," called M. Paul Déroulard. Poirot also helpfully situates his own religious identity in this story, noting explicitly that he is a "*bon catholique*" for the first time in the Poirot canon.[22] In fact, in reminding Hastings of his religious identity, Poirot points out that Déroulard's death "seemed to me fortunate."[23] Soon after, a young woman named Virginie Mesnard (who later becomes a nun) engages Poirot to investigate this death. Poirot is obviously hesitant, not only because of his religious allegiances but also because Mme. Mesnard is adamant that she doesn't want to involve the police, and Poirot was at this time "a member of the Belgian detective force."[24] However, romantic that he is, he is persuaded to take up her cause and begins his investigation.

Poirot as a Catholic

Even though it's clear Poirot is a Catholic from the 1924 short story "The Adventure of the Egyptian Tomb," the first time chronologically his religious identity is specified in dialogue is here in "The Chocolate Box." In the former story, Poirot and Hastings travel to Egypt and Poirot has to ride a camel, which Hastings finds enormously amusing. In his narration, Hastings notes, "He started by groans and lamentations and ended by shrieks, gesticulations and invocations to the Virgin Mary and every Saint in the calendar." Poirot's Catholic identity is also mentioned in *Murder in Mesopotamia* (1936), in which he describes himself as a "good Catholic" who knows "something of priests and monks." Later in that novel, he identifies himself as a "practicing Catholic" who knows "many priests and members of religious communities." We also learn that Poirot was raised as and still is a Catholic in 1947's "The Apples of the Hesperides," which I discuss in Chapter 11.

Again, as we saw in Parts One and Two, this story contains phrases and terms that indicate a particular worldview and context for the characters, one which assumes knowledge of a particular kind of religion on the part of the reader. For example, as Poirot interviews the doctor who treated Déroulard as to the other occupants of the house at the time of his death. One of these was M. de Saint Alard, whom the doctor describes as "a Catholic of the most fanatical," whose "friendship [with Déroulard] was being ruined by this question of church and state." The doctor concludes his statement

---

[22] See Christie, "The Chocolate Box."
[23] Ibid.
[24] Ibid.

by telling Poirot that "To M. de Saint Alard, Déroulard appeared almost as Antichrist."[25] The data included in the text box on this term from the world behind the text helps us understand better how Déroulard was viewed by M. de Saint Alard. Put differently, in the doctor's estimation, M. de Saint Alard sees Déroulard as someone with discordant views about the Church, who's trying to deceive others regarding his intentions to destroy it. And after all, as Poirot tells Hastings, de Saint Alard "was a fanatic, and there is no fanatic like a religious fanatic."[26]

Antichrist

This term is obviously a loaded one, as it seems to indicate a figure wholly in opposition to and dedicated to the destruction of the "correct" practice of Christianity. It only appears in one set of texts within the New Testament, and these are the Johannine Epistles (1, 2 and 3 John). As Paul Anderson writes, it seems that both the Gospel of John and the Johannine letters are concerned with "interreligious squabbles." That is, these texts are dealing with problems of belief and practice *within* groups of Jesus-followers. Here, it seems that the "squabbles" are about Christology, i.e., how Christ is to be understood. Those who hold a belief about Christ at odds with the way in which the author of these letters believes are "antichrists" (1 John 2:18, 22) who have left the community (2:19-20) because they "deny that Jesus is the Christ" (2:22). The author is writing "these things to you concerning those who would deceive you" (2:26), so even though these "antichrists" have split from the community, they're still trying to "deceive" those who remained.

The assumed religious/scriptural literacy we've been examining is most evident, perhaps, after Déroulard's mother, Madame Déroulard—who is described as *très pieuse*—admits to killing her son by means of poisoned chocolate.[27] For example, she describes her son as an "evil man" who "persecuted the Church" and "led a life of mortal sin" before murdering his wife.[28] More importantly for our purposes, she quotes Psalm 37:35 to describe the character of her son, that is, "He flourished as the green bay tree."[29] Finally, Madame Déroulard tells Poirot she's "willing to answer for my action before the good God," and asks him if she must "answer for it on earth also?"[30] Following this exchange with Madame Déroulard, Poirot agrees not to pursue his investigation any further or report any of it to the police. In his retelling to Hastings, Poirot offers no clarity for his decision to let her escape justice. Was it pity for her loss? Consideration

---

[25] Ibid.
[26] Ibid.
[27] Ibid.
[28] Ibid.
[29] Ibid. Hastings uses this same scriptural reference in "The Mystery of the Hunter's Lodge," discussed in Chapter 5.
[30] Christie, "The Chocolate Box."

for her age? His own sense of religious justice? That is, does he agree with Madame Déroulard's claim that God will punish her, and that should be good enough? In the end, though, Poirot claims this is his one big failure, and exhorts Hastings to "remember it, and if you think at any time that I am growing conceited – it is not likely, but it might arise."[31]

This short story was adapted in the series *Agatha Christie's Poirot*, and it's a perennial fan favorite mostly owing to its romantic overtones and insight into Poirot's past. The episode indicates right from the start that it'll carry through on the theme of Catholicism and anti-clericalism in the short story. For example, at the outset we hear Paul Déroulard (James Coombes), a government minister in Belgium, say to his wife Marianne (Lucy Cohu) that while he's thinking of Belgium's future, "the Catholic Church has narrowed your mind . . . just as it has my mother's." Marianne responds that Paul is "asking me to choose between you and my faith." Angered, Paul says, "My God, we're into a new century, but you are stuck in the last, just like your damned clergy." Marianne tries to explain that "Attacking the church won't help Belgium . . . [Instead] It'll turn the people against you," but Paul counters that he "won't attack it," he just wants "it to open its eyes." As they're having this conversation, the camera shows us Paul's mother's (Rosalie Crutchley) room, which not only has a Bible open on a lectern, but also a small altar with a cross and a candle burning, to which she crosses herself before she leaves her room to see what's going on. She sees Marianne run away from Paul and then fall down a flight of stairs, stopping dead at the bottom. Paul runs down after her, and looks up to meet his mother's eyes when he realizes Marianne is dead.

The scene then shifts to Japp and Poirot arriving in Brussels in the present. They're visiting so Japp can be "made a *Compagnon de la Branche d'Or*," what Poirot calls "the highest honor my country can bestow." When Poirot runs into his old friend Chantalier, (Jonathan Hackett) who's now the new Police Commissioner, Chantalier who brings up the Déroulard case. Despite Chantalier's claim, Poirot insists that Marianne's death wasn't an accident. Then Poirot begins to narrate Déroulard's death in a flashback sequence.

It's clear from this sequence that our earlier sense of Madame Déroulard's religiosity is correct. After Paul explains a new law that requires military commands to be given in both French and Flemish, she says sternly, "All I pray is that you and your friends in government have no plans for the mass to be said in Flemish, Paul."[32] There's an uncomfortable silence, until le Comte du St. Alard (Geoffrey Whitehead) stands and says, "Now I see it. This law is just the tip of the iceberg. Your late wife always said that one day you'd get your claws into the church." Even though Paul strenuously denies this, St Alard says, "The press knows you're against the Catholic Church, Paul." Paul tells St Alard not to say any more, but he accuses Paul of being willing to "appease the Kaiser as well. Then I suppose we'd all be speaking German." St Alard then leaves.

Poirot continues, and relates that about midnight everyone left the Déroulard's house, and "*Madame* retired to her nightly devotions." As we hear this, we're also shown

---

[31] This is clearly an allusion to the 1893 Holmes story "The Yellow Face."
[32] As Cook, *Belgium*, 80–83, notes, the debates over which language would be used for what functions in the new Belgian state were very contentious. Cook especially emphasizes the elements of class and education in these controversies, as Flemish was assumed to be the language of uneducated commonfolk (see p. 81).

Madame Déroulard kneeling before the small altar in her room crossing herself and kissing her rosary before going to bed. Paul, though, is a "slave to insomnia," and so he returns to his study to work. Poirot tells us that Paul had a reputation for "austerity and discipline," but had two vices: his career and chocolates. As if to put a fine point on her religious identity, we're shown Madame Déroulard praying the rosary interspersed with scenes of Paul working.

As in the story, Poirot agrees to take some leave time to accept the request of Virginie (Anna Chancellor) to look into Paul's death. And also, when he interviews the staff and occupants of the Déroulard house, shared religious language is at the fore. For example, Poirot asks the butler if he ever had any disagreements with Paul about "his easy ideas about religion." The butler responds by describing how M. Déroulard was "attacked for being a liberal" at dinner the evening he died. Poirot then asks if Madame Déroulard is also a liberal, but the butler says, "Sadly, no. A good Catholic, *monsieur*. Devout like St Alard."

In this adaptation, after Poirot visits a friend called Jean-Louis (Jonathan Barlow) who's a chemist and learns that crumbs of chocolate contained a medicine for high blood pressure called Trinitrin, Virginie volunteers to get St Alard to confess while Poirot listens in from another room. She tells St Alard she "can't help thinking that his death was a just punishment." Even though he assures her Paul's death was from heart failure, Virginie says, "Some people do anything for their faith, Xavier. I admire that. Suppose someone knew that Paul had plans to limit the church's power in Belgium. Would it be a sin to remove him?" Xavier asks, "To murder him?" "Oh, but such people would never be seen as common murderers, though, but as saviors. Well, at least by the church, don't you agree?" Virginie asks him. Xavier then admits, "I'm the one responsible for his death, Virginie." She asks him flatly, "You killed him?" and Xavier says, "As surely as if I had fired a pistol at his heart."

After, Madame Déroulard returns unexpectedly and finds Poirot in her house, Police Superintendent Boucher, (Mark Eden) who has already warned Poirot about his ideas regarding this case, orders Poirot to visit her and apologize. It's during this conversation with her and Virginie that Poirot realizes that it was Madame Déroulard who killed her son by putting the Trinitrin in his chocolates. She then admits it, and Virginie asks her why she did it. Madame Déroulard tells her, "Because of what he was doing to our country, Virginie, and our church." She then tells Poirot, "I pray, monsieur, that no woman in the world need ever choose again between love of God and the love of her child." Poirot responds, "But to take a life is a mortal sin, *madame*. How can a woman of such conviction so deny her faith?" Madame Déroulard reveals that "Paul was a murderer, monsieur. She [Marianne] did not die from an accident." We're then shown a flashback to the night when Marianne dies, and we see Paul pull the rug out from Marianne's feet, causing her to fall to her death.

Madame Déroulard then says, "He knew I had seen him do it, but we never spoke of it. Each of us afraid to admit he was capable of doing such a thing." She tells Poirot, "Before I died, I had to see justice done. My doctors tell me I have no more than six months left in this world. Will the truth wait six months, monsieur?" Gently, with a kind smile, Poirot leans forward, puts his hand on Madame Déroulard's shoulder, and says, "Perhaps longer, *madame*." She's adamant, though, telling him, "No, you must tell it. Tell all, when I've gone."

Both Japp and Chantalier ask Poirot why he never told. Poirot tells them that Virginie agreed that it'd be his decision, then explains, "Paul Déroulard, he was a murderer. His mother acted for the greater good of the country. I admired her sacrifice, her moral courage. Who does anything these days for the greater good?" At the end of the episode, Poirot sees his chemist friend Jean-Louis, who introduces him to his two sons, one of whom is named Hercule. Obviously flattered, Poirot says they look familiar, and Jean-Louis tells him that's on account of his wife, Virginie, who then enters the restaurant. Their reunion is quite touching, as Poirot, flushed with emotion, says that he was just telling Jean-Louis that "he was the most fortunate of men."

The episode, then, help us understand why Poirot let Madame Déroulard escape justice by concretizing his admiration of her action and motives. However, the question of whether this admiration bleeds over into sympathy with her views regarding the Church is left open. Even so, the short story "The Chocolate Box" and its adaptation are central in helping understand how Poirot's character reflects the role religion plays in Christie's Poirot canon, as it foregrounds and details his Catholic identity in contrast with a maximalist discordant example (Madame Déroulard) and a more unaffiliated paradigm (Paul Déroulard).[33] This quality of the short story is also pertinent in terms of the expectations of genre, i.e., Christie supplies more biographical detail than one would expect at this point in the development of the genre of crime fiction. By focusing that detail on a non-heroic Catholic foreigner, she's again showing herself to be a bucker of inherited traditions, as we've seen in previous chapters.

*   *   *

Our second example of Poirot's religious identity is a scene from the 1948 novel *Taken at the Flood*. In this novel, which is on the whole a rather bleak portrayal of post-War England, Poirot is drawn into another familial squabble over money after a man called Gordon Cloade impulsively marries a young widow named Rosaleen Underhay. Before Cloade can return home with his new bride, he's killed in a bombing. Much to their dismay—as they've been living off his financial goodwill—his family discovers Gordon left his entire estate to Rosaleen. Once her brutish brother David arrives and threatens to cut them all off, tensions flare, and members of the Cloade family decide to seek Poirot's help.

In Book 2, chapter six, the narrator describes two churches seen from the market square in the town: "In front of Poirot, set back a little, was the Roman Catholic Church of the Assumption, a small modest affair, a shrinking violet compared to the aggressiveness of St. Mary's which stood arrogantly in the middle of the square facing the Cornmarket, and proclaiming the dominance of the Protestant religion."[34] We're then told that Poirot goes into the former, "removed his hat, genuflected in front of the altar and knelt down behind one of the chairs."[35] He's obviously praying, as we hear that Rosaleen's crying interrupts "his prayers"—and this is, in fact, the *only* time we see

---

[33] By "maximalist," I mean the idea that religion should be maximally determinative for a person's behavior and interactions. See Bruce Lincoln, *Holy Terrors: Thinking about Religion after September 11* (Chicago & London: The University of Chicago Press, 2003), 5.

[34] Christie, *Taken at the Flood* (1948; reis. New York: HarperCollins, 2011), Kindle edition, ch. 6.

[35] Ibid.

Poirot praying in his entire textual existence. The two have a very revealing exchange in the church, and it gives us a fascinating glimpse into Poirot's religious thought and details several of the qualities we noted in Chapter 6.

After Poirot asks if he can help her, Rosaleen replies, "No one can help me. I can't go to confession, even. I've got to bear the weight of my wickedness all alone. I'm cut off from the mercy of God." Poirot responds that no one is so cut off, but Rosaleen protests that she'd have to confess her sins, a seemingly terrifying prospect for her. When Poirot presses her as to the purpose of her visit to the church, she tells him she came seeking comfort, but asks, "But what comfort is there for me? I'm a sinner." Poirot reminds her that "We are all sinners," but Rosaleen again protests, saying "But you'd have to repent – I'd have to say – to tell. . . . Oh, the lies I've told – the lies I've told."[36]

This conversation not only reinforces Poirot's "father confessor" quality, it also lays bare some of his key beliefs and attitudes and makes obvious their origin in his Catholicism. For example, in his claim that "We are all sinners," we see the root of his suspicious nature. Catholicism, like many branches of Christianity, views the human race as substantively or inherently sinful, i.e., born with "original sin." Put differently, humanity always falls short of the mark of holiness demanded by God, and engages in what are considered immoral and rebellious lifestances and practices. This is a position that hearkens back to the early history of the Church. It's a viewpoint perhaps best explored in the work of the African theologian Augustine (354–430 CE), and his position has been determinative for how Christianity understands sin. It's easiest to understand Augustine's view of original sin if we begin with his idea of predestination.

Around the turn of the fourth century CE, a prominent British monk named Pelagius made a splash in his claims that God could not be seen as just if humanity were punished for its sins without providing a way to help ourselves. In other words, there must be a way for humans to work their way out of sin; God will help those who help themselves. Augustine disagreed vehemently, arguing that God helps precisely those people who cannot help themselves. If we could save ourselves somehow, he asked, then of what use was Jesus's suffering and death? As William C. Placher writes,

> Through grace, God saves some people in spite of their inability to save themselves. Nothing they have done merited that salvation. Yet Scripture insists that God's grace does not extend to all. There are goats as well as sheep; some are consigned to eternal fire. God must therefore simply decide to save some and leave others, no worse in their characters, to the consequences of their sins. Is that unfair? Augustine argues that everyone sins, everyone deserves punishment. God gives some better than they deserve, but no one gets less."[37]

The implication of this position is that "no can claim to have earned salvation," i.e., salvation is not attainable through works but only through God's grace.[38] So, how does this help us understand Augustine's view of original sin?

---

[36] Ibid.
[37] Placher, *A History of Christian Theology: An Introduction* (Louisville, KY: Westminster, 1983), 115.
[38] Ibid., 116.

The presupposition of Augustinian predestination is that humanity is sinful, even babies. Why is this the case? Why is humanity steeped in sin? Augustine, interpreting the narration of the disobedient act in the Garden in Genesis 2-3, claims that it's because humanity in general has inherited original sin. More specifically, Adam committed a heinous sin by disobeying God, and that sin is somehow transmitted to all of his descendants. As Alister McGrath puts it, "By 'original sin,' Augustine meant a flaw, defect, or infection from the moment of birth, rather than something that was acquired later in life through sinful action. For Augustine, sinful human nature gives rise to individual sinful actions. Sin causes sin. Or, to use a medical analogy, sin is an illness, while individual sins are its symptoms."[39] Taking a cue from the idea of Jesus's virginal conception and birth, Augustine asks what it is about human sexuality that necessitated Jesus be born in that fashion. His answer is that in some way, the sin of Adam is transmitted through sexual intercourse or semen, and as such Jesus needed to be born without those measures in order to rescue humans from sin. It's important to note that Augustine doesn't feel sex in and of itself is evil. It's a gift of God and is to be celebrated. Adam and Eve had even had sex in the garden, but since we're all now drowning in sin, sex, like all other activities, has become tainted. Our will has been subsumed to our desires, when it should be the other way around. Spoiler alert: this insistence on the inherent sinfulness of humanity, as well as the physical cause for that condition, led to an increased interest in monasticism, asceticism, and a greater interest in Mary as an intercessory figure, all key traits of Medieval Christianity.

Just as understanding Augustine's view of original sin is easier once we grasp his ideas regarding predestination, understanding Poirot's comment regarding "sinners" makes it easier to comprehend the significance of his phrase "the mercy of God" and his mention of confession. Mercy as a quality of God towards humanity is suffused in biblical literature, and in the Catholic faith is most obvious in God's offering of God's son Jesus as an atonement for the sins of humanity. That is, God can be seen as merciful precisely because God doesn't allow humanity to wallow eternally in sin. However, in spite of Augustine's insistence on humanity's inability to work their own way out of their sinfulness, the Church had historically held that humans required an intermediary presence to facilitate processes—like interpretation of Scripture and the administration of ritual practices (such as the "Sacraments")—that put humans in contact with God. One of the ideas/practices of the Church that was challenged by a host of Catholics bent on reforming the Church was this insistence on humans needing a mediating presence in order to access God. And one of the most important of these reformers was Martin Luther.

Among his many theological claims, Luther felt that original sin was so pervasive that it had destroyed our free will, so that only God's grace could enable faith, which would then spawn good works—an idea Luther called *sola gratia* ("grace alone"). This idea of divine grace coming to humans unmediated and only from God was a challenge to the Church, as was Augustine's idea of original sin, oddly. Both seemed to contradict the Church's insistence on good works and penance playing a role in salvation. After all, if we're all writhing in sin, how are we able to do any good works?

---

[39] McGrath, *Theology: The Basics*, 2nd edn (Malden, MA: Blackwell, 2008), 156.

Luther and the movement he and other reformers spawned, what we now call the Protestant Reformation, was so influential, that Catholics felt the need to respond in some way. In a fit of historical creativity, those measures taken by the Catholics in response to the Protestant Reformation(s) are usually called the Counter-Reformation. The highlight of these measures was the Council of Trent, which was held from 1545–1563. The Council's views on the issues of grace and original sin are a direct response to Luther's ideas. Trent claimed that even though free will had been handicapped by original sin, it was not extinguished. Also, Luther had argued that justification—the act of being seen as innocent of sin—is solely an act of God, a gift to a completely undeserving humanity. Again, Trent saw matters differently:

> The bishops [at Trent] believed that salvation cannot be achieved without grace, but they rejected Luther's claim that justification comes from grace alone. Human efforts matter too.... Luther had focused on an instant of justification ... Trent pictured justification as a process in which divine grace and human efforts cooperate at every step and not only lead God to count us as justified but also begin to transform us so that we more nearly deserve that status.[40]

These "human efforts" include the sacrament of penance (or reconciliation), which was "the ritual act by which a person is reconciled to God and to the Christian community after the commission of personal sin."[41] Over time, what was originally a public ritual act morphed into the act of a private confession, which included a number of steps: "The penitent should feel real sorrow for sins (contrition), confess them to a priest, receive absolution from the priest, and perform whatever penance the priest enjoined upon the penitent."[42] The priest here serves an intercessory role, and the penance he assigns represents the actions by which the penitent is mercifully restored to their position as a member of the community in good standing.

In sum, Poirot's statements here are rooted both historically and theologically within Catholicism, from his claim that "Nobody ... is cut off from the mercy of God," to his query regarding Rosaleen taking confession to his flat assertion that "We are all sinners." It's his Catholic tradition that helps us grasp many of his predispositions and repeated statements in this novel. But how is this scene adapted in the world the text creates?

In the version produced for *Agatha Christie's Poirot*, the scene between Poirot and Rosaleen (Eva Birthistle) appears, and is fundamentally the same. However, unlike some of the episodes of this series that downplay or excise religious themes and/or language, there are two scenes here which serve to deepen Poirot's Catholic identity. First, after a service ends, Poirot initiates a conversation with the obviously troubled Rosaleen by telling her a bit of ecclesiastical trivia dealing with the burial of priests. The

[40] Placher, *History*, 203–204.
[41] Lawrence S. Cunningham, *An Introduction to Catholicism* (Cambridge & New York: Cambridge University Press, 2009), 111.
[42] Ibid., 112.

remainder of the conversation accords more or less with the novel, but this insertion highlights even more just how ingrained Catholicism is within Poirot's character.

A second, and more significant addition, to the Suchet version reinforces how that TV series emphasizes Poirot's religious identity. In the novel, there's a fairly conventional "Big Reveal" scene in which Poirot identifies David Hunter (Elliot Cowan) as the murderer of the real Rosaleen (who Hunter had replaced with an impostor called Eileen Corrigan), before David bolts from the room and escapes. In the TV adaptation, Poirot explains with acute emotion and disgust what David had done to Eileen, who here survives his attempt at murder and who's present during the scene. Poirot says, "You had seduced her, had deliberately impregnated her. And had had the baby disposed of." David protests, but Poirot shouts him down, saying "Outside of the church, Eileen Corrigan told me that she'd been cut off from the mercy of God." David says, "She miscarried," but Poirot, alternately angry, horrified, and near tears, counters,

> No monsieur! She endured abortion. As it was always your intention that she should. You wanted to crush the very soul of this simple Catholic girl, to make her so terrified by the state of her own life that she would deliver it to you. And maintained by morphine, ruled by terror, Eileen Corrigan would do whatever you told her to do. Why? WHY? Because you, monsieur, offered her salvation if she did, and, the fires of hell if she did not.

At the end of the scene, a disgusted Poirot confronts David, and asks, "How depraved and how evil does a man have to be to cause the slaughter of so many innocent people for the concealment of a single murder? If God should withhold His mercy from anyone on earth, monsieur, it surely will be you." Here it's obvious that Poirot is not simply righteously indignant at David's actions. He's also religiously offended at how David has systematically abused and perverted young Eileen's Catholic faith to keep her subservient. This offense is clear in Poirot's use of religious language throughout this scene, especially regarding abortion and murder.

It's well-known that Catholicism views human life as sacred, and in his survey of Catholic history and beliefs, Lawrence S. Cunningham discusses the scriptural foundation for such a view.[43] He focuses on the Decalogue in Exodus 20, specifically the prohibition of murder in 20.13, and writes,

> The Fifth Commandment against murder involves a discussion of the dignity of human life, life as sacred, and the general Catholic insistence that all life must be protected – from human conception to death. Obviously, under this broad rubric, there ramified out Catholic teaching on everything from the prohibition of abortion, direct euthanasia, when and under what conditions life may be taken in self-defense, in times of war, and whether it is legitimate for the State to inflict death as a punishment.[44]

[43] See also Christine E. Gudorf, "Contraception and Abortion in Roman Catholicism," in *Sacred Rights: The Case for Contraception and Abortion in World Religions*, ed. Daniel C. Maguire (Oxford & New York: Oxford University Press, 2003), especially pp. 60–62.

[44] Cunningham, *Introduction*, 236.

The "discussion" and "teaching" that flows from Exodus 20:13 is buttressed by several biblical texts in Cunningham's examination, but perhaps Genesis 1:27 is most obviously important.

In that verse, we're told that, "God created humans in his image [*tselem*] / in the image of God he created them / male and female he created them." Unsurprisingly, there's disagreement among scholars as to what being created in God's image means, but Ellen van Wolde's judgment represents a helpful and common explanation:

> The word *tselem* is never used for a concrete visual representation, but only for the pure image that has no concrete content or form. It is a general word which denotes a relationship, indicates an analogy and makes present something that is absent. Thus for example the ark of the covenant stands for the footstool of [God] on earth, and the portrait of Queen Elizabeth on British postage stamps indicates the monarchy. *tselem* can therefore best be rendered 'sign': a sign indicates something or someone that is absent. This means that according to Gen. 1.26–27, the human being is put in the world as a sign of God, to make God present. What makes the human being the image of God is not the corporeal person who stands for the (in) corporeal God, but the human being who makes God present in the world.[45]

Cunningham references this understanding of Genesis 1:27 in his discussion of the moral ramifications of Exodus 20:13 and, more broadly, the "fundamental truths" that "form the basic theological anthropology of Catholic Christianity."[46] The first of these "truths" is

> the conviction that all human life comes from God and that every individual person, class, gender, human capacities notwithstanding, are made in the image and likeness of God. From this fundamental datum flows any number of moral imperatives: Every person is made in the image of God; to harm any person or to degrade or oppress them, or in any way erase their humanity, is to somehow besmirch the image and likeness of God which is their mark.[47]

Based on this understanding of human identity and the creational/covenantal connections between God and humanity, Poirot's outrage becomes more easily understandable. That is, from his Catholic viewpoint, David has indeed diminished Rosaleen's humanity, her essential connection to God, via his murderous manipulations. Because Poirot understands life to be sacred, David's forcing Rosaleen to abort their child and his attempted murder of her are not simply physical actions; they represent violations of her sacred status as a human created in the image of God.[48]

---

[45] See van Wolde, "Genesis I: The Story of the Creation of Heaven and Earth," in *Stories of the Beginning: Genesis 1-11 and Other Creation Stories*, trans. John Bowden (Ridgefield, CT: Morehouse Publishing, 1997), 27.

[46] Cunningham, *Introduction*, 237.

[47] Ibid.

[48] Poirot states specifically that he values human life in *Curtain: Poirot's Last Case* (1975; reis. New York: HarperCollins, 2011), Kindle edition, Postscript.

David Suchet concurs with this view in his memoirs of playing Poirot, and singles out this film as the point at which the show "reveals yet another of Poirot's psychological qualities: his moral beliefs, and, in particular, his Catholicism."[49] His comments help explain the emphasis on religious language in this ending—and perhaps alludes to Poirot's vocation, adumbrated in *Peril at End House*—as he writes, "For me, as essential part of what made Poirot the man he was lay in his conviction that God had put him on this earth so that he could rid the world of evil. That was the *raison d'être* at the heart of every single one of his actions."[50] That conviction is obvious here, as it forms the basis of his opinion that the ultimate justice David must endure will be divine, and that he will escape neither that, nor the earthly justice he meets when we're shown him hang for his crimes.

This expanded and theologically rich ending is absent in the BBC 4 radio version, which follows the novel far more closely. The exchange between Poirot and Rosaleen is also present, and likewise hews closely to the novel.[51] Unlike the TV adaptation, no substantive addition is made to this exchange, but the choice to retain the deeply Catholic scene is evidence that later renderings recognize how central that identity is for Poirot.

We must be careful, though, in claiming too much based on what is clearly not intended to be a theological text. Christie didn't set out to write theological tractates, and since she was *not* Catholic (even though her second husband Max Mallowan was), we cannot assume too much resonance between what Poirot says and does with the actual practice and beliefs of Catholicism in Belgium during his formative years. Nevertheless, it's key to recognize the foregrounding of Poirot's religiosity when we encounter it here, as it helps illuminate the world of the text *and* the world the text creates. Put differently, this "telling" reinforces much of the "showing" we've encountered in previous stories in the Poirot canon regarding his religious proclivities and ideas.

These data also help us in understanding the world the text creates, and how these demonstrate an ongoing interest not just in Poirot, but also in the religious aspects of his character as ingredients for more compelling storytelling. And it's to some of these examples of later popular interpretations we'll turn in the next three chapters.

---

[49] Suchet and Geoffrey Wansell. *Poirot and Me* (London: Headline, 2013), 275.
[50] Ibid.
[51] This program was broadcast in October 2003. It was dramatized by Michael Bakewell and directed by Enyd Williams.

8

Murder on the Orient Express

In Chapters 6 and 7, I examined how Poirot's religious identity is presented in Christie's work, and paid attention to how the world behind the text can illuminate the choices she makes. In this and the following two chapters, I want to acknowledge the immense influence of later interpretations of the Poirot stories in shaping understandings of our little Belgian. This focus is an acknowledgement of the fact that many fans of Poirot encounter him in a mediated fashion. Not all fans of Poirot become fans through reading Christie's stories and novels; many do so as a result of later interpretations and renderings of those primary texts. Thus, we'll focus on TV and film renderings of her Poirot stories to discuss more specifically how the character has been received and adapted in the world the text creates. To do so, I'll perform three "Deep Dives," each of which focuses on a specific novel and its adaptations. These three novels are among Christie's most famous works, and two of them have been the subject of radically distinctive interpretations in TV and film. All three, though, demonstrate a deep interest in exploring the relationship between Poirot and religion.

Murder on the Orient Express (1934)

This novel is one of Christie's most popular, but it's also somewhat anomalous in her output up to this point, as it's essentially a narrated mystery thought experiment, a kind of extreme procedural, narrated in the third person, and not by Hastings.[1] That is, plot details aren't foregrounded; what we know of what happens is revealed via Poirot's investigation and questioning of other characters. Briefly put, Poirot boards an oddly already-full Orient Express, and is approached by a man called Rachett to serve as his bodyguard. Poirot refuses, Ratchett is murdered via twelve different stab wounds (and is revealed to be an infamous and heinous criminal called Cassetti), and Poirot is left to untangle a mystery laden with bluffs, blinds, and ultimately two very different solutions.[2]

---

[1] As Anne Hart, *Agatha Christie's Poirot: The Life and Times of Hercule Poirot* (1990; reis. London: HarperCollins, 1997), 155, reminds us, "Of Poirot's exploits, twenty-six stories and eight books are narrated by Hastings."

[2] For more on this novel, see Charles Osborne, *The Life and Crimes of Agatha Christie: A Biographical Companion to the Works of Agatha Christie*, rev. and updated ed. (London: HarperCollins, 1999), 111–115; and more recently, Mark Aldridge, *Agatha Christie's Poirot: The Greatest Detective in the World* (London: HarperCollins, 2020), 75–81.

Despite it being one of Christie's most popular and adapted works, the novel seems to contain little data for our examination. There are some telling sections, of course, of which four are helpful. First, as we saw in Chapter 6, there is religious-sounding language applied to Poirot. Second, there is a continued use of key terms like "evil" and "justice," e.g., Poirot comments to Bouc that, when Ratchett passed him in a restaurant, "I could not rid myself of the impression that evil had passed me by very close." Bouc replies, "It may be so. There is much evil in the world."[3]

Third, only one character has a direct connection with religion, and that's Greta Ohlsson, who's described as a "kind of missionary—a teaching one."[4] When the train gets stuck in the snow, she cries, but says, "All for the best, whatever happen."[5] The narrator describes this as her "Christian spirit." Later, Poirot is said to be cornered by her as she was "listening to a confused account of [her] missionary aims."[6] She also describes herself as a "matron in a missionary school near Stamboul."[7]

Finally, one of the most interesting pieces of data from this novel is the lack of "moral outrage" on the part of Poirot that someone has been murdered. After all, as recent as the previous novel, 1933's *Lord Edgware Dies*, Poirot states that murder is "the most repugnant of human crimes."[8] We have seen that Poirot has a consistently dim view of murder. Here, though, once Poirot establishes a connection between "Ratchett" and the Armstrong case, that view seems to be modified. For example, not long after this connection is made, Bouc says, in a "tone . . . redolent of heartfelt disgust" that "I cannot regret that he is dead—not at all!" whereupon Poirot responds, "I agree with you."[9]

So, why the change? It obviously could be an outrage at the nature of Cassetti's crimes—which is shared by all the other characters—or it could be that Cassetti was found guilty and sentenced to death. The novel, though, seems confused on that point. In Poirot's retelling to Bouc, he states that Cassetti was "acquitted on some technical inaccuracy" because of his "enormous wealth . . . and by the secret hold he had over various persons."[10] However, Linda Arden says later that "society had condemned him; we were only carrying out the sentence," and also mentions "the sentence of death that Cassetti had escaped."[11] It's possible that Linda meant that everyone knew Cassetti was guilty—as Poirot stated—but this is even more troubling for our understanding of Poirot and his religious views. If Cassetti was never found guilty, then Poirot's attitude toward his murder should be less casual. Or is it that Poirot shares Bouc's disgust at *both* Cassetti's crimes *and* his manipulation of the criminal justice system?

[3]   Christie, *Murder on the Orient Express* (1934; reis. New York: HarperCollins, 2011), Kindle edition, ch. 2, "The Tokatlian Hotel."
[4]   Ibid., Part 1, ch. 4, "A Cry in the Night."
[5]   Ibid., Part 1, ch. 5, "The Crime."
[6]   Ibid.
[7]   Ibid., Part 2, ch. 5, "The Evidence of the Swedish Lady."
[8]   Christie, *Lord Edgware Dies* (1933; reis. New York: HarperCollins, 2011), Kindle edition, ch. 6, "The Widow."
[9]   Christie, *Murder on the Orient Express*, Part 1, ch. 8, "The Armstrong Kidnapping Case."
[10] Ibid.
[11] Ibid., Part 3, ch. 9, "Poirot Propounds Two Solutions."

Either way, it's true that Bouc and Poirot's view of Cassetti's murder is shared and even heightened by other characters. MacQueen, "Mrs. Hubbard," Princess Dragomiroff, Col. Arbuthnot, and Foscarelli all express relief and even provide different kinds of justifications for the murder. Especially interesting for us are the comments of Greta Ohlsson and Hildegarde Schmidt. The former exclaims, "That there are in the world such evil men! It tries one's faith," and even admits to Poirot that "I did so rejoice that evil man was dead—that he could not any more kill or torture little children."[12] Like Greta, Hildegarde responds with theological incredulity to Cassetti's crimes, "It was abominable—wicked. The good God should not allow such things." We're then told "tears had come into the woman's eyes. Her strong motherly soul was moved," and Poirot "gravely" responds, "It was an abominable crime."[13]

In any case—and no surprise here—none of the passengers have any remorse for Cassetti. This is to be expected, obviously, but the interesting thing, again, is that Poirot seems to share their view. This leads to an uncomfortable question, exacerbated by the novel's conclusion: Does Poirot support extralegal murder? We've already seen several instances in which Poirot allows a criminal, even a murderer, to kill themselves and avoid a trial. Is he here saying that even if a trial is conducted and someone is acquitted, it's acceptable for injured parties to take justice into their own hands?

In the end, Poirot puts forward two versions/explanations of the evidence, and asks Bouc and Dr. Constantine to pick. One explanation is simple and obvious, all the more so because it is the one the passengers have been promulgating through their fabricated evidence and coordinated testimony: a lone assassin boarded the train, murdered Cassetti, and then fled. The more complicated and concerning version of events is the one Poirot deduces: all the passengers are complicit in the murder, and all of their motives stem from the victim's involvement in the kidnapping and murder of little Daisy Armstrong, as each of them were involved with/related to the Armstrong family in some way. Given this, how will Bouc and Constantine decide? What are the criteria for their judgment? Bouc is obviously motivated to choose based on what's best for the train line, and Constantine seems to choose based on Linda Arden's appeal. That appeal is central in determining the fate of the passengers. Linda's rationale for Cassetti's murder isn't just focused on what he'd done in the past to children; she claims, "there might be others in the future."[14] Both Bouc and Constantine are moved and persuaded by Linda's apologia/explanation and decide that Poirot's first solution is the one they'll present to the Yugoslav police.

The key point for our purposes about the ending of this novel is that Poirot offers no resistance, no counter-argument; there's no hand-wringing, no prayer, no moral discernment, just a simple acceptance of their decision. In Chapter 6, we discussed the issue of how Poirot understands his own calling or vocation, and based on an example from *Peril at End House* (1928) concluded that he saw himself as being divinely created

---

[12] Ibid., Part 2, ch. 5, "The Evidence of the Swedish Lady" and Part 3, ch. 8, "Further Surprising Revelations."
[13] Ibid., Part 2, ch. 12, "The Evidence of the German Lady's Maid."
[14] Ibid., Part 3, ch. 9, "Poirot Propounds Two Solutions."

to "interfere . . . on the side of the innocent."[15] Here, though, Poirot does not ultimately interfere, yet the novel fails to explain his decision. We might conjecture that Poirot has decided that no one is innocent—including the victim—and thus he will remain aloof from involvement, but again, the novel provides scant evidence for this conclusion. This rather stark, ambiguous, pregnant ending raises myriad questions regarding Poirot's religious views, and obviously, these questions—as well as the "thought experiment" aspect of this novel—have led to interesting and elaborate narrative insertions in later adaptations.

*   *   *

To date there have been four feature-length adaptations of the novel. The first, and the only cinematic adaptation of any of her works that Christie herself was even mildly positive towards, is the 1974 film version, directed by Sidney Lumet.[16] This film has been one of the most successful and profitable adaptations of Christie's work, and with its all-star cast—headed by Albert Finney as Poirot—and luxurious sets, it established the tenor for future cinematic renderings that are still in place to this day.[17] The second adaptation is a 2001 made-for-TV film from CBS directed by Carl Schenkel from a screenplay by Stephen Harrigan. This is something of an anomalous rendering of the novel, as it's not set in the original time period but instead in the modern era. It's also unique in that it's not widely available, either on DVD or via streaming services. This is perhaps due to the fact that it's one of the least successful and most reviled adaptations of a Christie novel in recent memory.[18] Because neither of these adaptations contains significant data for our examination, we'll focus on the two most recent renderings.

Murder on the Orient Express (2010)

The adaptation of *Murder on the Orient Express* in *Agatha Christie's Poirot* takes place in the twelfth series of the show, so Poirot is a *much* older man than in the novel.[19] The film begins with two scenes that set the stage for the moral questions at its heart, namely, the consequences of volitional and knowledgeable choice, and, more obviously, the problem of evil (or theodicy). First, we're shown the incident alluded to at the beginning of the novel. Here we see Poirot accusing a suspect, who suddenly shoots himself in the head right in front of Poirot, spraying blood on his face and clothing.

---

[15] Christie, *Peril at End House* (1932; reis. New York: HarperCollins, 2011), Kindle edition, ch. 12, "Ellen." Marty S. Knepper, "The Curtain Falls: Agatha Christie's Last Novels," *Clues* 23, no. 4 (2005): 69–83, even goes so far as to claim that in *Murder on the Orient Express*, Poirot is "playing God," i.e., "acting according to his own extra-legal concept of justice" (75; see also 78).

[16] As noted by Janet Morgan, *Agatha Christie: A Biography* (London: William Collins Sons & Company, 1984; repr. New York: Alfred A. Knopf, 1985), 375.

[17] For more specifics, see Aldridge, *Agatha Christie On Screen*, Crime Files (London: Palgrave Macmillan, 2016), 122–129.

[18] Again, for more information, see ibid., 314–315.

[19] By my calculation, David Suchet would've been 64 years old when the episode aired. For a brief overview, see Aldridge, *Screen*, 276–277.

This experience clearly traumatizes Poirot, as is obvious from his distracted and distraught behavior on the boat in the next scene. His army escort even tells Poirot that he thinks "it unjust that one mistake cost Lieutenant Morris so dearly. He was a good man who was involved in an accident." Poirot asks, "Unjust?" The escort says, "He made an error of judgment. He was a good man." Poirot counters that "It did not have to end in suicide," but his escort says, "I think he believed he had no choice." Poirot says that "a man like [Morris] always has choice. And it was his choice to lie that brought him into difficulty with the law." This comment ends the exchange.

The second scene occurs when Poirot arrives in Istanbul. He's witness to Mary Debenham (Jessica Chastain) and Arbuthnot (David Morrissey) finding themselves in the middle of a struggle between a woman and her husband. The husband has accused his wife of carrying another man's child and the wife is fleeing in terror. She grabs Mary's arm, but is ripped away by her husband, who's followed by a mob of people. As they and Poirot (from the top of a staircase) watch, the woman is stoned in public. Poirot simply observes all this, then turns away slowly and walks to his hotel, seemingly unaffected by this violence. Later, when he and Mary speak for the first time, they talk about the woman being stoned. Mary is clearly upset about what she witnessed, and Poirot says he is, too, but adds, "Justice is—is often upsetting to witness." Mary protests and asks, "Justice?" but Poirot explains, "It's like the gallows in England. But, in another culture it is best not to intervene, mademoiselle." Mary presses him, "The woman was adulterous. She had not killed anyone," and he responds, "No, but she had broken the rules, and she knew what that would mean." As Mary enters the washroom, he adds, "I also found it upsetting, eh? It is not pleasant," as she closes the door.

In this version, another important addition is that we're shown more content regarding the character of Ratchett (Toby Jones), which problematizes the flat characterization in the novel and the two previous film adaptations. Once the trip is underway, Ratchett approaches Poirot as in the novel, but here asks, "Do you believe in God, M. Poirot? I never used to, but I do now. I think he's like an extra gun. An extra piece of protection. And I think we all need some extra protection sometimes, don't we?" At this point, Poirot turns his back on Ratchett to continue smoking at the bar. Ratchett persists, telling him "You're gonna take on a job for me." Curiously, when Poirot asks Ratchett what he's doing on the train, Ratchett replies, "Penance. I need to give something back before I'm forgiven. But I could be killed before I do it." But when Ratchett says, "You start now," Poirot simply refuses. Angrily, Ratchett takes back the money he'd laid by Poirot and storms out of the car. Obviously, this exchange affects the audience's understanding of Ratchett, as it shows us a man disturbed by his actions, seeking to even the scales before he dies. The intent seems to be to make viewers more sympathetic to him because he's doing self-imposed "penance" for his crimes, thus presenting us with a more complicated presentation of the aforementioned issue of how one deals with the consequences of one's actions.

The subsequent scene, not found in the novel, is central for our examination. When Poirot gets to his own compartment, the first thing we're shown is a segment of him pulling his large rosary from its case and him arranging it carefully on his bedside table. The next scene with Poirot shows him on his knees, hands collapsed together in prayer with his rosary wrapped around his left hand. If we recall that Poirot is only shown praying once in all of Christie's works, then we can appreciate the importance of seeing him engage in that practice here. He prays in a whisper in French: "Lord, I thank thee for having created me, for having made me a Catholic." This scene is juxtaposed with a restless Ratchett sitting on his bed, pistol next to him, clearly agitated about the threats he's received. He, too, clasps his hands and begins to pray quietly, saying, "Pardon me for all the evil I have done this day." The shot then returns to Poirot, who says, "and if I have done any good, deign to accept it." Back to Ratchett: "Watch over me while I take my rest, [looking suspiciously around his cabin] and deliver me from danger." Back to Poirot, who unrolls his rosary and says "Amen" before kissing it. We then see Ratchett looking very anxious, saying, "Amen" and drinking his sleeping draught before one last shot of Poirot with hands held together looking up to God. Then we're shown the Express speeding down the tracks.

As with the previous scene, the inclusion of this near-contrapuntal scene of victim and detective, villain and hero, both praying, both demonstrating their religious identity, colors our assumptions about both men. Instead of superficially seeing Ratchett as evil, we're invited to think of him as a man who's done evil deeds but who's haunted by them, seeking to rectify them before it's too late. Similarly, Poirot's prayer belies the turmoil and seeming apathy he's demonstrated thus far and we see a man whose sights are set on an ideal, even though he's forced to live among the real.

As in the novel, the religious identity of Greta (Marie-Josée Croze) is highlighted, and nowhere more so than when Poirot interviews her. She tells him that Mary—with whom she shares a compartment—"does not pray. I prayed she needs to pray." She also tells Poirot that she's been to America "To speak for Jesus. To raise funds for the mission in India. To help the children." As Greta is leaving, Poirot asks if she's Catholic. She smiles and says, "Oh, no. I prayed for Catholics. Because they have it all wrong, don't they?" Poirot asks, "In what way?" She says, "The Catholic penance and forgiveness is false, isn't it, M. Poirot?" He looks thoughtful and then asks, "Because there are certain things that God will never forgive?" "Ja," answers Greta. "Like when you violate his law?" asks Poirot. Greta agrees, saying, "Ja." Poirot continues, "Violence against children," and Greta, emotionally, repeats, "Violence against the children. This man who is dead— Maybe God came last night on this train and refused to forgive." Poirot pauses, perhaps thinking of his own actions, then asks Greta, "You have been religious a long time?" Touching her St. Christopher and smiling, she answers, "I saw Jesus. . . who protects me now, as I protect the children. Five years ago. Five years I have been with him." She then leaves.

In this reworking, the train loses power and there's no heat or hot food, exacerbating the tense situation and fraying everyone's patience. Once Poirot begins to question everyone and unravel the mystery, we're shown a flashback of the murder in which Princess Dragomiroff (Eileen Atkins) talks to Cassetti as the others stab him. She tells him, "The people that you killed are all in heaven, Mr. Cassetti, while you are going to hell. That baby must have been so scared when you killed her. Did you not think that we would not search the world to get justice for those good people that we loved?" After Dragomiroff explains everything to Poirot, he's righteously angered, and spits out at them, "You people! With your kangaroo jury, your kangaroo justice! You have no right to take the law into your own hands!" Hildegarde objects, saying Daisy was only "five years old," then Linda says, quietly, "We were good, civilized people. And then evil got over the wall, and we looked to the law for justice. And the law let us down." Poirot shakes his head furiously,

> No, you behave like this, and we become just . . . savages in the street! Where juries and executioners, they elect themselves! No, it is medieval! The rule of law, it must be held high! And if it falls, you pick it up and hold it even higher! For all society, all civilized people, will have nothing to shelter them if it is destroyed!

Greta interrupts, "There is a higher justice than the rule of law, monsieur," and Poirot screams at her, "Then you let God administer it, not you!" She rises and asks Poirot, "And when he doesn't, when he creates a hell on earth for those wronged, when priests who are supposed to act in his name forgive what must never be forgiven? Jesus said, "*Let those without sin throw the first stone.*" "Oui," replies Poirot. Greta notes simply, "Well, we were without sin, monsieur. *I* was without sin."

This exchange is interrupted by Dragomiroff, who asks Poirot to let everyone else go when they get to Brod and hand her over to the police. He grabs the murder weapon and whispers, "Non," as he turns to leave the car. As he leaves, Arbuthnot yells that Cassetti was "the worst kind of murderer . . . the devil incarnate!" Bouc even tells Poirot that these are all "good people," and that Cassetti "deserved to be executed for what he did, and the world knows it was a travesty that he was not!" Poirot, though, continues to say "Non" louder and louder and tells Bouc to "Lock the door!" so no one can leave.

In a startling addition to the novel, Arbuthnot takes out a revolver and begins to load it, saying: "We have assigned one murder to the assassin. We can assign two more." Greta objects, saying, "Killing Cassetti was God's law." Arbuthnot starts to rush at Bouc and Poirot, but after he knocks Mary aside, Linda intervenes and talks him down. Mary gets up and tells Arbuthnot that if they kill Bouc and Poirot, they'll be no better than gangsters, saying, "God knows how hard it will be to carry Cassetti's murder through our lives. But how unconscionable will it be to carry murders that are wrong?" She then tells Arbuthnot she's proud of him for "getting justice for your friend," but exhorts him, "We don't do what is wrong."

A few minutes after this intense and emotional exchange, Mary brings tea to Poirot. She reminds him what he said about the woman in Istanbul knowing what the rules of her culture were, and she tells Poirot that Cassetti knew those rules, too. When he replies, "And so do you," Mary tries to explain again. In a heart-wrenching exchange, she tells him, "When you've been denied justice, you are incomplete. It feels that God has abandoned you in a stark place. I asked God—I think we all did—what we should do. And he said do what is right. And I thought if I did it would make me complete again." Poirot asks, "And are you?" Mary looks down, starts to cry, and says, "But I did what was right," and walks away.

As help and the police arrive, we see Poirot in his compartment trying to decide what to do while he runs the rosary through his left hand and smokes one of his little cigarettes. In his memoirs of playing Poirot, David Suchet helps us to understand this scene when he writes, "I am convinced that when he returns to his compartment after the denouement, to consider exactly what he should do, he spends his time alone there not only praying for God's guidance, but also painfully aware that he may not be able to follow it."[20] We don't hear all the dialogue, but it's clear that Poirot tells the police at Brod that a lone assassin did it. After he does, he looks at Mary, and one wonders if she understands what she has cost Poirot, the toll his lie has taken (and will take) on him, his understanding of law and justice, his relationship with God? Poirot then turns to walk away from the police, passengers, and the train. As he does so, he pulls his rosary out of his pocket and holds it. As Suchet writes, "He is carrying the pain of going against his Catholic faith, but at the same time is conscious that sometimes there is no alternative other than to do so."[21] The camera pushes in on his face, and he tries not to weep as the film ends.

This whole film frames the issue of solving the crime in terms of religious identity and language. As opposed to the previous two filmic adaptations and the novel, here Poirot recoils at the suggestion that justice not be served. He wrestles mightily with the issue, as it offends his judicial and religious sensibilities. To Poirot it is unthinkable to budge on this point. After all, we know that he does not approve of murder. Yet when the issue is no longer abstract, when Mary stares him in the face, does he see their suffering? Does he comprehend their misery, their sense of being abandoned by God (as both Mary and Greta note)? Is this why he lies to the police at Brod? And why does Poirot begin to cry at the end of the film? Is it because his faith has been tested and found wanting? Is it because he's betrayed his faith? Again, the film offers no answers.

In the same way, the film offers no on-screen answer to the key religious issue it raises, the issue of theodicy. This issue is related to the broader problem of evil and religion. Lawrence S. Cunningham et al. lay bare this problem, writing,

> In general, one can say that the problem of evil arises whenever certain "brute facts" of everyday experience suggest a contradiction between the world of ordinary existence and the sense of reality suggested by a particular notion of the sacred. In the first place, religious people identify evil as an inconsistency between *what is* (the facts of experience) and *what ought to be* (the reality of the sacred).[22]

This understanding of evil is closely tied to the classical definition of theodicy, and its applicability to our examination should be obvious. Put plainly,

> The problem of theodicy arises when the suffering of innocent persons is set against two beliefs traditionally associated, in the West, with ethical monotheism. One is the belief that God is absolutely just. The other is the belief that God controls all events in history, being both all-powerful (omnipotent) and all-knowing (omniscient). Taken together, these three ideas—the fact of suffering, God's justice, and God's power—seem contradictory ... Theodicy in its classical Western forms is the effort to resist the conclusion that such a logical trilemma exists. Theodicy

---

[20] Suchet and Geoffrey Wansell, *Poirot and Me* (London: Headline, 2013), 309.
[21] Ibid.
[22] Cunningham, et al., *The Sacred Quest: An Invitation to the Study of Religion*, 2nd edn (Englewood Cliffs, NJ: Prentice Hall, 1995), 115.

aims to show that traditional claims about God's power and goodness are compatible with the fact of suffering.[23]

Clearly, the characters in this 2010 adaptation are struggling with this issue of theodicy in a more profound and serious way than we find in the previous cinematic adaptations, not to mention Christie's novel. Through the dialogue of Greta and Mary, it seems obvious that the murder of an innocent like Daisy and the subsequent divine silence has shaken their understanding of God and the presence of justice in God's creation. Similarly, Poirot has been introspective and perturbed by the end result of his insistence on the truth from the beginning of the film, when we're shown the blood spatter across his face as a result of the officer's suicide. His prayerful attempts to reconcile his actions with his sense of purpose and God's presence are interrupted by Ratchett's murder, and now all the façades and pretensions of honest and good people have been ripped aside by their murderous actions. Poirot reacts with disbelief and fury at their attempts to rationalize the murder of Ratchett/Cassetti, and one can't help but hear in his anger and pleas a self-reproach, a sense of guilt at what his own actions have wrought, and a nagging suspicion that perhaps his simple faith can't sustain the burden of those "brute facts" he has too often experienced. Again, Suchet helpfully explains Poirot's dilemma here,

> Poirot is fighting both his Catholic faith and his moral reasoning as he confronts what should be done at the end of the story. He faith tells him firmly that man should not kill, but he also knows that the Bible instructs that man should love his neighbour and forgive their sins. He wants to please God and stay true to his belief that part of his role in life is to defeat evil wherever it may be, but that faith contradicts what his moral reasoning suggests: that sometimes people deserve to be forgiven.[24]

Put simply, we're shown Poirot's crisis of faith, his dark night of the soul, which remains sadly unresolved at the close of the film as he walks away from the train in the snow, rosary in hand. In the end, the film raises the question of theodicy, but offers no answers. It's a tragic, weary, disconsolate and older Poirot we see at the end of the film. And I think that's the point. The two previous filmic interpretations show tidy endings in which Poirot simply says, "Well, that's that." This film wants to problematize that approach, but it does so in a way that honors Poirot's and the passengers' experience of life as well as their suffering. It's a messy ending, but I venture to say that it's a more honest one than we've seen before, or since.

Murder on the Orient Express (2017)

The other adaptation we need to examine is the 2017 film (directed by and starring Kenneth Branagh as Poirot) which, for our purposes, promisingly opens at "The

---

[23] "Theodicy," in *The HarperCollins Dictionary of Religion*, ed. Jonathan Z. Smith (San Francisco: HarperCollins, 1995), 1065.

[24] Suchet and Wansell, *Poirot and Me*, 309.

Wailing Wall" in Jerusalem in 1934.[25] However, just as that promise goes unfulfilled, the opening of the film is also significant for how it depicts Poirot, which, also, is a disappointment. Branagh's version of Poirot is a much younger man than in the novel or other adaptations and he's also portrayed as a man of action, which is totally out of character with this and other novels.

First, let's note how the film depicts Poirot. It first tries to explain his characterization by having him explain how he solved the case: "I have the advantage. I can only see the world as it should be. And when it is not, the imperfection stands out like the nose in the middle of a face. It makes most of life unbearable. But it is useful in the detection of crime." The film also clumsily tries to establish a moral core to Poirot in this same exchange. The officer escorting Poirot to his ferry comments that Poirot seems to be able to see into people's hearts to their true nature. Poirot responds by observing rather disconnectedly, "There is right, there is wrong. There is nothing in between." The serious tone of this remark is belied when Poirot, in an odd fashion, asks the officer to adjust his tie.

As in the 2010 film, the scene between Poirot and Ratchett is also key for us in our attempt to understand how this film renders the former. We're shown Poirot in the dining car reading Dickens and laughing, almost cackling, to himself. When Ratchett (a menacing Johnny Depp) joins him, saying he feels silly enjoying dessert alone, Poirot tells him with a straight face, "I am at my happiest alone." He agrees to let Ratchett join him in exchange for sharing his dessert with him (another odd choice). After Poirot refuses Ratchett's offer, Ratchett tells him, "I know I'm not the best guy born, not by a long shot. And if there's a world after this one, I will face judgment just like you." Ratchett then puts his pistol on the table under a napkin, and comments, "But I ain't in no goddamn rush to do it." As in the novel, Poirot tells him simply he doesn't like his face, and exits the car with his book.

Later, When Bouc (a roguish Tom Bateman) asks Poirot to investigate, Poirot says, "Your faith touches me, *mon cher*. But I must have this rest." The film seems to imply that Poirot's approach to solving crime is more taxing than simply a mental exercise, that it costs him more than sitting in a chair and thinking, as Bouc says. Bouc tells him that if he lets the police handle it, they'll simply pick someone and punish them whether or not they did it. Ultimately, Bouc tells Poirot, "You are the only one who can bring justice," and then Poirot agrees, telling Bouc, "I do not approve of murder, my friend. Every day we meet people the world could do better without yet we do not kill them. We must be better than the beasts. So let us find this killer." In another telling scene after his investigation begins in earnest, Poirot and Mary (Daisy Ridley) have tea outside the train in the snow so he can interview her. These interviews with different characters overlap instead of having a single interview in a single scene, and at one point she tells him, "You live crime. You see evil every day." Poirot says, "Not so. I see enough crime to know that the criminal act is the anomaly. I believe it takes a fracture of the soul to murder another human being."

---

[25] For more on this film, see Aldridge, *Agatha Christie's Poirot*, 429–437.

Next, in an obvious departure from previous films, not to mention the novel, Greta Ohlsson is not a character in Branagh's film. Instead, there is a young woman named Pilar Estravados (Penelope Cruz).[26] In this film, Pilar is—as was Greta—very religious. She refuses the champagne offered by Bouc, and he asks if it doesn't agree with her. "Sin doesn't agree with me," she says. "Vice is where the devil finds his darlings." Pilar is often shown with a Bible, too, and later, when the passengers are complaining about the train, Pilar says, "Yes, some things, they are in God's hands. It is not for us to say if we deserve to arrive safely at our destination, or if, like Lucifer, we must fall." More significantly, once Poirot begins interviewing the passengers, we get a better sense of Pilar's backstory, as we do in all the versions I mentioned already. That backstory reveals Pilar's religiosity; she's a "missionary," but was trained as a nurse. When Poirot asks her about this career change, she says she "owed it to God." Poirot asks, "You owed Him a debt?" She answers, "There were. . . indulgent times in my life. . . when I took more than I gave." We're shown Pilar's hands, which are calloused "like a boxer's." Poirot asks about this, and she tells him, "I do my work in dangerous cities where I cannot be governed by fear. I trained to fight." Poirot asks, "But you do not trust your God anymore" and she replies, "No, in case He is busy." Poirot snaps back, "God is always busy." Finally, during the reveal, Poirot notes a functional view of Pilar's religiosity by singling her out as the "nurse in charge of Daisy, her newfound religious zeal born of guilt at allowing her charge to be abducted."

It's not simply the dialogue that bears on our investigation. It's also the staging of certain scenes, as when all the passengers are asked to leave the train while it's put back on the rails, and they all sit in the mouth of the tunnel, arranged like an imitation of the *Last Supper* (see Figure 8.1).

As Poirot approaches them, his arm in a sling as a result of an attempt on his life earlier by Arbuthnot (another major variance between film and novel), he monologues, "You tell your lies and you think no one will know. But there are two people who will know. Yes, two people. Your God, and Hercule Poirot. It is time to solve this case." After

Figure 8.1 Still from *Murder on the Orient Express* (2017), Alamy, © 20th Century Fox.

---

[26] Confusingly, this is also the name of a character in the 1938 novel *Hercule Poirot's Christmas*.

he identifies everyone's connection with the Armstrong murders, Poirot says emotionally,

> A murder should have one victim. When Ratchett kills Daisy Armstrong, a dozen lives are broken, deformed, ended. They demand justice! Of all these wounded souls, we must finally answer, who among them is a killer? Who takes up the knife? The answer is . . . [long pause] No single one of you could have done it. Nor any pair. It can only have been done, by all of you together.

After Mrs. Hubbard, aka Linda Arden, (Michelle Pfeiffer) admits it was her plan, she describes it and we're shown Ratchett's murder in a flashback sequence while oddly calming music is played. Poirot then comments, "And so it is done. For the death of the innocent. *A life for a life.* Revenge."

Arden begs Poirot to blame it all on her. She tells him that the others "are good people. They can be good again." Poirot, though, responds by saying, "There was right, there was wrong. Now there is you. I cannot judge this. You must decide. You wish to go free without punishment for your crime, then you must only commit one more." At this point he slams Hardman's revolver down on the table in front of Linda Arden, and says, "I will not stop you." Bouc protests, "You can't let them kill you," but Poirot says, "You give my body to the lake, and you walk away innocent at the station. You must silence me. Bouc can lie. I cannot. Do it! One of you!" Arden picks up the gun, points it at Poirot, says "I already died with Daisy," then puts it under her mouth to kill herself, but soon discovers the gun isn't loaded. Poirot turns away, and the scene ends.

Later, Poirot stands on the end of the train, and Pilar approaches him, saying, "You said your role was to find justice." Poirot asks, "What is justice here?" "Sometimes the law of man is not enough," she tells him. Turning his head to her, Poirot asks, "Where does conscience lie?" "Buried with Daisy," Pilar responds. After this, we see one brief segment where Poirot is obviously conflicted in the hallway outside his compartment.

The film ends with Poirot's response to a letter the late John Armstrong had sent him asking for his help with Daisy's case. Poirot narrates it as he walks the length of the train from his cabin to the other end of the train, where all the passengers are. The letter includes the following lines:

> I have now discovered the truth of the case, and it is profoundly disturbing. I have seen the fracture of the human soul. So many broken lives, so much pain and anger giving way to the poison of deep grief, until one crime became many. I have always wanted to believe that man is rational and civilized. My very existence depends upon this hope, upon order and method and the little gray cells. But now, perhaps, I am asked to listen, instead, to my heart.

It is instructive to compare this quotation from Poirot's letter and the previous quotation I reproduced from Suchet's memoir that also speaks of this key moment, the moment in which Poirot must decide which solution to present to the police. In Suchet's text, he emphasizes the role Poirot's religious faith plays in that decision; here, the deciding factor is the reliance on Poirot's "heart," as opposed to his intellect. The absence of religious language at this central juncture is telling, and reflects the absence of Poirot's Catholicism more broadly in this rendering.

Once he joins the passengers, Poirot tells them, "I have understood in this case that the scales of justice cannot always be evenly weighed. And I must learn, for once, to live with the imbalance. There are no killers here. Only people who deserve a chance to heal." He then tells them that the police believed his simpler solution to the crime, and ends by saying, "You are all free to go. And may you find your peace with this. May we all."

So, what does his decision cost Poirot? What's at stake for him? We're shown what appears to be a simplistic moral code at the outset of the film, but we have no religious background, no theological foundation with which to understand that code's origin or its function or its application. Because of this aporia, Poirot's struggle with his conscience—minimal though it is—is void of substance. Poirot is characterized at times as a simplistic child-man, giggling at Dickens, then deeply serious and dramatic. It's this schizophrenic depiction of Poirot—as well as the sometimes playful, sometimes action-packed tone of the film—that ultimately prevents the audience from understanding Poirot as deeply as they need to develop sympathy with/empathy for him and the decision that he must make. We simply don't feel his moral struggle as we do with the 2010 interpretation. There, at the end, Poirot walks away weary and more than a little broken but still holding his rosary, committed to his faith even though it is more difficult now. Here, the film ends with Poirot getting summoned to Egypt because there's been a murder on the Nile, a clumsy attempt to link this outing with the next film in Branagh's rebooted series, the 2022 film *Death on the Nile*.

In sum, Branagh's film does include religious language, but in a haphazard, ambiguous fashion. The religious and ethical issues and stakes seem ill-defined when compared with the 2010 adaptation. And while this is most likely due to market concerns and appeal, and perhaps the increasing decline in traditional religious affiliation, the cursory employment of religious language reflects a larger conceptual confusion underlying the film.[27]

Given the flat portrayal of the characters in the novel, including Poirot, in favor of a more procedural focus, it's only to be expected that later renderings would attempt to provide deeper characterization for audiences. As we've seen, though, the 2010 rendering does so with a far greater emphasis on Poirot's religious identity and with more subtlety. It raises a key religious issue (theodicy), and even though it doesn't provide an answer for that issue, it shows us how characters—especially Poirot and Mary—struggle to make sense of religion, justice, and evil in the world. In contrast, the 2017 rendering seems constrained in its treatment of religion by what I assume are box-office interests. As such, we see little of Poirot's Catholicism, and it's certainly not depicted as a resource for meaning-making in light of the terrible events he experiences and uncovers. In Chapter 9, we'll delve more deeply into that Catholic identity as we examine a remarkable rendering of Christie's novel *The A.B.C. Murders*.

---

[27] For this decline, see Part 1.

9

The A.B.C. Murders

One of Christie's more famous novels is *The A.B.C. Murders* (1936). This book is notable in her Poirot canon for its tone, and for the development of detective fiction for an innovative approach to crime-solving that still resonates today.[1] The story shows Poirot being contacted by a killer who's targeting victims based on the spelling of their names and locations, e.g., Alice Ascher in Ansford, Betty Barnard in Bexhill, and Sir Carmichael Clarke in Churston. Poirot and Hastings must find this lone, seemingly maniacal murderer before they work their way through the alphabet, and in this they're assisted by the friends and relatives of the victims, as well as Chief Inspector Japp and Inspector Crome, a younger officer. Poirot eventually discerns that ABC is actually Franklin Clarke, Sir Carmichael's brother, and that his other victims were only chosen to disguise the murder of his brother. That is, Franklin's primary target was his brother, but he created a concealing fog of confusion by inventing and adopting the persona of a "serial killer" in order to hide his motive. I must admit at the outset that there is precious little substantive data in the novel for our examination of religion. Nonetheless, let's explore the novel's tone and innovation briefly before discussing how it can help us understand how Poirot and religion have been presented in the world the text creates.

First, this novel has more than a twinge of melancholy related to a rather low view of humanity and their fate. For example, a woman named Mary tells Poirot and Hastings that her murdered aunt told her that her husband was a "fine handsome figure of a man" when they married. She then comments, "It's dreadful to think, sir, what people come to."[2] When the two detectives arrive at Mrs. Ascher's shop after her murder, Hastings comments on the crowd gathered outside, "What we saw was a mass of average human beings looking with intense interest at the spot where another human being had been done to death."[3] Once inside Ascher's house, Hastings remarks on the

---

[1] For an examination of Christie's technique of plotting in this novel, see Martin Edwards, "Plotting," in *The Routledge Companion to Crime Fiction*, eds. Janice Allan, et al (London & New York: Routledge, 2020), 188–190. For more on this novel, see Charles Osborne, *The Life and Crimes of Agatha Christie: A Biographical Companion to the Works of Agatha Christie*, rev. and updated ed. (London: HarperCollins, 1999), 131–135, who gushes that it's "positively brilliant in its imagination and originality" (133). More recently, see Mark Aldridge, *Agatha Christie's Poirot: The Greatest Detective in the World* (London: HarperCollins, 2020), 92–97.

[2] Christie, *The A.B.C. Murders* (1936; reis. New York: HarperCollins, 2011), Kindle edition, ch. 5, "Mary Drower."

[3] Ibid., ch. 6, "The Scene of the Crime."

wedding photo of Mr. and Mrs. Ascher, "I recalled the leering drunken old man, and the toil-worn face of the dead woman — and I shivered a little at the remorselessness of time."[4] Finally, Mrs. Merrion wonders if the second murder in Bexhill will adversely impact her tea shop business. When Inspector Kelsey assures her that people will come precisely because of the murder, she comments, "Disgusting, truly disgusting. It makes one despair of human nature."[5]

Along with melancholy, the novel also has a tone best described by Hastings when he notes his "sickening sense of insufficiency," the feeling of helplessness in the face of a lone serial killer like ABC.[6] Not only is this out of character for Hastings as a "man of action," it also represents a slight shift in the Poirot and Hastings stories. That is, the comedic/jovial sense of adventure is less evident in this novel.

The seriousness of ABC's crimes necessitates an innovative approach to detection in the novel, as well. This is first seen in the introduction an "alienist" named Dr. Thompson. He explains that, "A deadly logic is one of the special characteristics of acute mania," and as his first example, he notes that someone might believe themselves "divinely appointed to kill clergymen."[7] Thompson's presence and ABC's crimes lead to a lot of language regarding madness and mania. This language is directly connected to the fact that this is the first time that Poirot comes across "the 'chain' or 'series' type of murder."[8]

This kind of serial murder causes Poirot and Hastings to argue about what they should be doing to help. In chapter seventeen, the novel returns again to the already well-worn theme in the Poirot stories of the importance of "reflection" and "thought" over "action." Here, though, Poirot especially stresses the imaginative entering-into the perspective of the murderer, an empathetic identification with the killer (which we see early on, after the first murder). Only in this way, Poirot asserts, can he "know" the man, and only in this way will he be able to "go fishing."[9]

At the same time we note the tonal and innovative character of the novel, there is scant data of the presence of religion here. This is in itself notable. For example, After Poirot gathers the family members of the victims, he tells them that, "he [ABC] is a madman in an advanced state of mania."[10] What's so interesting to note here is that even though there's a lot of talk about what a "madman" or "maniac" ABC is, and the resultant "horror" that knowledge brings, not one character invokes any kind of religious language, theology, or praxis to deal with that horror or anxiety. What does this tell us? Given the Christian hegemony we noted in Part One, wouldn't we expect someone to do this? Is this lack of religious language connected to the theme of melancholia we observed in the novel? That is, could Christie be depicting a societal situation in which the modern age is somehow worse than a/the previous age? Might

4   Ibid.
5   Ibid., ch. 9, "The Bexhill-on-Sea Murder."
6   Ibid., ch. 23, "September 11th. Doncaster."
7   Ibid., ch. 8, "The Second Letter."
8   Ibid., ch. 9.
9   Ibid., ch. 17, "Marking Time."
10 Ibid., ch. 18, "Poirot Makes a Speech."

this deficiency be due to a lessening of religious certainty?[11] These are all questions which the novel doesn't answer.

The only biblical reference in the novel—aside from a lyric from the popular song "Some Sort of Somebody"—occurs in chapter twenty-four when we're told that Cust sees the film *Not a Sparrow* for the second time. This is significant, as the theater serves as the location for the fourth and final murder. Cust had seen this film once before in chapter sixteen, but we learn more about it here. First, it's not a real film, unlike so many actual references to popular culture in Christie's works. The film is described as an "all-star thrilling drama of pathos and beauty," with an "emotional and semi-religious end."[12] To illustrate this flowery description, we're provided a bit of dialogue from a "soul-stirring moment" in which the heroine gave "vent to a hoarse cry of indignation," and says, "Never. I would sooner starve. But I shan't starve. Remember those words: *not a sparrow falls*."[13]

Both this dialogue and the film's title seem to reference Matthew 10:29 ("Are not two sparrows sold for a farthing? And one of them shall not fall on the ground without your Father"), which is part of Jesus's instructions to the disciples before sending them out (see 10:5 and 11:1). The reference to the sparrows comes in the context of 10:26-31, in which Jesus tells the disciples not to be afraid of "them which kill the body, but are not able to kill the soul: but rather fear him which is able to destroy both soul and body in hell" (10:28). The note regarding sparrows seems to imply that God is ultimately in control of the disciples' fates, just like the sparrows. Just so, David Hill asks, "Since [sparrows] are the object of God's concern, how much more is the apostles' welfare his concern?"[14] Similarly, Douglas Hare writes, "Your father, who even cares for sparrows, cares so much for you that even the hairs of your head are numbered."[15] What might be the significance of this reference?

Let's keep in mind two key details. First, when Cust saw the film earlier, he "murmured to himself" upon leaving, "It's an idea . . ."[16] Second, when Cust sees the film for the second time and emerges, he notices the "really beautiful evening" and "a quotation from [the poet Robert] Browning came into his head": "God's in his heaven. All's right with the world."[17] We're told in chapter twenty-five that although Cust "had always been fond of that quotation," that "there were times, very often, when he had felt it wasn't true."[18]

If we put the Browning quotation in conversation with the quotation from Matthew, what kind of theology is the novel positing? And don't forget, Cust isn't entirely certain

[11] J. C. Bernthal makes a similar case for Christie's late works in his "'A Dangerous World': The Hermeneutics of Agatha Christie's Later Novels," in *The Bible in Crime Fiction and Drama: Murderous Texts*, eds. Alison Jack and Caroline Blyth; Scriptural Traces: Critical Perspectives on the Reception and Influence of the Bible, 16; LHB/OTS, 678; (London & New York: Bloomsbury, 2019), 167–182.
[12] Christie, *The A.B.C. Murders*, ch. 24, "Not from Captain Hastings' Personal Narrative."
[13] Ibid.
[14] Hill, *The Gospel of Matthew*, NCBC (Grand Rapids, MI: Eerdmans, 1972), 193.
[15] Hare, *Matthew*, IBC (Atlanta: John Knox Press, 1993), 116.
[16] Christie, *The A.B.C. Murders*, ch. 24.
[17] This is a quotation from Browning's 1841 verse-drama *Pippa Passes*.
[18] Christie, *The A.B.C. Murders*, ch. 25, "Not from Captain Hastings' Personal Narrative."

of the veracity of the Browning quotation. First, I think Cust's "idea" after seeing the film for the first time isn't related to murder—as the book implies until the reveal. Rather, it's a theological idea regarding God's providential control/power/protection. That is, in Matthew, Jesus is telling the disciples that God cares for them, that God's knowledge of them extends to counting hairs. This would obviously be a happy thought for Cust, given his life and suffering. However, that passage in Matthew *doesn't* say the disciples will never be persecuted, as Hare notes, just that God knows and will care for them.[19] This could very well be why Cust doubts the veracity of the Browning quotation, because things aren't "right with the world."

What this leaves us with is a sense of divine providence, the idea that God indeed has a plan, but humans still suffer within that plan. In Chapter 6, we saw Poirot wrestling with the notion of providence in *Peril at End House*, too, and there he rejects human passivity—specifically his own—in the face of God's plan. Finally, we must also ask if it's significant that it's Cust who's dealing with these theological issues? In a later exchange with Poirot, Cust tells him, "Everyone's hand has been against me—always," which could be a reference to either Genesis 16:12 or Lamentations 3:3.[20] How could this affect the reader's view of Cust as a persecuted "other"? How does this data overlap with the melancholy, helpless tone of the novel? Again, these are questions not engaged in the novel.

Finally, the ending of the novel is curious. In the "Big Reveal"—the solution of which is suggested by an offhand remark by Hastings, in an obviously Holmesian echo—Poirot identifies Clarke as the murderer. But, when Clarke pulls a gun to kill himself, Poirot reveals that he'd had an associate pick his pocket and remove the bullets. Poirot tells Clarke, "No, Mr. Clarke, no easy death for you. You told Mr. Cust that you had had near escapes from drowning. You know what that means — that you were born for another fate."[21] Here, Poirot doesn't allow the guilty party to kill themselves or escape instead of facing justice, but why? What's different about Clarke? Is it because he's a man? Probably not, since Poirot has let men go before (as in *Three Act Tragedy* the previous year). Could it be because of what Clarke did to the "innocents" by his actions? It could be, as Poirot notes, what Clarke did to Cust: "It was abominable — not so much the murder of his brother — but the cruelty that condemned an unfortunate man to a living death."[22] The language used here obviously brings to mind Genesis 4 and the murder of Abel by his brother Cain, not to mention the "mark" placing Cain in a kind of "living death." If his treatment of Cust is why Poirot wanted to see Clarke tried, that'd help explain the happy ending provided to Cust in part two of the final chapter.

* * *

Aside from the allusion to Matt. 10.29 and what it implies regarding the theology of the novel, there's very little on-point data for our examination. Luckily, like *Murder on the Orient Express*, the world the text creates is a particularly rich one, with four adaptations

---

[19] Hare, *Matthew*, 116.
[20] Christie, *The A.B.C. Murders*, ch. 33, "Alexander Bonaparte Cust."
[21] Ibid., ch. 34, "Poirot Explains."
[22] Ibid., ch. 35, "Finale."

of note. These include the rather loony 1965 comedy film *The Alphabet Murders*, starring Tony Randall as Poirot; the wonderful 1992 film in *Agatha Christie's Poirot*; and—oddly, given the subject matter—a four-part anime adaptation with a young female protagonist that appeared in the 2004 series, *Agatha Christie's Great Detectives Poirot and Marple*.[23] For our purposes, there's only one central interpretation we need to explore, and this is the fourth and most recent one, the 2018 three-part miniseries from BBC One and Amazon TV, directed by Alex Gabassi.[24]

Like the novel, the tone of this adaptation is thematically and technically melancholy, and it also emphasizes the theme of the depravity of human nature. In his examination, Mark Aldridge places the responsibility for "this extensive reworking of the Agatha Christie book" at the feet of Sarah Phelps, the screenwriter. Phelps, who also scripted the 2014 adaptation of *And Then There Were None*, evidently was more interested in delving into and inventing a new backstory for Poirot than in creating a faithful rendering of the novel or the character.[25] In a 2018 interview with the BBC, Phelps stated that she wanted to problematize the audience's assumptions about Poirot's identity. That is, she wanted to ask,

> Who is this man who is hidden behind the cartoon? Take that cartoon quality, that has come from decades and decades of being entirely habituated, and almost comforted by this familiar, rotund, irritating figure who is going to come in and be waspish and wax his moustache and have all the answers to the questions. I want to know who is hiding behind that mask and why he hides there.

Let's see how Phelps fared.

The most important change Phelps made is that the depiction of Poirot is starkly different than in the novel, and it's this depiction, his new backstory, that's so crucial for our purposes. If we focus on the first few scenes of the first episode, this variant depiction becomes clear. This adaptation leads us to believe that Cust (Eamon Farren) is obsessed with Poirot. In the first episode, we're shown Cust writing a letter, and the voiceover by Cust makes us aware that the letter is to Poirot. Cust says he followed Poirot recently, and that he looked old and tired. We're then shown the Poirot of this adaptation (John Malkovich) and he looks nothing like Poirot is described in the novels. When we see Poirot sitting on his bed, looking as if he's sitting upright with some difficulty, our eyes are immediately drawn to a large crucifix above the head of his bed. Poirot sits on the edge of his bed, holding his head in his hands. We then see Poirot dyeing his goatee—not a moustache!—pitch black, as Cust says that even though some people may laugh at Poirot and think he's pompous and vain, Cust doesn't think that. Instead, "I think you're trying to roll back the time to when you were a famous detective, when you were celebrated, when you were wanted, when you were loved." Cust's letter

[23] In *Agatha Christie On Screen*, Crime Files (London: Palgrave Macmillan, 2016), Aldridge discusses the 1965 film on pp. 105–108.
[24] For more on this film, see Aldridge, *Agatha Christie's Poirot*, 438–442.
[25] See Aldridge, *Agatha Christie's Poirot*, 438–439. For Phelps's interview, see https://www.bbc.co.uk/mediacentre/mediapacks/the-abc-murders/phelps.

then tells Poirot, "I have never been loved. But I will be feared. I will be a faceless beast, leading lambs to the slaughter." Obviously, this letter is radically different than the first letter in the novel.

We next see Poirot at Scotland Yard asking for Japp, only to discover that his old friend has retired. He's told that Inspector Crome (Rupert Grint) has taken over from Japp, and is asked to wait "with the other members of the public" on a bench until Crome returns. As in the novel, Inspector Crome is depicted as an example of a "modern" detective and is also "patronising" to Poirot.[26] As such, he's representative of a theme in the novel of younger characters underestimating Poirot, something Hastings bemoans therein. This obviously reinforces Poirot's sense of irrelevancy, the fact that no one recognizes his importance any longer. When Crome finally arrives, the desk officer tells him Poirot is waiting to see him, but Crome simply walks up the stairs without acknowledging Poirot at all. Poirot realizes he's being dismissed, and turns and walks out of the station.

Poirot goes to visit Japp (Kevin McNally), and we hear more of Cust's letter: "I'm going to do something for both of us, Hercule. I'm getting my ducks in a row, as they say. I'll let you know when I'm ready. Until then, chin-chin. A.B.C." Poirot even shows Japp other letters he's received from ABC, but shockingly, after Japp warmly invites Poirot to stay for supper, Japp falls over dead. We're shown Japp's funeral, and as we might expect, we hear the Vicar say, "The Lord giveth and the Lord taketh away. Blessed be the Lord. Man that is born of a woman hath but a short time to live." Following this, we see dirt being thrown on Japp's casket.

Poirot finally manages to speak to Crome, and the scene shifts to Crome's office. He's dismissive of Poirot, asking him if he still does "murder parties" for rich people. He then tells Poirot that "you appear to be melting," a reference to Poirot's hair dye running down his neck. Crome gets ever more dismissive and hostile towards Poirot in this scene, and as Poirot leaves, the desk officer (Yelland) is heard laughing at Poirot.

Back in Poirot's apartment, we see him rinsing all the dye from his beard as the camera moves to the crucifix on his wall again, situated close to a picture of Mary and the infant Jesus. Poirot's reflection comes into focus in the glass, as we see a lit candle and hear him praying the Hail Mary in French. He stops as we hear a voiceover of Crome teasing him again. Poirot is then kneeling on a prayer bench directly facing the image of Mary to say his prayer. Poirot tries to pray again, but stops as we hear Crome's voiceover again. After we hear and see repeated dialogue from Poirot's visit to Crome's office, Poirot mutters, "Assassin" twice before we hear a gunshot and see a young man's face. At that point, Poirot stands up and blows out the candle.

These opening scenes tell us quite a bit about how the miniseries views Poirot, and how this view differs from the Poirot we encounter in the novel. First, Poirot is a far older man than in the novel, one who's definitely past his prime. Both the letter and Crome's comments testify to this quality, not to mention Poirot's attempt to appear younger. This sense of irrelevancy dovetails nicely with the overall pallid and pensive tone of the film. Additionally, Poirot's religious identity is punctuated in what we're

---

[26] Christie, *The A.B.C. Murders*, ch. 9.

shown and what we hear. Finally, these scenes strongly hint that Poirot has a secret that will be slowly revealed as the miniseries progresses. In what follows, these characteristics will be obvious in our discussion of the two key components of the film most relevant to our examination. The first is that Poirot isn't who he says he is, who he's claimed to be since immigrating to England. This is related to the second component: Poirot's flashbacks and what they reveal about his past and his character. Both components are infused with the issue of Poirot's religious identity, as we'll see.

Towards the end of Episode 1, Poirot returns to his apartment to find Crome executing a search warrant and boxing up Poirot's letters and papers. Poirot and Crome have an exchange that presages the significance of this adaptation for our discussion, in which Crome accuses Poirot of lying to Japp for years about his identity. Crome explains, "You told him you were a policeman in Belgium before the war, a detective, but you weren't. Questions were asked about you, high up in the food chain.... You were looked into, and there's no record of you." Poirot tries to explain that in an invasion, like the one he experienced in Belgium, "Things are burnt. Buildings. People. Records turned to ash." However, Crome persists, noting, "No one had ever heard your name. No Hercule Poirot registered anywhere in the Belgian police before 1914.... You're not who you say you are. Who the hell are you?" Crome's question here echoes Phelps's goal for the miniseries: to peek behind the mask Poirot has adopted since arriving in England to ask who he really is, or was. The question is answered through the use of increasingly detailed flashbacks.

Episode 2 begins with one such flashback to Poirot arriving as a refugee to England in 1914. When asked his profession, he replies, "Gendarme." Back in the present, we then see Poirot in a church where the Priest is presenting worshipers with the host, repeating the phrase "Corpus Christi" as each approach him to receive it. Poirot, remaining in his seat apart from the other worshippers, has another flashback, very similar to the one at the end of Episode 1. We see the beleaguered face of a young man interspersed with shots of a community praying indoors in French, then the same people outside and recoiling as a shot rings out. Poirot then leaves the church.

Later in Episode 2, Poirot returns to the church and has another flashback. Scenes appear of the young man's face, a man running across golden fields yelling in French that soldiers are coming, a small girl inside a building repeating his warning in French, the running man being shot, and again the people outdoors shrinking in response to the shot. The priest of the church, Father Anselm (Cyril Nri), then tells Poirot that he wishes he'd take Communion, as "It grieves me to see you leave the mass without the Eucharist." The ensuing dialogue is telling, as Poirot replies, "I cannot take Communion without confession. I do not confess." The Father pushes back, saying, "I believe it would bring you some peace." Poirot asks, "Why should we have peace? Why should anyone here now have peace? We should be raging" as he rises from the pews. "Is that what you are, raging?" asks the Father, but Poirot continues, "And doubtful and terrified." "Of what?" "Failure," says Poirot, as he approaches the altar. "Of not being enough." The Father scoffs and replies, "You can't possibly know that you would fail." Turning back to the Father, Poirot says, "Oh, I do. I have failed—failed terribly, catastrophically. I was not enough." Turning back to the altar and looking at the painting of the Crucifixion, Poirot continues, "Nor was He. I doubt Him. I doubt all of it. So, Father Anselm, what do you say to that?" "I say that the confessional is just a few short steps over there. Come with me. You've already spoken it out loud. Say it in there so that I can absolve you, and you can receive the sacrament." As Poirot starts to walk out, the Father says, "God forgives all." Poirot responds, "But I do not," as he leaves the church.

Episode 3 brings more flashbacks from Poirot and they are becoming more intense. It also brings a closer relationship between Crome and Poirot, as the former begins to thaw in his view of the older man and actually begins to collaborate with him in investigating ABC. In a scene in which the two are examining evidence, Crome suggests to Poirot that since ABC seems to know so much about Poirot's life that he might be someone who followed him to England, that the killer might be someone who hated Poirot from "before, in Belgium." Poirot dismisses the idea as "not relevant," but it causes him to have another flashback. We again hear the man running across the golden fields, warning that "They're coming." And we again see the young man, but here he seems to get shot as we watch soldiers advance on the group of people who hide in a building that we now see is a church.

As we might expect, this final episode shows us a series of scenes that explain the plan and actions of ABC (revealed to be Franklin Clarke, the brother of the third victim, Sir Carmichael Clarke), but in a significant departure, there's no "Big Reveal" here. After this revelation, as Poirot is leaving Crome's office, the episode returns to the theme of Poirot's identity when Crome asks him, "What were you? If not a policeman, then what?" Poirot doesn't answer. Instead, we're shown another flashback. It's at this point that we finally see the full content of Poirot's memory, the secret he's been keeping from everyone all these long years. We see the young man running across a field and being shot again, but now Poirot enters the frame, wearing a priest's robe. In French, he tells the people, "In the church! Everyone in the church!" As he enters, he calls them "*Mes enfants*," and reassures them, "This is the house of God, and Christ holds you in his hands. No harm can come to you in here." We see soldiers walking closer across the fields, and Poirot says, "Do not move. Do not shout out." He then exits the church, and we see him approaching the soldiers with his arms outstretched, palms up, seeking to calm and petition them. We finally learn that the young man whose face Poirot continually sees is one of the soldiers. He's obviously terribly conflicted about holding a gun on a priest, but we hear someone shouting, "Shoot him!" and "Don't be a coward," as Poirot continues walking towards him with his arms outstretched. Weeping, the boy lowers his rifle but an officer standing behind Poirot shoots the young boy for disobeying his order. Shocked, Poirot stands and turns to the officer, who knocks him unconscious with his pistol. Poirot wakes to discover that the church is engulfed in flames, his congregation burned alive inside. He falls to his knees in the field and screams, "*Assassin!*" ("Murderer!").[27]

The episode ends with Poirot paying a visit to Franklin where he's being held prior to his execution. The latter tries to rationalize what he's done by claiming his actions had a positive effect on Poirot, that they "restored" him, but Poirot rejects this claim

---

[27] This scene could be a reference to the so-called "Rape of Belgium" which I mention in Chapter 6.

categorically. The killer even goes so far as to say that it was Poirot's "murder parties" that sparked his imagination, and Poirot simply responds, "Franklin, I didn't cast a spell on you. You were kindling lying in wait for a spark. I fear your soul is a charnel house. I grieve for you." Franklin grows angry, and yells at Poirot to tell him his secrets. When Poirot refuses, we see a man holding a book, presumably a priest with a Bible coming to escort Franklin to the gallows. Franklin looks at Poirot and snarls, "As if prayers are going to make the slightest difference." He then stands, walks to Poirot, gently touches the scar on Poirot's head from the officer's pistol, and whispers to him, "You're going to miss me, Hercule." We hear Franklin being hung, and the camera steadies on Poirot's face as the episode ends.

As Aldridge writes, this adaptation is set in a "deliberately provocative, dark and difficult world that doesn't make for comfortable viewing."[28] Further, as we've seen, "Poirot's new backstory [is] directly at odds with what we know of Christie's character."[29] Let's be more precise: what Phelps has done here is to "retcon" Poirot. The term "retcon" is borrowed from literary studies and describes what happens if a later author or filmmaker or, in our case, screenwriter, changes a significant number of details to an established narrative or character. If this happens, they invent what scholars have termed "retroactive continuity" or, have performed a "retcon." Using an example from comic books, Andrew J. Friedenthal defines this performance as follows: "Retconning is the process whereby a comic book creator in some way alters some of the events of the origin, back-story, and/or history of a particular character—changing, for example, the identity of the mugger who killed Batman's parents."[30] Let's continue listening as he helpfully elaborates, sticking with the example of Batman:

> Retconning is most often utilized to literally rewrite some aspect of a character's past, in order to keep that character more contemporary (Batman could not have been active during World War II, or else he would now be in his eighties), to erase stories from continuity that no longer fit by today's standards (Batman either as carrying a gun, in his first appearances, or as a goofy, often-spacefaring, well-adjusted father figure in the 1960's), or to create future story potential (adding a character into the life of Batman from before his parents' death, who then becomes an important ally or enemy of the hero in the present day).

What Phelps and Gabassi have done, then, is to "retcon" Poirot's origin story "to excite a modern television audience used to more hard-edged dramas."[31] The question we must ask—and indeed the question with all retcons—is whether to consider this portrayal of Poirot as "canon." That is, should we accept Phelps's new backstory of Poirot as canonical, or authoritative? Must all future discussions and/or depictions of

---

[28] Aldridge, *Agatha Christie's Poirot*, 440.
[29] Ibid.
[30] Friedenthal, "Monitoring the Past: DC Comics' Crisis on Infinite Earths and the Narrativization of Comic Book History," *ImageTexT: Interdisciplinary Comic Studies* 6:2 (2011) par. 20; available online at https://imagetextjournal.com/monitoring-the-past-dc-comics-crisis-on-infinite-earths-and-the-narrativization-of-comic-book-history/.
[31] Aldridge, *Agatha Christie's Poirot*, 439.

Poirot explicitly agree that he was a priest, not a police officer, in Belgium prior to fleeing to England? The answer seems obvious: no. For many reasons, no.

Even so, we must contend with this rendering of Poirot, and note that this retcon does build on some of the issues I discussed in Chapter 6. Most obviously, here the characterization of Poirot as a prophetic figure, a "father-confessor" who's devoted to "truth" and advocates for the innocent is taken to its logical conclusion in presenting him as a former priest. At the same time, it's a curious rendering of one of England's most popular fictional characters, given the numerical decline in dominant forms of Christianity in England in the twentieth century. That is, why choose to "church up" Poirot at a time when fewer and fewer folks are going to church? One answer could be that even though numbers are indeed declining, the socio-cultural influence (what we characterized as "soft power") of Christianity is still present in the twenty-first century. In other words, characterizing Poirot as a self-loathing, doubt-filled, former priest could resonate with more viewers than one might think. And this choice is certainly an important one for us to explore as we seek to understand how Poirot and his religious identity are rendered in the world the text creates.

10

Curtain

Our final example of how later interpretations of Christie's works address the religious identity of Poirot is *Curtain: Poirot's Last Case*. This novel has always occupied a liminal space in the Poirot canon for two reasons. First, it has a curious publication history. Christie wrote it (and a Marple book eventually called *Sleeping Murder*) in the early 1940s "during the first years of the war," as a kind of insurance policy.[1] She had both of them locked away for several decades, assigning the rights of *Curtain* to her daughter Rosalind, and giving her husband Max rights to the Marple novel. It was finally published in 1975, not long before Christie herself died in January 1976. And second, it tells the story of Poirot pursuing and then murdering a criminal before he himself dies. Obviously, this novel and its sole adaptation are important for our understanding of Poirot and religion.

    Curtain is narrated by Hastings, who'd been absent from Christie's Poirot stories since *Dumb Witness* in 1937.[2] Charles Osborne observes that, "*Curtain* is a sad, muted and nostalgic book," while Marty S. Knepper sees it as "elegiac in tone—for days gone by, lost youth, lost family, lost friendship."[3] And as R. A. York notes, this tone is signaled early on by Hastings, who's is in a pitiful state.[4] His wife (whom he adorably calls "Cinders," short for Cinderella, a pet name he gave her when they met in *The Murder on the Links*) has died and he misses her and her guidance terribly. Further, we learn that Hastings now has four children, one of whom (Judith) is a major character in the novel, and from whom Hastings is alienated. Hastings is returning to Styles to see Poirot, who'd sent for him. In keeping with the themes of sadness and nostalgia in the novel, Hastings reports that Poirot is "very old" and "almost crippled with arthritis" so that he must be in a wheelchair.[5] Despite his physical condition, Poirot maintains that his brain "functions magnificently."[6] Styles has fared no better, and serves as a physical symbol of the ravages of changing times; it's deteriorated and been remodeled as a hostel of sorts.

---

[1] Christie, *An Autobiography* (1977; reis. New York: HarperCollins, 2011), 509.
[2] As noted by Charles Osborne, *The Life and Crimes of Agatha Christie: A Biographical Companion to the Works of Agatha Christie*, rev. and updated ed. (London: HarperCollins, 1999), 368.
[3] Ibid., 369; Marty S. Knepper, "The Curtain Falls: Agatha Christie's Last Novels," *Clues* 23, no. 4 (2005): 75.
[4] York, *Agatha Christie: Power and Illusion*, Crime Files (New York: Palgrave, 2007), 156.
[5] Christie, *Curtain: Poirot's Last Case* (1975; reis. New York: HarperCollins, 2011), Kindle edition, ch. 1.
[6] Ibid., ch. 2.

We learn that Poirot summoned Hastings to Styles so that they could go "hunting" again, a clear reference to the ending of their first adventure and Christie's first novel, *The Mysterious Affair at Styles*.[7] However, he won't tell Hastings who their target is. And since Poirot is incapacitated, Hastings must be his eyes and ears, gathering evidence and reporting back to him. Hastings becomes convinced at one point that he's identified the murderer, a man called Allerton. And what's worse, Hastings also thinks his beloved daughter Judith is falling for him. Always the man of action, Hastings actually plans to kill Allerton, but seemingly falls asleep during his vigil. After the poisoning of Mrs. Franklin and Poirot suffering a serious heart attack, a man called Norton is discovered murdered. Not long after this, Poirot dies of a heart attack in Hastings is understandably crushed, and has him buried at Styles.

For our purposes, the most significant piece of the novel is its Postscript. This section consists mainly of a letter Poirot wrote to Hastings while still at Styles, which Poirot sent to a lawyer to deliver to Hastings four months after his death (which sounds a little like what Christie did with *Curtain*). Astonishingly, it's in this letter that Poirot reveals that he murdered Norton. There are several key points relevant to our attempt to understand how Christie presents Poirot and religion.

Poirot explains to Hastings that, "I had come across at last, at the end of my career, the perfect criminal."[8] Laura Thompson writes of this claim that "the terrible sadness of *Curtain* lies, above all, in its lack of resolution. The murderer is a man who can never be accused and never be caught. He has perfected the technique of inducing other people to commit murder: he has perfected evil."[9] As many commentators have noted, the villain in *Curtain* is modeled on Shakespeare's Iago, from his 1603 drama *Othello*.[10] In fact, *Othello* as a piece of what Jeremy Black calls "living culture" is central for the plot of *Curtain*, and a copy of the play also appears as a key clue in the novel.[11] One of the hallmarks of Iago is that he convinces others to undertake actions that will benefit him and his desires, even murder, yet he himself remains aloof from those actions.[12] Could it be this quality of the murderer, their indirect approach that renders them oblivious to criminal charges, that persuades Poirot to usurp the right to kill for himself? Or could it be the manipulation of those who are innocent—a key concern for Poirot, as we saw in Chapter 6? Earlier, in the first of three philosophic discussions contained in the novel, Dr. Franklin had posed the following hypothetical to Hastings with Poirot present: "Suppose a man thinks he has a divine right to kill a dictator or a money-lender or a pimp or whatever arouses his moral indignation. He commits what *you* consider a guilty deed – but what *he* considers is an innocent one."[13] Franklin's question is, Is this evil or not? Hastings responds that, "there must always be a feeling

7 Ibid.
8 Ibid., Postscript.
9 Thompson, *Agatha Christie: An English Mystery* (London: Headline, 2007); repr. *Agatha Christie: A Mysterious Life* (New York: Pegasus Books, 2018), Kindle edition, "God's Mark."
10 See, e.g., Knepper, "Curtain," 75 and 77; and York, *Agatha Christie*, 158.
11 Black, *The Importance of Being Poirot* (South Bend, IN: St. Augustine's Press, 2021), 182.
12 For example, in Act 3 Scene 3, Iago plots to plant a napkin belonging to Desdemona in Cassio's house so to make Othello jealous.
13 Christie, *Curtain*, ch. 7.

of guilt with murder," but Franklin dismisses this. Surprisingly, Poirot makes no comment, except to say he hopes Franklin "does not practice what he preaches." This example highlights the emphasis on ethical quandaries surrounding justice and the psychological workings of human nature in the novel that will come to a head in a startling climax.

Poirot also claims in his letter that, "Everyone is a potential murderer."[14] While this is a natural corollary to his axiom to "suspect everyone," it's also the point that the unnamed killer exploits by his genius of manipulating others to kill for him (as Poirot notes). As if to prove this claim, Poirot admits to Hastings, "the crime, you see, was to be committed by myself."[15] That is, in a shocking admission, Poirot states, "I, who do not approve of murder—I, who value human life—have ended my career by committing murder. . . . It is my work in life to save the innocent – to prevent murder – and this – this is the only way I can do it!"[16] In his letter, Poirot identifies Norton as the killer for whom they've been hunting. Norton, Poirot claims, was the driving force behind Hastings's decision to kill Allerton. Luckily, Poirot drugged Hastings to prevent him from doing so, but became afraid that Norton would start to focus on Judith. So, Poirot confronts Norton and tells him he knows everything. Norton "smirks" at Poirot and asks what he's going to do about it, to which the elderly detective replied, "I told him that I proposed to execute him."[17] Poirot then describes how he drugged Norton and the various actions he undertook to return him to his room and then kill him by shooting him "symmetrically," directly in the center of his forehead.[18]

Poirot has been apostrophizing Hastings throughout the letter, and does so at this point again in a moving declaration and exhortation: "And you, my poor lonely Hastings? Ah, my heart bleeds for you, dear friend. Will you, for the last time, take the advice of your old Poirot? . . . Go to find Elizabeth Cole"—a woman who Poirot wants Hastings to marry, thus alleviating his loneliness—and be her friend.[19] Poirot then becomes ruminative, cogitating on the morality of his actions:

> I do not know, Hastings, if what I have done is justified or not justified. No – I do not know. I do not believe that a man should take the law into his own hands . . .
> But on the other hand, I am the law! As a young man in the Belgian police force I shot down a desperate criminal who sat on a roof and fired at people below. In a state of emergency martial law is proclaimed. By taking Norton's life, I have saved

---

[14] Ibid., Postscript.

[15] Ibid., Postscript. That Poirot commits a crime that goes undetected seems the logical conclusion of a series of comments about the possibility/potential of him being an expert criminal (which is another legacy of Holmes). See, e.g., several of the stories collected in *Hercule Poirot: The Complete Short Stories* (New York: HarperCollins, 2013), Kindle book, viz., "The Million Dollar Bond Robbery," "Jewel Robbery at the Grand Metropolitan," "The Veiled Lady," "The Market Basing Mystery" and "The Dream." See also *Death in the Clouds* (1935; reis. New York: HarperCollins, 2008), Kindle edition, ch. 3, "Croydon;" and "Murder in the Mews," in *Murder in the Mews: Four Cases of Hercule Poirot* (1937; reis. New York: HarperCollins, 2011), Kindle edition.

[16] Christie, *Curtain*, Postscript. Again, see Thompson, *Agatha Christie*, "God's Mark."

[17] Christie, *Curtain*, Postscript.

[18] Ibid.

[19] Ibid.

other lives—innocent lives. But still I do not know ... It is perhaps right that I should not know. I have always been so sure—too sure ... But now I am very humble and I say like a little child "I do not know ..."[20]

Here we see Poirot documenting his internal debate over the morality of his actions. On the one hand, as a policeman he has sworn to uphold the law, and thus to reject the kind of vigilante justice he grapples with in *Murder on the Orient Express*. On the other hand, though, he must acknowledge that the murder of Norton will undoubtedly save innocent lives—something that is preeminent in his mind. As Patricia D. Maida and Nicholas B. Spornick describe it,

> When all ordinary means of bringing him to justice fail, Poirot takes the law into his own hands. He acts alone but with the conviction of his conscience.... The ultimate rationale then is a pragmatic one—murder or execution is sometimes necessary for the protection of society (just as it is in time of war). Thus Poirot's actions may be viewed as a kind of self-sacrifice in behalf of his fellowmen.[21]

This idea of self-sacrifice fits well with our discussion in Chapter 6 regarding how many characters (including himself) see Poirot as a kind of religious figure. An echo of this theme is found in J. C. Bernthal's writing on this section of the letter. He writes that Poirot "believes that he embodies 'the law', but also knows that this is dangerous, and ultimately gives himself up to God's judgement by evoking the words of Christ in Matthew's gospel, who commanded the faithful to 'humble [themselves] as little children' in order to receive the love of God (Matt. 18.4)."[22] Nevertheless, that he is wrestling with the ethical implications of murder is seen in his final comments regarding his suicide and God's judgement, which are obviously key in our examination. He writes, "Goodbye, *cher ami*. I have moved the amyl nitrate ampoules away from beside my bed. I prefer to leave myself in the hands of the *bon Dieu*. May his punishment, or his mercy, be swift!"[23]

It is also key for us to recall that the novel ends not with Poirot's death, but with a comment from Hastings. After reading Poirot's letter, he notes in passing that "The mark on Norton's forehead—it was like the brand of Cain...."[24] As the text box shows, this biblical imagery was resonant in some fashion for Christie, as she employed it to describe murders in the exact same way in works published closely together. But what could it mean?

[20] Ibid.
[21] Maida and Spornick, *Murder She Wrote: A Study of Agatha Christie's Detective Fiction* (Bowling Green, OH: Bowling Green State University Popular Press, 1982), 103.
[22] Bernthal, "'A Dangerous World': The Hermeneutics of Agatha Christie's Later Novels," in *The Bible in Crime Fiction and Drama: Murderous Texts*, eds. Alison Jack and Caroline Blyth; Scriptural Traces: Critical Perspectives on the Reception and Influence of the Bible, 16; LHB/OTS, 678; (London & New York: Bloomsbury, 2019), 171.
[23] Christie, *Curtain*, Postscript.
[24] Ibid.

The Mark of Cain

There are two points to make regarding the so-called Mark of Cain. First, the image of a mark or brand on the forehead of Adam and Eve's son Cain is found in Genesis 4:15 at the culmination of the narrative of the first human murder, one of fratricide. As Eva Mroczek points out, there are numerous understandings of what this mark might mean. Some think it's a protective mark, others feel it's a physical indicator of a cursed nature, and still others understand it as a sign of moral deformity associated with dark skin. In the end, Mroczek writes, "These diverse explanations . . . do not tell us what the text's original writers intended. But they do reflect the conflicted attitudes that Bible readers, ancient and modern, have had toward Cain himself." A second point concerns Christie's 1939 novel *Ten Little Niggers* (later republished in the US in 1940 as *And Then There Were None*). In the final chapter, we learn the identity of the ingenious murderer by their own admission, which is also a letter meant to be read after their death. The culprit, Justice Lawrence Wargrave, describes how he'll commit suicide following the completion of his letter and its depositing in a bottle in the sea. Wargrave notes in his letter that the way he was killed will be the third of three clues he's leaving for the police. He writes, "The manner of my death marking me on my forehead. The brand of Cain." Again, we see that not only does Christie assumes a modicum of biblical literacy from her readers, but also that exploring her biblical allusions leads to a deeper understanding of the function of such symbolism.

Black comments on the "theme of biblical judgment" indicated by Hastings's description, but Bernthal delves more deeply, writing,

> the bullet-wound can be read not so much as evidence of murder or execution as of branding; he has identified and judged a murderer, as the law cannot do. The mark of judgment is neat and symmetrical, so distinctly Poirot's, not [God's] – but if we take Poirot and Norton to be two sides of a coin, then the bullet-wound might also be the visible sign that God says his prophets must 'fix' upon their foreheads when they have understood his commandments (Deut. 11:18).[25]

Bernthal's interpretation has the benefit of connecting Poirot's murderous act with the characterization of him as a prophetic figure, but he and Black have hit on an important theme present in both *Curtain* and Christie's 1939/1940 novel *And Then There Were None*, namely, the theme of judgment on criminals who have or will escape the law. York highlights the parallels between Judge Wargrave (the killer in *And Then There Were None*) and Poirot without mentioning the biblical allusion:

[25] Black, *Importance*, 182; Bernthal, "'Dangerous'," 172.

There are great differences between the judge and Poirot. Poirot does not have the judge's wholehearted certainty of the justification of his acts and he certainly does not have the sense that the punishments are a virtuoso demonstration of lethal ingenuity. He stops short of suicide, merely failing to take the medicine which would counter the heart attack he expects. But he resembles the judge in stepping over the line between investigation and intervention, and in doing so he usurps the right to punish which is properly the responsibility of the legal apparatus of the state.[26]

In this description, one also sees the emphasis on "intervention" in Poirot's vocation. Here, we also need to note Knepper's claim—which York tries to temper—that in her last works, with their "emphasis on psychological aberration as a cause of evil, the suffering of innocents, and secret crime undetected or unpunishable by establishment justice," Christie alters the fundamental characterization of her sleuths.[27] According to Knepper, Christie "puts the detectives—particularly Poirot and Miss Marple—in the role of avenger, not just investigator."[28] That is, these late works show Poirot et al., "as agents of justice working to protect the innocent from characters whose evil is particularly insidious and dangerous."[29] Before we address the potential meaning(s) behind the ending of the novel and the characterization of Poirot, let's examine how the novel was adapted for the final season of *Agatha Christie's Poirot*.

* * *

In the 2013 adaptation of the novel—the only adaptation I know of in any genre—the melancholy, nostalgic tone of the novel is replicated nicely, beginning with Frédéric Chopin's Prelude, Op. 28, No. 15 in D-flat (aka the "Raindrop" Prelude) being played over the intro of the film. Since the film was released in the thirteenth and final series, both Hugh Fraser and David Suchet were of an age to depict Hastings and Poirot as much older men. Like several other adaptations in this show, the film contains several scenes not found in the novel that bear mention. Let's focus on three of these and see what they can tell us about Poirot's religious identity.

First, as in the novel, Poirot berates Hastings for not using "his grey cells." Afterward, though, the former talks aloud to the as yet unknown killer: "At it again, are you. . . at your deadly exercise? I knew you would be. For my sins, I knew you would. But while I have breath in my body, I will. . ." and his speech trails off while he has trouble breathing because of angina. He takes his medicine (amyl nitrite), then grabs his rosary from the nightstand, and caresses it as he gasps out, "I will damn you to hell, whatever the cost!" The use of religious language here, coupled with the repeated image of Poirot with his

---

[26] York, *Agatha Christie*, 161.
[27] Knepper, "Curtain," 78.
[28] Knepper's word choice here is deliberate, as both Poirot and Marple are referred to as an "avenger" in later works. See *Third Girl* (1966; reis. New York: HarperCollins, 2011), Kindle edition, ch. 21; and *Nemesis* (1971; reis. New York: HarperCollins, 2011), Kindle edition, ch. 22, "Miss Marple Tells Her Story."
[29] Knepper, "Curtain," 81.

rosary—an echo of the scene in the 2010 Suchet adaptation of *Murder on the Orient Express*—establishes a much more confrontational relationship between him and Norton, one that's grounded in a good vs. evil dichotomy. This kind of dichotomizing is often found at the root of religious violence, and often leads to "what the sociologist of religion Peter Berger refers to as *cosmization*, activities that occur in the ordinary routine world of human existence but are simultaneously enacted in a supernatural realm of divine truth whose significance transcends all human understanding."[30] Put differently, if Poirot views Norton as wholly evil via this lens of cosmic dualism, then it's far easier to justify murdering him, as he's clearly on the wrong side of the universal moral equation. This dichotomy will be emphasized again in our third example.

Second, after Norton is found dead, Poirot asks Hastings if he believes that Poirot has always strived to do his best. When Hastings responds in the affirmative, Poirot begins to cry slightly, and asks, "Do you think God will forgive me?" Hastings reassures him that God will certainly forgive him, as he's "a good man, the best a fellow could know." After Poirot expresses a sincere sympathy for "my poor, lonely Hastings," he asks his friend to leave him. As Hastings gets up to go, Poirot tells him that Norton's death "was not suicide. It was murder." Hastings turns to look at him, and Chopin's "Raindrop" Prelude begins as Hastings walks out of the room. Poirot then whispers, "*Cher ami*," as an attack of angina hits him. Instead of reaching for his amyl nitrite, he grasps his rosary. Praying to God one last time, he gasps out "Forgive me . . . forgive . . ." as he dies. The scene then shifts to Hastings walking into the room where Miss Cole (Helen Baxendale) is playing the Chopin Prelude. She stops, rises, and says "Captain Hastings?" A startled Hastings then bolts, rushing upstairs to Poirot's room, where he discovers that Poirot has died.

Third and finally, after the previous scene, the remaining thirty minutes of the ninety-nine-minute film consist of a voiceover from Poirot reading his letter, while we see the events described therein. For example, we're shown in a flashback sequence the exchange between Norton and Poirot, which we don't see in the book. Part of that exchange is relevant for our purposes. After Poirot tells Norton he plans to execute him, Norton makes light of Poirot's plan. Poirot then angrily responds, "Justice is no joking matter, Monsieur. I do what I can to serve it, but if I fail, there is a justice that is higher, believe me." Norton sneers, "You pathetic, self-important little man. Murder me? There's a mortal sin if ever there was. And then what? Suicide to escape the ignominy of hanging? Ah. Your God will give you a hell of a time. All those years of piety up in smoke because of me." Poirot then begins to have an attack of angina, but as he wheels over to a table to fetch his medicine, Norton takes it before he can reach it. As Poirot pleads for his medicine, Norton elucidates their situation: "You see, if you don't succeed, I am a free man, and even if you do, it will still be a victory of sorts, because in the eyes of the law, I would be innocent, whereas you and your reputation, your precious reputation—blown to bits." Norton eventually gives Poirot his medicine, but continues to taunt him, "See how good I am to you, old man? . . . Take your time, and see how it all pans out, shall we? Who will be there at the final curtain?"

---

[30] Charles Selengut, *Sacred Fury: Understanding Religious Violence* (Walnut Creek, CA: AltaMira Press/ Lanham, MD: Rowman & Littlefield, 2003), 21.

Again, the cosmic dualism I noted earlier returns with Poirot's mention of a higher justice. For his part, Norton plays into this scheme by taunting Poirot's faith and referring to "Your God," to make it obvious that he sees himself outside of the discourse of Poirot's Catholicism. The exchange continues, and as Poirot tries to antagonize Norton, he realizes Norton is simply playing with him. Poirot then offers him a cup of hot chocolate, which is drugged with sleeping pills. In this adaptation, we're shown that Norton wakes up right as Poirot is about to shoot him, and he smiles at Poirot right before the fatal gunshot.

We hear Chopin again, and again are shown Hastings running up the stairs to find his dear friend dead. At this point, Poirot's voice says, "I have no more to say. Am I justified in what I have done? I do not know. I do not believe that a man should take the law into his own hands, but by taking the life of Norton, *have I not saved others?*" Poirot then voices his uncertainty, saying "I have always been so sure, but now ..." At this point, his voice trails off as he picks up his rosary and kisses the cross. Finally, Poirot concludes, "When the moment comes, I will not try to save myself, but humbly offer my soul to God and pray for his mercy. It is for Him to decide." After he signs his name to the letter and removes his *pince-nez*, Poirot looks directly into the camera as we hear an echo of the famous saxophone solo from the theme of the series before the screen goes dark.

As we saw in the novel, even though Poirot is convinced that his actions will result in the saving of innocent people and others' lives, he's clearly ambivalent about the ultimate result of his actions. Part of this ambiguity may lie in the world behind the text, as Christie was writing during the War in the early 1940s. One could argue that up to this point, readers could easily "identify Poirot and Miss Marple as Christians with a strong sense of morality and justice."[31] More specifically, "Poirot stands for justice, in large part, to defend and protect the innocent but also to punish the guilty—generally, but not always, by operating through conventional legal channels."[32] However, it could be that the experience of a second World War had Christie asking uncomfortable questions about the certainty of her inherited Empire and faith. Along these lines, Knepper argues that in *Curtain*, as in other late works, "Christie explores abnormal human psychology and the importance and limits of human justice within a religious context," as she "found herself intrigued with the moral and theological implications of the form" of detective fiction.[33] York likewise feels that Christie is presenting a far more ethically ambiguous world here, writing, "Morally, the novel falls short of a condemnation of murder, and so of the sense of an unchallenged rule of justice. . . . Even Poirot's assertion, frequently made in the other novels, that he disapproves of murder, is abandoned."[34] Ultimately, York claims, "We have, rather than a world of good and evil, a world of conflicting wills or conflicting personalities, Norton's viciously random murderousness competing with Poirot's reluctant and carefully targeted murderousness. The detective story approaches a justification of murder; and perhaps

---

[31] Knepper, "Curtain," 78.
[32] Ibid.
[33] Ibid., 80.
[34] York, *Agatha Christie*, 162.

Christie may have reflected on how far the genre's fascination with murder itself implies some sympathy for it."[35] If you're thinking that this moral confusion sounds terrifying and out-of-step with the overarching assumptions of Golden Age detective fiction I mentioned in Chapter 1, then you get a gold star.

In his memoir of playing Poirot, Suchet has written of this scene and points out that in his reading, Poirot is terrified, too, of this religious and ethical uncertainty. That is, "there is a part of this final story that has made him wonder whether God will truly ever forgive him for his actions, and, as a good Catholic, that thought troubles him deeply."[36] He clearly has earned divine punishment, like so many of the killers he has identified in his long career, and is "struggling with the fear that there might be no redemption."[37]

But could it be that God will be merciful? Might Poirot himself reap the benefit of God's beneficence and escape judgment, as he himself often allowed criminals to do? Neither the novels nor the adaptations answer those questions for us, nor could they. What seems clear, though, is how Christie situates all of these issues within a framework of Christian hegemony and normativity. That is, both the religious language and the way in which religious issues are framed are via the dominant form of Christianity of her day. At the same time, though, we've seen how she pushes back against that normative Christianity. In *Curtain*, this resistance is seen most obviously in the fact that it's Poirot who murders and questions his own religious faith over that murder. Yet Christie cannot abandon or completely abrogate her inherited Christianity. Because of that, Poirot must not only commit a sinful act, but also await with trepidation the eschatological result of that act. That is, the assumptions of the dominant form of Christianity are still in effect, even if there are cracks in the universal acceptance of those assumptions.

Conclusion(s) to Part Three

In Chapters 6 and 7, I've brought together a variety of data from roughly a half-century of Christie's Poirot stories (focusing mainly on the worlds behind and of the text) to try and piece together what we can of Poirot's worldview. Obviously, I've privileged the religious content of that worldview to determine how it helps us see him using that component of his identity in his ethical thought and moral action. I've also foregrounded how these discourses are dealt with (or not) in the world the text creates, especially in Chapters 8–10. So, what have we learned?

To restate the obvious, Christie never intended to write a biography of Poirot, much less a spiritual one. This recognition is in keeping with the broader observation that in general, her characterization was never particularly deep. Nevertheless, it seems clear that Poirot was born into an area (Belgium) that was overwhelmingly Catholic, and

---

[35] Ibid.
[36] Suchet and Geoffrey Wansell *Poirot and Me* (London: Headline, 2013), 5.
[37] Ibid., 11.

thus would have been reared and socialized in a content of Christian hegemony. My brief investigation into education in Belgium in Chapter 7 demonstrates that whatever educational experiences Poirot might have received would have been compulsorily Catholic and supervised by Church representatives. This early experience of Catholicism functions determinatively for Poirot, as even after his emigration to England, he defines himself as a *bon catholique*, and his Catholic outlook shapes his beliefs and actions in the novels.

The importance of understanding this aspect of religion in Christie's Poirot stories is twofold. First, this understanding helps us interpret the attitudes and choices Poirot demonstrates and makes in the stories and novels. This, in turn, allows us a greater depth of insight into not only his character, but also the Christian hegemony and normativity of Christie's fictional world. And this awareness permits us a fuller appreciation of all of the worlds (behind the text, of the text, and that created by the text) that intersect in the diminutive figure of our little Belgian. Second, it assists us in grasping the modernist nature of her choice of Poirot as her sleuth. Put differently, Christie chooses a foreign, feminine, cerebral, urban, cosmopolitan, and *Catholic* detective. By doing so, she's kicking against the goads of her inherited literary tradition hard enough to crack but not break.

As we'll see in Part Four, one clear indication of those cracks lies in the presence and socio-theological existence and problems associated with other religious orientations. Traditionally, the Christianity of Christie's time saw these other traditions as inferior, a position that followed naturally from the internal belief in Christian superiority.

To wit, Khyati Y. Joshi—echoing some of the points I made in Chapters 2 and 6 regarding schooling and religious literacy—relates a story about when she was in the ninth grade and her teacher brought up the story of the Good Samaritan in an English class.[38] Because of her background, she didn't understand the reference, and draws two meaningful conclusions from this example in her work. First, "Due to Christian normativity, these sayings and stories are often used with the assumption that everyone understands what they mean."[39] And second, "a person who doesn't know or understand the metaphor can't participate in the conversation."[40] Put differently, in a culture characterized by Christian hegemony and normativity, it seems "natural" that everyone *should* understand Christian language and stories and symbols (Joshi's structural/external dimension) since the underlying assumption of such a culture is that Christianity is a superior religion (Joshi's attitudinal/internal dimension). If someone *doesn't* understand, then they're not really "our type" of people. In Joshi's terms, this example highlights how Christian hegemony creates both a "norm" and an "other."[41] This "othering" and how Christie pushes back against it is exactly what we'll discuss in the final four chapters.

[38] Joshi, *White Christian Privilege: The Illusion of Religious Equality in America* (New York: New York University Press, 2020), 148–149.
[39] Ibid., 148.
[40] Ibid., 149.
[41] Ibid., 134–135.

Part Four

"Other" Religions in Christie's Poirot Stories

Introduction to Part Four

Agatha Christie was a product of her time—that world behind the text we explored in Part One. As Patricia D. Maida and Nicholas B. Spornick put it, she was "a person shaped by the forces of family and environment and imbued with the pervasive values of Edwardian society," someone who was "stalwart in her Victorian values."[1] More specific to our purposes, that means she was reared in an environment characterized by the dominance of an establishment Christianity, one that conditioned all aspects of life, from architecture to politics to education to food.[2] This Christian normativity, as Khyati Y. Joshi calls it, is echoed in her Poirot stories in the way in which she uses religious language and scriptural citations and allusions, like the ones we examined in Parts Two and Three. More than that, though, it serves to create a sense of shared identity, a common worldview, between author and reader.

In Part One, we also explored the worldview imparted to the young Christie as a product of the Victorian and Edwardian periods, focusing specifically on the aforementioned normative Christianity in which she was socialized and which is reflected in her work. To reiterate, Christie assumes a certain amount of religious literacy on the part of her reader, and this literacy is built upon the discourse of a normative Christian culture in which that particular type of Christianity suffuses one's individual and communal identity deeply and thoroughly. However, I've also argued that Christie pushes back against these ideological forces in her work. I, along with other scholars, see Christie as a modernist author, meaning that she felt free to reexamine inherited assumptions and to revise both genres and influential literary influences (such as the Bible) in her work. As such, and given how we've defined the baseline of Christian hegemony and normativity, it'll be much more apparent that Christie is resisting those ideologies in her treatment of non-majority Christian groups and minority religious traditions. That is, we've seen how Christie engages in subtle inversions or alterations to the biblical texts she employs. However, her resistance will be far more obvious when applied to groups that exist beyond the fray of the in-group audience she assumes in her work. Another way of broaching that issue is to ask what happens when the normative status of Christianity is challenged by someone outside it? How do characters who either aren't Christian or are the wrong kind of Christian fare in Christie's Poirot stories? And what can these non-normative or discordant groups tell us about religion in the Poirot canon?

As an initial answer to these questions, let's return to Khyati Y. Joshi's work. We've discussed her analyses of Christian hegemony and normativity and used these as frames

---

[1] Maida and Spornick, *Murder She Wrote: A Study of Agatha Christie's Detective Fiction* (Bowling Green, OH: Bowling Green State University Popular Press, 1982), 5 and 32.
[2] Ibid., 33.

for understanding Christie's use of Christian language and imagery. As we saw, Joshi also discusses the impact of these phenomena on non-Christians, or members of minority religious traditions. Her thoughts are worth quoting in full here, as she writes that

> Christian normalcy implies that what is not Christian is not merely different, but is different in a way that diminishes it. A *norm* defines and is defined by its opposite: the "other," the exclusion of that which is simultaneous with, and mirrors, the inclusion of that which is normal. The norm encompasses everything from theological "truth" to manners and customs of practice; by comparison, the "other" religions come to be seen as deviant, wrongful, evil, or sick. That which is associated with the Christian norm is considered religious or spiritual, while that which is not is rendered exotic and illegitimate and relegated to cult status. By attributing to a population certain characteristics in order to categorize and differentiate it as an "other," those who do so also establish criteria by which they themselves are represented. In the act of defining religious minorities as deviant, Christians represent themselves as good, normal, and righteous.[3]

Warren J. Blumenfeld argues similarly to Joshi in noting that a hegemonic Christian culture has a deleterious impact on non-Christians. He defines Christian hegemony as "the overarching system of advantages bestowed on Christians. It is the institutionalization of a Christian norm or standard, which establishes and perpetuates the notion that all people are or should be Christian, thereby privileging Christians and Christianity, and excluding the needs, concerns, religious cultural practices, and life experiences of people who are not Christian."[4]

Obviously, Blumenfeld is interested in the privileges Christian hegemony affords to Christians, and he writes that privilege constitutes

> a seemingly invisible, unearned, and largely unacknowledged array of benefits accorded to Christians, with which they often unconsciously walk through life as if effortlessly carrying a knapsack tossed over their shoulders. This system of benefits confers dominance on Christians while subordinating members of other faith communities as well as non-believers. These systemic inequities are pervasive throughout the society. They are encoded into the individual's consciousness and woven into the fabric of our social institutions.[5]

And how are they "encoded"? Blumenfeld emphasizes the role of "the ideas, written expressions, theoretical foundations, and language of the dominant culture. These are implanted within networks of social and political control ... which function to

---

[3] Joshi, *White Christian Privilege: The Illusion of Religious Equality in America* (New York: New York University Press, 2020), 134–135.
[4] Blumenfeld, "Christian Privilege and the Promotion of 'Secular' and Not-So 'Secular' Mainline Christianity in Public Schooling and in the Larger Society," *Equity & Excellence in Education* 39 (2006): 196.
[5] Ibid., 195.
[6] Ibid., 196.

legitimize what can be said, who has the authority to speak and be heard, and what is authorized as true or as the truth."[6] The point of noting how Joshi and Blumenfeld describe the way(s) in which hegemonic and normative Christianity view discordant religious groups is that this would've been the dominant view that Christie inherited about this issue. That is, if the kind of establishment Christianity in England in the nineteenth to the mid-twentieth centuries was, indeed, hegemonic and claimed to be normative, then the attitudes Joshi and Blumenfeld note regarding non-dominant groups would've been in the air, so to speak. Because of this, it's more apparent and significant when we find Christie pushing back against those viewpoints.

I'll show in Part Four, then, that these often-subtle processes of Christian hegemony vis-à-vis "other" religions are present in Christie's Poirot works. Put differently, this process of creating an "other" in order to solidify the positive qualities one wishes to present about oneself and one's own group, the social marginalization, and even the religious exclusion implicit in the phenomena Joshi and Blumenfeld describe can all be found in one way or another in the works we'll discuss in Chapters 11–14. Further, I'll demonstrate that Christie doesn't simply go along with these processes or viewpoints, but in almost every case challenges her inherited worldview. Before we go too much further in this direction, though, let's begin with the world of the text.

First, let's remind ourselves that Christie's stories are populated with stock characters and stereotypes. Mary S. Wagoner notes that Christie's "stories rarely offer complex character analysis and involve only vestigial character development in the sense of a character's growing or changing."[7] Part of this is due to the limitation of genre, or what Earl F. Bargainnier calls the "requirements of characterization in detective fiction."[8] In other words, characters in detective fiction don't need to have "extensive psychological development" since they exist mainly "to accomplish the action of the plot."[9] In addition to recycling stock characters, Christie also made use of stereotypes in her characterization. We'll explore this issue in more detail when we examine her treatment of Jews and Muslims, but suffice it for now to echo how Callum G. Brown and Hugh McLeod describe the way in which religion impacted the way(s) in which practitioners understood themselves and others. As will become clear, this issue of sectarian identity is important for our subject. McLeod writes, "Children were brought up from an early age to be aware of the symbols of their own religion, and to regard adherents of the rival faith in terms of a series of hostile stereotypes."[10] Even though he focuses mainly on the "cleavage between Catholics and Protestants," this cognizance of the stories and images of one's own tradition as normative coupled with the sense of otherness in other forms of religiosity has a significant impact on how we'll understand Christie's works.

The importance of pointing out the values and the ideological/theological hegemony with which Christie was raised and how she constructs and populates her fictional

---

[7] Wagoner, *Agatha Christie*, Twayne's English Authors Series (Boston: G. K. Hall & Co., 1986), 16.

[8] Bargainnier, *The Gentle Art of Murder: The Detective Fiction of Agatha Christie* (Bowling Green, OH: Bowling Green University Popular Press, 1980), 38.

[9] Ibid., 38.

[10] McLeod, *Religion and Society in England, 1850-1914*, Social History in Perspective (New York: St. Martin's Press, 1996), 84.

world is that aberrations within that world become much more obvious. As Robert Barnard writes, Christie "was of the middle-middle class, and had some of the prejudices of the middle-middle class. Most of the characters in her novels are 'her sort of people,' and the outsider marks himself clearly off as such."[11] R. A. York agrees, noting that in Christie's construction of character, she exhibits a "profound ambiguity." That is,

> On the one hand, there is a firm assertion of the strength and self-sufficiency of the individual. On the other, people are perceived as justified by membership of an established class, as being "like us," as being what we expect and think normal, and those outside the given frame, by reason of nationality, class, race, gender role or sexual preference, are considered with a concern sometimes amounting to a puzzled distrust.[12]

As we'll see, this "distrust" of people "outside the given frame" will be seen in all four of the "others" we discuss in Part Four. At the same time, though, this "othering" will remain incomplete for three of the four groups we're examining thanks to Christie's questioning of this process of alterity.

In the same way, Bargainnier's work is very helpful in understanding how Christie reflects the values and presuppositions of the "world behind the text." He summarizes what he calls the "social setting" of Christie's works by opining that Christie was part of the "English upper middleclass, and the world of this class forms the social scene of her fiction. . . . Her values were those of her class: trust in reason, desire for stability, belief in civilized conduct, faith in property and a strong sense of morality."[13] He continues, "Social forms and attitudes are integral to the action of the classic detective story. Christie uses them as a framework of cause and effect to make explicable the actions of her characters. They act as they do because of the social class to which they belong."[14] Some of these attitudes include "Snobbery and narrow chauvinism, even xenophobia," the latter of which would include negative views of "foreigners" and "anti-semitism," the latter of which we'll discuss later.[15] Bargainnier then treats the expression of these attitudes in Christie's work, pointing out that "the prejudices of [her] class do occasionally appear in her fiction." Even so, Christie was "craftsman enough to suppress them to the extent that readers of all classes and nationalities have responded to other elements and never been troubled by those prejudices that do appear."[16]

In what follows, we'll examine several of these prejudices in both Christie's Poirot canon and later adaptations thereof in various genres. Along the way, we'll explore a discordant form of Christianity (Chapter 11), Spiritualism (Chapter 12), and minority

---

[11] Barnard, *A Talent to Deceive: An Appreciation of Agatha Christie* (New York: Mysterious Press, 1980), 31.

[12] R. A. York, *Agatha Christie: Power and Illusion*, Crime Files (Hampshire & New York: Palgrave Macmillan, 2007), 61–62. I'd obviously add "religion" to York's list.

[13] Bargainnier, *Gentle Art*, 30.

[14] Ibid., 31.

[15] Ibid., 33–34. See also the chapter titled "Xenophobia" in Jeremy Black's book *The Importance of Being Poirot* (South Bend, IN: St. Augustine's Press, 2021), 68–83.

[16] Bargainnier, *Gentle Art*, 34.

religions in England like Judaism and Islam in Chapters 13 and 14. Finally, we'll see that while Christie indicates through various means the received viewpoint that these religious expressions are not in keeping with the "acceptable" religion of her class, neither are they completely disregarded or vilified, as in other Golden Age crime fiction.

11

A Christian "Cult"

The Victorian period was, by all accounts, an age of rapid transformation and transition. As Sherri Lynne Lyons writes, "Issues that had supposedly been settled for centuries were now open to vigorous debate. Religious beliefs, ethical theory, and human nature were all topics subjected to critical discussion and scrutiny."[1] Among the causes of these discussions and the loss of prestige and authority one sees in traditional ecclesiastical and social institutions, we may include industrialization, urbanization, the rationalistic legacy of Enlightenment thought, the rise of higher-critical approaches to biblical interpretation, the dissemination of Darwin's theories, the demonstrable decline of church and chapel attendance, and changing views of gender roles.[2]

Speaking of church attendance—an aspect of that "hard power" of Christianity I mentioned in Chapter 2—one of the most important pieces of data we have for the prevalence of Christianity in Victorian England in the modern era is the religious census conducted in March of 1851. The snapshot of attendance on Sunday the 30th in that month tells us that "approximately 40 per cent of the adult population attended some kind of service."[3] Scholars break that figure down further to note that "51 per cent of those attending church on the day of the census went to an Anglican service," while "44 per cent of those counted at worship attended one of the Nonconformist chapels."[4] The remaining attendees were primarily made up of Catholics at about 4 percent, with a whole host of miscellaneous other minority religions accounting for the rest of the 1 percent left over. Imperfect as it may be, what this data tells us is that the vast majority of those attending religious services on that specific day in 1851 identified as Christian.

While attendance figures declined significantly in the remainder of the nineteenth century—as they did precipitously in the twentieth century as well—these numbers

---

[1] Lyons, *Species, Serpents, Spirits, and Skulls: Science at the Margins in the Victorian Age* (Albany: State University of New York Press, 2009), 3.

[2] Herbert Schlossberg addresses higher biblical criticism, rationalistic science, and Darwin's work in *Conflict and Crisis in the Religious Life of Late Victorian England* (New Brunswick & London: Transaction Publishers, 2009), 21–58.

[3] Hugh McLeod, *Religion and Society in England, 1850–1914*, Social History in Perspective (New York: St. Martin's Press, 1996), 20.

[4] Ibid., 11. On pp. 30–31, McLeod breaks down the Nonconformist groups into three categories, but for our purposes it's enough to mention the most well-known examples, including Congregationalists, Wesleyans/Methodists, and Presbyterians.

don't speak to piety or belief.[5] That is, the census didn't ask about individual beliefs or practices, so we must imagine some variance in how those attending (and not attending) on Census Sunday performed and thought about their beliefs. As we've seen, Christie reflects yet resists an acceptable, normalized version of religion that evinces a dominant form of Christianity current in her time. We'll also see soon how Christie's early home life conditioned this view of acceptable religion, as it was practiced by both her father and her "Nursie." On the other hand, Christie acknowledges that her mother's religious quests took her off the beaten path, so to speak, to engage with some of the forms of religious practice that Christie would later paint as discordant in her Poirot stories, such as Spiritualism, which we'll examine in Chapter 12. Christie's early life, then, sowed the seeds of both her recognition of/affinity with what we've been calling hegemonic Christianity, as well as her critical, modernist response to it. Let's begin, though, with an example of an unacceptable version of Christianity.

* * *

The Labours of Hercules is one of Christie's more interesting conceptual books.[6] A collection of twelve Poirot stories published elsewhere from 1939–1947, they're all thematically linked by the central image of the labors performed by Hercules in classical Greek myth. These stories are generally well-regarded, and Mary S. Wagoner even goes so far as to call them Christie's "best single-figure collection."[7] As Wagoner notes, these stories are a "complex comic adaptation" of "the myths of Hercules" in which Christie "wittily juxtaposes her little detective's heroism with Hercules' and modern with classical social pests."[8]

In one of these stories called "The Flock of Geryon," a woman named Miss Carnaby—who first appeared in another story in this collection called "The Nemean Lion"—returns.[9] In the previous tale, Poirot discovered that Carnaby was running a kind of animal kidnapping ring along with other domestic servants to offset their lack of retirement money. He so admired her organization and motives that he agreed to convince the husband of his client not to prosecute if she'd return the money from her most recent mark, the woman who'd hired him in the first place. In fact, Poirot even

[5] For this decline, See, e.g., Aimee E. Barbeau, 'Christian Empire and National Crusade: The Rhetoric of Anglican Clergy in the First World War', *Anglican and Episcopal History* 85, no. 1 (2016): 32–33; Callum G. Brown, *The Death of Christian Britain: Understanding Secularization, 1800–2000*, 2nd edn (London & New York: Routledge, 2009), 5; and Matthew Grimley, 'The Religion of Englishness: Puritanism, Providentialism, and "National Character," 1918–1945', *Journal of British Studies* 46, no. 4 (2007): 886–887.
[6] Unlike other examples of the world the text creates, I won't examine the adaptation of these stories in *Agatha Christie's Poirot*. The version that appeared in Series 13 of the show was very loosely based on a few stories in the collection, and the story I'm focusing on here isn't among them. For a more detailed summary of this collection see Charles Osborne, *The Life and Crimes of Agatha Christie: A Biographical Companion to the Works of Agatha Christie*, rev. and updated ed. (London: HarperCollins, 1999), 226–230; and more recently, Mark Aldridge, *Agatha Christie's Poirot: The Greatest Detective in the World* (London: HarperCollins, 2020), 183–190.
[7] Wagoner, *Agatha Christie*, Twayne's English Authors Series (Boston: G. K. Hall & Co., 1986), 26.
[8] Ibid.
[9] 'The Flock of Geryon' was originally published in the US under the title 'Weird Monster' in *This Week* on 26 May 1940, then in *The Strand* later that year in August. 'The Nemean Lion' was first published in *The Strand* in November 1939.

sends her the sum of two hundred pounds as a kind of grant to the retirement fund she's established. Later, in our story, Carnaby comes to Poirot with a problem. Her friend Miss Emmeline Clegg has become involved with an "odd sect" called "the Flock of the Shepherd."[10] However, she also admits to him that "I came to you, M. Poirot, because I hoped it might be possible to—to sublimate that craving for excitement by employing it, if I may put it that way, on the side of the angels."[11] After all, she says, "we all know the use the devil has for idleness."[12]

In explaining her predicament, Miss Carnaby notes, "Religion, M. Poirot, can be a great help and sustenance — but by that I mean orthodox religion." When Poirot asks if she means "the Greek Church," Miss Carnaby is "shocked," and elaborates,

> Oh no, indeed. Church of England. And though I do not *approve* of Roman Catholics, they are at least *recognised*. And the Wesleyans and Congregationalists — they are all well-known respectable bodies. What I am talking about are these odd sects. They just spring up. They have a kind of emotional appeal but sometimes I have very grave doubts as to whether there is any true religious feeling behind them at all.[13]

The language Carnaby uses leaves little doubt as to her inclinations. She specifically distinguishes between established, "*recognized* . . . well-known respectable bodies," and more transient "odd sects." Further, she doubts the veracity of the "religious feeling" of these sects, even though she admits they have a certain "emotional appeal." Carnaby's comments present the reader with an interesting case of socially approved vs. disapproved religiosity. Put differently, this is one of the clearest examples in Christie's writings of a discordant religious identity, as the quotation from Miss Carnaby mentions all the dominant forms of Christianity found in the 1851 Census I noted at the outset of this Chapter, and juxtaposes them with the aforementioned "sects." Even more so than the "spiritualist" tendencies in stories we'll examine in Chapter 12, this seems to be a straightforward example of an unacceptable religion. We hear Miss Carnaby specifically state this, and we're not shown any disagreement from any other characters in positions of authority. In fact, Poirot specifically refers to this as "a cult."[14]

The term "cult" is a loaded one in the field of Religious Studies, as it's often associated pejoratively with violent and counter-cultural movements, often led by charismatic leaders that abuse the trust of their followers in the cause of personal economic and/or sexual gain.[15] Relevant examples of the stereotypical "cult" would be the People's Temple at Jonestown or the Branch Davidians at Waco, TX. However, because of the widespread, derogatory, and loaded use of "cult," scholarly investigators now prefer the term "New

---

[10] Christie, 'The Flock of Geryon' in *The Labours of Hercules* (1947; reis. New York: HarperCollins, 2011), Kindle edition.

[11] Ibid.

[12] Ibid.

[13] Ibid (emphasis original).

[14] Ibid.

[15] For why "cult" is an unhelpful analytic term, listen to *Keeping It 101: A Killjoy's Introduction to Religion*: 'Smart Grrl Summer: What are "cults"? Why do we hate that word so much?', 10 June 2020; available online at https://keepingit101.com/smartgrrlsummer1.

Religious Movement" (NRM). Relying on the work of Eileen Barker, Judith Fox points out seven common characteristics in NRMs, including, "communal ownership of property, charismatic leadership, relationships based on personal trust rather than on institutional regulation, a message of salvation, liberation or transformation, a high turnover of members, and deviance from the wider community."[16] We shall see a number of these characteristics present in the Flock of the Shepherd, but it's also important for us to acknowledge the influence the world behind the text has on the discordant depiction of the Flock here.

Around the turn of the nineteenth century the times were ripe for religious experimentation, the development of NRMs, and a more public presence for minority religions. Barker reminds us that:

> it was not until the second half of the nineteenth century that full civil and political rights were extended to all religions—in 1871 Parliament passed the Universities Test Act that opened Oxford and Cambridge to members of all religions, and in 1890 all government posts became open to members of the Jewish faith. Around the turn of the century, a number of alternative religions (widely defined), such as Theosophy, Spiritualism, Deism, Auguste Comte's Positivist Church of Humanity, and the Salvation Army, began to make their presence known. During the first half of the twentieth century, other new religions, most notably those of Eastern origin such as SUBUD, Vedanta, and the followers of Krishnamurti, gained popularity among a small but significant group of middle-class intellectuals.[17]

Christie herself would have been familiar with the existence of NRMs and various sects, as they were part of her family history. In her *Autobiography*, she describes her mother Clarissa's religious searches as follows:

> She was, I think, of a naturally mystic turn of mind. She had the gift of prayer and contemplation, but her ardent faith and devotion found it difficult to select a suitable form of worship. My long-suffering father allowed himself to be taken to first one, now another place of worship. Most of these religious flirtations took place before I was born. My mother had been nearly received into the Roman Catholic Church, had then bounced off into being a Unitarian (which accounted for my brother never having been christened), and from there become a budding Theosophist.... After a brief but vivid interest in Zoroastrianism, she returned, much to my father's relief, to the safe haven of the Church of England, but with a preference for "high" churches.[18]

[16] Fox, 'New Religious Movements', in *The Routledge Companion to the Study of Religion*, 2nd ed., ed. John Hinnells (London & New York: Routledge, 2010), 343.
[17] Barker, 'General Overview of the "Cult Scene" in Great Britain', in *New Religious Movements in the Twenty-First Century: Legal, Political, and Social Challenges in Global Perspective*, eds. Phillip Charles Lucas and Thomas Robbins (New York & London: Routledge, 2004), 22.
[18] Christie, *An Autobiography*, (1977; reis. New York: HarperCollins, 2011), 25. See also p. 91. Curiously, in 'The Tape-Measure Murder'—a Miss Marple short story published first in the US in November 1941, then under the title 'The Case of the Retired Jeweller' in *The Strand* the following year—there's a character called Mrs. Spenlow whose religious journey is *very* similar to that of Clarissa's here.

In her biography of Christie, Janet Morgan also claims that Clarissa's children believed "she has second sight ... an impression that must have been fortified by her fickle but profound interest in various bizarre philosophies."[19] Christie herself recalled her father Frederick's and Nursie's Christian beliefs and practices as more straightforward, and her own (as she recalls them) fit snugly alongside theirs. What this indicates is that Christie's childhood experiences inculcated her into a fairly normal discourse of Christianity for her day. As such, she would have been sensitive to deviations from that norm, especially so due to what Morgan calls Clarissa's "spiritual and intellectual recklessness."[20]

Back to the world of the text. Miss Carnaby goes on to note that this specific sect, "The Flock of the Shepherd," is "stupid," but nevertheless, people attend a "Retreat" they hold, i.e., "a period of a fortnight—with religious services and rituals."[21] These rituals include "three big Festivals in the year, the Coming of the Pasture, the Full Pasture, and the Reaping of the Pasture."[22] The Flock is led by a Dr. Anderson, "a very handsome-looking man ... with a presence" who calls himself "the Great Shepherd," and who is "attractive to the women" who make up "at least three quarters of them [the Flock]."[23] It's not just that Anderson attracts women; they also provide funds for his movement. And "Several wealthy women have been among the devotees. In the last year *three* of them, no less, have died," leaving their money to the Flock.[24]

After hearing her out, Poirot suggests that Miss Carnaby go undercover while he investigates. Her reaction to this plan is immediate and acquiescent. For his part, Japp pulls no punches: "I hate these long-haired religious cranks like poison. Filling up women with a lot of mumbo-jumbo."[25] Clearly, Japp's view of this movement is consonant with Carnaby's in that both view it not only with suspicion, but as an illegitimate gathering, one whose purpose isn't religious, but deceptive and pecuniary.

Carnaby gains entry to the group through her friend Miss Clegg, but then has to undergo an entrance interview with Andersen himself. Therein, she restates her earlier position by telling him, "My father was a clergyman of the Church of England and I have never wavered in my faith. I don't hold with heathen doctrines"[26] Andersen tries to reassures her by emphasizing the syncretistic nature of his group, "Believe me, our doctrines are not heathen. Here all religions are welcomed, and all honoured equally."[27] When Miss Carnaby, "the staunch daughter of the late Reverend Thomas Carnaby," replies, "Then they shouldn't be," Andersen quotes John 14.2, "In my Father's House are many mansions."[28] Miss Carnaby soon finds herself "surrendering only too easily to the spell" of the Flock, and from the narrator's description, one can see why: "The peace, the simplicity, the delicious though simple food, the beauty of the services with their chants

---

[19] Morgan, *Agatha Christie: A Biography* (London: William Collins Sons & Company, 1984; repr. New York: Alfred A. Knopf, 1985), 13.
[20] Ibid., 1.
[21] Christie, 'The Flock of Geryon'.
[22] Ibid.
[23] Ibid.
[24] Ibid.
[25] Ibid.
[26] Ibid.
[27] Ibid.
[28] Ibid.

of Love and Worship, the simple moving words of the Master, appealing to all that was best and highest in humanity—here all the strife and ugliness of the world was shut out. Here was only Peace and Love."[29]

We as readers are privy to one of the aforementioned festivals of the Flock (the "Festival of the Full Pasture"), and the "call-and-response" dialogue is telling, as it enhances in-group identity and functions as a ritual in which core beliefs are expressed.

"Where are my sheep?"
The answer came from the crowd.
"*We are here, O Shepherd.*"
"Lift up your hearts with joy and thanksgiving. This is the Feast of Joy."
"*The Feast of Joy and we are joyful.*"
"There shall be no more sorrow for you, no more pain. All is joy!"
"*All is joy. . .*"
"How many heads has the Shepherd?"
"*Three heads, a head of gold, a head of silver, a head of sounding brass.*"
"How many bodies have the Sheep?"
"*Three bodies, a body of flesh, a body of corruption, and a body of light.*"
"How shall you be sealed in the Flock?"
"*By the Sacrament of Blood.*"
"Are you prepared for that Sacrament?"
"*We are.*"[30]

In the midst of this festival, Miss Carnaby "fiercely" told herself, "most blasphemous, the whole thing! This kind of religious hysteria is to be deplored."[31] Evidently, Carnaby takes umbrage with the kind of ecstatic worship employed by the Flock. Nevertheless, Andersen comes to her, pricks her arm and says, "the Sacrament of Blood that brings joy."[32] Soon after, she begins to feel and see differently, and it becomes obvious that she is undergoing a kind of hallucinatory episode. In keeping with the characterization of her being staunchly Christian, she even quotes Mark 8:24 "to herself reverently" to explain her experience, the Bible verse apparently intended as a kind of grounding or talismanic tactic in the face of the unfamiliar spiritual venture.[33]

Another important scene in the story for our purposes occurs between Carnaby and another Flock member named Mr. Cole. Cole tells her of a convoluted vision he had, which included "Elijah descending from heaven in his fiery chariot" as well as "altars of Baal" and a voice commanding him to "write and testify that which you shall see" along with the Norse high-god Odin.[34] This is a mélange of scriptural language and

---

[29] Ibid.
[30] Ibid.
[31] Ibid.
[32] Ibid.
[33] Ibid. Miss Carnaby simply says, "Like trees walking," but this is evidently an abridgement of the King James translation of this verse, which reads "And he [the blind man Jesus is healing] looked up, and said, 'I see men as trees, walking."
[34] Ibid.

allusions, including 2 Kings 2:11:12 and possibly Revelation 1:11. Miss Carnaby is actually relieved that Mr. Cole's vision isn't more esoteric and is rooted in Scripture, even if erratically so. The narrator tells us, "Miss Carnaby breathed a sigh of relief. Elijah was much better, she didn't mind Elijah."[35] Nonetheless, Miss Carnaby raises a concern about Mr. Cole's sanity to the Master. In response, he quotes 1 John 4.18, "Perfect love casteth out fear," evidently with the intention to engender that love in Carnaby, which would encourage both her resignation and compliance.[36]

After this encounter with Andersen, we see Miss Carnaby meet with Poirot for an update, and she makes a public scene disavowing Poirot in favor of her Shepherd. However, we quickly discover this was all an act on her part; she discovered she was being followed and needed to make a public scene to reassure those watching her of her loyalty to Andersen. As it turns out, Carnaby's pretended support couldn't help Andersen. Not long after her repudiation of Poirot, we're told the "great shepherd" is arrested during the "sacrament" by none other than Mr. Cole, who was an undercover police officer all along.[37] And as if to put a fine point on the religious meaning his real followers attached to his person, the narrator describes how the Sheep view the Shepherd as a martyr, "suffering, as all great teachers suffer, from the ignorance and persecution of the outside world."[38]

Poirot and Japp then reveal the truth to Miss Carnaby: Andersen had been dosing his followers with "Cannabis Indica," aka "Hashish or Bhang." As Poirot tells her, the drugs "bound his devotees to him. These were the Spiritual Joys that he promised them."[39] He also poisoned those wealthy women and was planning to poison Miss Carnaby as well. Far from being an upright, authentic spiritual leader interested in the betterment of those in his charge, Andersen—and the kind of charismatic, insular Christianity he represents—is shown to be a fraud and a criminal, interested only in mammon.

If we want to understand how this story reflects a discordant or improper form of Christianity, then it behooves us to return to Fox's seven characteristics of NRMs, which I mentioned earlier in the chapter. Of these, all save communal property are present, with a special emphasis on the charismatic leadership of Anderson, his personal appeal to women, and the group's deviance from not only its community but also from other forms of Christianity. These features of the Flock mark it as separate and unseemly when considered alongside the kind of Christianity Miss Carnaby embraces, as well as the kind of Christianity that Christie assumes in her Poirot stories.

* * *

As a reminder of who and what counts as "acceptable" religious practice, let's flip a few pages in *The Labours of Hercules* to the very next story in the collection. Titled "The Apples of the Hesperides," it recounts Poirot's search for a golden, jewel-encrusted

---

[35] Ibid.
[36] Ibid.
[37] Ibid.
[38] Ibid.
[39] Ibid.

goblet for a rich man named Emery Power.[40] Eventually, Poirot tracks it down to a convent on the coast of Ireland. Despite being a foreigner in that land, once he hears the bell of the convent toll and is granted an audience with the Mother Superior, "He understood the atmosphere in which he found himself," as he "was a Catholic by birth."[41] Poirot had tracked down the last known person to possess the goblet to this convent, but unfortunately, she had died two month earlier. In a not-strictly-legal move, Poirot hires a local man to help him enter the convent after hours and find the goblet. Although the man is worried about having "a mortal sin upon my conscience," Poirot assures him by means of quoting Mark 12:17 that he is "only restoring to Cæsar the things which are Cæsar's."[42]

Successful in his quest, Poirot returns to England and delivers the goblet to his client. He explains to Power that the girl he sought took the goblet to the convent "to atone for her father's sins. She gave it to be used to the glory of God."[43] However, when Power asks Poirot what he wants in return for finding the goblet for him, Poirot surprises him by requesting that the goblet be returned to the convent. He explains to his client that it has a history of evil attached to it, and exhorts him to return it to the convent to "Let the evil of it be purified there." Poirot asks Power to "Let it stand once more on the altar, purified and absolved as we hope that the souls of men shall be also purified and absolved from their sins."[44] After Power hears Poirot's plea, along with a description of the serene, stark beauty of the Irish coast—a coast in which he was raised—Power agrees, but still bemoans his loss. Poirot assures him, though, that "The nuns will say masses for your soul."[45] Power is appeased by this gesture, and the story closes with Poirot returning the goblet to the Mother Superior, who indeed volunteers to pray for the unhappy rich man.

So, how does this help us to see the distinction between acceptable and unacceptable forms of Christianity? If we pay attention to the kind of language employed to describe the goblet, the setting in which it's found, and how Poirot regards it and the Mother Superior he encounters, we see that all this language is in the service of portraying this kind of Catholic Christianity as a moral force for good, in opposition to the way in which the more trans-denominational Flock is characterized. That is, in Poirot's words and actions, there is a tone of reverence for the goblet and those who care for it (especially in the way the convent is depicted as an oasis of reflection and repentance) and this tone is connected to his religious identity as a *bon Catholique*. Taken together, Christie's language and Poirot's tone—as well as the decision Power makes at the conclusion of the story—indicate that kind of religion and the effect(s) it has on the characters is a positive, familiar force for good, unlike the narcissistic, drug-fueled, ultimately murderous kind of religious practice Anderson has concocted for his personal gain as the Shepherd of the Flock.

*   *   *

[40] This short story was first published in *The Strand* 597 in September 1940.
[41] Christie, 'The Apples of the Hesperides', in *The Labours of Hercules*.
[42] Ibid.
[43] Ibid.
[44] Ibid.
[45] Ibid.

I've been arguing that Christie resists the hegemonic Christianity which she inherited, so how do the examples in this chapter show that? In "The Flock of Geryon," why does she depict the Flock as she does? One possible answer is that Christie might be more sympathetic with normative Christianity here because of the obviously fraudulent and criminal practices of the Flock. At the same time, though, she does take time to point out the positive characteristics of the Flock via Miss Carnaby's experiences. Recall how the narrator describes what Carnaby encounters there: words and practices "appealing to all that was best and highest in humanity—here all the strife and ugliness of the world was shut out. Here was only Peace and Love." We see here that Christie doesn't stereotype the Flock (as Carnaby does), nor does she dismiss it out of hand (like Japp). This shows at least an openness to the ideas of new and non- and/or trans-denominational forms of syncretistic Christianity, even if she ultimately finds the Flock unacceptable in its implementation. And by placing the story of the Flock side by side with "The Apples of the Hesperides," she makes this unacceptability more prominent. How, then, did Christie view Spiritualism, a much less insular form of "religious" practice that had potential to challenge Christian hegemony?

12

Spiritualism

Among many responses to the changing, unsettling times of the Victorian age was Spiritualism.[1] Never a centralized movement, Spiritualism is best understood as originating in New York in the mid-nineteenth century and as a product of the spiritual marketplace atmosphere that characterized the Second Great Awakening in the States.[2] This was a period in American religious history in which old traditions morphed to accommodate to the changing times, and new traditions like the Church of Jesus Christ of Latter-day Saints and Christian Science arose.[3] Spiritualism was one of these new groups, but it's better to see it as a series of nonhierarchical movements built around two central convictions: "The first, quite ancient, is that there is continuity of life after death. Some immaterial essence survives that is referred to as the spirit or soul of that person. Second, it is possible for the living to communicate with these spirits through certain special people—mediums."[4] These beliefs and the practices they spawned, both private and public, soon hopped the pond to England where they "spoke to the growing crisis in faith that permeated all classes of society."[5]

Just as in the States, Spiritualism became popular as a response to the times. J. Jeffrey Franklin writes, "The first half of the nineteenth century witnessed first the arrival to England from the Continent of the 'mesmeric mania' and then the invasion from the United States of Spiritualism, all during a period when the Church of England was losing congregation to Nonconformist denominations and experiencing internal revolutions."[6] Mesmerism is a fascinating example of the kind of alternative science prevalent in the Victorian period, and I have mentioned the difficulties faced by

---

[1] There seems to be some variance in the secondary literature over whether or not to capitalize "Spiritualism." For the sake of clarity, I'll capitalize it in what follows with the caveat that "Spiritualism" isn't a clearly delineated movement.

[2] In Martin E. Marty's rightly lauded *Pilgrims in Their Own Land: 500 Years of Religion in America* (New York: Penguin, 1984), he calls this period a "Soul Rush. . . . a textbook example of free enterprise in the marketplace of religion, a competition in which the fittest survived" (169).

[3] Marty only mentions Spiritualism in passing, but this is most likely due to its diffuse nature and lack of membership data. Nevertheless, he opines that "indirectly it influenced thousands if not millions, though its institutions remained all but invisible to most Americans" (*Pilgrims*, 452).

[4] Sherri Lynne Lyons, *Species, Serpents, Spirits, and Skulls: Science at the Margins in the Victorian Age* (Albany: State University of New York Press, 2009), 90.

[5] Ibid., 6.

[6] Franklin, *Spirit Matters: Occult Beliefs, Alternative Religions, and the Crisis of Faith in Victorian Britain* (Ithaca & London: Cornell University Press, 2018), 30.

established religions, or *religion*, in Chapter 11.[7] More pressing here is the continuing impact of Spiritualism in the early twentieth century. And it made a large impact, indeed.

In her book *Modern Spiritualism and the Church of England, 1850-1939*, Georgina Byrne writes that "Spiritualism was a strange and fascinating American import; it became tremendously popular in England and appealed . . . to a wide variety of people."[8] This broad appeal, though, shouldn't cause us to disregard "how quickly and easily it became embedded into a receptive common culture. Put simply, despite its originality, spiritualism nevertheless contained many features that were already familiar to countless English men and women, and it connected with some long-established cultural tropes."[9] That is, Spiritualism found a well-tilled garden of socio-cultural assumptions and "religious" ideas upon its arrival that ensured its widespread diffusion. What were some of these conditions that made Spiritualism so attractive, even to Christians?

Hugh McLeod makes three points salient to our investigation in his history of religion in England. First, he points out that Spiritualism "had an obvious attraction for those who had suffered tragic bereavement, and the First World War, in particular, saw an upsurge of interest."[10] But McLeod also rightly notes that "Spiritualism as an ideology appealed mainly to those who wanted a middle path between Christian orthodoxy and atheism."[11] In other words, Spiritualism—often practiced in a semi-scientific fashion— can be seen as a kind of compromise or middle ground between a totally rationalistic rejection of religion and a maximalist religious identity. And, as Alex Owen points out, "Spiritualism was fully capable of containing the full spectrum of beliefs" one might find in various settings. What's more, Spiritualism and the dominant form of Christianity could exist in a state of "happy accommodation," as the former "did not undermine Christian belief, just as it was not necessary to believe in God in order to witness the reality of the spirits."[12] Owen's point here regarding the "happy accommodation" between Spiritualism and Christianity is a key one for our discussion, and is taken up in Byrne's book.

Therein, Byrne focuses on the malleable nature of "Christianity" and reminds us that while hegemonic, it's not immobile. She claims a reciprocal relationship existed between "Church teaching" and the "common culture" in this time, with the result that "religious belief in the nineteenth century, within the Church as well as beyond it, was fluid, dynamic and subject to accretion." Put differently, "Church teaching emerges . . . as susceptible to change, and religious belief – which is not the sole preserve of the

---

[7] For more on Mesmerism and England, see Logie Barrow, *Independent Spirits: Spiritualism and English Plebeians, 1850-1910*, History Workshop Series (London & New York: Routledge & Kegan Paul, 1986), 76–91.

[8] Byrne, *Modern Spiritualism and the Church of England, 1850-1939*, Studies in Modern British Religious History (Suffolk: The Boydell Press, 2010), 22.

[9] Ibid.

[10] Hugh McLeod, *Religion and Society in England, 1850-1914*, Social History in Perspective (New York: St. Martin's Press, 1996), 52.

[11] Ibid.

[12] Owen, *The Darkened Room: Women, Power, and Spiritualism in Late Victorian England* (Chicago & London: The University of Chicago Press, 1989), 22–23.

Church, but rather lies within and without it – is seen to be constantly in a process of negotiation."[13]

The negotiation Byrne claims here is exactly what we find in Christie's work: a playfulness and a dickering with dogma that interrogates rather than reifies the normative claims made by hegemonic Christian culture. With regards to Spiritualism more specifically, Byrne claims that since "the language and ideas of modern spiritualism . . . had become embedded in the common culture by the late nineteenth century," they actually impacted the Church of England's views on the afterlife.[14] For Bryne, this indicates a key point: "Religious belief in this analysis did not 'decline'; it adapted and changed."[15] This polyvalency, this twisting and turning of meaning will have obvious significance for how we understand the presence and depiction of Spiritualism *and* religion in Christie's works.

But let's return to McLeod, whose third and final point is that different kinds of spiritualist practices appealed to different social classes.[16] We have evidence that some more organized forms of Spiritualism coalesced around "working-class and lower middle-class" groups and became part and parcel of these groups' interests in more radical politics and "unorthodox healing" practices.[17] On the other hand, McLeod also identifies a kind of Spiritualism prevalent in middle- to upper-class groupings around the late nineteenth to early twentieth century. As he points out, "This form of Spiritualism tended to lack the socio-political dimension that was so important to its plebian counterpart. Its significance was primarily intellectual. It appealed to those who wanted a free-ranging and unprejudiced investigation of bizarre psychic phenomena, untrammeled by the dogmas either of orthodox Christianity or of orthodox science."[18] Many artists and writers explored this kind of Spiritualism in their work. An important example of the latter was Wilkie Collins, whose 1868 novel *The Moonstone* was a milestone in detective fiction.[19] Famously, one of the most prominent advocates of this more intellectual variety of Spiritualism was Arthur Conan Doyle.[20] And like the central model for her Poirot stories, Christie's use of spiritualist belief and practice in those stories is characterized by this variety of Spiritualism. Also, like Conan Doyle, Christie had personal experiences with Spiritualism which impacted her work.

Three examples of her early encounters with Spiritualism will suffice. First, as I note Christie's mother Clarissa flirted with Spiritualism for a time. As Laura Thompson puts it, "Her spiritualism was both profound and unsettled, as if she felt its importance but did not quite know what to do with it."[21] The impact of her mother's spiritualistic

---

[13] Byrne, *Modern Spiritualism*, 8.
[14] Ibid., 9.
[15] Ibid., 9.
[16] See ibid., 22.
[17] McLeod, *Religion and Society*, 52–53.
[18] Ibid., 53–54.
[19] For how this novel may have influenced Christie's work, see Patricia D. Maida and Nicholas B. Spornick, *Murder She Wrote: A Study of Agatha Christie's Detective Fiction* (Bowling Green, OH: Bowling Green State University Popular Press, 1982), 41–42. Collins's 1885 story "The Ghost's Touch" is a clear example of the fascination Spiritualism held for writers in the late nineteenth century.
[20] See Byrne, *Modern Spiritualism*, 72–75. Christie was aware of Doyle's interest in spiritualism and séances, as she mentions him in this connection in chapter eleven of *The Sittaford Mystery* (1931).
[21] Thompson, *Agatha Christie: An English Mystery* (London: Headline, 2007); repr. *Agatha Christie: A Mysterious Life* (New York: Pegasus Books, 2018), Kindle edition, "The Villa at Torquay."

dabbling left its imprint on Christie's work, as Patricia D. Maida and Nicholas B. Spornick note: "It is possible that some of her mother's dabbling in the occult may have influenced Christie's frequent use of seances, ouija boards and spiritualism in her works."[22] Second, in several of her juvenilia, Christie seems to have experimented with spiritualistic themes and practices. Janet Morgan writes that Christie's first story, "The House of Beauty," was "about madness and dreams, echoing the writings about the occult that Agatha and her friends were reading at the end of 1908. . . . There was at this time a great interest in mysticism and spiritualism."[23] Morgan also notes that other early stories explored "psychic phenomena" and included features like a "séance."[24] Finally, Christie encountered Spiritualism via the courting of a young man called Wilfred Pirie, who began pursuing Christie around 1910–1911. In her *Autobiography*, she recalls,

> He became interested in spiritualism, therefore I became interested in spiritualism. So far all was well. But now Wilfred began to produce books that he was eager for me to read and pronounce on. They were very large books—theosophical mostly. The illusion that you enjoyed whatever your man enjoyed didn't work; naturally it didn't work—I wasn't really in love with him. I found the books on theosophy tedious; not only tedious, I thought they were completely false; worse still, I thought a great many of them were nonsense![25]

Based on these three experiences, we can see that by the time Christie began to write her Poirot stories, she was already familiar with spiritualist thought and some of its basic practices. And despite the fact that poor Mr. Pirie doesn't seem to have made such a favorable impression on the young Ms. Agatha Miller, as Mrs. Christie she would continue to incorporate Spiritualism into her Poirot stories for years to come.

In what follows, we'll examine four examples of these spiritualistic beliefs and practices in Poirot stories ranging from 1923–1937, a period in which Spiritualism was extremely popular.[26] It was also a period in which Christie herself suffered the loss of her beloved

---

[22] Maida and Spornick, *Murder*, 12.

[23] Morgan, *Agatha Christie: A Biography* (London: William Collins Sons & Company, 1984; repr. New York: Alfred A. Knopf, 1985), 48.

[24] Ibid., 49.

[25] Christie, *An Autobiography* (1977; reis. New York: HarperCollins, 2011), 203. See also Morgan, *Agatha Christie*, 55.

[26] See Callum G. Brown, *Religion and Society in Twentieth-Century Britain* (Harlow: Pearson Education Limited, 2006), 141. There are obviously other, minor examples of Spiritualism and the occult more broadly in the Poirot canon which we won't engage. Example include the short stories "The King of Clubs," "The Adventure of the Egyptian Tomb," and "The Under Dog." The 1948 novel *Taken at the Flood* includes an encounter between Poirot and a Mrs. Katherine Cloade, who is depicted as a practitioner of Spiritualism. Unlike the other examples in this chapter, Poirot has little sympathy at all for Katherine's Spiritualism, and dismisses her coldly. Spiritualism is key in two Miss Marple short stories, as well: "Motive v. Opportunity," and "Tape-Measure Murder." And in other works, Christie often dabbled in the supernatural, as in her 1930 anthology of short stories titled *The Mysterious Mr. Quin*. In his work on Spiritualism and detective fiction, Chris Willis catalogues more of Christie's spiritualistic stories—like the 1931 novel *The Sittaford Mystery* and the 1933 short story collection *The Hound of Death and Other Stories*—in his "Making the Dead Speak: Spiritualism and Detective Fiction," in *The Art of Detective Fiction*, eds. Warren Chernaik, Martin Swales, and Robert Vilain (Hampshire & New York: Palgrave Macmillan, 2000), 65-67. Curiously, he omits her 1962 novel, *The Pale Horse*, which contains numerous references to spiritualistic phenomena.

mother Clarissa and underwent a painful and highly publicized separation from her first husband before traveling to Baghdad by herself on the Orient Express and ultimately meeting and marrying her second husband, Max Mallowan. Even though Christie herself disparaged some of her work in the 1920s (most famously the 1928 novel *The Mystery of the Blue Train*), all of the works we're discussing in this section are classic Christie.

*   *   *

"The Tragedy at Marsdon Manor"

Let's proceed chronologically in our survey, meaning we'll begin in 1923 with "The Tragedy at Marsdon Manor." In this story, Poirot is commissioned by an insurance company to investigate the death of a Mr. Maltravers after the deceased took out a rather large life insurance policy with them. After a discussion with Dr. Bernard, Maltravers's physician, Poirot and Hastings encounter a recent guest of the dead man, Captain Black. Black had evidently been to dinner recently and related a story about a man who committed suicide by shooting himself in the mouth up through the brain in such a way as to disguise the fact he killed himself. Once Poirot hears this, he is able to confirm that Maltravers was indeed killed in a similar fashion.

Mrs. Maltravers is devastated when Poirot informs her, and in an attempt to comfort her, Poirot remarks, "Madame, you of all people should know that there are no dead!" When she questions him, he asks, "Have you never taken part in any spiritualistic séances? You are mediumistic, you know." Mrs. Maltravers replies that she's been told that before, and asks Poirot, "You do not believe in Spiritualism, surely?" He responds ambiguously, "Madame, I have seen some strange things. You know that they say in the village that this house is haunted?"[27]

Mrs. Maltravers seems to be comforted by Poirot's attitude, and asks him and Hastings to stay for dinner. During that dinner, and unbeknownst to Mrs. Maltravers, Poirot uses the beliefs in Spiritualism and that the house is haunted—along with a hefty dose of theatrics—to force (or frighten) a confession from her.[28] Evidently, Poirot hired a local actor named Mr. Everett to dress up like Mr. Maltravers, tap on windows, stand in the house, and point at Mrs. Maltravers, using special effects to create an eerie light as he does so.[29] Meanwhile, Poirot has slyly smeared red paint on her hands to resemble blood, so that when she sees a figure she mistakes as her dead husband accusing her of his murder and what appears to be blood on her hands, she admits she killed him.

This is the first time that we encounter Spiritualism in Christie's Poirot stories, and this example demonstrates a rather basic awareness of the phenomenon. That is, we see

---

[27] Christie, "The Tragedy at Marsdon Manor," in *Hercule Poirot: The Complete Short Stories* (New York: HarperCollins, 2013), Kindle edition.

[28] Ibid.

[29] Upon seeing Everett as Maltravers, Hastings admits it made him think of "the old superstition that a suicide cannot rest" (loc. 1912). This is likely an inheritance from Dante, who in Canto XIII of his *Inferno* describes the fate of those commit suicides. If so, then this would be more evidence for Christie's use of shared religious language.

little more than an acknowledgment that those who have died can continue to communicate with the living—especially via "noises and sounds," i.e., "nonvisual experiences" like tapping, as well as the phenomenon of "materialization" in which physical objects might move about, or, more on point here, even the apparitional appearance of the dead.[30] Here, though, Poirot exploits the presupposition that generally those who die make compliant communicators. In her work, Simone Natale writes, "Antagonistic spirits are very rare in reports of spiritualist séances, and the interaction between sitters and spirits was usually described as one of sympathy and community."[31] There is certainly neither sympathy or community indicated in Mr. Everett's performance, and it may be this aspect of what Mrs. Maltravers believes is a visitation from her dead husband that disturbs her the most. To be fair, it is unclear as to whether Mrs. Maltravers confesses because of her spiritualistic beliefs or because she's terrified. Either way, she outs herself as a murderer, and Poirot pronounces her a "shrewd and scheming woman" who "only married [Maltravers] for his money."[32]

Interestingly, Spiritualism isn't the only minority religious practice we encounter in this story. Early in their investigation, the local doctor tells Poirot and Hastings that the victim, Mr. Maltravers, was a "Christian Scientist—or something of that kind," and as a result he'd never been examined.[33] This not only assumes that the sleuths (and the reader) understand the reference to Christian Science and its tenets regarding medicine, but also provides a major clue. At the end of the story, Poirot reasons that "The doctor seemed to think the deceased was a Christian Scientist, and who could have given him that impression but Mrs. Maltravers?"[34] Like Spiritualism, Christian Science also arose during the Second Great Awakening, but it has developed into a recognized American form of Christianity, where it's known for its idiosyncratic views regarding modern medicine.

When we examine the world the text creates, we find the genuineness of Mrs. Maltravers's spiritualistic beliefs called into question. "The Tragedy at Marsden Manor" was one of the mystery stories chosen to be adapted for "a new series called 'Murder Clinic' on WOR, the flagship [radio] station for the Mutual network."[35] Originally broadcast on 6 October 1942, Lee Wright and John A. Bassett's version of Christie's story includes shared religious language not present in the story, but also retains much of the spiritualistic tenor and content of the 1923 short story.

Most obviously, the spiritualistic theme is found in the séance that Mrs. Maltravers holds to contact her dead husband so that he can confirm her claim that Black murdered him. This differs from the short story, as there Mrs. Maltravers's spiritualistic beliefs seem much more genuine. After all, it's the appearance of the actor Poirot hired

---

[30] Simone Natale, *Supernatural Entertainments: Victorian Spiritualism and the Rise of Modern Media Culture* (University Park, PA: The Pennsylvania State University Press, 2016), 53; and Byrne, *Modern Spiritualism*, 21–22.

[31] Natale, *Supernatural*, 48–49.

[32] Christie, "The Tragedy at Marsdon Manor."

[33] Ibid.

[34] Ibid.

[35] See Victor A. Berch, Karl Schadow & Steve Lewis, "Murder Clinic: Radio's Golden Age of Detection," available online at https://mysteryfile.com/M_Clinic.html.

that causes her to admit her culpability, but there's no hint of duplicity on her part. In this radio version, she tries to use Spiritualism as a mechanism to cast guilt on Black, and as such it's implied that she doesn't really hold those beliefs.

This view that Spiritualism is simply a tool Mrs. Maltravers uses with nefarious intent is echoed in the 1991 television version of the short story in *Agatha Christie's Poirot*. There are numerous overlaps with the 1942 radio adaptation, in that Mrs. Maltravers's spiritualistic language and claims are obviously false, a tool she uses to deflect suspicion away from herself. Whether she genuinely believes in Spiritualism more broadly is left a more open question in this television rendering.

Peril at End House

Spiritualist practices also play a role in our second example: the 1932 novel *Peril at End House*.[36] Here, Poirot and Hastings are relaxing at a resort hotel in a town called St Loo when they meet a charming young woman named Nick Buckley. Nick owns an old home (the titular End House) and recently has been in several near-accidents, which Poirot soon divines are attempts at murder. Once her cousin Maggie is killed at End House, Nick agrees with Poirot, and the little Belgian sets out to discover who the culprit is.

The key section for our examination occurs after Maggie's murder and in the wake of Poirot's idea to fake Nick's death in order to draw the murderer out. In chapter eighteen, Hastings opens his mail, and he notes that the first letter is an announcement of a "spiritualist meeting." He jokingly suggests to Poirot—who is still having difficulty with the case—that "If all else fails, we must go to the spiritualists," since "The spirit of the victim comes back and names the murderer. That would be a proof."[37] Once Poirot has his breakthrough in this same chapter, though, he decides to take Hastings's suggestion seriously and stage a play at End House, but with a ghost in attendance. Sure enough, after Nick's will is read to everyone seated in the dining room, Poirot proposes to have a "seance," since—unbeknownst to his companion—"Hastings, here, has pronounced mediumistic powers."[38] Poirot even comments that "To get through a message from the other world—the opportunity is unique! I feel the conditions are propitious."[39] Soon after, the lights are dimmed and Nick silently walks into the room. Everyone is in shocked silence until Ellen, the maid, shrieks that "She's walking! Them that's murdered always walk!"[40] Poirot's ruse succeeds in identifying one criminal—the forger of Nick's will—and exposing another—Nick's friend Frederica's drug-running husband. However, in the "Big Reveal" in chapter twenty-one Poirot announces that, far

---

[36] For more about this novel, see Charles Osborne, *The Life and Crimes of Agatha Christie: A Biographical Companion to the Works of Agatha Christie*, rev. and updated ed. (London: HarperCollins, 1999), 95–97; and Mark Aldridge, *Agatha Christie's Poirot: The Greatest Detective in the World* (London: HarperCollins, 2020), 64–69.
[37] Christie, *Peril at End House* (1932; reis. New York: HarperCollins, 2011), Kindle edition, ch. 18, "The Face at the Window."
[38] Ibid., ch. 19, "Poirot Produces a Play."
[39] Ibid.
[40] Ibid. Interestingly, this is comparable to Hastings's claim in "Tragedy at Marsdon Manor" that "a suicide cannot rest."

from being a victim, Nick herself is the killer of Maggie. Curiously, though, he allows Nick the mercy of killing herself via an overdose of cocaine, courtesy of Frederica.

Nick and Mary Magdalene

Perhaps Poirot should have surmised a sinister streak in Nick earlier, given her name. In chapter two, Poirot becomes frustrated that Nick isn't taking the so-called accidents that have been happening to her more seriously, and tells her she's "obstinate as the devil." Not long after this comment, we learn that Nick's name has a devilish antecedent, and also that her real name is Magdala. She responds to Poirot, saying "That's where I got my name from. My grand-father was popularly supposed to have sold his soul to the devil. Everyone round here called him Old Nick. He was a wicked old man — but great fun. I adored him. I went everywhere with him and so they called us Old Nick and Young Nick. My real name is Magdala." Other sections in the novel, too, reinforce a devilish aspect to Nick's character, but this name will be a key point in Poirot's solution to the murder, as Nick's cousin Maggie is also named Magdala ("tower" in Greek). The name is, of course, significant for our purposes, as it refers both to a village called Magdala on the west coast of the "Sea" of Galilee, as well as to Mary of Magdala, more commonly known as Mary Magdalene. Mary Magdalene is obviously an important figure in the New Testament and non-canonical works, especially since in John's Gospel, she's the first of Jesus's followers to witness his resurrection (20:11-18). Even though this connection is tantalizing, I'm not sure the name Magdala is meant to call to mind any key character traits shared by Nick and Mary Magdalene. Even if we assume that Christie has uncritically accepted the popular (yet inaccurate) view that Mary Magdalene was a prostitute, Nick doesn't engage in any sexually suspect behavior in the novel. In fact, Maggie seems to be closer to the portrayal of Mary Magdalene in New Testament literature in terms of the "Christian works" we hear she performed. Nevertheless, by using both "Nick" and "Magdala" Christie invites us to consider the impact of names on how we regard her characters.

Now that we've encountered two examples of séances let's delve more deeply into this primary feature of spiritualist practice.[41] Obviously, as with "The Tragedy at Marsdon Manor," the séance that Poirot hastily arranges in this novel isn't intended to be a genuine attempt to contact the dead, but it is important nonetheless for us to

---

[41] Fuller accounts of genuine séances can be found in chapter two of Christie's novel *The Sittaford Mystery*, as well as her short stories "The Voice in the Dark" and "The Bird with the Broken Wing" (both originally published in the 1930 collection *The Mysterious Mr. Quin*). The former short story is a helpful example of a female spiritualistic medium, and the latter (as well as the novel) centers on a spiritualistic practice Christie doesn't mention in her Poirot works: table turning. For this practice, see Natale, *Supernatural*, 50ff.

understand how central this practice was in spiritualistic culture. Simone Natale points out that "Although mediums often performed on the theatrical stage, Victorian spiritualist séances were most frequently held in domestic spaces.... that were dedicated to social and familial gatherings. Such spaces, which were simultaneously private and public, allowed spiritualists to shape their events as religious experiences and, at the same time, as occasions for social encounters and playful activities."[42] The dining room in End House would certainly fit this bill, but Natale's description reminds us of the distance between what Poirot arranges and what other séances would have entailed. Normally, a séance would involve establishing contact with either a family member or a famous figure, and some kind of test to prove the identity of the spirit with whom the medium is communicating. More on point with *Peril at End House* is Natale's account of the emotions of those participating in this event. She writes,

> Victorian spiritualist séances were fueled by emotions and feelings similar to those excited by literature, theater, and film, such as an emotional high, amusement, and fascination with the unknown. Sittings were ruled by a recurring dramaturgy, which, no different from a theatrical sketch, manipulated the attention and the reactions of sitters. The contact with spirits elicited a climax of excitation that was similar in many ways to what, in overtly spectacular contexts, we call "suspense."[43]

Suspense is exactly what Poirot wants to generate by this faux séance. As we saw, his interest is to capitalize on the popularity of spiritualistic beliefs in order to create a situation in which a supposed murder victim presents themselves to a group which he believes to contain their attempted murderer. And his tactic is successful in that eventually he reveals that Nick, herself, is the murderer. But for our discussion, the key points are that the method Poirot employs involves the central practice of Spiritualism, the séance, and the fact that no one objects to the practice as being invalid or heretical. In fact, several of those involved are shocked upon seeing the apparitional figure of Nick enter the room, perhaps a sign that they, too, share the core belief of Spiritualism: that we can contact the dead. The lack of objection and the reaction from those assembled serves as evidence for broad acceptance of Spiritualism in both the world behind and the world of the text.

The adaptation of this novel in the television series *Agatha Christie's Poirot* also relies on this core belief and retains the scene with the séance and its function. The only alteration of note is that it's not Hastings but Miss Lemon who Poirot taps to lead the séance, since, as he notes with exaggeration, "Mlle. Felicity LeMon has the pronounced powers of the medium." As we'll see later in this chapter, Miss Lemon's participation is more apropos of the role women normally played in domestic séances, especially in the nineteenth-century heyday of English Spiritualism. As such, it makes sense to include her here as the medium in an attempt to communicate with the dead. And it very much appears that she does do so in the séance scene, as this adaptation hews closely to the novel with regards both to its setting and outcome.

[42] Natale, *Supernatural*, 42–44.
[43] Ibid., 48.

"Dead Man's Mirror"

Communicating with the dead is also prominent in the short story "Dead Man's Mirror,"[44] published in the 1937 collection, *Murder in the Mews: Four Cases of Hercule Poirot*.[45] Here, though, we also find other, more minor aspects of Spiritualism, including reincarnation and a preoccupation with ancient Egypt, when Poirot is summoned by a fabulously wealthy man called Sir Gervase Chevenix-Gore. When Poirot arrives for dinner, it's soon discovered that Sir Gervase has evidently committed suicide. However, Poirot soon realizes that something fouler is afoot amidst the family and servants of the dead man, leading to his discovery of the murderer.

Obviously, we're most interested in the fact that a major character professes spiritualistic beliefs. At the party Poirot attends at the beginning of the story, Sir Gervase's wife Vanda is described to him as "mad," since she has "a leaning towards the occult.... [and] Wears amulets and scarabs and gives out that she's the reincarnation of an Egyptian Queen."[46]

Egypt in Christie

The emphasis on Egypt in "Dead Man's Mirror" is telling, as Christie herself had a lifelong interest in Egypt and Egyptian imagery. In 1910, her mother took her on a trip to Cairo for three months. While she didn't lose her heart to Egypt on this inaugural trip, it wasn't the last time she visited. In fact, Christie published a mystery novel set in ancient Egypt in 1944 (*Death Comes as the End*), and sixty-three years after her first visit, her play *Akhnaton* was published. Additionally, interest in Egyptian religion was widespread in the late Victorian period. In fact, J. Jeffrey Franklin devotes the entire seventh chapter of his 2018 book *Spirit Matters: Occult Beliefs, Alternative Religions, and the Crisis of Faith in Victorian Britain* to the subject, and writes, "The period 1880–1910 was a culminating moment in the history of European engagement with its idea of Egypt and with modern Egypt itself. In those decades, political-colonial, scientific-archaeological, literary, and religious and spiritual discourses about ancient Egypt all came to a head in conjunction with one another with unprecedented intensity" (144). That interest in Egypt is also reflected in Golden Age detective fiction, especially after the discovery of King Tutankhamen's tomb in 1922 by Howard Carter. For examples, see S. S. Van Dine's 1930 novel *The Scarab Murder Case* and 1932's *The Egyptian Cross Mystery* by Ellery Queen.

---

[44] This short story is an expanded version of an earlier effort called "The Second Gong," which first appeared in the *Ladies Home Journal* in the States in June 1932, then one month later in *The Strand*.
[45] For more on this collection, see Osborne, *Life and Crimes*, 158-160; and Aldridge, *Agatha Christie's Poirot*, 109–113.
[46] Christie, "Dead Man's Mirror," in *Murder in the Mews: Four Cases of Hercule Poirot* (1937; reis. New York: HarperCollins, 2011), Kindle edition.

At one point, she tells Poirot and another guest named Major Riddle that her dead husband is standing right behind them and, perhaps more significantly, she also claims to be a reincarnation of "Hatshepsut" and a "Priestess in Atlantis."[47] Instead of viewing these claims as evidence of some sort of mental instability, though, Poirot seems to view Vanda's beliefs as a coping mechanism. He tells Major Riddle, "It is possible she finds it helpful. . . . She needs, at this moment, to create for herself a world of illusion so that she can escape the stark reality of her husband's death."[48] We're not certain here if Poirot is reducing Vanda's spiritualistic beliefs solely to a psychological need, but his recognition of the function these beliefs play relative to her husband's death coincides with Lyons's explanation of the emotional appeal of Spiritualism during the later nineteenth century. She writes that a wide swath of people "turned to spiritualism for solace as well as hoping the séance would provide evidence for the existence of the immaterial world, most importantly for the existence of the immortal soul. It provided an alternative to what appeared to be an increasingly bleak, amoral world devoid of meaning."[49] In the end, Poirot discovers it was Mr. Chevenix-Gore's assistant Miss Lingard who killed him because he planned to disinherit her daughter Ruth (even though Ruth didn't know Lingard was her mother). However, Poirot takes pity on Lingard and tells Ruth that Lingard won't be put through a trial because she has a terminal heart condition and "will not live many weeks."[50]

The adaptation of this story in Series 5 of *Agatha Christie's Poirot* retains this emphasis on the occult. Vanda (Zena Walker) is again shown to be deeply invested in Spiritualism, appearing first in the garden, stroking an Egyptian necklace, and telling Poirot about her "spiritual guide," a woman named "Safra," who was "a servant of Amenhotep." Ruth (Emma Fielding) tells Vanda that Poirot wouldn't want to hear about that, but as in the short story, Poirot seems to encourage Vanda, telling Ruth that "Poirot interests himself always in matters of the occult." He then examines Vanda's necklace, which she tells him belonged to Safra and is three thousand years old. She adds that Safra "is never wrong."

The episode takes pains to demonstrate how Vanda's practices are abnormal. For example, we see her in the following scene with outstretched arms, looking as if she's engaged in some sort of communicative ritual. And just to make sure we don't misunderstand the "otherness" of this, the music playing during these scenes with Vanda is described as "eerie" by the subtitles provided. Finally, as if to put a fine point on Vanda's spiritual practices, when her husband Gervase's body is discovered, Vanda stoically reiterates, "I told you. Safra is never wrong." Vanda's Spiritualism is also evident when Japp interviews her. Amidst a cloud of incense, she tells him that she and Gervase met on the "spiritual plane." Japp's skepticism is obvious, as is his misunderstanding, since he asks Poirot and Hastings where he can get ahold of Safra, presumably to question him. Also, at the "Big Reveal," Vanda protests when Poirot mentions Gervase's death, saying "He is not dead. He is on a different spiritual plane, that's all."

[47] Ibid.
[48] Ibid.
[49] Lyons, *Species*, 88.
[50] Christie, "Dead Man's Mirror."

Poirot accuses Ruth of being the murderer, as in the story, but the episode also includes an elaborate scene after the "Big Reveal" in which we hear a voice address Vanda while she's in bed. The voice claims to be Safra and tells Vanda to go downstairs amidst more "eerie music." The voice says, "It was you, Vanda. You killed him." When Vanda protests, the voice says, "You know it was. You killed Gervase. . . . Now you must make amends!" The voice then asks, "What have you hidden in your locket, Vanda?" As Vanda opens the locket, the voice says, "The bullet that killed your husband!" It continues, "You must write a note admitting it! And then. . ." as we're shown a noose hanging in the room.

At this, Hastings and Poirot rush into the room as Vanda faints. The former catches her, as Poirot opens two wall panels to reveal Miss Lingard (Fiona Walker). Japp righteously calls her actions "diabolical," as we learn that she's Ruth's mother. Miss Lingard is taken into custody by Japp here, after Poirot agrees to her request that Ruth never be allowed to see her. So, unlike the novel, Miss Lingard doesn't escape justice. However, this adaptation exhibits the seriousness with which Vanda embraces her spiritualist beliefs in Christie's short story. Again, these beliefs consist mainly of the two core attributes I noted—the dead aren't really gone, and we can contact them—as well as the Egyptian flair so prevalent when the story was composed.

Dumb Witness

Our final example is the novel *Dumb Witness*, published in 1937.[51] In this novel and its adaptation, we find a clearer comparison between Spiritualism and what some characters identify as "real" religious practices. That is to say, in the previous three examples, Spiritualism is presented as a fanciful yet essentially harmless form of meaning-making, perhaps a foolish one, but not in a specifically pejorative sense. In *Dumb Witness*, though, Christie is more deliberate in her characterization of Spiritualism and its practices as markedly different from the normative Christianity of her time, albeit a difference that doesn't disqualify spiritualistic practices as definitively deviant. But let's not get ahead of ourselves.

In *Dumb Witness*, Poirot's curiosity is kindled when he receives a letter dated 17 April on 28 June from a woman called Emily Arundell. He and Hastings (who narrates the novel) travel to Market Basing, but soon discover that Emily is dead and that she left her large estate and fortune to her domestic companion Minnie Lawson, instead of her family. Familial disputes over money always make for good motives, and so Poirot and Hastings begin their investigation, aided this time by a wire-haired terrier called Bob, who'd belonged to Emily. With Bob's help, Poirot discovers Emily's murderer and Bob returns to Argentina with Hastings.

Emily, the victim in this novel, is shown early on to be religiously active; for example, she fasts before the morning Easter service. Her companion Minnie tries to get her to

---

[51] For more about this novel, see Osborne, *Life and Crimes*, 155–158; and Aldridge, *Agatha Christie's Poirot*, 122–126.

eat, saying, "the vicar at Southbridge—a most conscientious man, told me distinctly that there was no obligation to come fasting," but Emily dismisses her suggestion haughtily, telling Minnie, "I've never yet taken anything before Early Service and I'm not going to begin now. *You* can do as you like." We're also told specifically that she and Minnie did attend that early service.[52]

Nevertheless, one of the most obvious elements of the plot is the focus on Spiritualism. We're told early on that Miss Lawson engages in Spiritualism, and two local sisters (Isabel and Julia Tripp) are deeply involved in the practice. This data reinforces the claim by several scholars that "Spiritualism was seen as overwhelmingly a woman's domain, and its rise contributed to the churches' acknowledgment by the end of the war that women's position in religion and society had altered."[53] Obviously, not all the women in *Dumb Witness* are as enthusiastic about Spiritualism as these three. For instance, Emily clearly holds no truck with Spiritualism, and even warns Minnie that she "better not let the vicar hear you" talking about it.[54] We're also told by the narrator later on that Emily worries if "this spiritualistic business was really good for Minnie."[55]

The kind of Spiritualism found in the novel again consists mainly of contacting and communicating with the dead. However, we do hear something new here in a description from Minnie of her activities one afternoon that Emily had released her from her domestic duties. Minnie tells Emily,

> I had the most interesting time. We had the Planchette and really — it wrote the most interesting things. There were several messages ... Of course it's not *quite* the same thing as the sittings ... Julia Tripp has been having a lot of success with the automatic writing. Several messages from Those who have Passed Over. It — it really makes one feel so grateful — that such things should be permitted.[56]

There are several important details to note here. First, Minnie mentions "automatic writing."[57] As Natale details in her work, "Spirit-authored texts could be delivered in several ways. A common procedure was automatic writing, in which the medium fell into a trance and wrote under the influence of spirits."[58] This would confirm Minnie's report that Julia Tripp had received and transcribed messages from departed spirits. As I noted earlier, spirits of the departed were normally "compliant communicators," and these spirits are evidently cooperative and copacetic. Minnie says as much when she later gushes to Emily that "our Dear Ones change so—on the other side. Everything is

---

52 Christie, *Dumb Witness* (1937; reis. New York: HarperCollins, 2011), Kindle edition, ch. 1, "The Mistress of Littlegreen House."
53 Brown, *Religion and Society*, 104–105. See also Owen, *Darkened Room*, especially her first two chapters, pp. 1–17 and 18–40. Along these lines, it's worth mentioning that in *Murder in Mesopotamia* (1936), the Nurse—who narrates the novel—has a "mediumistic" experience in chapter twenty-three, which is titled, "I Go Psychic."
54 Christie, *Dumb Witness*, ch. 3, "The Accident."
55 Ibid.
56 Ibid.
57 Christie also mentions "automatic writing" in *A Pale Horse*, ch. 6.
58 Natale, *Supernatural*, 126.

love and understanding."[59] These "Spirit-authored" texts were important in Spiritualism, as they provided a kind of evidence for contact with the dead. In fact, when Emily gently chides Minnie to say that she better not let the vicar hear her talk about Spiritualism, Minnie's response includes almost scientific-sounding language. She tells Emily, that she wishes the vicar "would examine the subject. It seems to me so narrow-minded to condemn a thing that you have not even investigated."[60] In connection with this, it behooves us to remember again that Spiritualism was often associated with Mesmerism in the popular imagination, and as such contained an aura of pseudo-science.

A second key detail—and an example of the technology related to Spiritualism as a kind of "scientific" inquiry—is when Minnie references a Planchette that wrote out some messages from the spirits they contacted. Later in this same conversation, Minnie reiterates that it "spelt out something" at a recent session, so that contact with the dead spirits was successful.[61] Natale helps us understand what this device is, noting, "Invented by a French spiritualist in 1853, it [the Planchette] consisted of a small board supported by wheels, to which a pencil was attached to write signs or letters that were interpreted as spirit messages."[62] The popularity of the Planchette was assured when it began to be marketed and sold in bookshops in the mid-nineteenth century.[63] This widespread availability and its acceptability as a desirable, even faddish middle-class object helps to explain the fact that Minnie doesn't have to explain the Planchette to Emily, even though Emily is wary of Spiritualism.

However, Emily's wariness is tempered by two narratorial comments from Hastings. In their conversation, Minnie mentions communicating with the dead, and Emily gently chides her. But once Minnie mentions a more specific spiritual message about a key to a Boule cabinet, Emily is immediately interested, since she has a Boule cabinet in which her father used to hide his liquor bottles. Even though the narrator tells us that Emily wondered if "this spiritualistic business was really good for Minnie," we're also told, "It was little things like that [the cabinet key], things that surely neither Minnie Lawson nor Isabel and Julia Tripp could possibly know, which made one wonder whether, after all, there wasn't something in this spiritualistic business."[64] Second, even though Emily is generally skeptical about Spiritualism, the narrator still describes her walking about her house at night when she couldn't sleep, "as though ghosts walked beside her."[65]

To understand better how Christie situates Spiritualism and a more recognized, acceptable form of religion here, let me mention three subsequent scenes in the novel. First, we're shown a scene in which Poirot learns more about the character of the community. In his first visit to Market Basing, Poirot takes the time to visit its church, and "wandered seemingly aimlessly about the churchyard reading some of the

[59] Christie, *Dumb Witness*, ch. 3, "The Accident."
[60] Ibid.
[61] Ibid.
[62] Natale, *Supernatural*, 132.
[63] Natale clarifies this for us in ibid., 133–134.
[64] Christie, *Dumb Witness*, ch. 3, "The Accident."
[65] Ibid.

epitaphs."[66] He's actually looking for information about Emily's family, and the narrator helpfully provides epitaphic descriptions from their grave markers like "Fell Asleep in Christ," as well as three epitaphs that include biblical citations: "I will arise and go to my father" (Luke 15:18); "Ask and ye shall receive" (John 16:24); and "Thy will be done" (Matthew 6:10). This last epitaph is part of Emily's own headstone, again indicating her Christian orientation and piety. These epitaphic citations not only indicate a shared biblical language, they also signify the Christian character of Emily's family and, by extension, of Market Basing. However, I want to echo Byrne here and note that the presence of these markers of Christian culture don't in and of themselves refute the ideas, presence, and/or practice of Spiritualism in the minds and lives of the residents of Market Basing. As Byrne demonstrates in her work, it's not an all or nothing proposition; lived religion is a notoriously messy affair, after all.

Second, when Poirot and Hastings visit Littlegreen House (Emily's former home), one of the servants, an older woman, shows them around. While doing so, she tells Poirot about Minnie's interest in Spiritualism, and leaves little doubt as to her own feelings on the matter: "Sitting in the dark round a table and dead people came back and spoke to you. Downright irreligious I call it — as if we didn't know departed souls had their rightful place and aren't likely to leave it."[67] She also reiterates that Emily did not hold with spiritualism, quipping that "she found spiritualism one degree better than playing patience or cribbage."[68]

Third, this opposition between "real religion" and Spiritualism is reinforced when Hastings and Poirot visit the Tripp sisters—whom Hastings describes as "vegetarians, theosophists, British Israelites, Christian Scientists, spiritualists and enthusiastic amateur photographers."[69] Isabel bemoans the fact that others in Market Basing aren't interested in Spiritualism, noting, "I have often tried to discuss things with the vicar, but find him most painfully *narrow*. Don't you think, Mr. Parrot, that any definite creed is bound to be *narrowing*?"[70] The opposition I note is evident here in the way in which the novel trivializes the Tripp sisters by treating them as harmless curiosities whom no one takes seriously. That is, if they're the central representatives of Spiritualism, they're not especially effective or persuasive ones.

Nonetheless, the Tripp sisters unknowingly provide Poirot with a central piece of evidence that Emily was poisoned when they describe what happened to her during a séance they were holding the night she died. They tell him they saw "a kind of halo" or "a luminous haze" that surrounded her head, "an aureole of faint light."[71] The sisters admit to Poirot they were never quite sure where Emily stood on the matter of Spiritualism, but they saw this "haze" as "a sign that she was about to pass over to the

---

[66] Ibid., ch. 7, "Lunch at the George." As I've pointed out before, Poirot also visits graveyards in *Hallowe'en Party* (1969) and in *Elephants Can Remember* (1972) he does the same. Both of these visits include the use of scriptural language/allusions.

[67] Ibid., ch. 8, "Interior of Littlegreen House."

[68] Ibid., ch. 10, "Visit to Miss Peabody."

[69] Ibid., ch. 11, "Visit to the Misses Tripp."

[70] Ibid., (emphasis original). Ironically, the first part of Isabel's lament is a quotation from Proverbs 29:18.

[71] Ibid.

other side."[72] Later, in chapter 15, Minnie corroborates their spiritualist-influenced account, reiterating to him that Emily was more open to Spiritualism than anyone might have guessed. Minnie explains that what she saw during the séance was, in fact, "the beginning of a materialization."[73] She explains to Poirot what she witnessed, telling him that, "Ectoplasm . . . proceeds, you know, from the medium's mouth in the form of a ribbon and builds itself up into a form. Now I am *convinced*, Mr. Poirot, that *unknown to herself* Miss Arundel was a *medium*."[74] Even though Poirot reaffirms his suspicious nature to Hastings in the novel, he refuses to disregard what the Tripp sisters told him solely because of their spiritualist beliefs, going so far as to tell Hastings that he has "an open mind on the subject."[75] However, with not a little sexism, he still notes that, "Foolish women . . . are foolish women, whether they are talking about spiritualism or politics or the relation of the sexes or the tenets of the Buddhist faith."[76]

Low-key sexism aside, Christie provides a much more rounded depiction of spiritualist practices and beliefs in this novel than we've seen before. It's not just that the dead aren't really dead or that the living can contact them; we hear more about the techniques and apparatuses used to facilitate and preserve the results of that contact here. As we've seen, several characters juxtapose these spiritualistic ideas and practices with more acceptable views of normative Christianity in a way that posits the "otherness" of Spiritualism as a religious orientation and lived practice. However, by the end of the novel the ideas and practices of Spiritualism aren't dismissed or even denigrated as dithering. As such, Christie positions them as neither dominant nor detached, indicating the kind of inclusivism that Byrne argues for in her work. But do we find that inclusive attitude retained in the world the text creates?

In the 1996 television adaptation, the spiritualistic element is highlighted early on, when the Tripp sisters (Muriel Pavlow and Pauline Jameson) approach Poirot at a boat dock where he and Hastings have come to watch Charles (Patrick Ryecart) try to break a speedboat record. They deliver a message from "the General" (Emily's father) that Charles's race will end in blood. Sure enough, Charles's boat malfunctions and he's forced to jump from it.

The Tripp sisters are also invited to what was supposed to be Charles's celebratory dinner, and in the midst of it, one of them stands, welcomes, and serves as a medium for the General as a spiritual visitor. The General warns both Poirot (via a message from "MP," Marie Poirot, Poirot's grandmother) and Emily (Ann Morrish). She then speaks in Greek to say, "You have all been warned." After dinner, Hastings wakes Poirot up, disturbed by the mediumistic visitation. Poirot gives Hastings a demonstration as to how so-called mediums can pick initials, asking him about a "JH in your family past." When Hastings takes this "JH" to mean his Uncle Jack, Poirot explains to him that it's "guesswork" on the part of the medium. Unlike the novel, then, Poirot here adopts a very skeptical attitude towards Spiritualism.

This version also departs from the novel in showing us Emily's death. The scene is quite dramatic, with a greenish fog emanating from her, which the Tripp sisters happily

[72] Ibid.
[73] Ibid., ch. 15, "Miss Lawson."
[74] Ibid, (emphasis original).
[75] Ibid., ch. 12, "Poirot Discusses the Case."
[76] Ibid.

interpret as her spirit leaving her body. Additionally—as in several of the film adaptations—we're shown Emily's funeral. We hear and are shown the priest read from the Church of England's Service for the Dead, which here includes quotations from Psalm 103:14-17, 1 Timothy 6:7, and Job 1:21.

In the novel, Poirot can only hypothesize what caused the "halo" emanating from Emily the night she died, but this adaptation resolves that ambiguity. Here, Poirot details how Bella Tanios (Julia St John), Emily's niece, poisoned her with phosphorus in her liver capsules. This created, in his words, a "lethal chemical reaction within her body which emanated from her in the form of a green vapor." And he specifically notes that this vapor was "thought by some to be her spirit leaving her body," as the shot shifts from him to the Tripp sisters. This adaptation, then, problematizes spiritualism through Poirot's skepticism and the attention paid to scientifically explaining seemingly spiritualistic phenomenon.[77]

*   *   *

In sum, the portrayal of Spiritualism in Christie's Poirot works is more sympathetic than her description of sectarian Christianity, but is still shown to be "other." What I mean is that aside from the possible exception of Mrs. Maltravers, all those who profess a belief in Spiritualism and engage in its accompanying practices seem sincere and aren't shown to be nefarious. While it's true that in *Dumb Witness* we hear of "official" and lay Christian opposition to Spiritualism, that opposition isn't serious or backed up by any action. This reflects the "happy accommodation" between Spiritualism and Christianity which Byrne details in her work.[78] To review, Byrne argues, "Clergy responses to the phenomena of spiritualism and the theology of spiritualism were decidedly mixed. Yet throughout the period many were aware, and spoke about, how spiritualism was 'gaining ground', regardless of whether they welcomed this or feared it. The language and ideas, as much as the phenomena, of spiritualism had become part of the common culture."[79] And yet the interaction between the Church of England and Spiritualism was more complicated than simply an oppositional one. Indeed, Byrne claims that interaction was far more reciprocal.[80]

Even granting this porous, amalgamated relationship, the "otherness" of Spiritualism is highlighted in the adaptations of Christie's works, as when we're shown Emily's burial and the accompanying readings from the Book of Common Prayer—neither of which are present in the novel. These reassert the primacy of normative Christianity in socially recognized rituals necessary for communal well-being in a way that Spiritualism could never serve. That is, even though Christie depicts Spiritualism as non-threatening and even welcomed by many, the world the text creates still demonstrates a need for the collective, public function of normative Christianity. Now, let's examine how Christie engages and depicts more socially prominent and organized minority religious practices like Judaism and Islam.

---

[77] Likewise, the film also corrects the troubling fact that Poirot engineered Bella's suicide in the novel. That is, here, Bella doesn't kill herself after Poirot identifies her as the murderer.
[78] See Owen, *Darkened Room*, 22–23.
[79] Byrne, *Modern Spiritualism*, 181.
[80] Ibid.

13

Jews and Judaism

One of the most problematic issues when investigating the presence of religion in Christie's Poirot stories is the way in which Jews and Judaism are presented. Of course, there are references to Jews and Judaism in other Christie novels, and one could even argue that in terms of data, these examples outside of the Poirot canon are more significant in understanding her treatment of Jews.[1] However, in the Poirot stories we have several instances in which Jews are treated in a pejorative, stereotypical way that makes it clear they aren't insiders in the pattern of "acceptable" religiosity Christie maintains in her work as a result of Christian hegemony.[2] Nevertheless, as we'll see, Christie's Jews aren't ever her murderers nor are they definitively excluded from the more mainstream groups who demonstrate "Englishness."

Before we get to the specific examples from her works, let's remind ourselves of one way that Christian hegemony asserts itself: the establishment of a "norm" over and against an "other." At the outset of Chapter 11, I used Khyati Y. Joshi's and Warren J. Blumenthal's analyses of Christian privilege in the US to describe the process by which those in the majority use political and cultural means to define themselves as normal by a process of alterity, or, creating an "other." This "other" functions as a repository of all the characteristics, beliefs, and behaviors that the "norm" views as undesirable and discordant. Put simply, alterity functions to solidify in-group identity by claiming that "We are who we are because we're not *them*," whoever the *them* might be.

Prior to our examination, let's also spend some time considering the world behind the text by briefly summarizing the situation of Jews in England broadly from the

---

[1] In *Agatha Christie: The Woman and Her Mysteries* (New York: Free Press, 1990), Kindle edition, ch. 3, "Agatha Christie: Kings and Commoners," Gillian Gill examines both the 1925 novel *The Secret of Chimneys* and the 1930 book *Giant's Bread*, which she published under the name Mary Westmacott. More attention is paid to this issue in Jane Arnold's article, "Detecting Social History: Jews in the Works of Agatha Christie," *Jewish Social Studies* 49, nos. 3/4 (1987): 275–282. Arnold also focuses on *Giant's Bread*, and on pp. 280-281 provides a helpful list of all the Jewish characters in Christie's work. The most comprehensive treatment of Jews in Golden Age crime fiction is that of Malcolm J. Turnbull, *Victims or Villains: Jewish Images in Classic English Detective Fiction* (Bowling Green, OH: Bowling Green State University Popular Press, 1998), which includes a section on Christie (see pp. 77–87).

[2] Obviously, there are other Jewish characters in the Poirot stories, such as Dr. Bauerstein in *The Mysterious Affair at Styles* and Demetrius and Zia Papapolous in *The Mystery of the Blue Train* (1928). However, I chose the Jewish characters about which we have more detailed comments to examine.

Victorian period to the outset of World War II. Todd M. Endelman notes that at the outset of the nineteenth century, "most Jews in England were immigrants or the children of immigrants," and "By 1830, there were about twenty thousand Jews living in London and perhaps another ten thousand in the provinces."[3] In the Victorian period in general, England approached native and immigrant Jews somewhat differently than Russia or other countries in Europe in that Jews weren't asked or required by law to forego Jewish practices or customs to be integrated into society.[4] Nor did leaders and lawmakers see any real danger to English society resulting from such integration.[5] In part, this lack of concern was due to the fact that most English Jews weren't orthodox in their religious observances; in fact, many Jews—especially upper class Jews—favored more moderate practices and religious services.[6] As such, a cozy intermingling of English and Jewish identities was possible in the mid-nineteenth century, due in part to the socializing effect of secondary education.[7]

For a variety of reasons, in around 1870 this changed when the "Jewish question" and the issue of emancipation finally was foregrounded in England.[8] One of the key reasons for this change was the increase and shift in immigration. Not just the amount, but also the kind(s) of Jewish immigrants caused not only a reconsideration of English immigration law—culminating in the Aliens Act of 1905—and a concomitant attitude shift among socio-economically privileged Jews, but also a redeployment of latent antisemitic sentiment in popular culture.[9] Once the Great War began in 1914, many became suspicious of Jewish collusion and/or sympathy with Germany, as so many English Jews had immigrated from there.[10] The fact that "friendly aliens" from Russia were exempt from the military conscription instituted in 1916 didn't help to assuage feelings that Jews weren't doing all they could, and sporadic anti-Jewish mob violence and property destruction resulted.[11]

However, there were points on which English and Jewish interests aligned, such as the issue of Zionism.[12] Even though most Jews in England weren't fervent in their support for a far-off, idealized state, the prospect of ending Turkish rule and thereby increasing the imperial reach of Britain was appealing. Another point of alignment was the increase in the socio-economic status of immigrant Jews in the Interwar period. This led to a greater integration of Jews into the social and economic fabric of England, and subsequently to the decrease in importance of traditional neighborhoods for immigrants, such as the East End.[13] The enlarged presence of Jews in middle- to upper-class English society disrupted traditional organizational models, and predictably led

---

[3] Endelman, *The Jews of Britain, 1656 to 2000*, Jewish Communities in the Modern World (Berkeley, Los Angeles & London: University of California Press, 2002), 79.
[4] Ibid., 108, 115, and 161.
[5] Ibid., 104.
[6] Ibid., 117–118, 147, and 167.
[7] Ibid., 99 and 123.
[8] Ibid., 152–153.
[9] Ibid., 82–83 and 91.
[10] Ibid., 184.
[11] See ibid., 185.
[12] Ibid., 186ff.
[13] Ibid., 196–197.

to a collateral rise in periodic antisemitic and discriminatory behavior.[14] These developments were buttressed by contributing events such as the widespread and ongoing popularity of the forged *Protocols of the Elders of Zion* (published in 1903, but not widely circulated in England until after the Great War) as well as the Bolshevik Revolution (1917–1923) and ultimately the outset of World War II in 1939.[15] Unfortunately, several of the evergreen stereotypes about Jews and Judaism resurfaced during this period, including those found in Christie's works during (and even after) this period.[16]

John Ritchie, Jeremy Black, and Malcolm J. Turnbull all note as much, connecting Christie's characterization of Jews with broader attitudes specifically towards foreigners and the accompanying British xenophobia, especially in, but not limited to, the 1920s. For his part, Ritchie comments that "Christie's society demonstrates its conservatism and insularity is in its attitudes to foreign people and ideas. It is suspicious of aliens who embody a different code of behaviour. Jews, Frenchmen and Americans, if rarely tolerated, are resented for epitomizing some facet of undignified behaviour."[17] Similarly, Black reminds us that "Jews as villainous were not a new aspect of detective fiction" by Christie's time.[18] More specifically, he writes, "The foreign origin of many Jews had led to them being positioned in tales of international villainy. Yet this was pushed to the fore due to the association of Jews with imperial Germany, and then with Bolshevism even more so."[19] As I'll mention, Black engages the issue of immigration and how that impacted views of foreigners (especially Jews) at different points, but especially after 1933.[20] Finally, Turnbull also helps us to grasp the macro picture of the world behind the text, noting,

> Negative fictional renderings of Jews peaked in the 1920s and 1930s parallel with renewed fears of international conspiracies and Jewish manipulation of finance in the traumatic aftermath of the Great War, concurrent concerns at alleged Jewish connections to Bolshevism and the Russian Revolution, the rise of Fascism at home and abroad, economic turbulence and social discontent caused by the Great Depression, and influxes of refugee immigrants—all against the backdrop of a rapidly deteriorating Europe.[21]

Turnbull's work also assists us in understanding that already by the time Christie published *The Mysterious Affair at Styles* in 1920/1921, British crime fiction was heir to a whole host of stereotypical depictions of Jews in drama, fiction, and other popular

---

[14] Ibid., 198–199.
[15] Ibid., 202. For more on the impact of the *Protocols* in England, see Colin Holmes, *Anti-Semitism in British Society, 1876-1939* (London & New York: Routledge, 1979), 141–160.
[16] See Endelman, *Jews*, 199–200.
[17] Ritchie, "Agatha Christie's England, 1918-39: Sickness in the Heart and Sickness in Society as Seen in the Detective Thriller," *Australian National University Historical Journal* 9 (1972): 4.
[18] Black, *The Importance of Being Poirot* (South Bend, IN: St. Augustine's Press, 2021), 68.
[19] Ibid.
[20] Ibid., 74.
[21] Turnbull, *Victims*, 7.

cultural products.[22] And the creation and maintenance of stereotypes is one of the primary ways through which the process of alterity functions.

Jane Arnold has investigated Jews in Christie's work, and writes, "stereotypes (like caricatures) are not necessarily inaccurate descriptions; they are simply unbalanced. Stereotypes might be described as the distilled essence of the public perception of particular groups of people."[23] In their examination of anti-Muslim content in editorial cartoons, Peter Gottschalk and Gabriel Greenberg provide a definition of stereotypes that dovetails nicely with the analyses of Joshi, Blumenfeld, and Arnold. They write, "Stereotypes are simply descriptions of a group by outsiders using characteristics understood to be both shared by all members and to define them as different from 'normal' society. These characteristics may be physical (e.g., tall), behavioral (e.g., excitable), or moral (e.g., conservative). Stereotypes often generate specific symbols of difference from the norm."[24]

As you might have guessed, for our discussion, stereotypes can be useful in determining how religion is perceived and depicted as a way of creating and sustaining the socio-religious distinction of an "other." To help us set a baseline for how Jews were understood in England in the early to mid-twentieth century, Turnbull reproduces some of the work of Sidney Salomon from 1938 that describes "the conceptions with which British Jews were most frequently and persistently obliged to contend." These include:

(1) that the Jews were an international force intent on controlling world affairs through finance; (2) that Jews were Bolshevists; (3) that refugee Jews were overrunning the professions ... (4) that Jews had divided loyalties (and, by extension, were ultimately "aliens"); (5) that Jews controlled the press and chain-stores ... (6) that Jews were promoting British involvement in war so as to revenge themselves on Hitler.[25]

Many of these "conceptions" have legs and will emerge as persistent antisemitic stereotypes, as we'll see. In what follows, then, I'll discuss two primary examples from Christie's Poirot canon that depict Jews and Judaism in stereotypical ways, and point out how these often-distasteful depictions are minimized in later adaptations.

Three Act Tragedy

In the 1934 novel *Three Act Tragedy*, there's a Jewish character named Oliver Manders, and we can detect three common stereotypes about Jews and Judaism in comments

---

[22] Some representative examples of Jews in fiction (crime and otherwise), both before and after *The Mysterious Affair at Styles*, would include Baroness Emma Orczy's 1905 historical novel *The Scarlet Pimpernel*; Frank Froëst's first novel, the police procedural *The Grell Mystery* (1913); the 1915 novel *The Thirty-Nine Steps* by John Buchan; Dorothy L. Sayers's 1923 novel *Whose Body?*; and Victor L. Whitechurch's *The Templeton Case* (1924).

[23] Arnold, "Detecting," 275. Additionally, see Paul Hedges, *Religious Hatred: Prejudice, Islamophobia, and Antisemitism in Global Context* (London & New York: Bloomsbury, 2021), 19–23.

[24] Gottschalk and Greenberg, *Islamophobia: Making Muslims the Enemy* (Lanham, MD: Rowman & Littlefield, 2008), 63.

[25] Turnbull, *Victims*, 42.

made about him.[26] A friend of Poirot's called Mr. Satterthwaite first describes him at the initial dinner party (the first of the titular three acts), and his discordant identity is marked early on: "A handsome young fellow, twenty-five at a guess. Something, perhaps, a little sleek about his good looks. Something else – something – was it foreign? Something unEnglish about him."[27] He later realizes what this "something" is, as he thinks, "Of course, that's it—not foreign—Jew!"[28] This foreignness is augmented by the fact that Manders is a communist, which in 1934 would still invoke the specter of Bolshevism. Manders's outsider status is a manifestation of the stereotype of *the Jew as perennial foreigner or alien*.[29] By 1934, the trope of the "Wandering Jew"—a trope that indicates Jews are cursed to migrate without settling, always remaining unassimilated or alien—would've been firmly ensconced in the popular and literary imagination of the period, not to mention the cumulative historical impact of numerous European expulsions that took place from the twelfth to fifteenth centuries. In his survey of the development of the image of the "Wandering Jew," Richard I. Cohen analyzes publications in England up to the late eighteenth century, indicating its prevalence even at that late date.[30] The implication of this stereotypical view is that Jews can never *really* be part of a society, since they refuse to assimilate and have no real home. As we'll see later, this stereotype is often linked to concerns over immigration and economic issues.

Given that one of most enduring stereotypes about Judaism focuses on *money and financial power*, it's not surprising that we find this characteristic associated with Manders.[31] We have two examples of this particular stereotype. First, a character called "Egg" (aka Miss Hermione Lytton Gore) calls him a "slippery Shylock."[32] The name Shylock, of course, is a reference to a character in Shakespeare's play *The Merchant of Venice* (1594–1596). Shylock is a Jew and a money-lender and has been an influential paradigm for representations of Jews. However, Shylock as a character and symbol never always means only one thing.[33] Even so, the comments of Susannah Heschel are

---

[26] To learn more of the plot of this novel, readers should seek out Charles Osborne, *The Life and Crimes of Agatha Christie: A Biographical Companion to the Works of Agatha Christie*, rev. and updated ed. (London: HarperCollins, 1999), 125–128; and Mark Aldridge, *Agatha Christie's Poirot: The Greatest Detective in the World* (London: HarperCollins, 2020), 82–85. Turnbull treats it briefly; see *Victims*, 81.

[27] Christie, *Three Act Tragedy* (1934; reis. New York: HarperCollins, 2011), Kindle edition, First Act, ch. 2, "Incident Before Dinner."

[28] Ibid.

[29] This stereotype is closely related to the generalization of Jews as "disloyal," or having a "dual identity." See Turnbull, *Victims*, 25, 54, and 75.

[30] See Cohen, "The 'Wandering Jew' from Medieval Legend to Modern Metaphor," in *The Art of Being Jewish in Modern Times*, eds. Barbara Kirshenblatt-Gimblett and Jonathan Karp; Jewish Culture and Contexts (Philadelphia: University of Pennsylvania Press, 2008), 150–153.

[31] See Turnbull, *Victims*, 25 and 55. In a similar way, in the first chapter of *And Then There Were None* (1939), a Mr. Morris is characterized as a "little Jew" by Philip Lombard, and Lombard laments the "damnable part about Jews, you couldn't deceive them about money—they *knew*!" Also, in her 1925 novel *The Secret of Chimneys*, Christie includes a shady character called Herman Isaacstein, who not only is described as the leader of a financial syndicate interested in foreign oil, but also is called "Nosystein" in chapter ten.

[32] Christie, *Three Act Tragedy*, First Act, ch. 2, "Incident Before Dinner."

[33] See, e.g., John Gross, *Shylock: A Legend and Its Legacy* (New York & London: Simon & Schuster, 1992), *passim*.

important for our purposes, as she notes Shylock's importance as a symbol in Jewish–Christian relations. She writes,

> The figure of Shylock, who has been presented on stage since the seventeenth century in a range of interpretations ... can also be read for allusions to the question of the Jewish presence within the Christian realm and also for its connections with race.... *The Merchant of Venice* expresses Christian concerns, racial and theological, about Jews.[34]

Are there similar "concerns" in Christie's novel over Manders's Jewishness? If so, are these concerns focused on his status as a cultural and religious outsider, or have they more to do with his affection for Egg? Either way, it is possible to read Egg's reference to Manders as a "slippery Shylock" as a comment on his eventual semi-acceptance. After all, both Shylock and his daughter Jessica convert and are thus able to incorporate somewhat into Christian Venetian society—even though his conversion is forced. Might these conversions parallel when Manders and Egg wind up together at the end of the novel? Could Oliver be accepted into Christie's kind of society at that point? Poirot certainly thinks so, as after Manders assures him that Egg is "all I care about in the world," he hints to Manders that one day Egg will be ready to love him, and "looked kindly after the young man" as Oliver departs.[35] Even so, if Manders's incorporation is meant to parallel Shylock's, one has to wonder if the consequences for the former rise to the heights endured by the latter.

The second comment dealing with the stereotype connecting Jews and money is much easier for us to grasp. This is because it shares the pecuniary prejudice we saw with the comparison to Shylock, and it's a brief, flat statement. Again, it comes from Egg, who tells Satterthwaite that Manders "wants to get rich."[36] On its own, this might not signify much more than Manders's desire as a young man wanting to earn a good living to impress the girl he fancies. Coupled with the reference to Shylock, though—and the ambiguous reference to a "Jewish gentleman" who might be lending money to the designer Mrs. Dacres—this desire to attain wealth takes on a different meaning altogether.[37] Again, though, Manders's ultimate fate in the novel belies any sinister connotations associated with the stereotype of Jews and money. His fate underscores the extent to which Jews are able to acculturate to English society, to be included into a more mainstream social grouping. This evidence is an important indication as to how Christie depicts the socio-cultural acceptability of Jews and Judaism, despite an exclusionary tendency in her inherited culture.

---

[34] Heschel, "From Jesus to Shylock: Christian Supersessionism and 'The Merchant of Venice'," *HTR* 99, no. 4 (2006): 409.
[35] Christie, *Three Act Tragedy*, Third Act, ch. 15, "Curtain." Lest we think Poirot is immune to the tendency to associate Shylock with antisemitic stereotypes, in the novel *After the Funeral* (1953; reis. New York: HarperCollins, 2011), Kindle edition, he describes Jessica as "the daughter of the hated and despised Jew" (ch. 23).
[36] Christie, *Three Act Tragedy*, First Act, ch. 4, "A Modern Elaine."
[37] It is unclear who this moneylender is. In Arnold's list of Jewish characters in Christie's works, she lists him separately from Manders. See "Detecting," 280.

A similar connection between Jews and money can be found in Christie's 1932 novel, *Peril at End House*. Therein, we hear of a Jewish character who's "rolling in money" named Jim Lazarus.[38] Lazarus is an art dealer, and when he offers to buy a painting for far more than it's worth, Poirot makes the cringeworthy comment that the offer of "the long-nosed M. Lazarus" is "uncharacteristic of his race."[39] Poirot's comment obviously is taking aim at the fiscal oddity of Lazarus's bid, the upshot being that since he's Jewish (and rich), Lazarus should know better. I want to make two points here before we go any further. First, as Turnbull notes, "Jews rarely seem to intrude into the words of Miss Marple or Tommy and Tuppence Beresford, Christie's subsidiary series sleuths. The more cosmopolitan Poirot appears to enjoy contact with a broader, multicultural cross-section of humanity and, interestingly, appears to have no animosity towards Jews as Jews."[40] That is, Poirot's urban nature and international experience occasion a greater familiarity with Jews, and even so, we find no vehement prejudice in his comments, even if he does voice what more modern readers would identify as cancel-worthy comments. As an example, and second, Poirot's notice about Lazarus's nose also speaks to physiognomic caricatures of Jews that are common in artistic propaganda, but that otherwise are rare in Christie's Poirot works.[41] This is not to say, though, that an assumption regarding Jewish hereditary traits is absent from the Poirot canon. A year after *Peril at End House*, we also see the use of antisemitic stereotypes in *Lord Edgware Dies*.[42] Poirot observes that one of the main characters, Carlotta Adams, is a "Jewess," and Hastings claims he can see "the faint traces of Semitic ancestry."[43] Returning to the trope of Jews and money, Poirot also claims that Adams's Jewish identity "makes for success," but it also contains the "danger" of the "love of money." When Hastings says that love of money might be a danger to anyone, Poirot replies, "That is true, but at any rate you or I would see the danger involved. We could weigh the pros and cons. If you care for money too much, it is only the money you see."[44] Here, Poirot posits a distinction between him and Hastings (as Christians) and someone like Carlotta, who cares too much for money, presumably because of her Jewishness.

A final example from *Three Act Tragedy* is a report from Mrs. Babbington about an incident in which "Oliver made a rather ill-bred attack on Christianity." Young Oliver told Rev. Babbington that he'd "like to sweep away the churches all over the world." He confesses he "hate[s] everything the Church stands for. Smugness, security and hypocrisy. Get rid of the whole canting tribe, I say!"[45] Mrs. Babbington then says how

---

[38] Christie, *Peril at End House* (1932; reis. New York: HarperCollins, 2011), ch. 3, "Accidents."
[39] Ibid., ch. 13, "Ellen."
[40] Turnbull, *Victims*, 82.
[41] See, for example, the remark in *Lord Edgware Dies* (1933; reis. New York: HarperCollins, 2011), Kindle edition, ch. 13, "The Nephew," about Rachel Dortheimer and her "long Jewish nose." In the opening trial scene of the novel *Sad Cypress* (1940; reis. New York: HarperCollins, 2011), Kindle edition, Prologue, Elinor is listening to a lawyer described as a "tall man with the Jewish nose."
[42] Black, *Importance*, 70, notices this.
[43] Christie, *Lord Edgware Dies*, ch. 1, "A Theatrical Party." Similarly, in *Murder on the Orient Express* (1934; reis. New York: HarperCollins, 2011), Kindle edition, Part 3, ch. 3, "Certain Suggestive Points," Poirot points out "a strain of Jewish" in Linda Arden (Goldenberg).
[44] Christie, *Lord Edgware Dies*, ch. 1, "A Theatrical Party."
[45] Christie, *Three Act Tragedy*, Third Act, ch. 2, "Lady Mary."

Mr. Babbington pointed out that even if Oliver managed to wipe away all the visible institutions of religion, "You would still have to reckon with God."[46] This remark evidently disarmed and silenced Manders.

This outburst is evidence of a third and final stereotypical view of Jews: their *hatred of Christianity*. This is an ancient stereotype, originating with the charge of deicide and the acceptance of guilt over Jesus's execution in Matthew 27:25. Given this, it is curious that no one notes that Oliver might hold this view of the Church because he's Jewish. Instead, it simply sounds like something an angry, stupid young man might say as a result of conditions out of his control. More specific to our focus, R. A. York helpfully reframes Manders's outburst in the context of how Christie depicts the changing societal mores and institutions of her times, commenting that in several of her works, "Young people show an aggressive disrespect to their seniors, to the Church which has been the central voice of an English morality, to loyalty to school or Empire."[47] York continues, writing that Manders's, "attack on Christianity is characteristic of the style of some 1930s progressivism, and his bitterness is plausibly rooted in the disapproval his parents have met for not being married."[48] This attack "is gently but firmly rejected by the saintly clergyman, Babbington, but Christie at least shows that the Christian hegemony is no longer in force (one may regret however that Mandel is Jewish, and so might well have been more moderate in attacking a religion to which he has presumably not belonged)."[49] York here makes a good point: it's not just that Manders as a Jew critiques the Church and no one calls him out on his tirade because of his Jewishness, it's also significant that as early as 1935 Christie is depicting cracks in the "Christian hegemony" we've been investigating. However, at the level of the world of the text, we can assume Manders's little tantrum was included to set up a similarity between Oliver and Egg, so that when they wind up together at the end of the novel it's a more believable outcome, since she had earlier critiqued the Church as well. With that outcome in mind, it seems plain that the narrative ultimately views him positively, as good enough to be incorporated into the "in-group," despite his Jewish faults.

The Hollow

A little over a decade later, we meet another Jewish character in the novel *The Hollow* (1946). Here, Mme. Alfrege is a minor character, almost totally dissociated from the central plot. She runs (or perhaps even owns) a dress shop in which Midge Hardcastle (the cousin of Lady Angkatell, at whose house the murder takes place) works, and the few descriptions we get of her are enough to establish her as an antisemitic caricature. Because of the murder, Midge has to call Alfrege to let her know she'll be missing work. When the connection is made, the narrator tells us the "raucous voice of the vitriolic

---

[46] Ibid.
[47] York, *Agatha Christie: Power and Illusion*, Crime Files (Hampshire & New York: Palgrave Macmillan, 2007), 81.
[48] Ibid.
[49] Ibid., 81–82.

little Jewess" comes on the line.[50] Alfrege is unsympathetic to Midge's plight, and in words marred by what appears to be a Yiddish-based lisp, she expresses disappointment and concern about how "sordid" and "vulgar" it all sounds.[51] Mme. Alfrege asks Midge,

> What wath that, Mith Hardcathle? A death? A funeral? Do you not know very well I am short-handed? Do you think I am going to stand for these excutheth? Oh, yeth, you are having a good time, I dare thay!.... Who are thethe friendth of yourth? What thort of people are they to have the poleeth there and a man shot? I've a good mind not to have you back at all! I can't have the tone of my ethtablishment lowered.[52]

Once the connection is broken, Edward Angkatell asks Midge if Alfrege was "decent about it." Midge replies, calling her boss "a Whitechapel Jewess with dyed hair and a voice like a corncrake."[53]

Midge's comment is more than simply a throwaway line; it's an insult linked to economic and immigrational issues. Whitechapel is a section of the East End of London, and the East End was a major destination point for immigrants and transmigrants in the late nineteenth to early twentieth centuries. Turnbull reminds us of the "influxes of impoverished Eastern European Jews after 1880 [that] were swamping the East End," and the population explosion that occurred in the wake of those influxes.[54] In his work, Nicholas J. Evans has shown the ambiguous status these migrants held.[55] At one and the same time they were targets of suspicion and revilement from anti-alienist forces, but they were also needed for Britain to maintain/retain its shipping/passenger concerns. After the Royal Commission on Alien Immigration was convened in 1902, the Aliens Act of 1905 and the Merchant Shipping Act of 1906 led to a heightened emphasis on "ethnic labelling" of migrants. Jews were now classified as Hebrews, or racially alien.

Much of this concern focused on Jewish immigrants who were, as Ben Gidley notes, "Yiddish-speaking Eastern Europeans," mostly from the *shtetl* communities of western Russia.[56] Gidley writes that the late nineteenth century

> marks the start of the expansion of the Jewish ghetto in East London. From this time, the Jewish population in Britain rose from around 50,000 to nearly 200,000 (the majority in London, but with sizeable communities in Leeds, Manchester,

---

[50] Christie, *The Hollow* (1946; reis. New York: HarperCollins, 2011), Kindle edition, ch. 14.

[51] For this lisp, see Arnold, "Detecting," 275.

[52] Christie, *The Hollow*, ch. 14.

[53] Ibid.

[54] Turnbull, *Victims*, 19. Turnbull also notes, "The Jewish population of London alone grew from 47,000 to 150,000 through immigration between 1883 and 1902" (19). See also Endelman, *Jews*, 95.

[55] Evans, "Commerce, State, and Anti-Alienism: Balancing Britain's Interests in the Late-Victorian Period," in *"The Jew" in Late-Victorian and Edwardian Culture: Between the East End and East Africa*, eds. Eitan Bar-Yosef and Nadia Valman; Palgrave Studies in Nineteenth-Century Writing and Culture (New York: Palgrave Macmillan, 2009), 80–97.

[56] Gidley, "The Ghosts of Kishinev in the East End: Responses to a Pogrom in the Jewish London of 1903," in *"The Jew" in Late-Victorian and Edwardian Culture*, 100.

Glasgow and elsewhere). These immigrants, often arriving at the docks of the East End, settled in precisely the areas that the wealthier Jews were beginning to vacate. It was in this period that the phrase "the East End" entered the English language, swiftly passing into Yiddish.[57]

The use of Yiddish and the lower socio-economic situation of these Jewish migrants in the East End marked them as additionally "other"; along with being Jewish, they were still culturally distinct and on the lower end of the economic spectrum. Gidley notes that the East End became "London's internal Orient," a site of imperial otherness, and these mostly uncultured and unskilled Jewish migrants who spoke Yiddish were obviously and observably different.[58]

Since Gidley brings up Yiddish, let's talk briefly about Mme. Alfrege's lisp. Literary and theater critics seem to be in agreement that it was Charles Dickens who first attached the lisp to an identifiably Jewish character, that of an unnamed Jew in chapter twenty of *Great Expectations*, published in 1860–1861.[59] Of course, Dickens's most famous Jewish character is Fagin, who appears in his 1838 novel *Oliver Twist*. As Susan Meyer writes, Dickens seemingly takes pains to incorporate numerous stereotypes to depict Fagin as *the* classic Jew.[60] Fast-forwarding back to *Great Expectations*, Dickens's use of the lisp as one way to deepen his anonymous character's Jewishness is echoed not just in other nineteenth-century literature, but also in scholarly works that purport to describe Jewish culture and language.[61]

In Christie's novel, the overall picture of Mme. Alfrege we can derive from Midge's comments is one of an immigrant Jew herself, or a descendant of one who either arrived/lived in a section of the East End. We also see that she speaks Yiddish (or, at least, that could be what we're to assume from her lisp), and is now in a much-improved or higher economic position as a manager (or owner) of a dress shop. All of this accords with what we know of Jews in London right before the Great War. As Endelman notes, there were about 180,000 Jews in London at that point, many of them recent emigres. He continues, "The newcomers found employment in two broad areas of economic life—retail trade (shopkeeping, pawnbroking, street and market trading) and small workshop manufacture."[62] However, it's not just that shops like Mme. Alfrege managed were common among Jewish immigrants, it's also that more women were rejoining the workforce at this point.[63] As Endelman writes, "Women immigrants were also active in traditional areas of commerce. They kept food shops, sold clothing and household

[57] Ibid. See also Endelman, *Jews*, 129, 145.
[58] Gidley, "The Ghosts," 101. See also Endelman, *Jews*, 156.
[59] Lauriat Lane, Jr., "Dickens' Archetypal Jew," *PMLA* 73, no. 1 (1958): 94–100, mentions this use of the lisp in *Great Expectations* as well as two other late works (97-98).
[60] Meyer, "Antisemitism and Social Critique in Dickens's *Oliver Twist*," *Victorian Literature and Culture* 33, no. 1 (2005): 239.
[61] Of special interest here are investigations into Jewish folklore by German scholars called *Volkskunde*. Interested readers should seek out Aya Elyada's "Early Modern Yiddish and the Jewish *Volkskunde*, 1880–1938," *JQR* 107:2 (2017): 182–208.
[62] Endelman, *Jews*, 130.
[63] See ibid., 132.

items in markets and from their homes, worked as credit drapers, newsagents, tobacconists, and shop assistants."[64] The success of Mme. Alfrege's shop also indicates that a level of integration into English society more broadly, in contradistinction to a majority of Jewish immigrants, who preferred to silo themselves and their business within Jewish enclaves.[65]

To that point, Gidley points out that wealthier, more acculturated British Jews embarked on an "assimilation project" in which they sought "to re-make their arriving co-religionists into English citizens as swiftly as possible. The Anglo-Jewish leaders consistently sought to make the ghetto dissolve itself into English society at large and throw off its old-fashioned, particularistic, and peculiar rituals, its debased jargon, and, above all, its radical politics."[66] In the case of Jews like Mme. Alfrege, we may assume that this project worked. As opposed to the stereotypical view of Jews as "scavengers and hawkers who struggled to make a living by collecting, patching, and reselling clothing cast off by others," Alfrege's dress shop is obviously a high-end establishment, and she bears little resemblance to the Jewish "ragmen and street sellers" of the popular English imagination in the mid- to late nineteenth century.[67] However, in Midge's eyes, she is still nothing but "a Whitechapel Jewess with dyed hair and a voice like a corncrake," despite the economic and cultural progress she has made in assimilating to English society. As such, the description of Mme. Alfrege trades in the stereotype of the Jew as *perennial foreigner*, just as we saw earlier with Oliver Manders in *Three Act Tragedy*. As far as Midge is concerned, then, Mme. Alfrege's lisp sets her apart from respectable English society.

These stereotyped characterizations of Jews and Judaism are obviously distasteful, and we shouldn't dismiss them merely as products of their time, as some have tried to do.[68] It's helpful, though to keep in mind two points about Jews in Christie's works.

---

[64] Ibid., 133.

[65] See ibid., 134.

[66] Gidley, "Ghosts," 101. See also Endelman, *Jews*, 82–83 and 171.

[67] Adam D. Mendelsohn, *The Rag Race: How Jews Sewed Their Way to Success in America and the British Empire*, The Goldstein-Goren Series in American Jewish History (New York & London: New York University Press, 2015), 8. For more on the Clothes Exchange in the East End, see pp. 18–36.

[68] Let me provide two examples of apologists for Christie in this regard. First, Martin Forward brings up Christie's depiction of Manders under the subheading of "Anti-Semitism in Practice" in his *A Short Introduction to Inter-Religious Dialogue* (Oxford: Oneworld, 2001). Even so, Forward lets Christie off the hook by claiming she was "a creature of her time and location" (95). Second, in Janet Morgan's standard biography of Christie, Morgan comes close to absolving Christie, too, noting, "Agatha mirrored in her books the attitudes of her class and generation. . . . Agatha's unsophisticated generalisations about Jews and Jewishness are a reminder that she did not share the inhibitions of a generation sensitised by the sufferings of the Jewish people since 1933. . . . The phrases with which Agatha offended were painful not because they were vicious but because they seemed flippant" (*Agatha Christie: A Biography* [London: William Collins Sons & Company, 1984; repr. New York: Alfred A. Knopf, 1985], 265). However, her deep, abiding appreciation for Wagner (see, e.g., York, *Agatha Christie*, 144) and her trip to Oberammergau at Easter-time in 1970 cast a more troubling light on her views on Jews, given the antisemitic views held by the former and the "many anti-Jewish stereotypes and caricatures" found in the latter (the quotation is from A. James Rudin, "Oberammergau: A Case Study of Passion Plays," in *Pondering the Passion: What's at Stake for Christians and Jews?* ed. Philip A. Cunningham [Lanham, MD: Rowman & Littlefield, 2004], 99).

First, Arnold reminds us of a point I made earlier in the chapter—as well as a larger characteristic of much Golden Age detective fiction—when she writes, "Christie's characters are stereotypes, and her Jews are stereotypes."[69] Arnold sees this not as a weakness, but as an important source for data regarding social history. I concur, and add that these data are also helpful in understanding how religion is depicted. That is, by noting these stereotypical views of Jews in Christie's work, it allows us to see more clearly the "symbols of difference" she erects between insider/outsider or acceptable/unacceptable religious practices; or, to put it in Khyati Y. Joshi's terms, between the "norm" and the "other."[70] Paying attention to how Christie depicts Jews shows us another way in which she challenges the Christian hegemony of her day (as we saw clearly with *Three Act Tragedy* and Oliver Manders).

Secondly, it's important for us to realize that Christie's portrayal of Jews and Judaism never crosses the line into a menacing depiction, as we can find in other examples of Golden Age crime fiction. As Gillian Gill puts it, Christie's work evinces a "kind of jingoistic, knee-jerk anti-Semitism [which] colors the presentation of Jewish characters in many of her early novels," and that "Christie's anti-Semitism had always been of the stupidly unthinking rather than the deliberately vicious kind."[71] This emphasis on Christie's early novels is important, as in her autobiography, Christie tells a curious story from 1933. She was at the house of a Dr. Julius Jordan (whom Morgan identifies as the "Director of Antiquities in Baghdad"), listening to him play Beethoven, when suddenly someone mentioned Jews.[72] Christie describes how "his face changed," and he said, "You do not understand. Our Jews are perhaps different from yours. They are a danger. They should be exterminated." Christie was understandably shocked, and comments that "On that day ... I saw my first Nazi."[73] And while one might argue that the more antisemitic caricatures are only found in her works before this encounter—as Robert Barnard does—we have seen in this chapter that Jewish stereotypes persist even after this terribly upsetting incident.[74]

---

[69] Arnold, "Detecting," 270–280. As we saw in the chapter, Arnold isn't alone in her view of Christie's use of stereotypes. See also Robert Barnard, *A Talent to Deceive: An Appreciation of Agatha Christie*, rev. and updated ed. (Glasgow: William Collins Sons & Co Ltd, 1980), 111, see also 65; and Wagoner, *Agatha Christie*, 55.

[70] See Joshi, *White Christian Privilege: The Illusion of Religious Equality in America* (New York: New York University Press, 2020), 134–135; and Gottschalk and Greenberg, *Islamophobia*, 63.

[71] Gill, *Agatha Christie*, ch. 3. In *Talent*, 15–16, Barnard disagrees slightly.

[72] See Morgan, *Agatha Christie*, 265.

[73] Christie, *An Autobiography* (1977; reis. New York: HarperCollins, 2011), 465–466.

[74] Barnard, *Talent*, recounts Christie's encounter with virulent antisemitism and claims, "from that date offensive references to Jews cease in her novels" (16). As one can see from the opening chapter of 1939's *And Then There Were None*, this is simply not true. Black makes a similar claim, writing that Christie's treatment of Jews differs "later in [her] career, after of course the Holocaust" (*Importance*, 72). Further, Black argues that in her work, Christie subtly and sometimes not-so-subtly alters and critiques inherited forms and ideas, like the conventions of detective fiction (56ff.) and modernism (61ff.). While he tries to claim that Christie does this as well with "xenophobic views," he provides no evidence of this vis-à-vis Jews and Judaism (75). In his work, York, *Agatha Christie*, 69, reiterates the position I take here. Like Black, however, York then tries to soften this assessment, arguing Christie actually demonstrates "respect for Jewish people," and that Poirot's foreignness indicates that "she feels no systematic xenophobia" (70).

The fact is that Christie continued to draw on traditional Jewish stereotypes in her works, but for our examination it is key to note that the Jewish characters in the Poirot stories are *not* totally beyond the fray. That is, both Arnold and Gill remind us that Christie's Jews are merely *different*, not anathema. Their claim is echoed more broadly by Edelman when he notes that verbal abuse and antisemitic opinions "were rarely translated into social and political action" in England. That is, "Neither high society nor the educated middle class closed its doors to Jews, even while viewing them as not quite English or even worse."[75] This is a central point for us to understand, as it indicates a softening of the more strict-sounding dichotomy one finds in Joshi; it seems that the Jews we find in the Poirot canon aren't completely "other." Arnold notes, "Although Christie's Jewish characters are not an easy part of the society she describes, neither are they entirely alien. No particular Jewish characteristic is completely negative."[76] More importantly, she writes, "The ambiguity of the status of Christie's Jewish characters extends to their place in society. It should be quite clear that we are dealing here with already very assimilated Jews; no Hassidim, or even religiously observant Jews, shadow the pages of her mysteries. Nonetheless, the Jews are Jews and, as such, are not quite English."[77] Similarly, Gill points out that "even at her most thoughtless and prejudiced, Christie saw Jews as different, alien, and un-English, rather than as depraved or dangerous—people one does not know rather than people one fears."[78] This is obvious in the case of Oliver Manders: he clearly occupies a place within Christie's society—even if that place is marginal because of his Jewishness. Nevertheless, by the end of *Three Act Tragedy*, we know that he and Egg will be together because Poirot has predicted and blessed their relationship. And even though in *Peril at End House*, Jim Lazarus is "long-nosed" and seemingly unwise with money—despite being very well off, it seems—Nick tells Poirot that, "He's a Jew, of course, but a frightfully decent one."[79] That judgment is born out in the fact that Lazarus, like Manders, winds up with the girl he's loved throughout the novel, Nick's friend Frederica. In fact, Christie signals Lazarus's acceptability by the language she uses to characterize Frederica, i.e., several times "Freddie" is described in reference to "a Madonna." Surely if a Jew can wind up with a "Madonna" then he's culturally and religiously acceptable, right? And it doesn't hurt that it seems Lazarus's business isn't doing well, so he and Freddie might have to be "poor" together.

We know that at times, Christie's American publishers would edit/censor some of her works to avoid any public outcry or official complaints, as when in 1947 the Anti-Defamation League sent a letter of complaint to Christie's American publishers.[80] But at the level of the world the text creates, how did later adaptations deal with these

---

[75] Edelman, *Jews*, 163–164.
[76] Arnold, "Detecting," 275.
[77] Ibid., 277. See also Turnbull, *Victims*, 86.
[78] Gill, *Agatha Christie*, ch. 3.
[79] Christie, *Peril at End House*, ch. 3, "Accidents."
[80] See Morgan, *Agatha Christie*, 264–265. In fact, Morgan specifically mentions that, "An unidentified reference in *The Hollow* had been found especially offensive" (265; see also Turnbull, *Victims*, 85). Might we assume this offense resulted from Midge's comment about Mme. Alfrege? I have been unable to locate the letter of complaint, so further comment would be unsupported by the available evidence.

portrayals of Jews? In the 1986 made-for-TV film, *Murder in Three Acts*, the approach is fairly simple.[81] There is no Oliver Manders in the film. Instead, there's a character called Ricardo Montoya, who's a Communist and Egg's companion. On the other hand, in the version filmed for Series 12 of *Agatha Christie's Poirot*, Manders (Tom Wisdom) is a character, but we're never told he's Jewish. At one point, Egg (Kimberley Nixon) does tell Poirot that Manders "just wants to get rich," but instead of a Jew, she calls him a Communist. Similarly, in the 1990 adaptation of *Peril at End House* in Series 2, Lazarus (Paul Geoffrey) is still an art dealer who Freddie (Alison Sterling) thinks is rich, but he's never referred to as a Jew. Finally, Mme. Alfrege as a character is totally absent from both the adaptations of *The Hollow*, including the 1952 dramatic rendering and the interpretation in Series 9 of *Agatha Christie's Poirot*.[82]

It's not clear whether these alterations were made due to pragmatic issues of adapting long prose works to film, or the producers simply recognized that perpetuating Jewish stereotypes in a post-Holocaust context would be unethical. Either way, we can be grateful that the regrettable presence of caricatures of Judaism in Christie's novels have not been carried over into these later versions. Given the social media frenzy in January 2022 over charges of antisemitism in J. K. Rowling's *Harry Potter* series, it's sadly clear that concern over Jewish stereotypes in British literature is still present and necessary.[83]

---

[81] In his book on Poirot, Aldridge discusses this film briefly; see *Agatha Christie's Poirot*, 348–349.

[82] See Turnbull, *Victims*, 85.

[83] For this kerfuffle, see, e.g., Gordon Haber, "Think the goblins in Harry Potter are antisemitic? Try the rest of British literature," *The Forward*, 10 January 2022; available online at: https://forward.com/opinion/480578/think-the-goblins-in-harry-potter-are-antisemitic-try-british-literature/.

14

Muslims and Islam

By all accounts, Islam was a fast-growing presence in the English religious scene in the early to mid-twentieth century. Because of the imperialistic spread of British rule in the Middle East, north Africa, and India, the colonial interests of England impacted economies, technologies, and legal systems of numerous territories with high percentages of Muslims.[1] These impacts also had the perhaps unintended (and at times unwelcome) consequence of encouraging immigration to England. As Callum G. Brown notes, Muslim immigration "had developed very slowly in the late nineteenth century and continued in the First World War," but after the end of the War, the ensuing economic depression caused "widespread unemployment and poverty in the 1920s."[2] In fact, Brown points out that immigrant communities like those of Muslims were blamed in part for these economic and social woes, despite the fact that Martin Pugh estimates that there were only around ten thousand "British Muslims by 1924."[3] Yet, counter-measures were still undertaken to lessen their presence, including "enforced repatriation" and "the 1925 Special Restrictions Order that tried to control the perceived 'flood' of Muslim immigration."[4] Nevertheless, Muslim immigration continued and Muslim communities grew, especially in urban areas, so that from 1939–1951, the Muslim population had doubled from 50,000 to 100,000.[5] This figure grew rapidly, and by 1990 there were an estimated "1.5 million Muslims in Britain."[6] According to the 2019 Annual Population Survey, Muslims now account for around 5.7% of the population of England and Wales, with an estimated 3.37 million self-identifying as Muslim.[7]

---

[1] As noted by Humayun Ansari, *"The Infidel Within": Muslims in Britain since 1800* (New York & Oxford: Oxford University Press, 2018), 29ff.

[2] Brown, *Religion and Society in Twentieth-Century Britain* (Harlow: Pearson Education Limited, 2006), 136. See also Ansari, *"The Infidel,"* 45–46.

[3] Martin Pugh, *Britain and Islam: A History from 622 to the Present Day* (New Haven & London: Yale University Press, 2019), 123.

[4] Brown, *Religion and Society*, 136. See also Ansari, *"Infidel,"* 46–47.

[5] According to Houssain Kettani, "Muslim Population in Europe: 1950–2020," *International Journal of Environmental Science and Development* 1, no. 2 (2010): 159–160.

[6] Brown, *Religion and Society*, 293.

[7] The results can be found online under "Population estimates by ethnic group and religion, England and Wales: 2019," *Office for National Statistics*, 16 December 2021; available online at https://www.ons.gov.uk/aboutus/transparencyandgovernance/freedomofinformationfoi/muslimpopulationoftheuk.

Despite these facts, Christie treats Islam rarely in her Poirot stories. However, we do have two significant examples: the 1936 novel *Cards on the Table*, and the 1959 novel *Cat Among the Pigeons*.[8] At the level of the world behind the text, we should recall that Christie spent a good deal of her adult life traveling and working in areas with large Muslim populations. She had always enjoyed the adventure of travel, as is clear from her year-long so-called Empire Trip around the world with her first husband Archie Christie in 1922.[9] After she and Archie divorced—subsequent to her famous "disappearance" in 1926—she undertook a solo trip to Baghdad via the Orient Express in 1928. There, she visited the dig site at Ur run by the famous archaeologist Leonard Woolley, whose wife Katherine took a bit of a shine to her, so much so that Christie was invited back to the dig the following season in 1930. There, Christie met a young archaeologist named Max Mallowan, who would propose to her soon after. The couple wed on 11 September 1930, and her life rapidly changed, as for many years she would spend time assisting Max at his various digs while continuing to churn out an impressive amount of writing to keep the family financially stable.

One of the works Christie completed after her marriage to Max is a memoir of sorts called *Come, Tell Me How You Live*, in which she narrates some of her experiences working on a dig with her husband from roughly 1935–1938.[10] From her reminiscences, it's obvious that Christie interacted with Muslims on a daily basis and as such, had firsthand experience with Islam, albeit a kind of Islam that was obviously culturally distinct from the Islams she might encounter in London, for example.[11] Two examples from this memoir will suffice to help illuminate the impact of her encounters with Muslims and Islam on her thought and writing.

One of the workmen Christie mentions is named Michel, who often served as their driver. At one point, Michel is driving them when he swerves "across the road with diabolical intentions, steps heavily on the accelerator and charges a party of Arabs," intent on killing them. Christie's husband Max berates him, but Michel replies, "What would it have mattered? ... They are Mohammedans, are they not?" Christie opines that this was "according to his views, [a] highly Christian sentiment," and when it isn't echoed by the other passengers, Michel "relapses into the martyred silence of one misunderstood. What kind of Christians are these, he seems to be saying to himself, weak and irresolute in the faith!" Max then "lays it down as positive rule that no attempted murder of Mohammedans is to be permitted," and Michel replies, "It would be better if *all* Mohammedans were dead!"[12] This episode is telling, as it demonstrates

---

[8] For more on these novels, see Charles Osborne, *The Life and Crimes of Agatha Christie: A Biographical Companion to the Works of Agatha Christie* rev. and updated ed. (London: HarperCollins, 1999), 140–143, 297–299; and Mark Aldridge, *Agatha Christie's Poirot: The Greatest Detective in the World* (London: HarperCollins, 2020), 104–108, 231–235.

[9] Christie's grandson has edited together a travelogue of sorts documenting this eventful trip. See Matthew Prichard, ed., *The Grand Tour: Around the World with the Queen of Mystery* (London: Christie Archive Trust/HarperCollins, 2012).

[10] In his work, Osborne discusses this book. See *Life and Crimes*, 212–215.

[11] See Alison Light, "Agatha Christie and Conservative Modernity," in *Forever England: Femininity, Literature and Conservatism between the Wars* (London & New York: Routledge, 1991), 110.

[12] Christie, *Come, Tell Me How You Live*, The Agatha Christie Mystery Collection (1946; reis. Toronto & New York: Bantam Books, 1985), 83. Christie also mentions Michel's attempts to commit vehicular homicide against "Mohammedans" on pp. 118, 159–160.

the religious/ethnic animosity in the region, as well as Christie's exposure to views of Islam as a discordant religion on the ground, as it were. We should also note that neither she nor her husband objects to Michel's claims on moral or religious grounds; Max's concern is purely pragmatic regarding the dig.

The second example from her memoir is its ending. Christie concludes the book with a postscript consisting of three Arabic words: "El hamdu lillah," or, more properly, *Alhamdulillah*, which means "Thank God," or "Praise be to God." This is obviously an Islamic saying, and Christie's use of it indicates not only her engaging in a different kind of shared religious language than we've seen her use, but her specific familiarity with colloquial Islamic phrases. In other words, the portrait Christie paints of herself in *Come, Tell Me How You Live* is of a woman comfortable with different faiths who has lived experience with Muslims.

Nevertheless, as a widely-read Englishwoman of her time, Christie also inherited stereotypical views of Islam, Arabs, and Turks (categories of the "other" that were—and still are—often conflated) prevalent in the Edwardian and Victorian eras. I've touched on the issue of stereotypes already in Chapter 13, but let's remind ourselves of what the process of creating an "other" entails. Peter Gottschalk and Gabriel Greenberg's comments are helpful here. They note,

> When one describes others as being aberrant, one relies on an audience's implicit understanding of what is normal. The Other is distinguished from "us" by characteristics that "they" have (and, implicitly, "we" do not; e.g., disunity, wickedness, irrationality). Or they may be distinguishable by characteristics "they" lack (e.g., civilization, restraint, morality) that "we" presumably have. So the qualities that the person making the distinction uses usually reflect what is considered normal or natural to the group with which he or she associates—or, more specifically, with him- or herself.[13]

So, to review, in making an "other" via the complex process of alterity, one is really concretizing how one sees oneself and defines one's social/kin groupings. Again, simply put, "we are who we are because we're not them," whoever the "them" may be. So, to what kinds of images or understandings of the Muslim or Arab "Other" might Christie have been exposed?

As Jamal al-Asmar argues, these images probably stemmed from biblical texts as well as travel narratives from the seventeenth to nineteenth centuries, and included ideas that Arabs lacked "morality and civilization," that they were "naïve and simple," but also could be violent thieves.[14] Al-Asmar also claims that once *The Arabian Nights* was translated into English in 1712, "a more sympathetic understanding of Oriental culture" begins, even though much of this still views these "Others" as exotic, culturally

---

[13] Gottschalk and Greenberg, *Islamophobia: Making Muslims the Enemy* (Lanham, MD: Rowman & Littlefield, 2008), 63. See also Paul Hedges, *Religious Hatred: Prejudice, Islamophobia, and Antisemitism in Global Context* (London & New York: Bloomsbury, 2021), 19–23.

[14] Al-Asmar, "Victorian Images of the Arabs and Their Sources," *Bethlehem University Journal* 13 (1994): 74.

stagnant, and "sensualists."[15] Additionally, the political needs of empire led British politicians from across the spectrum to make denigrating and false claims about the Ottoman Empire and Islam more generally in the late Victorian and early Edwardian periods. Figures like W.E. Gladstone (Prime Minister from the Liberal Party for a period of four terms during the years of 1868–1894), Robert Cecil (aka Lord Salisbury, three-time Prime Minster from the Conservative Party at intervals between 1885–1902) and even a young journalist called Winston Churchill, through both proclamation and performance, fomented negative views and allowed stereotypes of Islam to continue. As Humayun Ansari writes,

> These opinions reflected more general perceptions of Muslim despotism, corruption, religious fanaticism, sexual depravity and inequality depicted in literature, painting and travel writing. They were further accentuated by reports of major policy decisions, diplomatic initiatives and military expeditions undertaken around the world in pursuit of imperial interests.... These themes and images came to inform popular attitudes towards the small but growing Muslim population in Britain [in the mid-19th century to the early 20th century].[16]

As a result, "Islam was identified as the ultimate source of all wickedness: a religion that regarded the 'killing and plunder of infidels' as being 'as much an act of worship as prayer'.... The negative views of Islam and Muslims generally continued to generate hostility and resentment towards Muslims in Britain."[17]

From an American context, Asma Gull Hasan points out that a lack of religious literacy affects the impact of stereotypical depictions and presentations of Muslims:

> Inaccurate portraits of Muslims are more harmful that the use of stereotypes of just about any other group, because Americans are unfamiliar with Islam and Muslims and yet are quite familiar with other groups. As a result, Americans are unable to distinguish between what is reality and what is an over-amplification, exaggeration, or stereotype. With groups they are familiar with, Americans can distinguish stereotype from fact.[18]

Hasan's concern regarding a lack of accurate, firsthand knowledge of Islam among Americans at the beginning of the twenty-first century—and *prior* to the 9/11 attacks—is perhaps even more applicable to average British citizens living in England during the Victorian and Edwardian periods, since contact with Muslims was even more improbable because of population size and dispersal. And even if Christie did have much more experience with and exposure to a particular form of Islam, as we noted, she still would've been reared with these unflattering and often pejorative images of Islam and Muslims. As such, the fact that she depicts Muslims as integrating into

---

[15] Ibid., 81.
[16] Ansari, *"Infidel,"* 88.
[17] Ibid., 89–90.
[18] Hasan, *American Muslims: The New Generation* (New York & London: Continuum, 2000), 86.

English (read "Western") culture and employs Islamic language and concepts shows that Christie is again resisting the narrow and negative religio-cultural inheritances of her time and place.

The longevity of these stereotypical views is signaled by the work of Faiza Hirji on the enduring images of Muslims in modern popular culture. In discussing the origins of these stock (mis)characterizations, Hirji mentions again the influence of "the travelogues written by Orientalists," and includes a helpful list of what these "writers and painters ... saw (or thought they saw) in the exotic lands of the Orient."[19] These include, "mysterious women living a secretive existence, multiple wives serving the whims of a dominant man, primitive cultural practices and simple binaries such as dominant men/silent women, virginal European women/overly sexualized women of the East, modern West/backwards East."[20] As we'll see, R. A. York is correct when he broadly claims that Christie's "interest in other races or nationalities, to say the least, lacks subtlety."[21] Our first example, *Cat Among the Pigeons*, trades in many of these stereotypical views of Muslims that seem to indicate that Islam is an unacceptable religion within a discourse suffused with Christian normativity, alongside heterodox or "cultish" Christianity, Spiritualism, and Judaism. However, we've seen how Christie tempers the hegemonic Christian view of these seemingly discordant religious practices. And, as will become clear, by the end of *Cat Among the Pigeons*, Christie depicts the central Muslim character as sufficiently "Western" and progressive that he is capable of being integrated into English society and culture.

Cat Among the Pigeons

The novel begins at Meadowbank, a highly selective girls' school, with the arrival of new students at the beginning of the academic year. The setting of a private, very properly English school is important in understanding how Christie depicts the presence of normative Christian culture in the novel. Warren J. Blumenfeld's comments are helpful in understanding the socialization function of public schools vis-à-vis normative ideologies. He notes, "Schools are another institutional means by which social norms are maintained and reproduced. Norms of Christian privilege and marginalization of members of other faith communities and non-believers in the schools are conveyed by curricular materials (curricular hegemony), which focus upon heroes, holidays, traditions, accomplishments, and the importance of a European heritage, Christian experience."[22] Blumenfeld then introduces Sonia Nieto's concept of the "monocultural school," which he describes as one

---

[19] Hirji, "Telling Our Own Stories: Changing Representations of Islam in Popular Culture," *Oxford Islamic Studies Online*, October 2018.

[20] Ibid.

[21] York, *Agatha Christie: Power and Illusion*, Crime Files (Hampshire & New York: Palgrave Macmillan, 2007), 69.

[22] Blumenfeld, "Christian Privilege and the Promotion of 'Secular' and Not-So 'Secular' Mainline Christianity in Public Schooling and in the Larger Society," *Equity & Excellence in Education* 39 (2006): 198.

in which school structures, policies, curricula, instructional materials, and even pedagogical strategies (comprising hegemonic discourses) are primarily representative of only the dominant religious culture. Students who are Hindu, Muslim, Sikh, Jewish, and of other faiths, and non-believers, for example, see few of their perspectives and few, if any, people who look like them, people who believe as they believe, or people who adhere to the cultural expressions that they adhere to introduced and discussed in their classroom lessons.[23]

This educational setting is juxtaposed with some key backstory to the plot that takes place in the fictional middle eastern country of Ramat that will be central to our examination of Islam. These plot lines are connected by two students enrolling at Meadowbank: a British girl called Jennifer Sutcliffe and a Princess from Ramat named Shaista. Their time at the school will be marked and marred by murders, stolen jewels, a kidnapping, and the presence of a short foreigner with an egg-shaped head who will eventually explain it all.

As I said, one of the novel's opening scenes is set in a country called Ramat, which appears to be an amalgam of Muslim territories like Iran and Afghanistan. This allows for both a return to the theme of foreigners and immigration we saw previously and when we discussed Judaism in Chapter 13, as well as a new kind of shared language. Evidently, Ramat is in the midst of civil unrest, and Prince Ali Yusuf (only 25 years old and a cousin of Shaista's) has already been shot at as he was trying to escape the violence with some of his family's fortune in the form of precious jewels. He even tells his friend and pilot Bob Rawlinson that, "I don't like the idea of running away. But I do not in the least want to be a martyr, and be cut to pieces by a mob."[24] This statement depicts the people of Ramat negatively, as ruled by a mob mentality, unable to think for or control themselves. Ali is also bitterly disappointed in his people for not embracing his "welfare" initiatives, such as hospitals. He even tells Bob,

> My grandfather was a cruel man, a real tyrant. He had hundreds of slaves and treated them ruthlessly. In his tribal wars, he killed his enemies unmercifully and executed them horribly. The mere whisper of his name made everyone turn pale. And yet—he is a legend still! Admired! Respected! The great Achmed Abdullah! And I? What have I done? Built hospitals and schools, welfare, housing . . . all the things people are said to want. Don't they want them? Would they prefer a reign of terror like my grandfather's?[25]

Here again, the people of Ramat seem to be characterized as backwards, preferring and respecting a violent despot instead of someone modern (read "Western") like Ali who

---

[23] Ibid. For Nieto's work, see "Affirmation, Solidarity, and Critique: Moving Beyond Tolerance in Education," in *Beyond Heroes and Holidays: A Practical Guide to K-12 Anti-racist, Multicultural Education and Staff Development*, 4th edn; eds. Enid Lee, Deborah Menkart, and Margo Okazawa-Rey (Washington, DC: Network of Educators on the Americas, 2008), 7–18.

[24] Christie, *Cat Among the Pigeons* (1959; reis. New York: HarperCollins, 2011), Kindle edition, ch. 1, "Revolution in Ramat."

[25] Ibid.

would've been "an enlightened ruler, with democratic principles."[26] His dilemma is reminiscent of our discussion earlier regarding the colonial disruption of indigenous economies and technologies that British imperial expansion caused in many traditionally Muslim areas. Ansari describes the "compromise" with "European ideas" many Muslims were faced with, and claims that "Engagement with the framework established by British authority increasingly appeared a necessary precondition for any future progress. Muslims had to acquire a 'modern' outlook and come to terms with the 'modern' world."[27]

In his role as leader of his country, Ali is very much engaged in this process of "compromise," of coming to "terms with the 'modern' world," but Christie depicts the people of Ramat as wholly resistant to his program of accommodation, or better, "Westernization." This is an important dichotomy in Christie's portrayal of Islam and "Islam" in the British mind, given the high value placed on societal and intellectual progress in European society generally since the Enlightenment.[28] As Pugh writes, "Fortified by what appeared to be British superiority, many Victorians took for granted the backwardness of Muslims, doomed as they were to obscurantism by their religion and trapped by beliefs that rendered them incapable of reform."[29] As we saw, this positive value of progress can be reinforced by declaring that the "other," in this case Islam, doesn't possess it, and this is "proved" in the novel by depicting the people of Ramat as opposed to Ali's advocacy of "progress."

At several points, the characterization of Islam we've seen thus far via dialogue is reinforced by narratorial comments, which carries weight/authority because our narrator is omniscient. First, the narrator tells us that Ali has indicated that the precious jewels he's trying to get out of his country ahead of the revolution are in the hands of Allah. That is, "It is as Allah wills," and "All will go as Allah wills." Ali even tells Bob that he's not "nuts," he's just a "fatalist."[30] Then, the narrator seems to critique Ali's plan of "sitting back quietly himself and leaving everything to Allah. Bob had not got that recourse. Bob's God expected his servants to decide on and perform their own actions to the best of the ability their God had given them."[31] The narratorial comment is telling because it seems to make a distinction between Allah and Bob's (presumably Christian) God. The issue of whether Allah is different than the God of the Old or New Testament is a fascinating one, but it has also been employed as a common anti-Muslim trope as a way of denigrating Islam and/or signaling the distance between Islam, Judaism, and/or Christianity.[32] This distinction could also be an inheritance of the influence of Christian evangelism, which had taken root in England in the nineteenth century. As Pugh notes, in addition to their critique of both Catholicism and Islam for being superstitious and opposed to progress, "evangelical Christians often embraced a

---

[26] Ibid., ch. 3, "Introducing Mr. Robinson."
[27] Ansari, *"Infidel,"* 32–33.
[28] As noted by al-Asmar, "Victorian," 74. Also see Pugh, *Britain,* 108.
[29] Pugh, *Britain,* 109.
[30] Christie, *Cat Among the Pigeons,* ch. 1.
[31] Ibid.
[32] Readers interested in this issue can consult Gabriel Said Reynolds, *Allah: God in the Qur'an* (New Haven & London: Yale University Press, 2020), 10–16 and 41–42.

militant imperialism, reflecting their belief that the British had a missionary duty to extend the benefits of good government to Indians and Africans."[33] Additionally, this distinction seems to be rooted in the stereotypical view of foreigners (especially "Arabs" and "Orientals") as lazy.

Hirji's comments about stereotypical images of Muslim women remind us that sex and gender play an important role in constructing the "other." In his work, al-Asmar also highlights these categories, writing, "In the Victorian times the East seemed to those travellers as merely a place of emirs, sheikhs and princes with courtesans, concubines, slaves and several wives. In short, a place of voluptuous people given up to luxury and sensual gratification."[34] Building on these comments, I believe we find additional evidence of a negative view of Islam in two comments on women in the novel. First, there's an undercover man called Ronnie from the Special Branch of the police posing as a gardener at Meadowbank who takes the pseudonym of "Adam Goodman."[35] In a letter to his superior, he comments on the fashion style of Princess Shaista, expressing surprise since, "I'd always understood these Oriental girls were brought up modestly behind the veil."[36] His comment betrays a stereotypical view of Islamic women and perhaps even a tone of disapproval that is adumbrated by Pugh: "Many Victorians convinced themselves that the Turks lacked self-control and had inflammable minds, so that English women were always at risk from them. Obsessed with the harems known to exist in Oriental countries as hotbeds of vice, they accused the Turks of sexual depravity, religious fanaticism and political corruption."[37] Second, Jennifer Sutcliffe comments to Poirot that women in Ramat "all wear veils and things like that. Though they take them off in Paris and Cairo, I believe. And in London, of course."[38] This is an example of the assumptions that Islam is a rigidly patriarchal religion and that Muslim women are both oppressed and secretly yearn to be free/Western.

Speaking of Meadowbank, the information we're provided about the school is also significant in both what we know, and what we don't know. That is, we're told that students write papers on Scripture and girls are required to gather for prayer in the evenings on campus. They also attend both Protestant and Roman Catholic services off-campus at times, accompanied by teachers. However, no mention is made of equitable accommodations for the religious needs of Muslim students, even though there are a number of international students present. Meadowbank thus fits the definition of a "monocultural school" we saw earlier. For example, there is no release time for Muslim daily prayers, and I'd bet folding money that the "Scripture" the girls write on doesn't include the *Qur'ān*. As such, we can again note that the English educational system is a key site for both the presence of Christian privilege and the inculcation of normative Christianity.

---

[33] Pugh, *Britain*, 113.
[34] Al-Asmar, "Victorian," 86.
[35] In a humorous example of shared religious language, Ronnie is asked what he'd like his undercover name to be. Jokingly, he replies "Adam Eden" (loc. 542).
[36] Christie, *Cat Among the Pigeons*, ch. 5, "Letters from Meadowbank School."
[37] Pugh, *Britain*, 122.
[38] Christie, *Cat Among the Pigeons*, ch. 20, "Conversation."

The end of the book is especially interesting for our purposes. A certain Mr. Robinson makes arrangements with Poirot for the jewels of Prince Ali to be taken out of Poirot's bank and given to a young woman named Alice, to whom Ali was married and with whom Ali had a son named Allen. Alice explains at one point how they were able to marry without anyone recognizing him: "There's so many of these foreign Moslem students, you see. We knew it didn't mean anything really. He was a Moslem and he could have more than one wife, and he knew he'd have to go back and do just that."[39] So, even though Ali loved Alice, he was aware of the expectations of lineage and assumed he'd be marrying Shaista. However, Alice's comment also assumes the presence of polygyny (not polygamy) in Ramat, which carries stereotypical implications about the kind of Islam practiced there. Recall that stereotypes are "the distilled essence of the public perception of particular groups of people."[40] In this case, the assumption is that all "Moslem" men are polygynous, and this was no more accurate in the mid-twentieth century than it is today.[41]

Also, when Robinson offers to let Alice keep one of the stones (before he takes them, sells them, and sets her up with lawyers and accountants to invest the money from the sale), she refuses: "You see, he and I—he was a Moslem but he let me read bits now and again out of the Bible. And we read that bit—about a woman whose price was above rubies. And so—I won't have any jewels. I'd rather not."[42] This bookended characterization of Ali is interesting, as it perpetuates what I see as his Western redemption. That is, we heard at the beginning of the novel that he's "pro-western" and has turned Ramat into a "Welfare State."[43] Now, at its conclusion, the novel portrays him as open to a Western wife and reading the (presumably Christian) Bible—even if the passage Alice mentions (Proverbs 31:10) is an androcentric fantasy. All this makes Ali, in effect, "our kind of Muslim." Put differently, his views are progressive and embrace a program of Western accommodation and integration that would've aligned with those of Christie's British audience.[44] Still, Ali is not unlike Jim Lazarus, the "frightfully decent" Jew of *Peril at End House*, in that while Ali is different, he's acculturated enough to English society to be acceptable.[45] That is, yes, Christie does employ stereotypical images of Muslims and Islam, but like her depiction of Jews and Judaism, they don't veer off into the sinister tradition of Islamophobic representations.

---

[39] Christie, *Cat Among the Pigeons*, ch. 25, "Legacy."
[40] Jane Arnold, "Detecting Social History: Jews in the Works of Agatha Christie," *Jewish Social Studies* 49, nos. 3/4 (1987), 275.
[41] See, e.g., Jane I. Smith, "Islam," in *Women in World Religions*, ed. Arvind Sharma (Albany: State University of New York Press, 1987), 237.
[42] Christie, *Cat Among the Pigeons*, ch. 25.
[43] Ibid., ch. 1.
[44] Pugh reminds us of those views and some of their components in his *Britain*, 114.
[45] Merja Makinen reinforces this claim in her discussion of Christie's use of Arabic in her *Agatha Christie: Investigating Femininity*, Crime Files (New York: Palgrave, 2006), 169.

Poirot and *Qur'ān*

If Muslims and/or Islam were viewed with suspicion and even hostility at times in British history, it appears that their sacred text was acceptable enough in the eyes of Christie to find its words placed in Poirot's mouth twice. Poirot quotes the *Qur'ān* at the end of chapter twenty-six and the beginning of chapter twenty-seven of the 1936 novel *Murder in Mesopotamia*, saying, "*Bismillahi ar rahman ar Rahim.*" He translates it as "In the name of Allah, the Merciful, the Compassionate," and explains it's "the Arab phrase used before starting out on a journey." He then grandly tells those assembled, "*Eh bien*, we too start on a journey. A journey into the past. A journey into the strange places of the human soul." And over thirty years later, in the novel *Hallowe'en Party*, Poirot quotes a proverb from *Qur'ān* 17:13, "the fate of every man we have bound about his neck." While these quotations don't demonstrate a deep engagement with Islamic scripture, they do betray a familiarity with Islamic literary culture, a familiarity that Christie herself shared at least in part, as evinced in the postscript of her memoir, *Come, Tell Me How You Live.*

In the sole TV adaptation of the novel (which appeared in Series 11 of *Agatha Christie's Poirot*) there are some remnants of the negative view of Islam we saw earlier. For example, the opening scene switches back and forth between preparations for the new school year at Meadowbank and Prince Ali (Raji James) attempting to escape an armed coup in Ramat. We see images of what we assume is the ruling palace being stormed by an armed mob, and the camera focuses on one of the invaders. He is wearing a light red turban and is obviously supposed to be an Arab. Here, though, both Bob and Ali die in a standoff with that armed mob. Similarly, "Adam" (Adam Croasdell) tells Poirot that Ali would've been "an enlightened ruler," and that he was a "democrat, which is probably what did the poor chap in." Both this comment and the choice to zoom in on one of the members of the mob reinforce the view that the locals in Ramat are backwards and primitive when compared with the characters at Meadowbank.

However, there's no ending in this episode with Ali's girlfriend, no exchange between Poirot and government officials or secret go-betweens. Poirot leaves to go arrange the return of the jewels to the real Shaista, but he gives Julia Upjohn (Lois Edmett)—a friend of Jennifer Sutcliffe's (Jo Woodcock) who helped him with his investigation— one of the rubies as a reward before he returns to London. So, virtually all the language about and dim view of Islam found in the novel is removed completely from this adaptation. This shouldn't be surprising to us, since a period of almost fifty years elapsed between the novel and the release of this episode, and stereotypical and harmful images of Muslims and Islam in popular media are thankfully growing scarcer as more and more viewers decry them and their impact. After all, many of the stereotypes we have encountered in Christie's novel—such as that Muslims are somehow both lazy and violent, and that Islam is averse to progress and unwilling to acculturate to non-Muslim societies—form the bedrock of modern Islamophobia, a pernicious and destructive ideology.[46]

Cards on the Table

Our second and final example in this chapter is a more subtle one, and comes from the 1936 novel *Cards on the Table*, an idiosyncratic work in the Poirot canon. As Gillian Gill notes, it was one of Christie's "personal favorites, and it is a detective novelist's detective novel."[47] This affection, and its idiosyncrasy, can be seen in the fact that the novel begins with a caveat from Christie herself—the only time she provided such a thing in her Poirot canon—that this will be a case in which "the deduction must be … entirely *psychological*," since there is virtually no physical evidence. This is fine, she writes, "because when all is said and done it is the *mind* of the murderer that is of supreme interest."[48]

What she means is that the novel centers around the game of bridge, and a specific game in particular. A mysterious man called Shaitana invites four representatives of the law (Poirot, Colonel Race, Superintendent Battle, and Ariadne Oliver) and four people whom he knows are murderers (Dr. Roberts; Mrs. Lorrimer; Major Despard; and Miss Meredith) to a dinner party followed by bridge. When Shaitana is found murdered, Poirot must unravel the truth using virtually nonexistent evidence, relying instead on the psychology and character of the other guests that he gleans from interviews and their bridge score cards.[49] Hence, this novel is a great example of how important shared language and assumptions are, even the non-religious kind. That is, if one doesn't know anything about bridge, one misses so much in terms of how the narrator describes the games and Poirot's process.[50]

As I mentioned, the victim is called Shaitana, and it is his nominal association with the Devil that serves as the dominant biblical or religious image in the novel. First, his name is obviously a reference to the Hebrew verb *śāṭān* and its corresponding noun *śāṭan* , the former of which means "'accuse,' 'slander,' and 'be an adversary.'"[51] In Old Testament texts like Psalm 109:4, 20, 29; 1 Samuel 29:4; 1 Kings 5:18; Numbers 22:22 & 32; and Zechariah 3:1-2, one encounters a variety of "satans," including terrestrial and

---

[46] For a definition of Islamophobia, see Todd H. Green, "What is Islamophobia?" in *The Fear of Islam: An Introduction to Islamophobia in the West*, 2nd edn (Minneapolis: Fortress Press, 2019), 9–40.

[47] Gill, *Agatha Christie: The Woman and Her Mysteries* (New York: Free Press, 1990), Kindle edition, ch. 5, "Mrs. Mallowan: Last Trump for Shaitana."

[48] Christie, *Cards on the Table* (1936; reis. New York: HarperCollins, 2011), Kindle edition, Foreword.

[49] For more on the puzzle aspect of this novel, see Patricia D. Maida and Nicholas B. Spornick, *Murder She Wrote: A Study of Agatha Christie's Detective Fiction* (Bowling Green, OH: Bowling Green State University Popular Press, 1982), 73–75; and Mary S. Wagoner, *Agatha Christie*, Twayne's English Authors Series (Boston: G. K. Hall & Co., 1986), 58–59.

[50] See, e.g., chapter three and especially Mrs. Lorrimer's recollection of the game to Poirot in chapter eleven.

[51] Victor P. Hamilton, "Satan," in *The Anchor Bible Dictionary*, ed. David Noel Freedman, et al (New York: Doubleday, 1992), 5:985.

celestial ones, to use the classification of Victor P. Hamilton.[52] The most prominent and influential appearance of a *śātan* is in the prologue to the book of Job, beginning in 1:6. In his translation of Job, Robert Alter renders *ha-śātan* as "the Adversary," explaining that the Hebrew "invariably uses the definite article [*ha* = "the"] because the designation indicates a function, not a proper name. The word *satan* is a person, thing, or set of circumstances that constitutes an obstacle or frustrates one's purposes."[53] Clearly, Shaitana encompasses the accusatory and slanderous aspects of his biblical namesake(s), and as we'll see, the novel is structured so as to make him and Poirot adversaries, though their relationship is much different than that of God and *ha-śātan*. Even so, the depiction of *ha-śātan* in the prologue of Job is one of the key building blocks of what will eventually become our modern, Western image of "Satan," or the Devil, but this development will take quite some time.[54]

However, the spelling of his name, the confusion as to Shaitana's origins, and the fact that he "has relatives in Syria," means it might be more fruitful for us to look at one stage of that development, namely, in the *Qur'ān*.[55] As we've seen, by the publication of *Cards on the Table*, Christie had married her second husband, the archaeologist Max Mallowan, and had become more familiar with Islam as a result of accompanying him on a dig in Chagar Bazar in northern Syria.[56] So, at the very least, Christie would've had some passing familiarity with qur'anic literature as well as exposure to colloquial, shared religious language in everyday encounters.

Briefly, the *Qur'ān* mentions two figures that will come to be conflated in later Islamic thought: Satan (*Shaytan*) and Iblis. Stefan Wild helpfully dissociates the two in the context of qur'anic literature, noting, "The devil in the role of the proud, disobedient rebel against God's command, who refuses to bow before Adam, was originally called Iblis, whereas the devil as a tempter of Adam and mankind is called *al-shaytan*."[57] Wild continues, describing the characterization of *al-shaytan* in the *Qur'ān* as "the opponent of God [who] plays the counterweight to the divine guidance for mankind." More specifically,

> Satan's pernicious cunning is everywhere and his deceit spares nobody: he often 'whispers evil' (7.20) to mankind; he leads astray (4.60) – an action, which in the Qur'an is usually ascribed to God (e.g. 13.27); he causes hatred and enmity

---

[52] Ibid., 986–987.

[53] Alter, *The Wisdom Books: Job, Proverbs, and Ecclesiastes: A Translation with Commentary* (New York & London: W. W. Norton, 2010), 12. See also Samuel E. Balentine, *Job*, Smyth & Helwys Bible Commentary (Macon, GA: Smyth & Helwys, 2006), 51–52, and the sidebar on 53.

[54] For more on this development, interested readers can seek out Philip C. Almond, *The Devil: A New Biography* (Ithaca: Cornell University Press, 2014).

[55] Christie, *Cards on the Table*, ch. 9, "Dr. Roberts."

[56] See Janet Morgan, *Agatha Christie: A Biography* (London: William Collins Sons & Company, 1984; repr. New York: Alfred A. Knopf, 1985), 210. Wagoner, *Agatha Christie*, 58 n. 8 (found on p. 147) even notes that Christie "expresses admiration for the Yezidis, the worshippers of Shaitan, and for their holy shrine." The reference is found in Christie, *Come, Tell Me How You Live*, 90-91, but she also mentions it in her *An Autobiography* (1977; reis. New York: HarperCollins, 2011), 81.

[57] Wild, "Devil," in *The Qur'an: An Encyclopedia*, ed. Oliver Leaman (London & New York: Routledge, 2006), 179.

(5.91).... He causes not only intercommunal strife among Muslims (*fitna*; 22.52) but is in general the enemy of mankind (17.53).[58]

Many of these deceptive and cunning traits are shared by *al-shaytan*'s literary descendant, Shaitana. Similarly, Fazlur Rahman's description of Satan in the *Qur'ān* should sound familiar to readers of the novel:

> The Devil's activity essentially consists in confusing a person and temporarily (or, in the case of evil people, almost permanently) clouding his inner senses.... Satan's tentacles alone are not strong; it is only man's weakness and lack of moral courage and alertness that make Satan look so strong. According to the Qur'ān, Satan's beguiling activity is rooted in his desperation and utter lack of hope.[59]

This, too, nicely parallels the descriptions of Shaitana, in that many characters describe him as not so much a physical threat as an emotional and/or intellectual one. That is, he finds their interior weakness and exploits it, much to his profit and pleasure.

In addition to the scriptural (both biblical and qur'anic) allusions, an obvious way the narrator indicates how Shaitana is to be viewed is by using more general language to describe him. For example, we hear him labeled as "Mephistophelian" or "diabolical." At times, characters simply call him Mephistopheles, and at other times imagery one could call "devilish" is used to characterize him.[60] Shaitana even dressed as Mephistopheles at a party, thus cementing on his own terms this identification.[61] This figure of Mephistopheles is found in German folklore, but the character as devil was captured most popularly (and perhaps most ambiguously) in Johann Wolfgang von Goethe's play *Faust* in the early nineteenth century.[62] And as has long been noticed, the Faust legend as it appears in Goethe's work is heavily indebted to the book of Job.[63]

Another important component of Shaitana's characterization is the way in which he and Poirot are pitted against one another, as I mentioned earlier. This contrast serves to heighten both the diabolic character of Shaitana as well as to reinforce the religious characteristics of Poirot we've noted in Part Three by comparison. For example, the novel obviously casts Poirot and Shaitana's dialogue at the outset of the novel (in which they are "like duellists *en garde*" and even have a kind of moustache competition, at least in Poirot's mind) in the same vein as the Faust legend.[64] Shaitana attempts to persuade Poirot that a successful murderer is an artist, a highly skilled laborer who produces an aesthetic work worthy of admiration. In response, Poirot grants that

---

[58] Ibid., 180.

[59] Rahman, "Satan and Evil," in *Major Themes of the Qur'ān*, 2nd edn (Minneapolis: Bibliotheca Islamica, 1994), 124.

[60] See, e.g., ibid., ch. 1, ch. 2, "Dinner at Mr. Shaitana's" and ch. 9.

[61] Ibid., ch. 14, "Third Visitor."

[62] For more on the contribution of Goethe's *Faust* to the developing image of the Devil, see Jeffrey Burton Russell, *Mephistopheles: The Devil in the Modern World* (Ithaca & London: Cornell University Press, 1986), 157–167.

[63] See, e.g., Charlotte Spivack, "Job and Faust: The Eternal Wager," *The Centennial Review* 15, no. 1 (1971): 53–69.

[64] See Christie, *Cards on the Table*, ch. 1.

"murder can be an art" and that a "murderer can be an artist," but at root for him the act will always be abominable, a sin and a transgression.[65] Shaitana counters that to do a thing well is a justification for the act itself, no matter how morally reprehensible that act might be.

In the midst of this dialogue, Shaitana brags that he "collects" those murderers "who have got away with it," i.e., he's learned who these people are and has cultivated some sort of relationship with them.[66] Poirot warns him of the danger of such a "hobby," but Shaitana merely "laughed, a very Mephistophelian laugh."[67] Of course, as I have mentioned, Shaitana invites these murderers to a dinner at which he's murdered.

As examples of how Poirot is contrasted with Shaitana and his ideas, let me mention two more scenes from the novel. The first can be found when the former interviews several of the "murderers" who attended the party. In his chat with Mrs. Lorrimer in chapter eleven, she and Poirot have a wonderful dialogue regarding God and humanity. Mrs. Lorrimer compliments Poirot as he's leaving, and he demurs, "I am as the good God made me, Madame." But, Poirot says, "Some of us have tried to improve on His pattern," like Shaitana, who Poirot says should've been content to collect "*bric-à-brac*" but instead collected "sensations." When Mrs. Lorrimer responds that was simply part of his character, Poirot objects, "He played the part of the devil too successfully. But he was not the devil. *Au fond*, he was a stupid man. And so—he died." Mrs. Lorrimer asks, "Because he was stupid?" to which Poirot replies, "It is the sin that is never forgiven and always punished, Madame."[68]

A second example is found in a telling exchange between Poirot and Superintendent Battle that reflects several data from our examination in Chapter 6. In chapter nineteen of the novel, the other four guests meet in Battle's office. After Col. Race provides some background information on Major Despard, a frustrated Battle says, "You can't have human beings judging other human beings and taking the law into their own hands. . . . It shouldn't happen." He asks for Poirot's input, who agreeably repeats his catchphrase, "I have always disapproved of murder."[69] Mrs. Oliver then asks him if he thinks "there are people who ought to be murdered," and Poirot's reply illuminates his view of crime and religion. He tells Mrs. Oliver, "You do not comprehend. It is not the victim who concerns me so much. It is the effect on the character of the slayer." Oliver asks, "What about war?" and Poirot responds at length:

> In war you do not exercise the right of private judgement. *That* is what is so dangerous. Once a man is imbued with the idea that he knows who ought to be allowed to live and who ought not—then he is half-way to becoming the most dangerous killer there is—the arrogant criminal who kills not for profit but for an idea. He has usurped the functions of *le bon Dieu*.[70]

[65] Ibid.
[66] Christie will return to this idea of collecting murderers who have evaded the legal system in her novel *And Then There Were None* in 1939.
[67] Christie, *Cards on the Table*, ch. 1.
[68] Ibid., ch. 11, "Mrs. Lorrimer."
[69] See also Poirot's comment to Shaitana and Mrs. Oliver that he has a "*bourgeois* attitude to murder" in ibid., ch. 1 and ch. 8, "Which of Them?."
[70] Ibid., ch. 19, "Consultation."

This emphasis on divine judgment and a yawning gap between human and divine, that boundaries are key and that arrogance and stupidity (ignoring those boundaries) are precursors to evil acts underlies Poirot's approach to crime in general and plays a central thematic role in the novel. After all, Poirot critiques Shaitana for seeking to "improve on God's pattern," which parallels the pride/arrogance that Satan displayed in seeking the worship due to Adam. This is certainly how the *Qurʾān* characterizes the actions of Iblis (later conflated with *al-shaytan*, as I have noted). And in the world the text creates, we find a similar view taken in John Milton's poem *Paradise Lost*, which has exerted a terrific influence on the modern image of Satan.[71] In sum, we find a panoply of shared language from several religious and cultural streams being used in the novel to designate Shaitana as cunning, deceptive, and evil, in explicit contrast to Poirot, who is allied with God.

In her work on Christie, Gill points out that, "Poirot does not like Shaitana. We readers also tend to dislike him, since Shaitana epitomizes the kind of exotic, alien, nonpukka, Dr. No character that British popular writers have enjoyed casting as villain."[72] This "othering" of Shaitana, as we've seen, is related to his devilish characterization and the importance of establishing him as a counter to Poirot, thus enabling the latter to clarify his view of murder. And these characterizations are carried over into the world the text creates. For example, in the 2002 BBC Radio 4 dramatization of the novel, Poirot (voiced by John Moffat) makes a special point to mention the Mephistophelian effect Shaitana produces.[73] The adaptation in *Agatha Christie's Poirot* in 2006 also highlights this "othering" of Shaitana in several obvious ways. First, Alexander Siddig (aka Siddig El Fadil), best known for his role as Dr. Bashear on *Star Trek: Deep Space Nine* (CBS, 1993–1999) was cast as Shaitana. A Sudanese actor, Siddig's long, lean frame, dark features, and exotic mustache certainly differentiate him from the other characters in the film. Another way Shaitana is set apart is through the costuming. For example, his attire at the party is distinctive, with a vest that seems to have jewels on it, large, colored rings, and even dark cigarettes. Later Major Despard (Tristan Gemmill) points out that Shaitana dressed oddly, and even that he wore perfume. Finally, the setting also emphasizes his otherness. When the guests arrive for the dinner party, we're shown his sumptuous house while we hear him say that it's "modeled on the Alhambra," with floral and calligraphic art adorning the walls.

Through these methods, as well as retaining the novel's confusion over his origins and offhand comments from characters—such as when Mrs. Lorrimer (Lesley Manville) says she doesn't know Shaitana, but she knows "he likes to be different"—the film replicates and even heightens Shaitana's otherness. At the same time, there is a lessening of the devilish language used in the novel, i.e., we don't find the same kind of imagery in the film. Nevertheless, Shaitana is still shown as a nefarious, hedonistic manipulator of human emotion, in stark contrast to Poirot.

In sum, the importance of discussing *Cards on the Table* in the context of Christie's treatment of Islam lies in her characterization of Shaitana. That is, by alluding to the

[71] See Milton, *Paradise Lost*, 1.39–44.
[72] Gill, *Agatha Christie*, ch. 5.
[73] This program was dramatized by Michael Bakewell and directed by Enyd Williams.

qur'anic understanding of Satan in how she depicts him, I believe she's pushing her audience to engage alternative understandings of religious figures, even if only implicitly, since she never mentions the *Qur'ān* specifically. It is also significant that she uses both biblical and qur'anic imagery and themes in her characterization, yet she leaves Shaitana's identity unresolved. It would've been easy and even expected to depict him as a Muslim "other," but Christie chooses not to do so. Gill agrees with my point and makes what seems to me to be an important point regarding Shaitana and Christie's writing here. She notes, "Shaitana seems a thoroughly stereotyped villain, but, interestingly, Christie casts him as victim, not villain. Though so often accused of using cardboard characters, Agatha Christie is in practice far more inclined to subvert the stereotypes invented by her male compatriots than to support them."[74] This reticence to accord with the orientalizing and Islamophobic tradition she inherited, along with her sympathetic portrayal of Islam in *Cat Among the Pigeons*, highlights how Christie pushes back yet again against the hegemonic Christian discourse and its view of discordant religious practices.

By the time *Cat Among the Pigeons* was published in 1959, interventionist policies and increased immigration had impacted old stereotypical views of Muslims due to events such as the impact of World War I on pan-Islamism and Islamic nationalism; the rise of Zionism and the declaration of the state of Israel in 1948; the dissolution of the Ottoman Empire; the partition of India and Pakistan in 1948; and—most immediately to the publication of *Cat Among the Pigeons*—British intervention into Iranian politics in 1953 after the abdication of Reza Shah in 1941, resulting in, among other things, the nationalization of the Suez Canal in 1956. While Muslim immigration to England steadily increased, as we have seen in this chapter, this imperialistic meddling brought into stark relief the failure of British foreign policy towards Muslim territories, and would lead to catastrophic consequences for many of the governments and peoples involved in the latter twentieth and early twenty-first centuries.

Conclusion(s) to Part Four

To be sure, there are other examples of discordant religiosity in the Poirot canon, such as the religious practices described by a character called Akibombo in *Hickory Dickory Dock* (1955).[75] However, our discussions of sectarian Christianity; Spiritualism; Jews and Judaism; and Islam suffice to show how Christie creates an "other" in contradistinction to her "norm" of Christianity. We've seen how the ideology of Christian hegemony and normativity serves to render Christianity as "natural" while other expressions of religious practice seem foreign or even dangerous. Examining

---

[74] Gill, *Agatha Christie*, ch. 5.

[75] Akibombo is from west Africa, and not only is his English depicted as, well, idiomatic, but as a character he also serves to portray indigenous practices as discordant and uncivilized forms of religion through the use of the terms "superstition" and "voodoo," which are contrasted with descriptors like "modern and scientific." See Christie, *Hickory Dickory Dock* (1955; reis. New York: HarperCollins, 2011), Kindle edition, ch. 16.

these discordant cases throws into harsh relief the way in which Christie presents Christianity as positive, acceptable, and even redemptive, not to mention necessary in order to grasp the shared language and imagery she employs in her works.

On the other hand, as we've seen in this chapter, Christie's depiction of these "others" isn't monolithically pejorative. That is, some kinds of New Religious Movements might be acceptable, as long as they're not exploitative (or murderous). Spiritualism is unthreatening and poses no real threat to the dominant form of Christianity, as it can't function publicly like the Church of England can. Likewise, her British Jews and Muslims are acculturated, if not assimilated, to "proper" English society. Despite their ethnic and/or religious qualities, it's possible for them to participate in the culture to a great degree. This incremental inclusivity, this permeability in the boundary between "norm" and "other" marks Christie's treatment of non-majority forms of religion as essentially banal, even if she trades in stereotypes and discomfiting dialogue at times. Put differently, we've tracked a tendency of resistant reception of the normative Christianity in Christie's works that marks her off as a modernist writer, one who felt free to disregard and redeploy elements of her inherited literary and religio-cultural traditions.

Conclusion

When I was in graduate school, one of my professors was fond of asking students, "So what?" That is, we might have written a technically insightful paper, but if we failed to explain the significance and/or contribution of our work to our larger field of study, our work was incomplete. And believe me, nobody wanted to be asked that question in the classroom or see it written in bright red ink on a graded paper.

Of course, now I understand the wisdom of making us consider the broader implications of our work. In the case of this book, answering the "So what?" question is actually pretty easy: Agatha Christie and Hercule Poirot are still going strong in the twenty-first century. As I said in the Introduction, Christie's work continues to be extraordinarily popular; in fact, after Shakespeare, Christie is the most popular author in human history. In her work, religion is a recurrent and obviously important presence, but to date there's been no book-length work on religion in her output. Therefore, a work that examines religion in various ways (remember the Three Worlds model?) will help readers delve more deeply into Christie's work, understand more fully the socio-historical backgrounds of that work, and critically engage later adaptations of her work. See? Easy peasy.

I've always been a fan of brief conclusions, so let me just summarize the key points we've covered in the preceding chapters, and note a few possibilities for future work in this area. Beginning in Part One, I've presented Christie as a modernist author, one who questioned and complicated her inherited literary, socio-cultural, and religious traditions, tropes, and practices. With regards to religion, she pushed back against the Christian hegemony and normativity of her day in a practice I've called "resistant reception." In Part Two, we paid special attention to religious language in the form of the Bible, noting her tendency to resist traditional and/or androcentric understandings of biblical literature. And this practice of resistance impacts not only how she depicts normative Christianity, but also how non-normative and/or minority religions are portrayed. That is, Christie presents challenges to religious hegemony in her presentation of Spiritualism, minority religions like Judaism and Islam, and what she characterizes as improper forms of Christianity. We engaged these examples in Part Four in an effort to understand better how these discordant forms of religiosity serve to highlight and interrogate the normative position of Christianity in Christie's works.

Beginning in Part Three, I focused more specifically on the character of Poirot. We discussed several components of his worldview, including his distaste for murder and love of truth; the necessity of protecting innocents; his suspicious outlook and view of humanity; and his sense of divine justice—all of which are nurtured and buttressed by his Catholic identity. Along the way in all this, but most obviously in Chapters 8–10, I paid attention to the world the text creates: later adaptations of Christie's novels in radio, TV, and film. In those adaptations, we saw that, generally speaking, the more mainstream the production, the less religious content from the novels was included. For example, in neither of the big-budget productions starring Peter Ustinov nor in the recent Kenneth Branagh films do we find an emphasis on Poirot's religious identity or the retention of religious language and/or imagery from the source material. In contrast, the long-running TV show *Agatha Christie's Poirot* not only retains much of Christie's religious content, but also augments it with scenes that deepen the characterization of Poirot as a *bon Catholique*. This summary of the world the text creates leads us to an important point about our little Belgian.

As I mentioned in the Preface, most of my research has dealt with religion and/or Bible and popular culture. In 2010, I wrote a short chapter about Jesus and American popular culture, and—after surveying a variety of, well, sketchy interpretations— concluded by claiming that, "Jesus functions as an empty shell into which various meanings or significations can be poured."[1] What I meant then is that we have very little historical and literary evidence for Jesus as a figure in time, so "various interpreters would see in him and his life and teachings a rationale for their current identities and practices."[2] I used these claims to buttress my answer to the "So what?" question. I wrote that we have to pay attention to how Jesus has been received in popular culture for a simple reason: "Popular and lay understandings of Jesus in various aesthetic genres within popular culture have arguably done more to shape how people understand Jesus than all the councils in church history."[3] Now, I'm not comparing Poirot to Jesus—even though I do think one could make that argument based on Part Three—but there are two important points of overlap here. First, in the world the text creates it does seem that "Poirot" also serves as a malleable mass that can be shaped in various ways according to the times and interests of the writer and director. This should be clear from the adaptations I explored in Chapter 8. And second, the emphasis on paying attention to what's done with Poirot (and Christie more broadly) in popular culture points us to five possibilities for future research.

First, I'm not aware of any large-scale research into religious language, imagery, and issues in Golden Age crime fiction, broadly speaking. In Chapter 13, I relied on Malcolm J. Turnbull's book *Victims or Villains: Jewish Images in Classic English Detective Fiction*, but there are numerous unexplored nooks and crannies and authors within the enormous literary output included in the parameters of that genre and timeframe.

Second, and perhaps most obviously, I can easily imagine someone turning from Poirot to Marple. That is, no one has yet undertaken a critical study of how religion is present and presented in Christie's twelve Marple novels and twenty short stories, not

---

[1] See "'Here, There, and Everywhere": Images of Jesus in American Popular Culture," in *The Bible in/ and Popular Culture: A Creative Encounter*, Semeia Studies, 65; eds. Philip Culbertson and Elaine M. Wainwright (Atlanta: Society of Biblical Literature, 2010), 57.
[2] Ibid., 58.
[3] Ibid.

to mention the later TV and film adaptations. In the preceding chapters, I've done my best to mention thematic and plot-related overlap from selected Marple stories, but an examination of all of them would, I imagine, yield a rich harvest of insights.

For my third suggestion, let's note a jab from Japp. In "The Flock of Geryon"—which I explored in detail in Chapter 11—Poirot is approached to investigate a semi-Christian new religious movement, and involves Chief Inspector Japp. At one point, Japp kids around with Poirot, telling him, "You might start a new religion yourself with the creed: 'There is no one so clever as Hercule Poirot, Amen, D.C. Repeat *ad lib*.'!"[4] As of this writing, Japp is correct, but we wouldn't want to push the issue as far as Robert Barnard does in the conclusion to his study of Christie. There, he boldly claims,

> Those who regard the Sherlock Holmes societies and re-enactments of the famous fatality at the Reichenbach Falls as a species of the higher lunacy we can well do without can surely rest assured that no similar cult will embrace Poirot, Hastings, George and Miss Lemon. They lack the recognizable humanity of Holmes and Watson, and the densely imagined physical environment as well. They do not have sufficient independence as creations to affect people's imaginations in that way.[5]

While it is true that Barnard wrote those words prior to the *Agatha Christie's Poirot* series (which has done much to flesh out Christie's characters and foment Poirot fandom) and that there is no group of Poirot fans analogous to "Trekkies," there are groups that organize themselves around Christie and Poirot to express, demonstrate, and perform their fandom.[6] For example, I am a member of two Poirot fan groups on Facebook with members from around the world: "The Hercule Poirot Fan Club," a closed group with almost 30,000 members, and a group simply titled "Poirot," with ca. 45,000 members. Many members routinely post about how the little Belgian detective enriches their lives; ask other members questions about the stories and/or adaptations; post pics/memes from the adaptations; and, of course, regularly engage in often heated debates about who's the "best" Poirot.

It would be revealing to dive into the deep end of this fandom, but first let's make sure to define our terms. Matthew Hills writes that "fans" can be described as "individuals who have a particular liking or affection for a range of popular cultural texts, celebrities, sports (teams), or artifacts," who "typically displaying an affective relationship with their fan object."[7] Some of those activities include exploration of, elaboration on, and embodiment of the object(s) of their adoration. Exploration could include creating a fan publication or magazine (a "fanzine") or, more currently, a

---

[4] Christie, "The Flock of Geryon," in *The Labours of Hercules* (1947; reis. New York: HarperCollins, 2011), Kindle edition.
[5] Barnard, *A Talent to Deceive: An Appreciation of Agatha Christie* (New York: Mysterious Press, 1980), 118–119.
[6] I explore these areas of fandom in my chapter titled "Crucifixions, Cosplay, and Fan Cultures," in *The Oxford Handbook of the Bible and American Popular Culture*, eds. Dan W. Clanton, Jr. and Terry R. Clark (New York: Oxford University Press, 2021), 488–502.
[7] See Hills, "Fans and Fan Cultures," in *The Blackwell Encyclopedia of Sociology*, ed. George Ritzer (Malden, MA: Blackwell Publishing, 2007), 1638.

website, Facebook/Instagram page, or Twitter hashtag. Examples of elaboration could include writing fan-fiction, creating amateur films in which fictional characters appear, or composing allusive TikToks. Finally, embodiment could involve costume-play or cosplay, which is "the art and craft of assuming both the appearance and persona of a fictional character." According to Lauren Orsini, "What differentiates cosplay and dressing-up is that cosplayers take on a theatrical persona while in costume."[8] Fans of a fictional character like, Poirot, then, could create forums to discuss him, his stories, and their adaptations; write their own stories involving him; and/or make/don clothing and/or apply other features (obviously his famous moustache) that allow them to embody his character and, per Orsini, adopt his characteristics, accent, and worldview.

A fourth area of potential future research is related to my third suggestion, and has to do with fan pilgrimage and religious tourism. Practically every week in one of the Facebook groups I have mentioned, someone posts an image of Florin Court, the building used in *Agatha Christie's Poirot* as Poirot's Whitehaven Mansions apartment. Located in Charterhouse Square in the London district of West Smithfield, the 1936 art deco structure has become a pilgrimage site for fans of David Suchet's Poirot. J. Caroline Toy helps us understand "pilgrimage," when she writes that in general, it "is usually understood as structured geographic travel to a place associated with events, people, or narratives that have a high degree of significance. It is often highly ritualized, but this does not necessarily mean that all participants closely follow a set script together."[9] Toy also notes that for many pilgrims, the ultimate value placed on the "significance" and the ritual/scripted nature of the "geographic travel" marks their pilgrimage as functioning religiously, whether or not the place holds any traditional religious meaning. This echoes the work of Michael Stausberg, in which he explores the possibility that tourism is a functional analog or substitute for traditional religious practice.[10] A related avenue of research is religious tourism, in which pilgrimage and tourism combine to mediate a sacred, embodied encounter of traditional holy sites.[11] Speaking of sites, in her work Toy examines seemingly "secular" fan pilgrimages to "*Harry Potter*-related sites [including] the Warner Bros. Studio Tour London; the Platform 9 ¾ photo op at King's Cross Station in London; and the Wizarding World of Harry Potter theme park in Orlando, Florida."[12] Given this model of analysis, I can imagine someone researching Poirot-related fan pilgrimages to Florin Court and other sites, and this would entail interviews with and surveys of participating pilgrims—an approach that Toy models in her work.

Fifth and finally, research related to Poirot in popular culture is a "gimme" as long as new Poirot adaptations and content continue to be created. For example, I discuss the

[8] Orsini, *Cosplay: The Fantasy World of Role Play* (London: Carlton Books, 2015), 8.
[9] Toy, "Ritual Doing, Religious Doing: Understanding Harry Potter Fan Pilgrimages," in *Understanding Religion and Popular Culture*, 2nd edn; eds. Elizabeth Rae Coody, Dan W. Clanton, Jr., and Terry Ray Clark (London & New York: Routledge), 103.
[10] Stausberg, *Religion and Tourism: Crossroads, Destinations and Encounters* (New York: Routledge, 2011), especially 22–25.
[11] For example, see the collection edited by Courtney Bruntz and Brooke Shedneck, *Buddhist Tourism in Asia*, Contemporary Buddhism Series (Honolulu: University of Hawai'i Press, 2020).
[12] Toy, "Ritual," 105.

2018 limited TV series version of *The ABC Murders* and the Kenneth Branagh cinematic adaptations in 2017 and 2022 in Chapters 3, 8, and 9. Branagh plans to continue making Poirot films, and his film *A Haunting in Venice* (based on *Hallowe'en Party*) premiered after this book was complete. I also want to mention the new Poirot stories, written by Sophie Hannah with the approval and endorsement of Agatha Christie, Limited. To date, Hannah has written five Poirot novels: *The Monogram Murders* (2014); *Closed Casket* (2016); *The Mystery of Three Quarters* (2018); and *The Killings at Kingfisher Hill* (2020); and *Hercule Poirot's Silent Night* (2023) While there are purists who decry anyone but Christie writing Poirot stories, the creation of new Poirot stories is good news for anyone who cares about the character.[13] All of these new Poirots and the possibilities of Poirot fandom and pilgrimages are especially good news for those of us who research Poirot. They validate Mark Aldridge's claims that "the character can thrive even as the world around him changes" and the "idea that there is only one Poirot is an increasingly untenable one."[14]

It's been decades since I first encountered Poirot on that pallet at my grandparents' house, and I feel privileged that I've been able to return to him (or variations of him) again and again. My hope is that my work in this book illuminates the role of religion in the changing worlds of these multiple Poirots, provides some paths forward for future research, and—maybe most important of all—inspires a return to Christie's Poirot stories.

So go on, make yourself your own pallet, put the kettle on, and enjoy.

---

[13] For a brief overview of these novels, see Mark Aldridge, *Agatha Christie's Poirot: The Greatest Detective in the World* (London: HarperCollins, 2020), 422–428.
[14] Ibid., 447 and 449.

Appendix: Biblical Allusions and Quotations

Title (in chronological order)	Biblical Reference
The Mysterious Affair at Styles, ch. 1	Luke 10:7
The Mysterious Affair at Styles, ch. 5	Reference to "Haman" (Esther)
The Mysterious Affair at Styles, ch. 10	Matthew 26:41
Murder on the Links, ch. 7	Judges 16: "Samson"
"The Mystery of the Hunter's Lodge"	Luke 15:11-32
"The Mystery of the Hunter's Lodge"	Psalm 37:35
"The Mystery of the Hunter's Lodge"	Acts 28:4
"The Kidnapped Prime Minister"	Matthew 14:29
"The Chocolate Box"	Psalm 37:35
The Murder of Roger Ackroyd, ch. 3	"Queen of Sheba" 1 Kings 10
The Murder of Roger Ackroyd, ch. 4	Exodus 21:22-25 / Deuteronomy 19:21
"The Lemesurier Inheritance"	Proverbs 13:15
"The Incredible Theft"	Matthew 24:48
The Big Four, ch. 4	Genesis 28:10-22
The Big Four, ch. 13	"Judas"; Mark 14:10-21
The Big Four, ch. 18	"Samson"; Judges 16
Peril at End House, ch. 7	Genesis 6:19
Peril at End House, ch. 16	Proverbs 11:21
Three Act Tragedy, ch. 11	2 Samuel 12:7
Three Act Tragedy, ch. 11	Isaiah 22:13; 1 Corinthians 15:32b; Ecclesiastes 8:15
Three Act Tragedy, ch. 15	Genesis 3:1; Matthew 10:16
ABC Murders, ch. 16	Matthew 10:29
ABC Murders, ch. 19	Reference to "Eden" in a song
ABC Murders, ch. 33	Genesis 16:12; Lamentations 3:3
Dumb Witness, ch. 6	Psalm 90:10
Dumb Witness, ch. 7	Luke 15:18
Dumb Witness, ch. 7	John 16:24
Dumb Witness, ch. 7	Matthew 6:10
Dumb Witness, ch. 11	Proverbs 29:18
"The Incredible Theft"	Matthew 24:28 / Luke 17:37
Appointment with Death, Pt. 1, ch. 10	Psalm 23:4
Appointment with Death, Pt. 1, ch. 12	Matthew 4:9
Appointment with Death, Pt. 1, ch. 12	John 11:50
Appointment with Death, Pt. 1, ch. 12	Ecclesiastes 4:1-3
Hercule Poirot's Christmas, Pt. 1, sec. 6; Pt. 2, sec. 1; Pt. 3, sec. 10	Luke 15:11-32
Hercule Poirot's Christmas, Pt. 6, sec. 6	Romans 14:7
Hercule Poirot's Christmas, Pt. 6, sec. 6	Judges 5; Judith
Hercule Poirot's Christmas, Pt. 6, sec. 6	Micah 7:5-7
Hercule Poirot's Christmas, Pt. 7, sec. 5	Genesis 2-3
Sad Cypress, ch. 1, sec. 1	Matthew 6:28
Sad Cypress, ch. 4	Psalm 92:7
Sad Cypress, ch. 6	Psalm 23:4

Title (in chronological order)	**Biblical Reference**
One, Two, Buckle My Shoe, ch. 1, sec. 2	Ecclesiastes 11:1
One, Two, Buckle My Shoe, ch. 3, sec. 10	Acts 2:17 / Joel 2:28
One, Two, Buckle My Shoe, ch. 6, sec. 1; ch. 9, sec. 2	Revelation 21:1
One, Two, Buckle My Shoe, ch. 6, sec. 5	1 Samuel 15
One, Two, Buckle My Shoe, ch. 6, sec. 5; ch. 10	1 Samuel 15:23
Five Little Pigs, Bk. 1, ch. 6	Acts 9.5
"The Nemean Lion," in *The Labours of Hercules*	Proverbs 16:18
"The Arcadian Deer," in *The Labours of Hercules*	"Bathsheba" from 2 Samuel 11
"The Augean Stables," in *The Labours of Hercules*	"Jezebel" from 2 Kings
"The Flock of Geryon," in *The Labours of Hercules*	John 14:2
"The Flock of Geryon," in *The Labours of Hercules*	Mark 8:24
"The Flock of Geryon," in *The Labours of Hercules*	Elijah and his fiery chariot from 2 Kings 2:11-12
"The Flock of Geryon," in *The Labours of Hercules*	Revelation 1:11
"The Flock of Geryon," in *The Labours of Hercules*	1 John 4:18
"The Apples of the Hesperides," in *The Labours of Hercules*	Mark 12:17
"The Capture of Cerberus" in *The Labours of Hercules*	Matthew 19:24
Taken at the Flood, ch. 13	Romans 6:23
Mrs. McGinty's Dead, ch. 13	Exodus 20:5-6
After the Funeral, ch. 6, sec. 2	Lamentations 3:59
Hickory Dickory Dock, ch. 16, sec. 5	Psalm 37:35
Dead Man's Folly, ch. 3	Matthew 6:28
Dead Man's Folly, ch. 12	Matthew 3:12
Cat Among the Pigeons, ch. 21, sec. 1	Joel 2:28/Acts 2:17
Cat Among the Pigeons, ch. 25, sec. 2	Proverbs 31:10
The Clocks, ch. 24, sec. 3	Luke 19:40
Hallowe'en Party, ch. 6	John 1:5
Hallowe'en Party, ch. 11	"Judith & Holofernes"
Hallowe'en Party, ch. 11	Judges 5:25
Hallowe'en Party, ch. 14	Psalm 127:2
Hallowe'en Party, ch. 14	Psalm 39:12
Hallowe'en Party, ch. 14	Matthew 20:1-16
Hallowe'en Party, ch. 14	1 Corinthians 3:9
Hallowe'en Party, ch. 14	Luke 10:29-37, quoting Leviticus 19:18b
Hallowe'en Party, ch. 27	Matthew 4:10 or Mark 8:33
Hallowe'en Party, ch. 27	"Garden of Eden"
Elephants Can Remember, chs. 12, 18, 20	2 Samuel 1:23
Elephants Can Remember, ch. 18	Matthew 6:12
Curtain, ch. 6	Psalm 105:18
Curtain, ch. 10, sec. 2; ch. 14, sec. 1	Mark 9:42 / Matthew 18:6
Curtain, ch. 13, sec. 3; ch. 18, sec. 2	"Judith & Holofernes"

Bibliography

Primary Literature

Christie, Agatha. *The Mysterious Affair at Styles* (1920/1921). Reissued: New York: HarperCollins, 2010. Kindle edition.

Christie, Agatha. "The Wife of the Kenite." *The Home*, September 1922. Collected in *The Last Seance: Tales of the Supernatural*. London: HarperCollins, 2019. Kindle edition.

Christie, Agatha. *The Murder on the Links* (1923). Reissued: New York: HarperCollins, 2011. Kindle edition.

Christie, Agatha. "The Affair at the Victory Ball." *The Sketch*, 7 March 1923. Collected in *Hercule Poirot: The Complete Short Stories*. New York: HarperCollins, 2013. Kindle edition.

Christie, Agatha. "Jewel Robbery at the Grand Metropolitan" (originally published as "The Curious Disappearance of the Opalsen Pearls"). *The Sketch*, 14 March 1923. Collected in *Hercule Poirot: The Complete Short Stories*. New York: HarperCollins, 2013. Kindle edition.

Christie, Agatha. "The King of Clubs." *The Sketch*, 21 March 1923. Collected in *Hercule Poirot: The Complete Short Stories*. New York: HarperCollins, 2013. Kindle edition.

Christie, Agatha. "The Disappearance of Mr. Davenheim." *The Sketch*, 28 March 1923. Collected in *Hercule Poirot: The Complete Short Stories*. New York: HarperCollins, 2013. Kindle edition.

Christie, Agatha. "The Tragedy at Marsdon Manor." *The Sketch*, 18 April 1923. Collected in *Hercule Poirot: The Complete Short Stories*. New York: HarperCollins, 2013. Kindle edition.

Christie, Agatha. "The Million Dollar Bond Robbery." *The Sketch*, 2 May 1923. Collected in *Hercule Poirot: The Complete Short Stories*. New York: HarperCollins, 2013. Kindle edition.

Christie, Agatha. "The Mystery of the Hunter's Lodge." *The Sketch*, 6 May 1923. Collected in *Hercule Poirot: The Complete Short Stories*. New York: HarperCollins, 2013. Kindle edition.

Christie, Agatha. "The Chocolate Box" (originally published as "The Clue of the Chocolate Box"). *The Sketch*, 23 May 1923. Collected in *Hercule Poirot: The Complete Short Stories*. New York: HarperCollins, 2013. Kindle edition.

Christie, Agatha. "The Adventure of the Egyptian Tomb." *The Sketch*, 26 September 1923. Collected in *Hercule Poirot: The Complete Short Stories*. New York: HarperCollins, 2013. Kindle edition.

Christie, Agatha. "The Veiled Lady." *The Sketch*, 3 October 1923. Collected in *Hercule Poirot: The Complete Short Stories*. New York: HarperCollins, 2013. Kindle edition.

Christie, Agatha. "The Adventure of Johnny Waverly." *The Sketch*, 10 October 1923. Collected in *Hercule Poirot: The Complete Short Stories*. New York: HarperCollins, 2013. Kindle edition.

Christie, Agatha. "The Market Basing Mystery." *The Sketch*, 17 October 1923. Collected in *Hercule Poirot: The Complete Short Stories*. New York: HarperCollins, 2013. Kindle edition.

Christie, Agatha. "The Incredible Theft" (expanded version of story originally published as "The Submarine Plans"). *The Sketch*, 7 November 1923. Collected in *Hercule Poirot: The Complete Short Stories*. New York: HarperCollins, 2013. Kindle edition.

Christie, Agatha. "The Cornish Mystery." *The Sketch*, 28 November 1923. Collected in *Hercule Poirot: The Complete Short Stories*. New York: HarperCollins, 2013. Kindle edition.

Christie, Agatha. "The Double Clue." *The Sketch*, 5 December 1923. Collected in *Hercule Poirot: The Complete Short Stories*. New York: HarperCollins, 2013. Kindle edition.

Christie, Agatha. "The House of Lurking Death." *The Sketch*, November 1924. Collected in *Partners in Crime: A Tommy and Tuppence Collection* (1929). Reissued: New York: HarperCollins, 2012. Kindle edition.

Christie, Agatha. *The Secret of Chimneys* (1925). Reissued: New York: HarperCollins, 2011. Kindle edition.

Christie, Agatha. "The Under Dog." *Mystery Magazine*, 1 April 1926. Collected in *Hercule Poirot: The Complete Short Stories*. New York: HarperCollins, 2013. Kindle edition.

Christie, Agatha. *The Murder of Roger Ackroyd* (1926). Reissued: New York: HarperCollins, 2011. Kindle edition.

Christie, Agatha. *The Big Four* (1927). Reissued: New York: HarperCollins, 2011. Kindle edition.

Christie, Agatha. "The Bloodstained Pavement." *The Royal Magazine*, March 1928. Collected in *Miss Marple: The Complete Short Stories* (1985). Reissued: New York: HarperCollins, 2011. Kindle edition.

Christie, Agatha. "Motive v. Opportunity." *The Royal Magazine*, April 1928. Collected in *Miss Marple: The Complete Short Stories* (1985). Reissued: New York: HarperCollins, 2011. Kindle edition.

Christie, Agatha. *The Mystery of the Blue Train* (1928). Reissued: New York: HarperCollins, 2011. Kindle edition.

Christie, Agatha. *Partners in Crime: A Tommy and Tuppence Collection* (1929). Reissued: New York: HarperCollins, 2012. Kindle edition.

Christie, Agatha. "The Blue Geranium." *The Story-Teller* 272, December 1929. Collected in *Miss Marple: The Complete Short Stories* (1985). Reissued: New York: HarperCollins, 2011. Kindle edition.

Christie, Agatha. "The Herb of Death." *The Story-Teller* 275, March 1930. Collected in *Miss Marple: The Complete Short Stories* (1985). Reissued: New York: HarperCollins, 2011. Kindle edition.

Christie, Agatha. "The Four Suspects." *The Story-Teller* 276, April 1930. Collected in *Miss Marple: The Complete Short Stories* (1985). Reissued: New York: HarperCollins, 2011. Kindle edition.

Christie, Agatha. *The Murder at the Vicarage* (1930). Reissued: New York: HarperCollins, 2011. Kindle edition.

Christie, Agatha. *The Sittaford Mystery* (1931). Reissued: New York: HarperCollins, 2003. Kindle edition.

Christie, Agatha. "Dead Man's Mirror" (expanded version of story originally published as "The Second Gong"). *The Strand*, July 1932. Collected in *Hercule Poirot: The Complete Short Stories*. New York: HarperCollins, 2013. Kindle edition.

Christie, Agatha. *Peril at End House* (1932). Reissued: New York: HarperCollins, 2011. Kindle edition.

Christie, Agatha. "Death on the Nile." *Cosmopolitan*, April 1933. Collected in *Parker Pyne Investigates* (1934). Reissued: New York: HarperCollins, 2010. Kindle edition.

Christie, Agatha. "The Pearl." *Nash's Pall Mall*, July 1933 (later retitled "The Pearl of Price"). Collected in *Parker Pyne Investigates* (1934). Reissued: New York: HarperCollins, 2010. Kindle edition.

Christie, Agatha. *Lord Edgware Dies* (1933). Reissued: New York: HarperCollins, 2011. Kindle edition.

Christie, Agatha. *Murder on the Orient Express* (1934). Reissued: New York: HarperCollins, 2011. Kindle edition.

Christie, Agatha. *Parker Pyne Investigates* (1934). Reissued: New York: HarperCollins, 2010. Kindle edition.

Christie, Agatha. *Three Act Tragedy* (1934–1935). Reissued: New York: HarperCollins, 2011. Kindle edition.

Christie, Agatha. *Death in the Clouds* (1935). Reissued: New York: HarperCollins, 2008. Kindle edition.

Christie, Agatha. "Problem at Sea." *This Week*, 12 January 1936. Collected in *Hercule Poirot: The Complete Short Stories*. New York: HarperCollins, 2013. Kindle edition.

Christie, Agatha. *The A.B.C. Murders* (1936). Reissued: New York: HarperCollins, 2011. Kindle edition.

Christie, Agatha. *Murder in Mesopotamia* (1936). Reissued: New York: HarperCollins, 2011. Kindle edition.

Christie, Agatha. *Cards on the Table* (1936). Reissued: New York: HarperCollins, 2011. Kindle edition.

Christie, Agatha. *Murder in the Mews: Four Cases of Hercule Poirot* (1937). Reissued: New York: HarperCollins, 2011. Kindle edition.

Christie, Agatha. *Dumb Witness* (1937). Reissued: New York: HarperCollins, 2011. Kindle edition.

Christie, Agatha. "The Dream." *The Saturday Evening Post*, 23 October 1937. Collected in *Hercule Poirot: The Complete Short Stories*. New York: HarperCollins, 2013. Kindle edition.

Christie, Agatha. *Appointment with Death* (1938). Reissued: New York: HarperCollins, 2005. Kindle edition.

Christie, Agatha. *Death on the Nile* (1938). Reissued: New York: HarperCollins, 2011. Kindle edition.

Christie, Agatha. *And Then There Were None* (1939/1940). Reissued: New York: HarperCollins, 2011. Kindle edition.

Christie, Agatha. *Hercule Poirot's Christmas* (1939). Reissued: New York: HarperCollins, 2011. Kindle edition.

Christie, Agatha. "The Nemean Lion." *The Strand*, November 1939. Collected in *The Labours of Hercules* (1947). Reissued: New York: HarperCollins, 2011. Kindle edition.

Christie, Agatha. "The Flock of Geryon" (originally published in the U.S. as "Weird Monster" in *This Week* on 26 May 1940) *The Strand*, August 1940. Collected in *The Labours of Hercules* (1947). Reissued: New York: HarperCollins, 2011. Kindle edition.

Christie, Agatha. "The Apples of the Hesperides." *The Strand*, November 1940. Collected in *The Labours of Hercules* (1947). Reissued: New York: HarperCollins, 2011. Kindle edition.

Christie, Agatha. *Sad Cypress* (1940). Reissued: New York: HarperCollins, 2011. Kindle edition.

Christie, Agatha. *Evil Under the Sun* (1941). Reissued: New York: HarperCollins, 2011. Kindle edition.

Christie, Agatha. "Strange Jest" (originally published as "A Case of Buried Treasure"). *This Week*, 2 November 1941. Collected in *Miss Marple: The Complete Short Stories* (1985). Reissued: New York: HarperCollins, 2011. Kindle edition.

Christie, Agatha. "Tape-Measure Murder." *This Week*, 16 November 1941. Collected in *Miss Marple: The Complete Short Stories* (1985). Reissued: New York: HarperCollins, 2011. Kindle edition.

Christie, Agatha. "The Case of the Caretaker." *The Strand*, January 1942. Collected in *Miss Marple: The Complete Short Stories* (1985). Reissued: New York: HarperCollins, 2011. Kindle edition.

Christie, Agatha. "The Case of the Perfect Maid" (originally published as "The Perfect Maid"). *The Strand*, April 1942. Collected in *Miss Marple: The Complete Short Stories* (1985). Reissued: New York: HarperCollins, 2011. Kindle edition.

Christie, Agatha. *The Moving Finger* (1942/1943). Reissued: New York: HarperCollins, 2011. Kindle edition.

Christie, Agatha. *Five Little Pigs* (1943). Reissued: New York: HarperCollins, 2011. Kindle edition.

Christie, Agatha. *Towards Zero* (1944). Reissued: New York: HarperCollins, 2011. Kindle edition.

Christie, Agatha. *The Hollow* (1946). Reissued: New York: HarperCollins, 2011. Kindle edition.

Christie, Agatha. *The Labours of Hercules* (1947). Reissued: New York: HarperCollins, 2011. Kindle edition.

Christie, Agatha. *Taken at the Flood* (1948). Reissued: New York: HarperCollins, 2011. Kindle edition.

Christie, Agatha. *The Witness for the Prosecution and Other Stories* (1948). Reissued: New York: HarperCollins, 2012. Kindle edition.

Christie, Agatha. *Crooked House* (1949). Reissued: New York: HarperCollins, 2011. Kindle edition.

Christie, Agatha. *A Murder is Announced* (1950). Reissued: New York: HarperCollins, 2011. Kindle edition.

Christie, Agatha. *Three Blind Mice and Other Stories* (1950). Reissued: New York: HarperCollins, 2012. Kindle edition.

Christie, Agatha. *They Came to Baghdad* (1951). Reissued: New York: HarperCollins, 2011. Kindle edition.

Christie, Agatha. *They Do It with Mirrors* (1952). Reissued: New York: HarperCollins, 2011. Kindle edition.

Christie, Agatha. *After the Funeral* (1953). Reissued: New York: HarperCollins, 2011. Kindle edition.

Christie, Agatha. *A Pocket Full of Rye* (1953). Reissued: New York: HarperCollins, 2011. Kindle edition.

Christie, Agatha. *Hickory Dickory Dock* (1955). Reissued: New York: HarperCollins, 2011. Kindle edition.

Christie, Agatha. *Dead Man's Folly* (1956). Reissued: New York: HarperCollins, 2011. Kindle edition.

Christie, Agatha. *Ordeal by Innocence* (1958/1959). Reissued: New York: HarperCollins, 2011. Kindle edition.

Christie, Agatha. *Cat Among the Pigeons* (1959). Reissued: New York: HarperCollins, 2011. Kindle edition.

Christie, Agatha. "The Mystery of the Spanish Chest" (expanded version of story originally published as "The Mystery of the Baghdad Chest" in *The Strand*, January 1932). *Women's Illustrated*, 17 September – 1 October 1960. Collected in *Hercule Poirot: The Complete Short Stories*. New York: HarperCollins, 2013. Kindle edition.

Christie, Agatha. *A Pale Horse* (1961). Reissued: New York: HarperCollins, 2011. Kindle edition.

Christie, Agatha. *A Caribbean Mystery* (1964/1965). Reissued: New York: HarperCollins, 2011. Kindle edition.

Christie, Agatha. *At Bertram's Hotel* (1965). Reissued: New York: HarperCollins, 2011. Kindle edition.

Christie, Agatha. *Third Girl* (1966). Reissued: New York: HarperCollins, 2011. Kindle edition.

Christie, Agatha. *Hallowe'en Party* (1969). Reissued: New York: HarperCollins, 2011. Kindle edition.

Christie, Agatha. *Nemesis* (1971). Reissued: New York: HarperCollins, 2011. Kindle edition.

Christie, Agatha. *Elephants Can Remember* (1972). Reissued: New York: HarperCollins, 2011. Kindle edition.

Christie, Agatha. *Curtain: Poirot's Last Case* (1975). Reissued: New York: HarperCollins, 2011. Kindle edition.

Christie, Agatha. *Sleeping Murder* (1976). Reissued: New York: HarperCollins, 2011. Kindle edition.

Christie, Agatha. *Miss Marple: The Complete Short Stories* (1985). Reissued: New York: HarperCollins, 2011. Kindle edition.

Christie, Agatha. *The Harlequin Tea Set and Other Stories* (1997). Reissued: New York: HarperCollins, 2012. Kindle edition.

Christie, Agatha. *Hercule Poirot: The Complete Short Stories*. New York: HarperCollins, 2013. Kindle edition.

Christie, Agatha. *The Last Seance: Tales of the Supernatural*. London: HarperCollins, 2019. Kindle edition.

Eliot, T. S. *Four Quartets* (1943). Reissued: San Diego & New York: Harcourt Brace & Company, 1971.

Goethe, Johann Wolfgang von. *Faust: A Tragedy, Parts One & Two*. Translated by Martin Greenberg. Fully Revised Edition. New Haven & London: Yale University Press, 2014.

Secondary Sources

Ackershoek, Mary Anne. "'The Daughters of His Manhood': Christie and the Golden Age of Detective Fiction." In *Theory and Practice of Classic Detective Fiction*, edited by Jerome H. Delamater and Ruth Prigozy, 119–128. Contributions to the Study of Popular Culture, 62. Westport, CT & London: Greenwood Press, 1997.

Al-Asmar, Jamal. "Victorian Images of the Arabs and Their Sources." *Bethlehem University Journal*, 13 (1994): 58–88.

Aldridge, Mark. *Agatha Christie On Screen*. Crime Files. London: Palgrave Macmillan, 2016.

Aldridge, Mark. *Agatha Christie's Poirot: The Greatest Detective in the World*. London: HarperCollins, 2020.

Almond, Philip C. *The Devil: A New Biography*. Ithaca: Cornell University Press, 2014.

Alter, Robert. *The David Story: A Translation with Commentary of 1 and 2 Samuel*. New York & London: W. W. Norton, 1999.

Alter, Robert. *The Book of Psalms: A Translation with Commentary*. New York & London: W. W. Norton & Co., 2007.

Alter, Robert. *The Wisdom Books: Job, Proverbs, and Ecclesiastes: A Translation with Commentary*. New York & London: W. W. Norton, 2010.

Anderson, Paul. "Johannine Community." *Bible Odyssey*. Available online: https://www. bibleodyssey.org/articles/the-johannine-community/. Accessed 14 September 2023.

Ansari, Humayun. *"The Infidel Within": Muslims in Britain since 1800*. New York & Oxford: Oxford University Press, 2018.

Arnold, Jane. "Detecting Social History: Jews in the Works of Agatha Christie." *Jewish Social Studies* 49, nos. 3/4 (1987): 275–282.

Balentine, Samuel E. *Job*. Smyth & Helwys Bible Commentary. Macon, GA: Smyth & Helwys, 2006.

Barbeau, Aimee E. "Christian Empire and National Crusade: The Rhetoric of Anglican Clergy in the First World War." *Anglican and Episcopal History* 85, no. 1 (2016): 24–62.

Bargainnier, Earl F. *The Gentle Art of Murder: The Detective Fiction of Agatha Christie*. Bowling Green, OH: Bowling Green University Popular Press, 1980.

Barker, Eileen. "General Overview of the 'Cult Scene' in Great Britain." In *New Religious Movements in the Twenty-First Century: Legal, Political, and Social Challenges in Global Perspective*, edited by Phillip Charles Lucas and Thomas Robbins, 22–28. New York & London: Routledge, 2004.

Barnard, Robert. *A Talent to Deceive: An Appreciation of Agatha Christie*. New York: Mysterious Press, 1980.

Barrow, Logie. *Independent Spirits: Spiritualism and English Plebeians, 1850–1910*. History Workshop Series. London & New York: Routledge & Kegan Paul, 1986.

BBC Interview with Sarah Phelps, 15 December 2018. Available online at https://www. bbc.co.uk/mediacentre/mediapacks/the-abc-murders/phelps. Accessed 14 September 2023.

Berch, Victor A., Karl Schadow & Steve Lewis. "Murder Clinic: Radio's Golden Age of Detection." Available online at https://mysteryfile.com/M_Clinic.html. Accessed 14 September 2023.

Bernthal, J. C. "'A Dangerous World': The Hermeneutics of Agatha Christie's Later Novels." In *The Bible in Crime Fiction and Drama: Murderous Texts*, edited by Alison Jack and Caroline Blyth, 167–182. Scriptural Traces: Critical Perspectives on the Reception and Influence of the Bible, 16; Library of Hebrew Bible/Old Testament Studies, 678. London & New York: Bloomsbury, 2019.

Binns, Amy. "Nobility, Duty and Courage: Propaganda and Inspiration in Interwar Women's and Girls' Pageants." In *Restaging the Past: Historical Pageants, Culture and Society in Modern Britain*, edited by Angela Bartie, et al., 132–157. London: UCL Press, 2020.

Birns, Nicolas and Margaret Boe Birns. "Agatha Christie: Modern and Modernist." In *The Cunning Craft: Original Essays on Detective Fiction and Contemporary Literary Theory*, edited by Ronald G. Walker and June M. Frazer, 120–134. Macomb, IL: Yeast Printing/ Western Illinois University, 1990.

Black, Jeremy. *The Importance of Being Poirot*. South Bend, IN: St. Augustine's Press, 2021.

Blenkinsopp, Joseph. *Ezekiel*. Interpretation: A Bible Commentary for Teaching and Preaching. Atlanta: John Knox Press, 1997.

Blumenfeld, Warren J. "Christian Privilege and the Promotion of 'Secular' and Not-So 'Secular' Mainline Christianity in Public Schooling and in the Larger Society." *Equity & Excellence in Education* 39 (2006): 195–210.

Bradford, Richard. *Crime Fiction: A Very Short Introduction*. Oxford: Oxford University Press, 2015.

Brothers, Thomas. *Louis Armstrong: Master of Modernism*. New York & London: W. W. Norton & Company, 2014.

Brown, Callum G. *Religion and Society in Twentieth-Century Britain*. Harlow: Pearson Education Limited, 2006.

Brown, Callum G. *The Death of Christian Britain: Understanding Secularization, 1800–2000*. 2nd edn. London & New York: Routledge, 2009.

Bruntz, Courtney and Brooke Shedneck, eds. *Buddhist Tourism in Asia*. Contemporary Buddhism Series. Honolulu: University of Hawai'i Press, 2020.

Bunson, Matthew. *The Complete Christie: An Agatha Christie Encyclopedia*. New York: Pocket Books/Simon & Schuster, 2000.

Burns, Arthur. "A National Church Tells its Story: The English Church Pageant of 1909." In *Restaging the Past: Historical Pageants, Culture and Society in Modern Britain*. edited by Angela Bartie, et al., 56–79. London: UCL Press, 2020.

Byrne, Georgina. *Modern Spiritualism and the Church of England, 1850–1939*. Studies in Modern British Religious History. Suffolk: The Boydell Press, 2010.

Camp, Claudia V. "1 and 2 Kings." In *Women's Bible Commentary*, edited by C. A. Newsom and S. H. Ringe, 102–116. Expanded Edition, with Apocrypha. Louisville, KY: Westminster/John Knox Press, 1998.

Carroll, John T. *Luke: A Commentary*. New Testament Library. Louisville: Westminster John Knox, 2012. Kindle edition.

Carvalho, Corinne L. *Primer on Biblical Methods*. Winona, MN: Anselm Academic, 2009.

Christie, Agatha. *Come, Tell Me How You Live* (1946). Reissued: The Agatha Christie Mystery Collection. Toronto & New York: Bantam Books, 1985.

Christie, Agatha. *An Autobiography* (1977). Reissued: New York: HarperCollins, 2011.

Clanton, Dan W., Jr. "'If I Perish, I Perish': Esthers in Film." In *Daring, Disreputable, and Devout: Interpreting the Hebrew Bible's Women in the Arts and Music*, 111–141. New York & London: T&T Clark, 2009.

Clanton, Dan W., Jr. "'Here, There, and Everywhere': Images of Jesus in American Popular Culture." In *The Bible in/and Popular Culture: A Creative Encounter*, edited by Philip Culbertson and Elaine M. Wainwright, 41–60. Semeia Studies 65. Atlanta: Society of Biblical Literature, 2010.

Clanton, Dan W., Jr. "The Divine Unsub: Television Procedurals and Biblical Sexual Violence." In *The Bible in Crime Fiction and Drama: Murderous Texts*, edited by Alison Jack and Caroline Blyth, 125–148. Scriptural Traces: Critical Perspectives on the Reception and Influence of the Bible Series. London & New York: Bloomsbury, 2019.

Clanton, Dan W., Jr. "Crucifixions, Cosplay, and Fan Cultures." In *The Oxford Handbook of the Bible and American Popular Culture*, edited by Dan W. Clanton, Jr. and Terry R. Clark, 488–502. New York: Oxford University Press, 2021.

Cohen, Richard I. "The 'Wandering Jew' from Medieval Legend to Modern Metaphor." In *The Art of Being Jewish in Modern Times*, edited by Barbara Kirshenblatt-Gimblett and Jonathan Karp, 147–175. Jewish Culture and Contexts. Philadelphia: University of Pennsylvania Press, 2008.

Cook, Bernard A. *Belgium: A History*. Studies in Modern European History, 50. New York: Peter Lang, 2002.

Craddock, Fred B. *Luke*. Interpretation: A Bible Commentary for Teaching and Preaching. Atlanta: John Knox Press, 1990.

Cunningham, Lawrence S., John Kelsay, R. Maurice Barineau, and Heather Jo McVoy. *The Sacred Quest: An Invitation to the Study of Religion*. 2nd edn. Englewood Cliffs, NJ: Prentice Hall, 1995.

Cunningham, Lawrence S. *An Introduction to Catholicism*. Cambridge & New York: Cambridge University Press, 2009.

Darr, Katheryn Pfisterer. "Ezekiel." In *Women's Bible Commentary*, edited by C. A. Newsom and S. H. Ringe, 192–200. Expanded Edition, with Apocrypha. Louisville, KY: Westminster/John Knox Press, 1998.

Declercq, Christophe. "The Odd Case of the Welcome Refugee in Wartime Britain: Uneasy Numbers, Disappearing Acts and Forgetfulness Regarding Belgian Refugees in the First World War." *Close Encounters in War Journal* 2 (2019): 5–26.

Dobbelaere, Karel and Liliane Voyé. "From Pillar to Postmodernity: The Changing Situation of Religion in Belgium." *Sociological Analysis* 51 (1990): S1–S13.

Edwards, Martin. "Plotting." In *The Routledge Companion to Crime Fiction*, edited by Janice Allan, Jesper Gulddal, Stewart King and Andrew Pepper, 185–193. London & New York: Routledge, 2020.

Elyada, Aya. "Early Modern Yiddish and the Jewish *Volkskunde*, 1880–1938." *The Jewish Quarterly Review* 107, no. 2 (2017): 182–208.

Endelman, Todd M. *The Jews of Britain, 1656 to 2000*. Jewish Communities in the Modern World. Berkeley, Los Angeles & London: University of California Press, 2002.

Evans, Ellen L. *The Cross and the Ballot: Catholic Political Parties in Germany, Switzerland, Austria, Belgium and the Netherlands, 1785–1985*. Studies in Central European Histories. Boston: Humanities Press, Inc., 1999.

Evans, Nicholas J. "Commerce, State, and Anti-Alienism: Balancing Britain's Interests in the Late-Victorian Period." In *"The Jew" in Late-Victorian and Edwardian Culture: Between the East End and East Africa*, edited by Eitan Bar-Yosef and Nadia Valman, 80–97. Palgrave Studies in Nineteenth-Century Writing and Culture. New York: Palgrave Macmillan, 2009.

Fitzmyer, Joseph A. *The Gospel According to Luke*. 2 Vols. The Anchor Bible 28 & 28A. New York: Doubleday, 1970, 1985.

Flood, Alison. "Hercule Poirot's real-life model may have been detected in Torquay." *The Guardian*, 13 May 2014. Available online at https://www.theguardian.com/books/2014/may/13/hercule-poirot-real-life-model-belgian-gendarme. Accessed 14 September 2023.

Fortescue, William. *The Third Republic in France, 1870–1940: Conflicts and Continuities*. Routledge Sources in History. London & New York: Routledge, 2000.

Forward, Martin. *A Short Introduction to Inter-Religious Dialogue*. Oxford: Oneworld, 2001.

Fox, Judith. "New Religious Movements." In *The Routledge Companion to the Study of Religion*. 2nd edn., edited by John Hinnells, 339–353. London & New York: Routledge, 2010.

Franklin, J. Jeffrey. *Spirit Matters: Occult Beliefs, Alternative Religions, and the Crisis of Faith in Victorian Britain*. Ithaca & London: Cornell University Press, 2018.

Friedenthal, Andrew J. "Monitoring the Past: DC Comics' Crisis on Infinite Earths and the Narrativization of Comic Book History." *ImageTexT: Interdisciplinary Comic Studies* 6:2 (2011). Available online at https://imagetextjournal.com/monitoring-the-past-dc-comics-crisis-on-infinite-earths-and-the-narrativization-of-comic-book-history/. Accessed 14 September 2023.

Gaines, Janet Howe. "How Bad Was Jezebel?" *Bible Review* 16, no. 5 (2000): 12–23.

Gidley, Ben. "The Ghosts of Kishinev in the East End: Responses to a Pogrom in the Jewish London of 1903." In *"The Jew" in Late-Victorian and Edwardian Culture: Between the East End and East Africa*, edited by Eitan Bar-Yosef and Nadia Valman, 98–112. Palgrave Studies in Nineteenth-Century Writing and Culture. New York: Palgrave Macmillan, 2009.

Gill, Gillian. *Agatha Christie: The Woman and Her Mysteries*. New York: Free Press, 1990. Kindle edition.

Goldstein, Phyllis. *A Convenient Hatred: The History of Antisemitism*. Brookline, MA: Facing History and Ourselves, 2012.

Gottschalk, Peter and Gabriel Greenberg. *Islamophobia: Making Muslims the Enemy*. Lanham, MD: Rowman & Littlefield, 2008.

Green, Barbara Green. *David's Capacity for Compassion: A Literary-Hermeneutical Study of 1–2 Samuel*. Library of Hebrew Bible/Old Testament Studies, 641. London: Bloomsbury T&T Clark, 2017.

Green, Todd H. "What is Islamophobia?" In *The Fear of Islam: An Introduction to Islamophobia in the West*, 9–40. 2nd edn. Minneapolis: Fortress Press, 2019.

Grimley, Matthew. "The Religion of Englishness: Puritanism, Providentialism, and 'National Character,' 1918–1945." *Journal of British Studies* 46, no. 4 (2007): 884–906.

Gross, John. *Shylock: A Legend and Its Legacy*. New York & London: Simon & Schuster, 1992.

Gudorf, Christine E. "Contraception and Abortion in Roman Catholicism." In *Sacred Rights: The Case for Contraception and Abortion in World Religions*, edited by Daniel C. Maguire, 55–78. Oxford & New York: Oxford University Press, 2003.

Haber, Gordon. "Think the goblins in Harry Potter are antisemitic? Try the rest of British literature." *The Forward*, 10 January 2022. Available online at: https://forward.com/opinion/480578/think-the-goblins-in-harry-potter-are-antisemitic-try-british-literature/. Accessed 14 September 2023.

Hamilton, Victor P. "Satan." In vol. 5 of *The Anchor Bible Dictionary*, edited by David Noel Freedman, et al, 985–989. 6 Vols. New York: Doubleday, 1992.

Hare, Douglas R. A. *Matthew*. Interpretation: A Bible Commentary for Teaching and Preaching. Atlanta: John Knox Press, 1993.

Hart, Anne. *Agatha Christie's Poirot: The Life and Times of Hercule Poirot*. 1990. London: HarperCollins, 1997.

Hasan, Asma Gull. *American Muslims: The New Generation*. New York & London: Continuum, 2000.

Hause, Steven C. "Anti-Protestant Rhetoric in the Early Third Republic." *French Historical Studies* 16, no. 1 (1989): 183–201.

Hedges, Paul. *Religious Hatred: Prejudice, Islamophobia, and Antisemitism in Global Context*. London & New York: Bloomsbury, 2021.

Heschel, Susannah. "From Jesus to Shylock: Christian Supersessionism and 'The Merchant of Venice'" *The Harvard Theological Review* 99, no. 4 (2006): 407–431.

Hill, David. *The Gospel of Matthew*. New Century Bible Commentary. Grand Rapids, MI: Eerdmans, 1972.

Hills, Matthew. "Fans and Fan Cultures." In *The Blackwell Encyclopedia of Sociology*, edited by George Ritzer, 1637–1641. Malden, MA: Blackwell Publishing, 2007.

Hirji, Faiza. "Telling Our Own Stories: Changing Representations of Islam in Popular Culture." *Oxford Islamic Studies Online*, October 2018. Available online at http://www.oxfordislamicstudies.com/Public/focus/essay1018_islam_in_popular_culture.html.

Holmes, Colin. *Anti-Semitism in British Society, 1876–1939*. London & New York: Routledge, 1979.

Janzen, David. "The Condemnation of David's 'Taking' in 2 Samuel 12:1-14." *Journal of Biblical Literature* 131, no. 2 (2012): 209–220.

De Jastrzebski, T. T. S. "The Register of Belgian Refugees." *Journal of the Royal Statistical Society* 79, no. 2 (1916): 133–158.

Jenkins, Philip. *The Great and Holy War: How World War I Became a Religious Crusade*. New York: HarperOne, 2014.

Joshi, Khyati Y. "Diversity, Pluralism, Secularism." In *Proceedings of the Fifth Biennial Conference on Religion and American Culture*, 42–43. Indiana University & Purdue University, Indianapolis: The Center for the Study of Religion and American Culture, 2017.

Joshi, Khyati Y. *White Christian Privilege: The Illusion of Religious Equality in America*. New York: New York University Press, 2020.

Keeping It 101: A Killjoy's Introduction to Religion. "Smart Grrl Summer: What are 'cults'? Why do we hate that word so much?," 10 June 2020. Available online at https://keepingit101.com/smartgrrlsummer1. Accessed 14 September 2023.

Kettani, Houssain. "Muslim Population in Europe: 1950–2020." *International Journal of Environmental Science and Development* 1, no. 2 (2010): 154–164.

Knepper, Marty S. "The Curtain Falls: Agatha Christie's Last Novels." *Clues* 23, no. 4 (2005): 69–83.

Knight, Stephen. "'..done from within' – Agatha Christie's World." In *Form and Ideology in Crime Fiction*, 107–134. London & Basingstoke: The Macmillan Press, 1980.

Knight, Stephen. "The Golden Age." In *The Cambridge Companion to Crime Fiction*, edited by Martin Priestman, 77–94. Cambridge & New York: Cambridge University Press, 2003.

Knight, Stephen. *Crime Fiction since 1800: Detection, Death, Diversity*. 2nd edn. New York: Palgrave, 2010.

Lane, Jr., Lauriat. "Dickens' Archetypal Jew." *Proceedings of the Modern Language Association* 73, no. 1 (1958): 94–100.

Lapsley, Jacqueline E. "Ezekiel." In *Women's Bible Commentary: Twentieth-Anniversary Edition*, edited by Carol A. Newsom, Sharon H. Ringe, and Jacqueline E. Lapsley, 283–292. Louisville, KY: Westminster John Knox Press, 2012.

Larsen, Timothy. *A People of One Book: The Bible and the Victorians*. Oxford & New York: Oxford University Press, 2011.

Light, Alison. "Agatha Christie and Conservative Modernity." In *Forever England: Femininity, Literature and Conservatism between the Wars*, 61–112. London & New York: Routledge, 1991.

Lincoln, Bruce. *Holy Terrors: Thinking about Religion after September 11*. Chicago & London: The University of Chicago Press, 2003.

Lloyd, Jennifer M. "Women Preachers in the Bible Christian Connexion." *Albion: A Quarterly Journal Concerned with British Studies* 36, no. 3 (2004): 451–481.

Lyons, Sherri Lynne. *Species, Serpents, Spirits, and Skulls: Science at the Margins in the Victorian Age*. Albany: State University of New York Press, 2009.

Maida, Patricia D. and Nicholas B. Spornick. *Murder She Wrote: A Study of Agatha Christie's Detective Fiction*. Bowling Green, OH: Bowling Green State University Popular Press, 1982.

Makinen, Merja. *Agatha Christie: Investigating Femininity*. Crime Files Series. New York: Palgrave, 2006.

Marty, Martin E. *Pilgrims in Their Own Land: 500 Years of Religion in America*. New York: Penguin, 1984.

Mays, James Luther. *Micah*. Old Testament Library. Philadelphia: Westminster, 1976.

McGrath, Alistair. *Theology: The Basics*. 2nd Edition. Malden, MA: Blackwell, 2008.

McLeod, Hugh. *Religion and Society in England, 1850–1914*. Social History in Perspective. New York: St. Martin's Press, 1996.

McLeod, Hugh. "Protestantism and British National Identity, 1815–1945." In *Nation and Religion: Perspectives on Europe and Asia*, edited by Peter van der Veer and Hartmut Lehmann, 44–70. Princeton: Princeton University Press, 1999.

Mendelsohn, Adam D. *The Rag Race: How Jews Sewed Their Way to Success in America and the British Empire*. The Goldstein-Goren Series in American Jewish History. New York & London: New York University Press, 2015.

Merrill, Robert. "Christie's Narrative Games." In *Theory and Practice of Classic Detective Fiction*, edited by Jerome H. Delamater and Ruth Prigozy, 87–101. Contributions to the Study of Popular Culture, 62. Westport, CT & London: Greenwood Press, 1997.

Meyer, Susan. "Antisemitism and Social Critique in Dickens's *Oliver Twist*." *Victorian Literature and Culture* 33, no. 1 (2005): 239–252.

Moorman, John R. H. *A History of the Church in England*. 3rd edn. Harrisburg, PA: Morehouse Publishing, 1980.

Morgan, Janet. *Agatha Christie: A Biography*. London: William Collins Sons & Company, 1984. Reprinted New York: Alfred A. Knopf, 1985.

Mroczek, Eva. "Mark of Cain." *Bible Odyssey*. Available online at https://www.bibleodyssey.org/articles/mark-of-cain/. Accessed 14 September 2023.

Natale, Simone. *Supernatural Entertainments: Victorian Spiritualism and the Rise of Modern Media Culture*. University Park, PA: The Pennsylvania State University Press, 2016.

Neill, Stephen and Tom Wright. *The Interpretation of the New Testament, 1861–1986*. New Edition. Oxford & New York: Oxford University Press, 1988.

Nieto, Sonia. "Affirmation, Solidarity, and Critique: Moving Beyond Tolerance in Education." In *Beyond Heroes and Holidays: A Practical Guide to K-12 Anti-racist, Multicultural Education and Staff Development*. 4th edn., edited by Enid Lee, Deborah Menkart, and Margo Okazawa-Rey, 7–18. Washington, DC: Network of Educators on the Americas, 2008.

Nye, Joseph S., Jr. "Soft Power." *Foreign Policy* 80 (1990): 153–171.

Orsini, Lauren. *Cosplay: The Fantasy World of Role Play*. London: Carlton Books, 2015.

Osborne, Charles. *The Life and Crimes of Agatha Christie: A Biographical Companion to the Works of Agatha Christie*. Revised and Updated Edition. London: HarperCollins, 1999.

Owen, Alex. *The Darkened Room: Women, Power, and Spiritualism in Late Victorian England*. Chicago & London: The University of Chicago Press, 1989.

Placher, William C. *A History of Christian Theology: An Introduction*. Louisville, KY: Westminster, 1983.

Plain, Gill. "'Tale Engineering': Agatha Christie and the Aftermath of the Second World War." *Literature & History* 29, no. 2 (2020): 179–199.

"Population estimates by ethnic group and religion, England and Wales: 2019." *Office for National Statistics*, 16 December 2021. Available online: https://www.ons.gov.uk/peoplepopulationandcommunity/populationandmigration/populationestimates/articles/populationestimatesbyethnicgroupandreligionenglandandwales/2019. Accessed 14 September 2023.

Prichard, Matthew, ed. *The Grand Tour: Around the World with the Queen of Mystery*. London: Christie Archive Trust/HarperCollins, 2012.

Pugh, Martin. *Britain and Islam: A History from 622 to the Present Day*. New Haven & London: Yale University Press, 2019.

Rahman, Fazlur. "Satan and Evil." In *Major Themes of the Qur'ān*, 121–131. 2nd edn. Minneapolis: Bibliotheca Islamica, 1994.

Reynolds, Gabriel Said. *Allah: God in the Qur'an*. New Haven & London: Yale University Press, 2020.

Ritchie, John. "Agatha Christie's England, 1918–39: Sickness in the Heart and Sickness in Society as Seen in the Detective Thriller." *Australian National University Historical Journal* 9 (1972): 3–9.

Ruden, Sarah. "The Good News according to Loukas." In *The Gospels: A New Translation*, 161–258. New York: Modern Library, 2021.

Rudin, A. James. "Oberammergau: A Case Study of Passion Plays." In *Pondering the Passion: What's at Stake for Christians and Jews?*, edited by Philip A. Cunningham, 97–108. Lanham, MD: Rowman & Littlefield, 2004.

Russell, Jeffrey Burton *Mephistopheles: The Devil in the Modern World*. Ithaca & London: Cornell University Press, 1986.

Scaggs, John. *Crime Fiction*. The New Critical Idiom. London & New York: Routledge, 2005.

Schlossberg, Herbert. *Conflict and Crisis in the Religious Life of Late Victorian England*. New Brunswick & London: Transaction Publishers, 2009.

Selengut, Charles. *Sacred Fury: Understanding Religious Violence*. Walnut Creek, CA: AltaMira Press/Lanham, MD: Rowman & Littlefield, 2003.

Shaw, Marion and Sabine Vanacker. "Women Writers and the Golden Age of Detective Fiction." In *Reflecting on Miss Marple*, 9–34. Heroines? London & New York: Routledge, 1991.

Shelley, Thomas J. "Mutual Independence: Church and State in Belgium: 1825–1846." *Journal of Church and State* 32, no. 1 (1990): 49–63.

Smith, Jane I. "Islam." In *Women in World Religions*, edited by Arvind Sharma, 235–250. Albany: State University of New York Press, 1987.

Spivack, Charlotte. "Job and Faust: The Eternal Wager." *The Centennial Review* 15, no. 1 (1971): 53–69.

Stausberg, Michael. *Religion and Tourism: Crossroads, Destinations and Encounters*. New York: Routledge, 2011.

Stevens, Jennifer. "The Victorians and the Bible." In *The Historical Jesus and the Literary Imagination 1860–1920*, 9–33. English Association Studies, 3. Liverpool: Liverpool University Press, 2010.

Strømmen, Hannah M. "Poirot, the Bourgeois Prophet: Agatha Christie's Biblical Adaptations." In *The Bible in Crime Fiction and Drama: Murderous Texts*, edited by Alison Jack and Caroline Blyth, 149–166. Scriptural Traces: Critical Perspectives on the Reception and Influence of the Bible, 16; Library of Hebrew Bible/Old Testament Studies, 678. London & New York: Bloomsbury, 2019.

Suchet, David and Geoffrey Wansell. *Poirot and Me*. London: Headline, 2013.

Sussex, Lucy. *Women Writers and Detectives in Nineteenth-Century Crime Fiction: The Mothers of the Mystery Genre*. Crime Files. Hampshire & New York: Palgrave Macmillan, 2010.

"Theodicy." In *The HarperCollins Dictionary of Religion*, edited by Jonathan Z. Smith, 1065–1067. San Francisco: HarperCollins, 1995.

Thompson, Laura. *Agatha Christie: An English Mystery*. London: Headline, 2007. Reprinted *Agatha Christie: A Mysterious Life*. New York: Pegasus Books, 2018. Kindle edition.

Towner, W. Sibley. "The Book of Ecclesiastes." In volume 5 of *The New Interpreter's Bible*, edited by Leander E. Keck, et al., 265–360. 12 Vols. Nashville: Abingdon Press, 1998.

Toy, J. Caroline. "Ritual Doing, Religious Doing: Understanding Harry Potter Fan Pilgrimages." In *Understanding Religion and Popular Culture*. 2nd edn., edited by Elizabeth Rae Coody, Dan W. Clanton, Jr., and Terry Ray Clark, 101–116. London & New York: Routledge.

Turnbull, Malcolm J. *Victims or Villains: Jewish Images in Classic English Detective Fiction*. Bowling Green, OH: Bowling Green State University Popular Press, 1998.

Van Wolde, Ellen. "Genesis I: The Story of the Creation of Heaven and Earth." In *Stories of the Beginning: Genesis 1–11 and Other Creation Stories*, 9–33. Translated by John Bowden. Ridgefield, CT: Morehouse Publishing, 1997.

Wagoner, Mary S. *Agatha Christie*. Twayne's English Authors Series. Boston: G. K. Hall & Co., 1986.

Watson, Colin. "The Little World of Mayhem Parva." In *Snobbery with Violence: Crime Stories and Their Audience*, 165–175. London: Eyre & Spottiswoode, 1971.

Watson, Colin. "The Message of Mayhem Parva." In *Agatha Christie: First Lady of Crime*, edited by H.R.F. Keating, 96–110. New York: Holt, Rinehart and Winston, 1977.

Whybray, R. N. *Ecclesiastes*. New Century Bible Commentary. Grand Rapids, MI: Eerdmans, 1989.

Wild, Stefan. "Devil." In *The Qur'an: An Encyclopedia*, edited by Oliver Leaman, 179–181. London & New York: Routledge, 2006.

Williams, Sarah C. "Is There a Bible in the House? Gender, Religion and Family Culture." In *Women, Gender and Religious Cultures in Britain, 1800–1940*, edited by Sue Morgan and Jacqueline deVries, 11–31. London & New York: Routledge, 2010.

Willis, Chris. "Making the Dead Speak: Spiritualism and Detective Fiction." In *The Art of Detective Fiction*, edited by Warren Chernaik, Martin Swales, and Robert Vilain, 60–74. Hampshire & New York: Palgrave Macmillan, 2000.

Wolff, Hans Walter. *Micah: A Commentary*. Continental Commentaries. Translated by Gary Stansell. Minneapolis: Augsburg, 1990.

Worsley, Lucy. *The Art of the English Murder: From Jack the Ripper and Sherlock Holmes to Agatha Christie and Alfred Hitchcock*. New York & London: Pegasus Crime, 2014.

Worsley, Lucy. *Agatha Christie: An Elusive Woman*. New York & London: Pegasus Crime, 2022. Kindle edition.

York, R. A. *Agatha Christie: Power and Illusion*. Crime Files. Hampshire & New York: Palgrave Macmillan, 2007.

Index of Biblical References

General Index